FIRSTBORN
OF
VENICE

The Johns Hopkins University Studies in Historical and Political Science
106th Series (1988)

FIRSTBORN
OF
VENICE

VICENZA
in the
EARLY RENAISSANCE STATE

James S. Grubb

The Johns Hopkins University Press
Baltimore and London

The book has been brought to publication with the generous assistance of the Gladys Krieble Delmas Foundation.

The Johns Hopkins University Press, 701 West 40th Street,
Baltimore, Maryland 21211
The Johns Hopkins Press Ltd., London

Library of Congress Cataloging-in-Publication Data

Grubb, James S., 1952–
    Firstborn of Venice.

    (The Johns Hopkins University studies in historical and political science;
106th ser., 3 (1988))
    Bibliography: p.
    Includes index.
    1. Vicenza (Italy)—History.   2. Venice (Italy)—History—697–1508.
3. Renaissance—Italy—Vicenza.   4. Renaissance—Italy—Venice.
5. City-states—Italy—History.   I. Title.   II. Title: First-born of Venice.
III. Series: Johns Hopkins University studies in historical and political
science; 106th ser., 3.
DG975.V7G78   1988   945′.31   87-33878
ISBN 0-8018-3613-1 (alk. paper)

Contents

Acknowledgments

It is a pleasure to thank those who have given so much to this book. Throughout years of research and writing, I have enjoyed the unstinting support of family members, teachers, colleagues, librarians, and archivists. Without their help this book would be meager in spirit and data. I am deeply grateful to them all.

Several institutions have aided my research and writing. A Fulbright Fellowship sponsored a year of research in Vicenza, and a grant from the Gladys Krieble Delmas Foundation allowed a summer in Venice. A summer faculty grant from the University of Maryland Baltimore County gave me the opportunity to complete primary research. During a year's leave funded by the National Endowment for the Humanities, I was able to pursue secondary studies and, finally, to write up a mass of notes into book form. Without that support this project could never have been undertaken.

Julius Kirshner of the University of Chicago first suggested Vicenza as a case subject for the study of Venetian territorial expansion. His guidance has been particularly valuable in fostering historiographic sensitivity and textual accuracy, and his moral support has provided constant encouragement. The late Eric Cochrane of the same university was a true friend and mentor. His own passion for the Renaissance was an inspiration for my work, and his research and writing set standards to which I can only aspire. Richard Goldthwaite of the Johns Hopkins University pointed out several useful secondary works and kept me up to date especially with Tuscan monographs.

The Veneto is an extraordinarily friendly region for historical studies. The professional hospitality and personal warmth of those engaged in Venetian research has been gratifying. Senior scholars such as Gaetano Cozzi, Reinhold Mueller, and Gherardo Ortalli of Venice, Paolo Sambin and Giorgio Cracco of Padua, Giorgio Borelli of Verona, and Giorgio Chittolini of Milan suggested sources and lines of enquiry, provided information on related topics, and welcomed me into that lively community. Archivists and librarians in many cities were patient in explaining manuscript holdings and most cooperative in making documents available. The staff of the Biblioteca Civica Bertoliana in Vicenza, above all Dottoressa F. M. Galante, Giovanni Dal Lago, and

Renato Zironda, fulfilled my requests with skill and forbearance. Ugo Soldà, formerly of the Vicentine state archives, revealed some of the valuable yet ill-catalogued resources of that rich repository.

Four young scholars merit special thanks. John Law of Swansea, Gian Maria Varanini of Verona, and Michael Knapton and Claudio Povolo of Vicenza gave freely of their time and friendship in assisting my research. Their unparalleled knowledge of sources immensely facilitated my entry into a complicated field, and their own studies provided invaluable points of comparison and perspective.

This book is dedicated to my family, which gave me a deep appreciation of the past, supported my choice of a historical career, and provided the moral and material support for the long haul of research and writing. The late Augustus and Julia Farnsworth encouraged further education and facilitated particularly my graduate studies. Thomas and Patricia Crawford shared their love for the Veneto and provided a marvelous base from which to work. My parents, Edward and Anne MacBurney, instilled in me a love for learning and for European culture. To them, as to my in-laws and grandparents, I owe my vocation.

Anne Crawford Grubb introduced me to Italy and directed my attention to the Renaissance. She has been my companion in tourism and study for many years, and her passion for Italian culture has enriched my own. Without her patience and unfailing support, the pleasure of historical discovery would have been seriously dampened. Thomas Edward Farnsworth Grubb is our firstborn, a fine young man whose delight in the world is unbounded. I love and thank them both.

Introduction

Venice's sea trade and overseas dominion are famous; the mainland dominion is much less so. The prevailing image of a maritime republic has obscured the fact that, by 1500, Venetian control extended over much of northern Italy, from Crema and Bergamo in the west to Friuli in the east, to the Polesine and Ravenna in the south. Governance of that dominion is little known compared with Venetian diplomacy in Italy and the wider European and Mediterranean theaters. General histories acknowledge that territorial expansion signaled a crucial turn in Venetian fortunes, but only a handful of specialists, most in the past two decades, have actually explored the internal workings of the mainland state.

This book examines that state through a case study of the governance of the city and countryside of Vicenza. The time is the fifteenth century, loosely defined: from 1404, when Vicenza's incorporation into the dominion began a quarter-century of Venetian territorial accumulation, to 1509, when the forces of the League of Cambrai shattered (albeit temporarily) that dominion. The approach is comparative, matching the Vicentine situation with that of other *terraferma* subjects and matching the Venetian state with Lombard and Tuscan counterparts. The enquiry moves beyond the traditional viewpoint of the state from the capital outward and seeks to give equal status to the perspective of the periphery, looking both at relations between Venice and Vicenza and at the location of power within Vicentine society. The issues involved are political in the broad sense: institutions and administrative praxis, certainly, but also the social bases of power, cultural differences and exchanges, fiscal policy, ecclesiastical management, and the ideologies that both defined authority and conditioned its exercise.

THE HISTORIOGRAPHIC PROBLEM

Niccolò Machiavelli, for one, was well aware of the importance of what he termed composite states, those consisting of formerly free polities brought under a dominant authority. He especially noted the lessons of

Venice's disastrous defeat at Agnadello in 1509, and he used the Venetian experience as a pointed example of ill-advised territorial expansion and administration. Francesco Guicciardini's rebuttal stressed Venice's wisdom in subjugating its neighbors, thereby securing a military buffer and a fiscal windfall.[1] Still, in declaring the didactic value of the mainland state, Machiavelli and Guicciardini pursued a solitary path. Students of Venice did not take their lead for well over four centuries.

This is no accidental gap in the historiographic record. From the Quattrocento to the present, a broad consensus of interests has led Venice's apologists, critics, and historians alike to overlook, even deliberately to ignore, relations between Republic and *terraferma*. The emerging myth that exalted Venetian institutions and deeds focused squarely on the "city built upon the sea." Indeed, location alone explained Venice's wealth, stability, and freedom from outside domination. The special destiny of Venetians was "to cultivate the sea and turn their backs on the land." Naval triumphs provided the basis for the rituals that impressed that destiny upon succeeding generations, most famously the yearly marriage of the doge to the sea as symbol of maritime dominion. Fleets, overseas commerce, and colonies in the East were the appropriate illustrations of Venetian magnificence.[2] As such, the myth of Venice proved ill equipped to describe the radically altered polity that resulted from mainland expansion. Fifteenth-century Venetians spoke little of mainland governance, in part because they lacked the conceptual vocabulary with which to discuss the union of islands and hinterland.[3]

Quattrocento Venetians preferred to hew to the old myths, particularly those that stressed the city's original independence from the mainland, and to leave in abeyance any definition of the territorial dominion or its relations with the capital. Many Venetians, indeed, were hostile to mainland expansion as a betrayal of the maritime-commercial orientation that had brought Venice to glory, as a source of political distraction and moral corruption to the city's patrician rulers. The humiliation of Agnadello, and the enormous costs of recapturing and holding the dominion thereafter, only reinforced their sentiments. Even those Venetians who accepted the necessity of mainland dominion thought it inconceivable that the *terraferma* be annexed on terms of parity with their ancient and proud state, and they continued to define the state as an urban polity alone. Early in the Quattrocento, for example, Lorenzo de' Monacis contrasted the glorious city with its savage and godless hinterland; few critics thereafter were as harsh, but none admitted the dominion to membership in the Most Serene Republic. Bernardo Giustiniani thought that Venice proper ended on the border with Padua; Gaspare Contarini in the next century felt it ended at the estuaries of rivers that emptied into the lagoon. The mainland dominion was considered extraneous to what was truly Venetian—when it was considered at all.[4]

When Contarini summed up the mature myth of Venice in the *De magistratibus et republica venetorum,* written in the 1520s and 1530s, he was obliged at least to mention mainland expansion. His scattered comments repeated suggestions from the previous century: that mainland peoples had invited Venice to expel tyrants, that the dominion merely reconstructed the ancient province of Venetia, that subject peoples retained their liberties and laws in a sort of federal state. These became commonplaces in apologetic historiography and were repeated well into the nineteenth century. But since the mainland was a marginal aspect of Contarini's myth, it remained marginal to a historiography that faithfully followed that myth. Too, Contarini's implicit disapproval of mainland expansion, reflecting the prevailing thought of his contemporaries, did nothing to stimulate study of the territorial state.[5] For their part, Venice's many critics were concerned to explode the myth, but they did not move beyond its terms.

Nor did historiography at large incline towards examination of the internal workings of the territorial state in the Renaissance. J. C. L. Sismondi, for example, lamented the extinction of communal freedoms as the medieval city-state passed under the authority first of domestic *signori* and then of regional states; Jacob Burckhardt, on the other hand, saw the creation of larger principalities as a positive (however brutal) step towards the modern state. To both models, state formation as decadence and as modernization, the sheer fact of the composite state was significant and sufficient. The situation of the provinces after the destruction of their independence did not warrant elaboration. Nineteenth-century writing and its twentieth-century reflexes favored the metropolitan center, the independent city-state, the republic, the "crisis of liberty," larger diplomatic and military movements. The title of Carlo Cattaneo's *City Considered as Ideal Principle of Italian Histories* fairly summed up a historiographic consensus.[6] Following a line of thought dating back at least to Machiavelli, historians knew that extinction of freedom brought only decadence to the unfree. Whereas spiritual impoverishment was of some interest to idealists such as Benedetto Croce, the political details of decadence were not.

The economic-juridical school of history, which rose to prominence in Italy just before the turn of the present century, seemed to offer a new perspective. Scholars from new disciplines such as economics, sociology, and legal history joined to study social relations within cities and juridical relations between cities and hinterlands. They subjected nonmetropolitan units, particularly rural communes, to un-precedented scrutiny. But the unit of analysis remained the simple binary of urban commune and agrarian *contado,* and the prevailing interest remained the free city-state as prototype or analogy for the Risorgimento Italian republic. Romolo Caggese, concerned to docu-ment the extinction of rural freedoms and the exploitation of the peasantry, took the "conquest of the *contado*" as a terminal event and chose not to examine the dispossessed after their subjection. Gaetano Salvemini, Gioacchino Volpe, and many others who explored the for-mation and internal struggles of communes were not much interested in the imperialism of those communes, and they were interested least of all in the subjection of smaller cities to greater. Attention waned with affirmation of the *signori* in the fourteenth century and ended with the absorption of most communes into greater regional states a century later.[7]

Study of the internal workings of the Renaissance state began only after around 1910, especially after the disappointments of World War I and Mussolini's rise to power. Manifest failure of the post-Risorgimen-to liberal state canceled the utility of the medieval commune as meta-phor for modern Italy. The original criteria for focus on that com-mune, especially the triumphs of bourgeois government and republican liberty, lost urgency and relevance. Following the lead of Antonio Anzilotti, historians as diverse as the Fascist Francesco Ercole and the Communist Antonio Gramsci thoroughly revalued the city-state, seeing replacement of autonomous communes by individual rulers as legitimate, because it was based on popular consent or imperi-al authorization, or at least as inevitable given the structural instabilities of communes.[8] By itself this viewpoint validated concentration postmedieval, signorial, composite states. It equally dictated a shift in focus. Modernity was still the primary test, but modernity evidenced in institutional maturation rather than rationalization or republicanism. The degree to which governments moved to level classes and munici-pal particularism, as necessary steps in unification, required study of the internal governance of the new political units. The leader in this movement was unquestionably Federico Chabod, whose famous stud-ies of the sixteenth-century Milanese bureaucracy and initial (though incomplete) steps towards the modern state have remained models of methodology.[9]

Venetian historiography, meanwhile, remained within Venetian myths. Diffusion of scientific historiography in the last century little affected the situation. Indeed, program statements of the regional historical commission, the Deputazione di Storia Patria, made the myths canonical. The mainland dominion remained a secondary concern. The prestigious Accademia Olimpica of Vicenza, for example, sponsored lucrative essay contests between 1891 and 1911 on topics relating to the *terraferma* and its administrative, military, and economic relations with Venice, but it received no worthy entries and never awarded the prizes.[10] Venetianists looked closely at the mainland dominion insofar as its administration necessitated creation or reform of the magistracies of the capital. When they studied the mainland, they looked at relations with local *signori* before 1404, or at relations with other Italian states thereafter, but seldom at relations with subjected cities. Local historians, often concerned to proclaim the oppression of their cities by the capital, did not contribute to a broader, regional field of study. The few studies that moved freely between lagoon and mainland, however excellent, have been more influential in our time than in their own. Even in modern times the myths that privileged the maritime over the mainland have not entirely died away. Notably, debate over Venice's decline as a European economic power, focusing on the loss of naval supremacy and the diversion of capital and energy to landed investment, did not ignore the *terraferma* but gave mainland expansion an essentially negative reading.[11]

Marino Berengo's *Società veneta alla fine del Settecento,* published in 1956, was the first major monograph to supersede insularity and parochialism. Drawing upon non-Venetian models to test for decadence or modernity, he placed the mainland dominion at the center of an examination of Venetian society and ignored the familiar commonplaces of Venetian historiography. The Venetian nobility, he wrote, was incapable of ceding power to a central bureaucracy and so preserved local municipal particularism in what was from the start a "disorganic and fragmentary" state. In keeping with its own aristocratic mentality, the Venetian governing class assisted local patriciates in closing ranks and assuming control of local communes. Yet, equally incapable of admitting mainland communes and elites to full membership in a unified state, Venice progressively stripped subject cities of real authority. Formation of the territorial state thus produced a double "crisis of liberty," excluding popular forces from power and subjecting mainland communes to exploitative Venetian rule, all without the compensation of unification or modernization for the state as a whole.[12]

Berengo's suggestions received elaboration and documentation by Angelo Ventura, whose *Nobiltà e popolo* of 1964 remains the standard, though not universally accepted, work in the field. In general terms, Ventura's conclusions diverged little from those of Berengo, though he relocated the origins of aristocratization and decadence in the fifteenth and sixteenth centuries or even earlier. Ventura also more directly targeted commonplaces of the Venetian territorial state: Ercole's assertion of "diarchy," with local communal institutions sharing authority with the dominant power, Romanin's vision of the Venetian state as federate, and Contarini's claim that mainland cities willingly submitted to Venetian rule and retained their liberties under it.[13] He abruptly dismissed the traditional images of Venetian benevolence and equity, of subjects' docility and gratitude. It was the first major assault upon the myths.

Gaetano Cozzi, already widely known for his work on Fra Paolo Sarpi and the Interdict Controversy, shortly thereafter offered a second model of mainland dominion. Cozzi, too, posited a conceptual separation between Venice and subject cities, but he attributed that "diaphragm" less to Venetian class privileges than to cultural differences. Above all, simple imposition of Venetian authority upon cities of the *terraferma* was impossible given distinct and incompatible legal systems, products of the very different historical evolutions of Venice and the mainland. Cozzi's several important essays examine the means by which Venice overcame that diaphragm to assert its sovereignty over the centrifugal forces of local particularism. It would be excessive, as Elena Fasano Guarini has noted, to see that "symbiosis" and reconstruction of regional unity as passage towards the modern state. On the other hand, Cozzi's more irenic vision gives no suggestion of the Venetian state as divisive or corrupt.[14]

The third prevailing vision of mainland dominion is not strictly speaking Venetian, having been formulated by Giorgio Chittolini for Lombardy, but in recent years, Venetianists have found it increasingly attractive. Chittolini has drawn upon the work of distinguished historians of the Visconti and Sforza states, long the only major school that concentrated on the internal constitution of the postcommunal polity, and, in common with that school, he has concentrated almost exclusively on political, juridical, and administrative relationships. He stresses the pluralism of the composite state, with independent jurisdictions and autonomous fiefs only imperfectly disciplined by the ruler. In a series of elegant essays, he has demonstrated the informal but effective division of powers between central and peripheral governments, with mutually limited ambitions and creation of only such central agencies as were necessary for maintenance of overall control.[15] His state is neither modern, nor mired in medieval particularism, nor consistently centralizing, nor rationally and systematically ordered. Hence Chittolini rejects traditional criteria of unification or decadence, and he insists upon *regional state* as the term for a polity sui generis.

Under the influence of these models, the mainland has assumed a primary position in Venetian studies, precisely at a time when insular

Venetian myths have lost much of their currency as historiographic guides. Venetian historical writing has, in consequence, become closely aligned with Italian studies for the first time. Throughout the peninsula historians have taken the path indicated by Chabod a half-century ago: his own pedagogic influence was widespread, and his writings provided strong topical and methodological models. Turning from diplomatic history to evaluation of the inner workings of the state, scholars test for modernity, or for exploitation of subject peoples, or, with more ideological overtones, for mechanisms and effects of class and hegemony. At the same time burgeoning universities have sent students into the countryside to professionalize provincial and rural studies. Conferences and collaborative volumes have strongly supported study of the regional, the composite, and the position of subordinates within the overall state. Rapidly accumulating work on the Lombard, Tuscan, and Papal states thus provides rich comparisons with that on the Veneto. The implicit context is even broader: Veneto authors, as do their counterparts throughout Italy, line up models of state development with those of the *ancien régime* as a whole. It is within that movement, as much as the specific context of Veneto historiography, that the present work has been conceived.

Renaissance state is a term that is rather out of fashion among European political historians. When John Law recently challenged Burckhardt's notion of political rationalism, of "the state as a work of art," he articulated a position that many recent scholars have assumed or implied. Few would accept the literal notion of a state broadly conceived in classical terms. Medievalists, concerned to break down ancient and pejorative periodization, have largely rejected even the limited sense of *Renaissance state* as a polity substantially distinct from those of the Middle Ages. Philip Jones, denying that fifteenth-century political forms represent any novelty with respect to earlier centuries, has declared that "the 'Renaissance state' is a fiction to be banished from the books."[16] Historians from many camps deliberately ignore the idea of Renaissance, preferring descriptive referents such as *regional* or *territorial state* (Chittolini), chronological referents such as *Cinquecento* (Berengo), or topographic referents such as *Venetian state* (Cozzi). Where the notion of a Renaissance state has survived, it usually carries a sharply reduced meaning, denoting political forms chronologically coincident with that movement in high culture that fairly constitutes a renaissance.[17]

Nonetheless this book retains the word *Renaissance* in the title and text not out of inertia and not because the term still resonates in Anglo-Saxon scholarship. It does so not in the expansive Burckhardtian sense, which would overwhelm a political case history, but in the restricted and literal sense that political actors required classical principles for governance. Even in provincial Vicenza, slightly outside the humanist mainstream, classical norms were crucial to justification or alteration of political relations. Vicentine patricians, in particular, found the Roman heritage—law, sanction for aristocratization, theories of corporation and clientage, universality of empire—indispensable to resisting Venetian pretensions and consolidating local power. The fact that classical ideas were often quarried from medieval commentary does not vitiate their antiquity, since people of the Quattrocento knew and revered the origins of those ideas. Nor is classicism diminished by its appearance as post facto justification rather than actual motivation, unless we are to deny all importance to apologetics.

Furthermore, *Renaissance state* preserves temporal precision and signals specific forms of organization and operation, which generic and timeless referents such as *regional* or *territorial state* do not. The Quattrocento state does show a radical change from medieval predecessors: composite, far larger, more sophisticated and systematic in its linkages, certainly more lasting than the unstable, ephemeral *signorie* of the Trecento. Students of the seventeenth and eighteenth centuries, in turn, will find the state outlined here a foreign place. Further revision may yet give a more defensible meaning to the notion of a distinctly Renaissance state—but that is a project for the future. This little-known territory needs detailed examination before the historian can affix labels with any certainty.

STUDYING VICENZA

Fifteenth-century Vicentines were fond of proclaiming their city the firstborn of Venice, the first to come under Venetian rule.[18] Because it was first and was ever loyal to the Venetian Republic, local partisans regarded Vicenza as a model subject among its *terraferma* colleagues. The first part of this image is not, strictly speaking, true, since Venice had governed Treviso with only a short hiatus since 1338. Still, during the Quattrocento such diverse and authoritative figures as Flavio Biondo and Doge Cristoforo Moro accepted the Vicentine claim to primacy, and it remained a staple of local self-perception thereafter.[19]

The second part of the image, Vicenza as exemplary, is the working hypothesis of the case study approach adopted here. It must, however, await verification in future syntheses. Since up to the present there have been no full-length studies of individual cities in the Veneto but only regional surveys and monographs on discrete sectors of governance, historiography offers a variety of comparisons but no single municipal norm by which to assess the Vicentine experience.

A preliminary, impressionistic valuation at least does not suggest any gross eccentricity that might disqualify the use of Vicenza as a case model. City and countryside were of middling size and proportion. As measured by Venetian fiscal demands, the only available index to the relative importance of mainland cities in the fifteenth century, Vicenza ranked squarely in the middle of the seven "noble cities" of the Venetian dominion, behind Brescia, Padua, and Verona, ahead of Bergamo, Treviso, and Crema (and a flock of lesser cities).[20] When firm demographic data are first available, in the next century, the Vicentine ranking is precisely the same.[21] Vicenza's topography, rather typically for the region, combined mountains and low-lying plains in about equal measure, with a thin but prosperous band of foothills separating the two. The countryside was not unusually rich or poor in soil, minerals, timber, or transport routes. Too, Vicenza seems to have been spared some of the local anomalies in Venetian governance: extraordinary controls on Padua, initially seething with rebellion and situated on the very edge of the lagoon; extraordinary privileges of autonomy for Brescia, on the border with Lombardy and always likely to accept Milanese rule; confirmation of deeply entrenched feudal jurisdictions in Friuli.

Vicenza's most evident deviation from the norm is its lack of a tradition of independence. Having fallen under the tyranny of Ezzelino da Romano in 1234, the city enjoyed less than a decade of freedom after his death in 1259 before passing under a loose Paduan "custody." A revolt in 1311 ousted the hated Paduans, but the city submitted almost immediately to the della Scala lords of Verona. The Visconti of Milan succeeded them in 1387, largely without opposition. Vicentine leaders did not make a serious bid for independence when Milanese rule crumbled after Giangaleazzo Visconti's death in 1402. Machiavelli was to observe that a people long accustomed to subjection was less likely to revolt against its lord, and thus could be more mildly ruled, than a people with a tradition of self-determination.[22]

The argument of lack of freedom, however, overstates Vicentine distinctiveness. In the Trecento, neighboring communes effectively ceded sovereignty to indigenous *signori* and retained only such authority as the ruler chose to delegate. By the second decade of Venetian rule, the other communes of the Veneto were about as docile as Vicenza. All offered fierce resistance to increased taxes and infringements of judicial prerogatives but seldom challenged overall Venetian control or conventional Venetian administration. Despite their history of subordination, Vicentines preserved a typical municipal patriotism through cults, rituals, civic chronicles, and enmity towards neighboring cities.

Vicenza was thoroughly like its neighbors, too, in its governing institutions. Two officials appointed by the ruler, a podesta with largely judicial competence and a captain with largely military competence, provided overall direction in Vicenza, as did their colleagues throughout the region. The legislative center was a large council (in Vicenza, the Council of Five Hundred), though a set of smaller elite bodies (in Vicenza, the eight deputies and, eventually, the Council of One Hundred) gradually acquired executive power and legislative initiative. Guild officials held ex officio council seats, despite a progressive loss of real power. The Vicentine judiciary, four consuls for civil cases and twelve consuls for criminal cases, was similar to that of Verona. So was the system of taxation, based on fixed quotas of imposts distributed according to separate assessments (*estimi*) for city and countryside.

The case study of Vicenza offers both a complement and a control to recent work on the Veneto. One advantage at this stage in research is place specificity. Ventura and Cozzi, ranging over dozens of mainland communes as well as myriad jurisdictions in Dalmatia and overseas, necessarily take a pointillistic approach and build up general patterns of governance from individual episodes. Anchoring a monograph to Vicenza alone permits subsequent overviews to decide which phenomena are locally idiosyncratic and which are characteristic of the region generally. Anchoring a monograph to the Quattrocento alone, in turn, provides time specificity. Ventura, for example, regards the fifteenth century as preamble to the sixteenth and seventeenth. Even if he is correct that there was no substantial change in the long run, it is necessary to establish the point of departure with greater precision. It is necessary to determine, as well, why certain aspects of the decadence attendant upon Venetian rule—the hostility of patricians to Venice, popular hostility to patricians, corruption of Venetian nobles and local patricians—were only latent in the earlier period.

A further advantage is the case study's capacity to follow small-scale but significant changes in governance. In a century that saw few grand constitutional statements or definitive confrontations, Venetians and their subjects defined and adjusted relations in a quiet fashion. Ideological positions emerge from apparently generic discourses such as preambles to laws or flattering orations. Minute, long-term shifts of jurisdiction disclose the dynamics of power. For example, Cozzi and several successors have stressed the importance of the Venetian magistracy of the *auditori nuovi,* sent on annual tours of the mainland to facilitate appeals to the courts of the capital. As bridging local and central judiciaries, the *auditori nuovi* apparently signal Venetian readiness to undercut local autonomies in the interests of sovereignty and equity. The story usually ends there. In fact, a succession of piecemeal Venetian reforms pared down the powers of the *auditori nuovi* as they consistently mishandled their task, as the central judiciary admittedly failed to provide good justice, and as local agencies proved able to safeguard or even expand their own prerogatives. This book must explore several such highly technical and unglamorous subjects as the necessary testing grounds of larger issues.

By restricting geographic and chronological range, the case study permits examination of Vicenza from several angles. A single line of enquiry—judicial, fiscal, rural—may in the long run prove tangential to general patterns. Only a test of different aspects of a single subject can separate the anomalous from the characteristic. Alternatively, fragmentary indicators from one sector may corroborate those from another. This book thus expands the traditional institutional focus of political history to a variety of concerns: the questions of who made law and by what principles, and who executed the law; the ways in which ruling groups established control and separated themselves from the unprivileged; the triangular relation of capital, civic commune, and rural communes; Venetian fiscal demands and local mechanisms for tempering them; ecclesiastical policy conjoining patronage with spiritual authority; the ways in which Venetians and Vicentines perceived their relationship; and the means used in everyday governance to reconcile sometimes divergent perceptions. High culture gets a passing glance: the degree to which subjects adopted or resisted Venetian styles is an important index to the capital's power. It is surely no accident, for example, that Vicentine patricians, far more than their Paduan and Veronese counterparts, crowded the city with palaces built in the Venetian Gothic manner.

The eclectic approach is hardly novel. Many years ago Federico Chabod, lamenting a tendency of the 1920s and 1930s towards specialization and compartmentalization in historical studies, decried the separation of political and cultural spheres and the division of the former into distinct subfields.[23] His lead has found admirable elaboration in the work of Ventura, who has studied aristocratic mentality and ideology along with such topics as food supply, charitable foundations, and criminal justice, and in the work of Cozzi, whose interests extend to painting, language, and ethical and spiritual beliefs as well as more conventional subjects such as legal administration. Deployment of multiple vantage points has not, however, been directed at the study of a single locale.

The case study, however much it points to larger issues, remains in itself a modest enterprise. Students of the composite state will find in Vicenza evidence for larger issues such as modernity or decadence, crisis of liberty, civic humanism and republicanism, rationalization, and unification. Nonetheless the single Vicentine case cannot be more than indicative. The present study, moreover, is written with specific historiographic questions in view, to test, document, sometimes confirm, and sometimes revise recent theses. It invites future syntheses but leaves to them many overriding considerations.

This is a task well suited to its subject. Vicenza was and is an unexceptional city, lacking in flashiness but not without significance for that fact. Often the ordinary detail is an accurate guide to what is characteristic of the whole.

PART I

The Making of
the Composite State

1

Creating the
Territorial State

*The fame of your justice, your prudence, and all your
other virtues has led us, Most Serene Prince and Most
Excellent Fathers, to come freely under your obedience
and submit to your dominion, which is the shield of all
Italy. We could not have borne the injuries of our most
bitter Paduan enemy, under whose cruel yoke we were
nearly forced to fall; we could not have borne his odious
tyranny, if we were not gathered into the breast of Venetian clemency . . . Therefore take this city, its countryside, and our riches, and defend them from the injuries of the Carrarese prince with that valor and
greatness of soul which this Most Serene Dominion has
always had. If you do so, you will have us as faithful
servants and friends, ready to spend not only our riches
but even our lives for the glory of your empire.*

—Giacomo Thiene, 1404

THE SUBMISSION OF VICENZA

By the spring of 1404 the Milanese dominion in the Veneto was on the
verge of collapse. Giangaleazzo Visconti's conquests, up to the shores of
the Venetian lagoon, had been due to the force of his personality alone;
and he had been dead for eighteen months. His widow, Caterina,
regent for his young heirs, could not maintain control. During the
winter, Francesco da Carrara had recovered lordship of Padua and sent
captains to raid the Vicentine countryside. Now he was building fortifications on Vicentine land. He could do so almost with impunity,
since the main Visconti garrison had been pulled back to Verona and
Visconti mercenaries in the field were more inclined to pillage than to
fight. Vicentines, loyal to the Visconti if only from an abiding hatred of
the Carraresi family and a bitter memory of earlier Paduan tyranny,

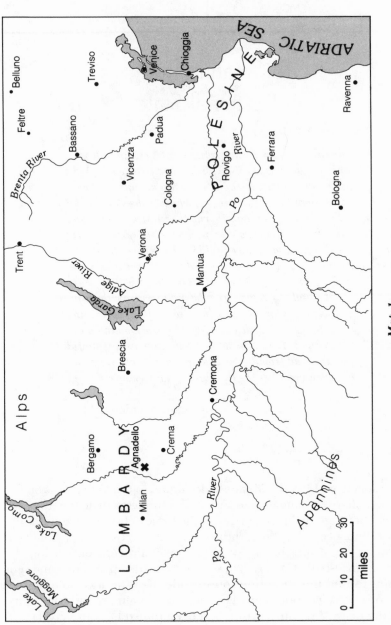

Map 1.
Northern Italy in the fifteenth century

took matters into their own hands. A ragtag militia of city dwellers and peasants marched forth bravely to redress "insupportable injuries"— and was cut to pieces, with the loss of 1,200 prisoners. In late March the Carraresi escalated the conflict, allying with Guglielmo della Scala to seize back lordship of Verona. On 8 April their combined forces captured Verona and besieged the Milanese garrison in the city's castle. Having installed the Scaligeri under firm Paduan patronage, the Carraresi sent an army eastwards towards a beleaguered Vicenza.[1]

That city, though declaring itself caught between Scylla and Charybdis, was not without resources. When on 11 April the "commune and people" of Vicenza sent out letters imploring Visconti assistance, they made certain that one letter was addressed to Giacomo Dal Verme, the Visconti ambassador in Venice. Four days later, Vicentines sent the ambassador Giacomo Thiene to press their case personally before Dal Verme, well aware that it was futile to expect Visconti aid but aware too that any such request would immediately reach Venetian ears.

A month before, appeal to Venice would have been in vain. Venetian negotiators had refused Caterina Visconti's offer of Verona and Vicenza in exchange for an anti-Carraresi league, optimistically declaring that "the lord of Padua was as a son to the [Venetian] Signoria, and always obedient to it."[2] The fall of Verona, however, made it very clear that the da Carrara had no intention of obeying Venetian calls for restraint. Venetian hopes of preserving an advantageous neutrality ended when the Carraresi laid siege to Vicenza, clearly signaling their ambition for regional domination. On 17 April the Signoria authorized sending two hundred crossbowmen and spending two thousand ducats for "the business at Vicenza and Bassano." The urgency of the situation was underscored a few days later when Guglielmo della Scala died—by Paduan poison, according to the inevitable rumors—and the da Carrara reinforced their control of his heirs. In Venice, Vicentine ambassadors dropped all pretense of loyalty to the Visconti and sought to place their city under the Republic's protection. Giacomo Dal Verme too gave up the lost Visconti cause and supported the proposal. His impassioned pleas on behalf of the Vicentine offer broke down lingering Venetian resistance to direct involvement.

On the night of 25 April a force of perhaps twenty-five Venetian crossbowmen slipped through Paduan lines to reinforce Vicentine defences.[3] The mere threat of full Venetian intervention was sufficient to cause Francesco da Carrara to lift the siege three days later. Even then Venetian intentions in Vicenza were uncertain: the doge on 3 May sent a bland letter congratulating Vicentines on their devotion and resistance and promised Venetian protection against hostilities by outside powers. Only a fortnight after that did the Venetian commander formally accept "dominion and governance" of Vicenza in the name of the Republic, establishing a rule that was to last for nearly four centuries.

MAINLAND EXPANSION

In the short term the taking of Vicenza precipitated, if it did not cause, a major redirection of the Venetian Republic. It propelled Venice into open war against the da Carrara and their Scaligeri clients. Success in that war led to annexation of Verona and Padua the next year. To keep those cities, the Republic found it imperative to exterminate former *signori*.[4] Some members of those families survived, however, and their cause attracted the support and armies of Sigismond of Hungary, King of the Romans and thus nominal overlord of the region. In fifteen years of sporadic war, Venice took Friuli and purchased much of Dalmatia when Sigismond acknowledged himself defeated.

The expansionist impulse, fueled by relatively easy success, proved difficult to curb. Ignoring the warnings of the dying Doge Tommaso Mocenigo to leave well enough alone, the Republic after 1426 seized Brescia, Bergamo, and Crema from the Visconti and defended them through two decades of war. Some Venetians aimed at Milan itself after the death of Duke Filippo Maria Visconti in 1447, or at least at establishment of an informal patronage over the Milanese.[5] Though that ambition failed, the peninsulawide Peace of Lodi in 1454 ratified Venetian conquests in the Veneto and Lombardy. In the parlance of the day, the lion of St. Mark had come ashore.

At the time, however, observers did not regard the taking of Vicenza, Verona, and Padua as a significant change in Venetian policy. Venetian council records made little mention of annexation, and chroniclers generally passed over the event with a few brief notices. It was no surprise to other Italian powers, which for the previous century had been building up their own states at the expense of petty *signori* and lesser communes. Venice was merely a late starter. Florentine councils, for example, ignored the taking of Vicenza and responded to the taking of Verona only with a flowery plea, building upon the inappropriate simile of King David and Absalom, that Venice not further castigate its wayward sons the della Scala.[6]

The very notion of a turn to the land would have seemed absurd to Venetians. Despite the insistence of mythmakers that Venice was "without fields, meadows, or vines, and live[ed] by trade and industry alone,"[7] the Republic had long been heavily involved in mainland politics. Even a maritime state required a pacified hinterland, a ready food supply, and open trade routes. To maintain regional stability the Republic granted trade concessions and signed alliances to maximize its influence in friendly cities and to neutralize hostile *signori*. From the thirteenth century onwards Venice supplied several dozen governors (*podestà*) to Padua and a score to Verona and Vicenza.[8] When diplomatic initiatives failed to keep the peace, the Republic was quick to send troops to keep river traffic and ports open and to protect its monopoly on salt production.

In the Trecento, Venetian intervention became more frequent and direct. The ever-expanding della Scala dominion prompted counterattack by a Venetian-Florentine-Paduan league in 1336–39. In the course of a successful campaign, Venice lent troops for a revolt within Vicenza and eventually assumed control over Treviso. When not itself fighting, the Republic was much in demand as arbiter in disputes between cities or, in the 1340s, between the della Scala and rebellious subjects within Verona. Indeed, one stated reason for the initial Venetian reluctance to take a more active role in the crisis of 1404 was that the Republic was already serving as guarantor of an earlier Milanese-Paduan peace treaty.[9]

Only with reluctance did Venetian councillors abandon a long-standing policy that emphasized diplomacy over conquest and preferred client *signori* to direct rule. In the spring of 1404, however, the threat posed by the resurgent da Carrara left little alternative. Paduan alliance with Genoa in the war of Chioggia (1378–81), which had paralyzed commerce and brought the enemy within the lagoon itself, provided an ugly precedent. Despite their defeat the da Carrara thereafter remained insensible to the advantages of allowing passage of goods to and from Venice. Nor could Venice pursue the traditional strategy of playing off dynastic enmities to its own advantage once the Carraresi had driven out the Visconti and effectively subordinated the della Scala. Probably only general exhaustion after the War of Chioggia delayed the final conflict. The Vicentine embassy of April 1404, then, was no more than a catalyst in precipitating the inevitable.

Nonetheless the taking of Vicenza (and Verona and Padua) was critical to the gradual transformation of Venice from a primarily maritime to a primarily landed power. It quickened investment in land until, for example, one-third of the Paduan countryside lay in Venetian hands. It obliged the Republic to devote a large and eventually predominant portion of administrative personnel and energies to maintenance of the mainland state. It established Venice as one of the five great Italian powers and drew the Republic into numerous alliances and wars in order to maintain a peninsulawide balance of power.

Furthermore, expansion not only established a mainland state but set the tone for its governance. Unlike Florentine or Milanese expansion, quite openly the product of aggression, early Venetian expansion was reactive and preventive. The Republic initially sought to ward off Carraresi hegemony and to protect trade routes, not to conquer. From the beginning, that is, the Venetian state was marked by limited central ambitions. Certainly expansion was not intended to absorb mainland cities into a greater union.

TERMS OF SUBMISSION

The first step in organizing the new state was adoption of articles regulating each city's submission to Venice. The Vicentine *capitula* are an unlikely sort of constitution, though that is what they became. An ad hoc assembly of "many citizens" drew up a jumbled list of forty-one requests barely two weeks after the Paduan siege had lifted. A Venetian army commissioner who had stayed on as provisional governor agreed to some, hedged on others, and suspended several "until the Dominante shall respond as it sees fit." Many articles addressed purely momentary concerns, requesting limited amnesty and confirmation of recent land transactions. Many were more hopeful than realistic, such as the requests that Venice not impose new taxes and that clergy be resident in their benefices. Several were contradictory or at least gave ambiguous signals. The articles ignored several crucial issues, in particular the urban commune's jurisdiction in the countryside. When the turmoil of the Veronese and Paduan conquests subsided, negotiators issued a more streamlined set of articles in March 1406, without changing basic terms of the *capitula* of 1404.

The first article was clear enough, asking that Venice receive dominion and administration (*regimen*) of Vicenza. Further articles assumed, though only indirectly, the transfer of supreme criminal and civil jurisdiction (*merum et mixtum imperium*) to Venice. Vicentine municipal statutes in 1425 elaborated this complex of powers, "transferring to [the Dominante] all force and power, with full criminal and civil jurisdiction and the power of the sword, and any jurisdiction whatever; and authority to create, supply, interpret, and change the law freely according to its will. Whatever that Dominante desire[d] by way of prerogative, burden, decree, or jurisdiction [should] be duly and properly commanded."[10]

Simultaneously, however, the *capitula* declared that justice would be rendered according to the statutes and ordinances of the commune of Vicenza. By logical extension, the articles preserved the municipal councils and offices defined in the statutes and guaranteed that the prerogatives and procedures of communal offices and tribunals would be supreme in ordinary administration. Additional articles ordered "integral and inviolate" observance of the privileges and statutes of municipal corporations, specifically the colleges of jurists and notaries, and ordered collection of indirect taxes (*dazi*) according to Vicentine norms. There was a strong suggestion that *merum et mixtum imperium,* at least in the countryside, remained with the Vicentine commune.[11]

Perhaps in agreeing to these requests the Venetian governor Giacomo Soranzo intended only to follow arrangements that had become customary in the ebb and flow of *signorie:* he spoke of "the usual procedure for changing lordships." In fact, the *capitula* mark a significant escalation of Vicentine powers. After 1329 the Scaligeri podesta of Vicenza had held legal authority to appoint or change municipal officers at will, without regard to local councils or statutes. The Venetian podesta certainly could not do so after 1404. The Venetian Republic had freely imposed its law upon Treviso after 1338. *Capitula* of 1387, regulating submission of Verona and Vicenza to the Visconti, had assigned full legislative and juridical authority to the new ruler but had offered no guarantees of local statutes and institutions.[12] On that basis the articles of 1404 and 1406, reducing the arbitrary authority of governors and restoring the integrity of Vicentine law and magistracies, came to be known as the "privileges" (*privilegia*) of the Vicentine commune.

Between the Venetian *arbitrium* conferring the capacity for unlimited intervention and the Vicentine *privilegia* protecting local prerogatives, the articles established an overall hierarchy but were decidedly ambiguous regarding the location of authority in everyday governance. In a similar vein the Venetian Senate's commissions to governors, which ordered execution of justice according to local custom and statutes "as long as these are in accordance with God and justice and our honor," only hinted at the relative competences of central and local governments.[13] Boundaries could never be precisely drawn. There remained ample space for conflict and ample space for adjustment.

But however improvisatory, erratic, and incomplete, the *capitula* established the basic relationship between ruler and subject.[14] They served as a constant point of reference for Venetians and Vicentines alike, almost as an anchor around which political discourse moved. That discourse was invariably conservative: politicians from both sides justified reform as a return to the strict sense of the *capitula* or resisted innovation as a deviation from original principles. A century of interpretation removed some of the ambiguity of the articles but none of their centrality.

PROTECTION OF PRIVILEGES

The Venetian guarantee of local rights need not be taken at face value. If Vicentines called the articles *privilegia,* Venetians sometimes called them *concessiones,* signaling that what the Dominante conceded it could revoke or override at will. The Veronese jurist Bartolomeo Cipolla, a leading professor at the University of Padua, was certain that "the prince can remove a privilege that he has conceded."[15] Among recent historians, Angelo Ventura has dismissed guarantees as fictions on more empirical grounds. The Venetian Republic was, he concludes, a conquering power. It issued the articles unilaterally after the "farcical ritual" of a supposedly spontaneous submission, which was in fact obtained with Venetian troops camped outside the city. He goes on to document systematic violation of privileges in crucial sectors such as taxation and control of the food supply.[16]

Ventura is entirely correct that rulers did not strictly enforce the *capitula:* Vicentine bishops were never resident, and Venetian taxation began soon after 1404. Nonetheless senior Venetian magistracies insisted that the core of the *capitula,* those articles protecting local law and administration of justice, receive the full backing of the Republic. Already by 1407, responding to mainland complaints, the Senate threatened Venetian officials who infringed local privileges with dire penalties. In doing so the Senate explicitly extended guarantees from the *capitula* to municipal statutes. Even the *arbitrium* conceded to governors in their commissions was insufficient to override local prerogatives: "We desire that the statutes and concessions made to this our most faithful commune be preserved to the letter, and that there be done nothing to contravene them in any way, indeed that they remain uncorrupted and inviolate . . . You should observe those statutes inviolably." The Council of Ten in 1444 was even more adamant, declaring that "no small terror and scandal" would arise among subjects if Venetian councils were to contravene privileges. The stability of the state itself would be undermined, "which is not to be tolerated." Decisions made by any Venetian official contrary to the *privilegia* were to be revoked and the offender fined a thousand ducats, thrown off the Great Council, and banned from office for five years.[17]

Those declarations followed generally accepted opinion. Most legal theorists of the day believed that privileges constituted a contract and established mutual obligations between ruler and subject as free and consenting parties. They were equally sure that rulers could not infringe that contract. It was the conclusion of the noted Paolo da Castro, sometime professor at the University of Padua, that "the Doctors have commonly held that when a ruler institutes a contract with his subject, he is obliged to maintain it. He cannot legally act otherwise even on the basis of his supreme power, because then he would be acting contrary to the primeval natural law."[18] That Venetian councillors admitted the contractual nature of the *capitula* is seen in their common use of another synonym for the articles, the *pacts (pacta)*, taken from the language of bilateral negotiation.

Alternatively, the protection accorded *privilegia* might only extend to those laws in effect when the *privilegia* were drawn up, that is, in 1404–6. Since the statutes of most cities were remade after that time—those of Padua in 1420, of Vicenza in 1425, of Verona in 1450—the Venetian guarantee of local prerogatives technically extended only to a body of law that was soon obsolete. Occasionally, it is true, Venetian magistracies declared their intention that privileges granted "at the time of first submission" be respected, with no specific protection accorded subsequent legislation. But such measures, apparently subversive of local rights, have quite another meaning.

In the middle decades of the century, senior Venetian magistracies fought a bitter internecine battle for primacy. One of the main issues of contention was various councils' claims to serve as sole protector of local privileges. In 1444 the increasingly powerful Council of Ten seized the legislative initiative, forbidding governors and other officials to act contrary to privileges and concessions except with express permission of four of the six ducal councillors, two of the three heads of the judicial magistracy of the Forty, and three-fourths of the Forty as a whole. By 1450, however, the Council of Ten held only the power to protect privileges made at the moment of submission. The Republic's chief legal officials, the *avogadori di comun,* guarded subsequent privileges.

The *avogadori* hastened to put the widest possible interpretation on their new jurisdiction, extending it in 1454 to the protection of local statutes drawn up after 1406.[19] But the Council of Ten was not prepared to accept curtailment of its patronage of mainland communes, and later that year it ordered that by *its* authority all Venetian officials were forbidden to act contrary to privileges, at time of submission or subsequent. In rapid succession the Ten attacked the *avogadori,* the *auditori nuovi,* and even its own leadership for breaches of local privileges. A decade later the Ten, in two decrees passed in a single day, singled out the *avogadori* as the greatest offenders against the rights of subjects. In March 1468 the Ten ruled that governors were not bound to obey any other council's mandates that contravened decrees of the Ten, because it wished "to preserve, and cause to be preserved, the statutes of Vicenza."[20]

The contest was far from over. On 18 September 1468 the Venetian Great Council, exasperated at continued bickering among higher magistracies, carefully defined jurisdictional boundaries. It stripped the Council of Ten of competence over observance of mainland privileges and assigned the task to the *avogadori.* In the next two decades, as a result, the *avogadori* several times curbed Venetian officials inclined to abrogate the "statutes and privileges of this most faithful commune of Vicenza." In 1486, however, the Great Council performed an about-face, assigning protection of subjects' privileges—those of the moment of submission to Venice and those subsequent—exclusively to the Council of Ten. A year later the Great Council reversed itself yet again, returning to the principles of 1450: the Council of Ten retained jurisdiction over the 1404 and 1406 *capitula,* while the *avogadori* gained jurisdiction over concessions made after the latter date.[21] This uneasy compromise remained in force for the remainder of the century but was little respected.

The long and dreary squabble, however undignified and corrosive to the nascent myth of a stable, harmonious Venetian government, had great significance for mainland cities. Most obviously, communes such as Vicenza could usually find a supportive magistracy in Venice, eager to uphold local rights in order to secure patronage over the mainland. Tribunals of the capital gave sympathetic hearing, in particular, to mainland protests against the intrusions of lesser Venetian officials. Furthermore, because senior councils had overlapping jurisdictions and were often at war among themselves, subjects could endlessly appeal unfavorable judgments until they secured more suitable verdicts. In 1472, for example, a civil case was heard successively by the podesta, the Forty, the Council of Ten, and finally the *avogadori,* whose ruling ordered "observation of the statutes and privileges of this most faithful commune of Vicenza."[22]

Secondly, competition to protect *privilegia* greatly raised the level of Venetian guarantees. Post-1404 statutes and later Venetian concessions soon acquired the inviolable status given to original *capitula.* Already by 1454 the Council of Ten had forbidden Venetian officials to perform any act "contrary to privileges . . . contrary to local statute . . . or contrary to the many decrees of the Senate or ducal letters." Vicentine customs and council decisions joined the list within a decade: "Provisions and statutes of this most faithful commune and its customs shall be preserved." By 1485 the doge confirmed that Venice was even inclined to expand the scope of guarantees. "We have deliberated and determined that you [governors] ought to observe the statutes, privileges, and ducal letters conceded to this most faithful commune, and that you should not involve yourself in things that pertain to our power. For we are more disposed to increase the privileges and concessions of this commune than to derogate them in any way."[23]

It is unlikely that such statements were mere propaganda. Venetians could hardly have regarded the *privilegia* as soothing fictions, casually conferred because easily violated, if senior councils spent so much energy defending them. The fact that both theoretical and practical protection of core privileges was consistent and intense over the course of a century indicates a basic Venetian resolve. Even if the issue of sincerity is suspended, it is well to recall that political language plays a dual role: it legitimates conduct and makes the ruler's actions appear in conformity with expectations and ideals of the public, but it equally places constraints upon the ruler's actions, which must at least approximately conform to the principles that he professes.[24] Examination of specific sectors of governance will demonstrate that Venetian resolve indeed translated into routine protection of Vicentine (and Paduan and Veronese) prerogatives, even at the expense of the overall Venetian capacity for intervention on the local level.

2

Definitions of State

Venetians produced no theory of the mainland state. They did not give separate consideration to issues such as the reasons why the Republic had annexed cities, the right by which they ruled cities, the proper relationship between ruler and subject municipalities, or the laws and principles by which they were to govern the dominion. The sole work addressed specifically to mainland administration, Marc' Antonio Sabellico's *De praetoris officio,* is short, freighted with classical clichés, and rather unrevealing.[1] General silence is hardly surprising, given the mainland's marginal position in the Venetian consciousness. Venetians were scarcely more voluble concerning their own government: the few surviving political treatises from the Quattrocento, principal sources for recent studies of Venetian political theory, were either unfinished, unknown, or unpublished in their own time.

Why this was so may be variously explained. Silence was largely intentional, as stringent laws forbade revelation of council discussions. Councillors largely respected the code of a closed governing process; even the semiofficial diaries of Marino Sanudo remained unpublished for four centuries. A compact ruling class may have so widely shared political assumptions that overall principles did not require articulation. Venetian nobles who did write were concerned to establish the Republic's greatness, not to examine its policies critically. They did not, for example, seriously undertake that humanist historiography which might explode the myths of Venice's privileged origins, and by half-hearted sponsorship of official histories they effectively discouraged others from doing so.[2]

So, to Burckhardt, Venice was a city of silence. He was quite correct, if the object of enquiry is the sort of fully developed thought found in the works of Salutati or Bruni. But though Venetians were not inclined to make grand constitutional pronouncements, they made frequent if smaller political statements: scores of chronicles, a few histories, hundreds of letters, and countless decrees and preambles to laws. The evidence is admittedly meager compared with the rich legacy of Florence in the Quattrocento or Venice itself in the Cinquecento, and some indications must remain fragmentary or inconclusive. Nonetheless there is sufficient evidence to reconstruct the thought that underlay or rationalized political action. If political assumptions can be recovered only from such second-level statements, that fact alone is a further clue to the basically pragmatic and empirical nature of Venetian governors. In any case, to dismiss the effort is to reduce the history of the *terraferma* state to a series of contingent political events.

EXPLAINING ANNEXATION

Venetians felt it imperative that expansion be accepted as the result of the uncoerced submission of subjects. The Republic could muster no precedent claims to mainland cities. For three decades after 1404 it held no formal title to those cities. When in 1435–37 Venice obtained imperial recognition of its expansion, the treaty specifically excepted Verona and Vicenza, and the basis for Venetian authority in those cities remained unratified for another century. This was a glaring omission in an age particular about formal legitimation of power. Even Giangaleazzo Visconti, quite openly bent on conquest, had been anxious to regularize his position by securing imperial title. Venetians, more vulnerable to charges of illegality because their own imperial title was at best partial, could find justification only in the notion that subjects had voluntarily submitted.

Apologists experimented with alternate strategies but soon found them unworkable and eventually discarded them. Right of conquest, for example, only fueled enemies' claims of Venetian imperialism and usurpation. Those few writers who dared even mention the military component of expansion were careful to stress the Republic's purely defensive intentions, particularly Venice's need to protect vital trade routes against Carraresi blockade. Even so, the commonplaces of the just war theory might have justified attack on Padua and preventive occupation of Vicenza, but they gave Venice a weak excuse for seizure of Verona, an even weaker excuse for annexation of Friuli, and no excuse whatever for expansion into Lombardy. Most authors preferred to deny bellicosity outright—though when Bernardo Giustiniani somewhat later claimed that "our empire was increased more through good political order than by arms," he offered no convincing alternative to military force. Only in the eighteenth century did apologists openly advance a justification of expansion by military conquest.[3]

Francesco Barbaro spoke for the majority in frequent and vehement denials that Venice was motivated by "lust for domination." Rather, he claimed, Venetian troops sought only to protect the freedom of mainland peoples against foreign or domestic tyrannies. His argument was congenial to subject peoples, as it embroidered their own declarations of submission, and it had considerable rhetorical appeal for Florentine civic humanists. Barbaro was ably supported by statesmen such as Ludovico Foscarini and Pietro Del Monte.[4] Still, this explanation rang increasingly hollow as Venice refused to restore local independence even after the demise of signorial dynasties. When Venetian troops seized cities that had no intention of seeking Venetian protection, continued their forward progress after the death of the last Visconti duke in 1447, and indeed aimed at Milan itself, Florentine support evaporated, and even the Republic's most fervent supporters deemed it best to avoid the subject of warfare altogether. In the later Quattrocento, justification by protection of mainland *libertas* suffered inevitable eclipse.

Several Venetian humanists took a rather different approach. From classical sources they recalled the Roman province of Venetia or the vast area once ruled by the Veneti, implying that mainland expansion merely reconstituted ancient jurisdictions.[5] A parallel line of thought claimed Venice as "new Rome" or successor to Rome, thus rightful heir to Rome as chief city of the peninsula. The paragon Venice-Rome was established in various ways: historically, asserting the descent of Venetians from the same Trojan stock; genealogically, demonstrating the literal descent of Venetian nobles from Roman patricians; ethico-politically, claiming the Republic's leaders as heirs to Roman valor. As Francesco Barbaro expanded the latter argument, Venetians had so excelled the Romans in *virtù* that "empire was properly transferred to better men."[6]

But all classicizing themes ran directly contrary to the myths' insistence on Venice as unique, independent of the Roman world in past history and present legal culture. Mere suggestion of an imperial destiny opened the Republic to charges of imperialism and contradicted the preferred line that Venice had only accepted invitations to protect the mainland against tyrants. Too, metaphoric affinity with ancient Rome was a feeble pretext for extending Venetian *imperium*. The *Romanitas* of Venice remained a literary conceit, widely diffused in cultured circles but without any real resonance in serious political discourse.

The theme of free submission had the additional and powerful quality of merely repeating a commonplace of subjects. Giacomo Thiene of Vicenza was the first to articulate the idea, in April 1404, and speakers and writers throughout the dominion followed his lead without significant variation. Whether from sincerity, sycophancy, hope for favorable treatment, or a desire to erase the stain of past opposition, peoples of the mainland were careful not to antagonize new masters by professing anything other than a warm welcome. Chroniclers, in particular, noted that heartily disliked neighbors had been "sold like steers" or "taken by siege and famine," but invariably painted their own cities as having enthusiastically sought Venetian assistance.[7]

Paduans, whose Carraresi lords had precipitated the war, and who were, in consequence, particularly nervous about Venetian good will, were the most obsequious of new subjects. They were also the best trained in fulsome oratory. As their ambassador explained at the ceremony of submission in 1405, Paduans had thrown off the yoke of tyranny and put on the pure white cloth of liberty, come forth from shadows into the glorious joy of light eternal, and realized the subjection, servitude, depopulation, and destruction suffered under the Carraresi. Now aware of the great justice, clemency, and liberty of a wise, powerful, and most excellent Venice, which by divine grace had brought then from an unjust and severe yoke of tyranny into liberty, the commune and people of Padua submitted happily to the doge.[8]

Vicentines, who really had chosen Venetian rule over unpleasant alternatives, were no less enthusiastic. They too could be theatrical. As the communal orator Matteo Bissari later reconstructed events of 1404, Lady Vicenza herself had cried out: "Take my laws and rights, my sacred halls, my public and private spaces, take my colonies and whatever surrounds me. Finally, take my free citizens and their fortunes!" Battista Trissino in 1462 cooperated in refuting charges of Venetian rapacity with the declaration that "our city was not taken by war or arms, nor bought for money. Stirred only by zeal of faith and singular devotion to the Venetian Senate, it surrendered itself freely and willingly to Venetian rule."[9]

Venetians, in turn, used the familiar theme to project an image of benevolent governance. Doge Pasquale Malipiero in 1459 reassured Vicentines of the ruler's good will: "When the city of Vicenza, together with its district, freely gave itself to our dominion, we promised by patents of privilege that we would accept the city and its district under the protection of our right hand and conserve it and increase it."[10] Hence the primary Venetian term for the events of 1404: *acceptatio,* simple acceptance of Vicentines' spontaneous offer.

The reward for professed loyalty was special Venetian favor, as Doge Cristoforo Moro declared in 1471: "[Vicentines] are especially worthy to be treated liberally, for before the citizens of all other cities they came to give themselves and their city—which they held in their own hands, their own power—into the hands and power of our Dominion, uncoerced by force of arms."[11] But in that soothing comment Doge Moro committed a serious indiscretion. The validity of Venetian rule, if derived from spontaneous submission, rested on the tacit assumption that in 1404 Vicenza was sovereign and legally able to transfer dominion. Moro made that assumption explicit. This distorted the historical record, since by all accounts Visconti lordship was technically intact when Venetian troops entered the city. Venetian-Milanese negotiations over Vicenza had broken down, and if Duchess Caterina thereafter released Vicentines from obedience, the document has not been preserved.[12]

Indeed, the very notion of spontaneous submission was flawed. It was patently untrue for many subject cities. Its theoretical implications for the rest, for those cities in which a philo-Venetian party had actually professed welcome, was corrosive to Venetian plans for permanent dominion. If Vicenza's original freedom was assumed and was reinforced by jurists' definition of the articles of submission as a contract between free consenting parties, dissidents could equally advance a claim that the submission of a free people need not be irrevocable.

The issue was far from abstract. In the frequent invasions of Lombardy and the Veneto in the second quarter of the century, most cities had the opportunity to resubmit to Visconti rule, and several did so gladly. They justified their actions with the precedent of a free transfer of allegiance at the time of initial submission to Venice, turning the pleasant Venetian commonplace against the Republic. They also learned that Venetians, however conciliatory in welcoming subjects into the dominion, were not prepared to accept their departure. Francesco Barbaro, for example, was normally the most mild of governors, but he took evident pleasure at the brusque suppression of a Veronese uprising, and when the people of Lecco rebelled, he suggested that they be chased out en masse and replaced by Lecchese exiles.[13]

Linguistic change after mid-century indicates a hardened Venetian resolve. Governors continued to define the act of mainland expansion with the generous *acceptatio* but first coupled it with and gradually replaced it by the harsher term *deditio*. Humanists and lawyers alike knew the *deditio* of the Roman law as a final, unconditional, irrevocable act of surrender. *Deditio* carried overtones of a capitulation in which the lesser party, far from ceding certain rights as a freely contracting body, gave over its entire existence, unilaterally and with hope only for the good will of its superior.[14]

Much of the terminology of Venetian expansion, in fact, assumed an authoritarian ring. This is particularly the case of the predominant term applied to the Venetian government, *Dominatio* (Italian *Dominante*). Linguistically it was related to traditional, relatively benign terms such as *dominus* (lord) or *dominium* (lordship). But *Dominatio* was also related to the verb *domare*, suggesting the power to subdue, to vanquish—to dominate. The Vicentine people, accordingly, were *subiecti*, not only subjects in the modern sense but equally those peoples subjected to Venetian rule, voluntarily or not. The communal orator Battista Trissino, for his part, accepted that reading in numbering his fellow citizens among "the peoples subjected to your governance on land and sea." The job of the Venetian captain in Vicenza, explicitly, was "to do what was necessary to maintain the total obedience" of local inhabitants.[15]

One final line of thought runs through the mass of Quattrocento documents. Both Vicentines and Venetians ascribed mainland expansion to divine favor. God willing, Vicentines wrote into their statutes in 1425, Venice should forever hold dominion of their city. Paduans and Veronese too saw God's will underlying Venetian expansion.[16] Divine sanction has, of course, been a commonplace of justification from Hammurabi to the present, but it is not less powerful for that fact. Its invocation throughout the Quattrocento was neither formulaic nor propagandistic. The very myth of Venice, then reaching maturity, had a primary spiritual component in stressing the constancy of Venetians' piety, their zeal to further the Church, their glorification of God in magnificent churches and cults, their special relationship with St. Mark. Wealth and empire were but rewards for an active faith. Deep religiousity, as Innocenzo Cervelli has remarked, informed Venetians' public policy as well as private devotions; indeed, the two can hardly be distinguished.[17]

Divine sanction had specific consequences for governance. Since territorial expansion was divinely favored, then rulers and subjects alike were entirely correct when they called the Venetian dominion sacrosanct. Subjects referred to the Republic as *Celsitudo* (Highness), a term hitherto reserved for God or his vicar the emperor. By implication, resistance to the central authority was not only illegitimate but impious. As Domenico Morosini noted pointedly, "God does not succor those who resist or rebel against him, but only those who are subject to him voluntarily and submissively."[18]

NAMING THE STATE

Quattrocento political discourse was relatively straightforward. Ruler and subject shared language and, to a large extent, values. But key words often meant different things to different parties and often carried multiple implications that provided alternate linguistic strategies. A century of governance, though generally peaceful, produced no consensus of meaning. To some degree this reflects the very different political cultures of island and mainland and indicates the degree to which governance never erased fundamental differences. But concep-

tual ambiguity was also a useful political instrument, containing conflicting intentions within apparent harmony. A technical term used
generically might paper over differences; or a generic term used with
technical connotations might press a claim or change a policy without
infringing the letter of agreements. Venetians made little effort to
render precise their principles of governance, it would seem, not because they were careless or inexpert but because they sought to avoid
the limitation on authority that would come from adoption of precise
labels.

The Vicentine commune's first request in March 1404 was that
Venice accept *dominium* of the city. The term was an old one, long
applied to the lordship exercised by *signori*. The Veronese in their
submission a year later reinforced this traditionalist approach, asking
that Venice be perpetual mistress (*Domina*) of their city. By retaining
the language of lordship, the Vicentines and Veronese evidently
intended to declare that the Republic simply replaced the previous
dynasty and established no new principle of authority.[19] In that sense
dominium implied a vague, open-ended capacity to govern, not far from
the English *dominion*.

But the word had alternate referents, and Venetians were not
inclined to distinguish between them. *Dominium* could refer not to a
principle of authority but also to the polity that exercised that authority: the *Dominium* as the totality of Venetian government heard petitions, ordered taxes, granted citizenship, and conferred privileges.[20]
Alternatively, *Dominium* referred to the executive magistracy of the
Signoria, composed of the doge, his six councillors, and the three
chiefs of the Council of Forty. Other magistracies, notably the Senate
and Great Council in appointing governors, frequently issued decrees
under the signature of the *Dominium*. Towards the end of the Quattrocento, *dominium* acquired territorial significance, as the area in which
the Republic exercised authority. Thus the Senate in 1506 complained
that "recently the evils and inequities of thieves have grown throughout our dominion."[21] Multiplication of referents only reinforced the
comprehensiveness of Venetian authority.

The fluidity of *dominium* had a more severe aspect. As was inevitable in a region permeated with the language of civil jurisprudence,
dominium also carried the technical implication of property ownership,
derived from the Roman law through the *ius commune*. From the earliest days of the state, subjects used verbs of property transfer in connection with Venetian dominion, as in the Vicentine request of 1404
that Venice not "give, sell, concede, or by any title alienate" its *dominium*
in Vicenza. Mainland expansion in that sense was not the generous
acceptance of subjects' free submission but a unilateral territorial ac-

quisition. Venetians wasted no time in borrowing the expression, announcing in 1406 that "by God's disposition . . . we have acquired *dominium* of the city of Padua with all its walled towns and fortresses."[22] Venetian reference to "lands and places acquired recently" or to "the time since we acquired Vicenza" became common, then formulaic.

Leading interpreters of the civil law reinforced the association of rulership with ownership. The Venetian Pietro Del Monte and the Veronese Bartolomeo Cipolla, in particular, followed traditional jurisprudence by concentrating on the *dominium* of property, but in a bold conceptual leap they transferred the qualities of goods (*res*) to governance (*auctoritas*). Their comments that *dominium* could signify "preeminence" or "jurisdiction" did not, it is true, advance the argument beyond the level of suggestion. Nonetheless, in conflating proprietary rights and political authority, they endowed *dominium*, hence endowed Venetian power, with a double potency.[23] This style of argumentation left *dominium* rich in implication yet versatile in application, hinting at central command without necessarily stripping subjects of traditional self-perceptions.

Other labels applied to the new territorial state had much the same fluidity. As was true in Florence and elsewhere in the peninsula, *state* (*status*) itself often had idealistic overtones, referring to the right ordering or just administration of the public welfare. An alternate use gave *status* a purely political signification, referring to the polity's constitutional format or ruling group. Or, indeed, *status* could be employed in both senses simultaneously, as in the description of a grave crime as *contra honorem et statum dominationis nostre*. By extension, *state* also took a territorial sense, embracing the region over which the polity held authority.[24] Mingling political ethics, coercive institutions, and regional hegemony in a single word, *status* magnified the stature of the Venetian government.

Imperium enjoyed much the same polyvalency. Often coupled or synonymous with *dominium*, it too began as an attribute of authority transferred to Venice at the time of submission, specifically supreme criminal and civil jurisdiction. In the words of Pietro Del Monte, *imperium* consisted of "the capacity to coerce and the power to punish."[25] In time *imperium* came to mean not so much the basis for Venetian governance as the Venetian government itself. From there it was a short step to territorial significance, *imperium* as the region in which that government exercised power. When decrees ordered preservation of the honor and dignity of the Venetian *imperium*, they intended any or all of these meanings and so added power to Venetian claims through multiple signification.

As Nicolai Rubinstein has pointed out, the very imprecision of *imperium* made it "particularly suitable for conditions in which the boundaries between immediate jurisdiction and political hegemony were liable to be blurred."[26] The distance from *imperium* to empire was short. Humanist apologists in particular found Venetian *imperium* a convenient vehicle for articulating expansionist ambitions without opening Venice to charges of imperialism. The trick was to raise parallels with the glories of Rome while stopping just short of advocating universal dominion in the peninsula. Hopes that the Venetian *imperium, status,* or *dominium* grow suggested territorial increase but could be explained away as referring only to consolidation of internal jurisdiction, or extension of a loose protectorate over helpless cities, or even realization of a bland ideal such as "good government." Vicentine partisans shared this line of argumentation, glorifying the Venetian *imperium* and hoping for its increase.[27]

In one respect, Venetian political language was entirely clear. Labels applied to the new polity were seldom free-standing but were generally qualified by a possessive: our dominion, our state, our *imperium.* The issue after 1404 was the geographic referent of that possessive. If "our dominion" included peoples of the mainland, if the geographic scope of the *dominium* were to be coterminous with the demographic scope of *nostrum,* then the Republic would have effected a radical change by expanding its political membership to include new subjects. In the early years this may indeed have been the Venetian intention. Citizens of most mainland cities, Vicenza's among them, received Venetian citizenship shortly after submission.

But, as Angelo Ventura has demonstrated, thorough absorption of the mainland would have swept away the aristocratic constitution of the Venetian state. If mainland nobilities had been given political access equivalent to that of their Venetian counterparts, the Venetian patriciate as a privileged class would have been disastrously diluted.[28] Rulers found the price of territorial integration too high to pay. Mere citizenship did not, in fact, entitle mainland peoples to hold significant office in the magistracies of the capital.

Other political discourse equally signals separation of capital from mainland. *Status* might be geographically inclusive of lagoon, mainland, and overseas possessions, but the invariable qualifier *noster* was politically exclusive. Venetian decrees ordered peoples of the mainland to love the state, honor it, and not create troubles (*scandala*) for it, but subjects had no share in it. As Lauro Quirini stated categorically, *imperium* belonged to the city of Venice alone. Subjects, in turn, accepted a political reality that rulers adamantly refused to alter: so Giacomo Thiene in 1404 declared Vicentines willing to sacrifice wealth and lives for "your empire."[29] *Dominium* too, however territorial, was qualified by possessives—*nostrum, Venetorum*—that made it evident that governance was the exclusive preserve of a Venetian patriciate to which non-Venetians could not hope to accede. Francesco Barbaro was explicit: the Venetian *respublica* did not include mainland cities or peoples.[30]

NAMING THE SUBJECT

Venetian magistracies never challenged Vicentines' definitions of their own polity. They protected local self-perceptions even when prevailing constructs, carried over from the era of free communes, suggested near-total autonomy. That is not to say, however, that rulers did not have a fundamentally different vision of Vicenza's status after 1404, or that they made no effort to impose their vision while leaving local definitions intact. The Ventian style was less to confront than to shift the terms of debate, sometimes investing similar language with different implications, often deploying generic terminology to devalue the precise claims of local, technical descriptive terms.

The most powerful name that Vicentines gave their municipal government was *respublica.* They did so in the face of the strict definition of jurists such as Bartolomeo Cipolla: "Those who call their city a republic speak improperly, except Venetians, because their city recognizes no superior."[31] Vicentines certainly did recognize Venetian superiority and hence could not claim sovereignty, but they clung tenaciously to an apparently outmoded civic identity.

What they meant by *republic* is suggested by the commune's chief magistracy, the office of the "eight wise men deputed for the utility of the Vicentine *respublica.*" These deputies, by the prescriptions of municipal statutes, protected the "public good of the city and district of Vicenza," flanked the podesta in ordinary administration, guarded against dissipation of the public patrimony, supervised guilds, and pacified violence. The Vicentine republic, by the inference of that commission, embraced more than urban commune alone: it was the collective public body of the Vicentine people, citizens and noncitizens, inhabitants of city and countryside, members of the closed municipal councils and the great mass of the population excluded from political power. Other documents spoke of the Vicentine republic as the collective political conscience of the populace, as the repository of justice and right governance. A governor's grant of illegal pardons insulted the *respublica;* tax evasion defrauded the *respublica;* admission of unworthy men as citizens offended the *respublica;* cheating in council elections brought shame upon the *respublica.*[32]

While Vicenza as republic was a centuries-old construct, its continued invocation in the Quattrocento actually expanded municipal pretensions. As guardians of the Vicentine republic, communal deputies laid claim to jurisdiction over city and countryside alike, notably over those urban corporations and rural communes that had often operated as independent authorities in the past. In particular, the commune as republic sought to handle ordinary rural administration, and to serve as intermediary between Venice and the Vicentine district. Venetians never challenged that potent attribute, but they avoided endorsing it by making no reference to the Vicentine republic and by keeping the word out of their political vocabulary.

Respublica was reserved for solemn occasions. In everyday discourse Vicentines referred to their polity as a *civitas*. The principal definition of *civitas*, a body of persons living under their own law, implied an authority and integrity to Vicentine law that the Dominante could not abrogate without direct assault upon local privileges. As *civitas* the Vicentine commune held, by definition, the capacity to make statutes and provisions and to grant citizenship. Bartolomeo Cipolla followed authoritative legal tradition in further endowing the *civitas* with territoriality, urban government exercising authority over and declaring the law for a subject countryside.[33]

Venetians too labeled Vicenza a *civitas*, but they meant something quite different by it. *Civitas* need not be translated as city-state, indeed need have no territorial connotations. The jurists, who were the most scrupulous lexicographers of the day, offered contrasting definitions: *civitas* as urban settlement alone or *civitas* as urban government with jurisdiction over the surrounding countryside.[34] If Vicentines preferred the territorial meaning, Venetians preferred the strictly urban. Occasionally, it is true, central magistrates used *civitas* as an all-encompassing term, but more frequently they referred to the *civitas et districtus* of Vicenza, defining urban core and rural surroundings as separate and independent entities. The imposition by Venetians of the lesser topographical meaning seriously devalued, if only implicitly, the claim of the municipal government to exercise authority over rural communes.

Venetian magistracies eventually bypassed *civitas* altogether, designating Vicentine municipal government (and the government of each mainland city) as a *communitas*. Evidently they intended to translate the term as "commune" and so to preserve traditional labels. But *communitas* was nonetheless subversive. It was not the locally preferred word for a commune—*communis* or *commune* was—and it tacitly denied the considerable authority that mainland communes claimed. The standard meaning of *communitas* was nearly that of "community" today, with connotations of social bonds and coresidence, perhaps a common law or common property, but not necessarily governmental powers.[35] Venetians' consistent deployment of *communitas* thus deflected the potent claims embedded in *civitas* or *respublica* and acknowledged no local autonomy or even capacity for self-government. *Communitas* also downgraded the privileged status of the Vicentine urban government, since even the smallest village communes were equally styled *communitates*. Nothing in *communitas* assigned any territorial jurisdiction to the urban commune, perhaps one reason why Vicentine lawmakers studiously avoided the term.

The first letter of the doge to his new subjects, dated only three days after Vicenza's submission, was addressed not to the commune but to "the citizens, community, people, and entirety of our city of Vicenza." It established a relationship, that is, between the ruler and a series of disjointed, distinct bodies and thereby downplayed the special authority of the urban commune. Subsequent correspondence and decrees replaced that unwieldy salutation with the clipped *lands*. Venetian councils sent legislation "to the lands and places subject to us," "to all our lands on the mainland," and so ignored the city government's claim to mediate and execute central decrees.[36] If *civitas* as an urban unit undercut the Vicentine municipal government as a regional authority, and the generic *communitas* devalued the specific jurisdiction of the commune, *terrae et loci* discounted local government altogether.

METAPHORS OF STATE

Rulers and subjects may have had rather different conceptions of the territorial state, but neither side inclined towards confrontation. Vicentines did not protest a terminology that reinforced Venice's broad capacity for intervention, despite that terminology's hard edge suggesting severe reductions in local autonomy. Venetians, in turn, respected even the most particularistic language of their subjects. Conflict, though frequent and sometimes bitter, was confined to specific cases of jurisdictional interference and did not spill over into disputes over principle. Potential friction between divergent ideals of governance was eased, as well, by consensus in a metaphoric discourse tending towards conciliation and accommodation.

Venetian councillors quickly adopted the paternalistic imagery that had long been applied by rulers to the proverbially loyal and compliant Vicentines. Thus the doge referred to Vicentines as "our dearest, best-loved, and most faithful children." Vicentines reciprocated, calling their Venetian governors "our true parents." Veronese, Paduans, and Trevisans too acknowledged Venetian parentage, while the Paduan commune in 1449, attempting to mollify ancient Vicentine enmity, stressed the sibling concord expected of "brothers born of the same parents."[37] Filiation conveniently acknowledged, yet also limited, the aspirations of center and periphery. It established subordination, certainly cut off local claims to independence, and reminded subjects of the obedience due to parents, but it left the subject as a distinct person with at least a limited freedom of action. Both sides ignored the metaphor's less soothing implications: on the one hand the totality of power enjoyed by the father under the *patria potestas*, on the other hand the certainty that the *filius* would eventually come of age and throw off parental authority. In a related image, Venetian humanists referred to mainland governance as tutelage or guardianship, invoking the Roman law's "right and power over a free person . . . to protect him who, because of his age, is not able to defend himself." Subjects shared the image;[38] and no one suggested that mainland wards would eventually reach maturity.

The equally common metaphor of a patron-client relationship admirably reinforced the notion of voluntary submission. Francesco Barbaro, for example, repeatedly stressed that, in extending its patronage over the mainland, Venice had acted only to protect endangered clients. The Vicentine orator Guglielmo Pagello in 1471 saw patronage as the basis of all Venetian territorial authority, in the East as well as on the Italian mainland: "I will not recall how many kings, how many nations, how many peoples have given themselves over as clients of the Venetians."[39] Subjects throughout the dominion shared his view. Variants on the theme identified the *patronus* with the local podesta, both as personal guardian of his city and as representative of a protective Republic. A symbolic reading identified the patron with St. Mark himself.[40] Like tutelage, even more than filiation, patronage preserved the free status of the subordinate without jeopardizing the superior's overall authority. No one was inclined to develop the metaphor beyond that point by suggesting that the client could dissolve the relationship, or that the patron could exercise iron control.

A final line of thought described the Venetian territorial state as a corporation, a body politic of head (Venice) and limbs (mainland cities). The image was a familiar one, a long-time staple of political theory that had achieved particular emphasis and refinement during the recent conciliar movement. In the Quattrocento, Venetian partisans found the corporate image generally descriptive of the composite state, and it entered Venetian myths in that form. Veronese councillors too found it apt and fixed it in municipal statutes of 1450. The previous year, Vicentines, accepting Paduan gestures of friendliness, commented that charity between mainland cities was both useful to those *membra* and glorious to their common head.[41]

Incorporation was, characteristically, suggestive but not threatening. For Venetians, corporation suggested an overall unity, reinforced by obligations of support by limbs and the directive capacity of the head. It was especially useful in justifying demands for financial assistance: "It is wholly necessary that these [peoples], who are the limbs of our state, shall give aid to us who are the head."[42] Mainland peoples found comfort in several conclusions of corporate and conciliarist theory: that the head could not operate without or usurp the proper functions of the limbs, and that those limbs enjoyed a limited autonomy of operation and a limited degree of consent in the movements of the whole.

When Lorenzo de' Monacis summed up the main themes of Venetian expansion in 1426, the result was a graceful jumble of mixed metaphors: "Divine Providence has ordained that this our island, Venice, which governs several mighty cities of the ancient province of Venetia with happy moderation, now adds others under the mild yoke of its dominance, combining them as limbs of its body. As it once preserved those peoples from the greed, ferocity, and violence of barbarians and pagans, may it now save their successors from tyrannical power."[43] His rhetoric was not vacuous, though it was perhaps excessively irenic. Nor was the state he described without conceptual foundations, however much its expressed principles were vague and inconclusive. Ruler and subject found real meaning in themes of expansion as providential, Venice as strictly insular, Venetian governance as gentle, the state as corporation, expansion as protection of the weak from tyranny. Apparent failure to define the state more precisely was, in fact, a shared strategy. It left both sides room for maneuver while establishing a broad consensus and a harmonious atmosphere in which to work out the relationship. Given the unbridgeable cultural differences that divided Venice and mainland in 1404 and continued to divide ruler and subject for the next century and more, neither side could aspire to greater precision.

3

Dominion and Law

Venetian territorial expansion did not constitute simple absorption of
cities by a more powerful neighbor, as was the case in Tuscany and
Lombardy, but rather superimposition of distinct and even incompatible cultures. Venice had had a radically different historical development and had generated different political values and institutions for
realizing those values than had the cities of the mainland. The Republic's partisans acknowledged that fact, setting Venice's original and
ongoing independence from the larger Western Empire as a primary
component of the emerging myths. Specifically, Venetians, unlike their
subjects, made no use of the *ius commune*, which was largely derived
from Roman law, and thereby created a fundamental contrast between
the political and legal systems of capital and hinterland.

Isolation from mainland ways posed formidable obstacles to thorough imposition of central authority. Complete adaptation to local
structures was out of the question, given the Venetians' deep pride in
their institutions. On the other hand the laws and procedures of the
capital were almost incomprehensible to subjects and could not be
simply imposed upon them. Lacking the resources and the inclination
to eradicate local usage, Venetians were inclined to endorse it—hence
the dual jurisdiction established in articles of submission, and hence
the contrary claims embedded in the language that defined the state.
Bicultural governance proved a generally workable compromise, but it
produced constant tension between center and periphery and, in the
end, heavily conditioned the effectiveness of Venetian rule.

VICENTINE LAW AND COMMON LAW

Judges in Vicenza, including the Venetian governor and the jurists on
his staff, were charged with administering justice according to municipal law. When local norms were inadequate to decide a case, the sole
recourse of judges was to the common or civil law. This principle, long
established by jurists, was written into Paduan as well as Vicentine
statutes. Indeed, no mainland city adopted Venetian law as a source for
resolving juridical conflict or uncertainty. As Pietro Del Monte noted,

Venetian law was not observed in areas in which the *ius commune* was normative. Venetian councillors in turn acquiesced in the exclusion of their law when they ratified mainland statutes. They accepted, as well, the common opinion that municipal law was to be interpreted strictly according to local custom, by those who had drawn up those statutes. In doing so they reinforced the juridical separation of capital and subject cities and, because Venetians were largely ignorant of the civil law, gave local governments a primary say in judicial administration. The Venetian state, accordingly, was potentially less centralized than the Florentine, where the statutes of the capital were used to fill lacunae in local law.[1]

Vicentines found a strong impetus to preserve the civil law tradition, both as the basis of the municipal judiciary and as a counterweight to Venetian pretensions. That *ius commune* already underlay legal discourse in Vicenza and other mainland cities. The leading historian of medieval Vicentine jurisprudence has concluded that "the written law that has been conserved in communal codices is all or nearly all Roman law." Quattrocento statutes continued to rely heavily upon the terminology and constructs of the *Corpus iuris civilis* and the *ius commune* generally. One rubric, for example, ordered that all published judicial sentences were to have the force of *res iudicata* as defined by the civil law. Vicentine notarial instruments took Roman titles (*donatio inter vivos, verba de presentis, confessio dotis, datio in soluto*) and largely replicated the terms of Roman jurisprudence. Roman law permeated everyday discourse as well: an orator invoked the *lex Iulia de annona* by name, a Vicentine ambassador paraphrased the venerable maxim *Quod omnes tangit* before the doge, and the local College of Jurists peppered its statutes with quotations from the Roman civil law.[2]

Vicentines knew that the civic utility of jurisprudence would suffer if its practitioners came to regard the profession as a mere guarantee of social prestige. They insisted that jurists be demonstrably proficient in the Roman law and medieval glosses and commentaries. Municipal statutes ordered that "no one shall henceforth be received into the College of Jurists of the city unless he has studied the law for a sufficient time or has acquired a doctorate or at least a license from an authentic university, and unless he is in possession of all books of the *Corpus iuris civilis*."[3] Vicentine students took that requirement to heart and achieved considerable prominence at the University of Padua: at least five Vicentines were elected rectors of the law students in the first half of the century alone, and at least twenty-one taught civil or canon law.[4] At least eight of those professors, including the distinguished Alessandro Nievo, left *consilia*.[5]

The College of Jurists was equally concerned to maintain the qualifications of its membership. College statutes required that each aspiring lawyer pass the same sort of examination given to university doctoral candidates, specifically that he read publicly "one paragraph or law of the Code or Digest and recite all the ordinary glosses of Accursius . . . Then he must hear and respond to any questions that members of the college wish to put to him." Tests were not mere formalities to give the stamp of legitimacy to young men qualified only by social prominence: many scions of noble families were denied admission.[6]

Having demonstrated their learning, Vicentine lawyers continued to immerse themselves in the civil law. Known Quattrocento library inventories are filled with copies of the *Corpus iuris civilis*, glosses, commentaries, lectures, and *consilia*. Several active typographies early established Vicenza as a center for the editing and printing of legal texts, including a *Vocabularius iuris* in 1482 and another in 1492, the notarial textbooks of Rolandinus and Pietro da Unzola, Maffeo Vegio's *Vocabula ex jure civili excerpta* in 1477, three editions of Vicentine statutes before 1499, and premier editions of the statutes of Verona (1475) and Padua (1482).[7] Vicentines could also draw, of course, on the flourishing printing and manuscript centers of Padua and Venice.

Vicentine jurists were, moreover, active in the interpretation of law. Either party in a civil lawsuit could submit the case for the formal opinion of a jurist. The resulting *consilia* were delivered orally, so there is no indication of their frequency; but notarial registers record dozens of commissions of disputes for expert advice. That the technical skills of lawyers were in constant demand is suggested also by the fact that most surviving manuscripts of municipal statutes, as well as several early printed copies, were more or less heavily glossed. Notably Girolamo da Schio, who enjoyed a distinguished forty-year career as councillor, deputy, and ambassador to Venice until his death in 1509, filled the 180 folios of his text with marginal exegesis, definitions, quotations from Roman law, explications, interpretations, corroborations from other cities' statutes, and citations of medieval authorities. His intention, following jurisprudential tradition, was twofold: to clarify local law and to ground it in Roman law and medieval interpretation. In doing so he used a far wider range of sources than was usually the case even among the academics: the *Corpus* and standard gloss, certainly, but also Jacopo da Ardizano, Cynus, Bartolus, Jacobus Butrigarius, Baldus, Giovanni da Platea, Francesco da Crema, Bartolomeo Belenzini, Bartolomeo Saliceto, Pietro Del Monte, and a dozen others.[8] His gloss is strong evidence for the vitality of Vicentine legal thought.

The strength of the civil law tradition is suggested, finally, by increased employment of legal specialists. The *capitula* of 1404 spoke of the city's dearth of *doctores legum;* it was the nadir of the demographic slump and a plague year as well. From that law point the College of Jurists grew steadily, then more than tripled its membership in the period 1469–1503, from twenty-one to seventy.[9] For its part the commune tried to stimulate such growth by offering a tax exemption to college members. It also pushed jurists into higher-level careers as consultants and ambassadors, forbidding them to serve as mere legal representatives or trial lawyers. As early as 1410 civic councils decreed that "no judge of the College of Jurists of the city of Vicenza can or ought to be a procurator or syndic in any legal cases or disputes heard in the communal palace of the city of Vicenza."[10] Still, the need for expert opinion exceeded even the resources of an expanded college, and cases were routinely sent to the faculty of the University of Padua for interpretation. Hundreds of *consilia* and *questiones* relating to Vicentine disputes are known, with probably hundreds more yet to be discovered.[11]

VENETIAN LAW AND EQUITY

Venetian law was altogether different. The great myth, that Venice had been founded in freedom and had never been subjected to imperial domination, claimed legal as well as political idiosyncracy. Mythmakers were not alone in making that claim. Several generations of jurists used very different sources to corroborate the Venetian self-perception. The obscure lawyer Alessandro Terzi summed up their conclusions in a *consilium* delivered before the doge in the mid-Cinquecento.[12]

Venice, he paraphrased Bartolus and Baldus, was exempt from the jurisdiction of the Roman Empire by virtue of a golden bull issued by Frederick Barbarossa. But that privilege was superfluous, according to Baldus, because Venice had been built upon the sea and thus, according to both the *ius gentium* and the civil law, belonged exclusively to those who had built it.[13] In either case the implications for Venetian justice were clear. As Raffaele Cumanus had asserted and Giason del Maino had repeated, Venetians did not live by those *leges communes* that derived from the emperor but by their own natural justice. And so, Terzi concluded from Giason, who had followed Baldus, who in turn had followed Cynus, Venetians followed not the imperial law but the dictates of natural reason in deciding cases.

Terzi was by no means exhaustive on the subject. Bartolus had argued from the law of prescription that Venice's unchallenged long-term independence conferred legitimacy. In the Quattrocento, Paolo da Castro used Bartolus's criterion for sovereignty to assert that, since

Venice recognized no superior, it held a status independent of and equivalent to the empire. Raffaele Fulgosio went a step further, claiming Venice as New Rome and hence freed of any obligation to follow norms emanating from Old Rome. Jacopo Alvarotti was not sure that the doge held legitimate authority since he was elected by councils and populace rather than the emperor; but the emperor had tolerated the situation for so long that the doge held power lawfully (*iuridice*). On a more practical level, Bernardo Giustiniani believed that the requirements of trade justified Venetian rejection of a cumbersome imperial law. That array of arguments reached a unanimous conclusion: "Venetians make no use of the *ius commune* in sentences delivered in Venice."[14]

Venetian law had not always been so insular. Well into the thirteenth century it had preserved notable traces of imperial law, both Roman and Byzantine. Civil lawyers stressed affinities between Venetian usage and Justinianic law and gave Venetian statutes of 1242 the same sort of glosses and commentaries that they gave statutes of the mainland. By the fifteenth century, however, Venetian statutes had fallen into disuse. They were seldom mentioned in the city and never on the mainland.[15] Exclusion of civil law norms and procedures, though long suggested by mythmakers and jurists, was now complete.

Venetians argued on the basis of divine or ethico-religious ideals such as justice or equity or *humanitas*, not from positive human law and certainly not from classical norms. In Venetian usage a crime was not so much an infringement of statute as an act "against God, right, and justice, against the rules of good behavior and against our proclamations." In specific applications of this principle, Venetian councils ordered capture of violent malefactors and punishment of fiscal abuses not because crimes broke any human law but because toleration of injustice offended the honor of God and Holy Scripture.[16]

Faith alone demanded good governance, but so did political good sense. To permit injustice was to permit impiety, which would jeopardize God's good will towards the Republic. This conflation of piety and pragmatism was the first principle of governance, as written into commissions of Vicentine governors:

> Those who hold the helm of cities must be careful above all to forbid those sins that can easily provoke the wrath and indignation of Omnipotent God. Nothing is more harmful than that, by failing to do what ought to be done, an unstained justice is perverted or (what is worse) faith in Christ be denied . . . Justice, in which the safety of cities especially consists, must be venerated and preserved in accordance with divine precept.[17]

As the Maggior Consiglio declared in 1435, justice was the principal foundation and singular ornament of Venice; but *iustitia*, to Venetians, rested upon application of abstract ideals rather than codified norms. Pier Paolo Vergerio noted at about the same time that "our civil law is hardly anything else besides equity."[18]

Having excluded the *ius commune* and statutory law, Venetian statesmen needed guides to just administration. Not surprisingly, they found models for right political behavior in the ancestors who had made the Republic an exemplar of just rule, and they found normative models in the specific acts of those ancestors. Councillors held deep reverence for *progenitores* and by extension deep reverence for the elders in their midst. Venetian law, accordingly, was case law, argument on the basis of past legislation and court judgments. Yet justice could not be served merely by following precedent, lest rigid adherence to bygone decisions unintentionally reproduce the flaws of positive law. It was necessary to apply universal principles according to the needs of the moment. Councillors justified empiricism by a maxim that runs throughout Venetian proclamations: "experience is the best teacher." That *experientia* pointed in two directions, to the lessons of past experience and to the situational demands of present experience. Nonetheless the Maggior Consiglio, for one, saw no contradiction between juridical conservatism and judicial flexibility: "The provisions of our ancestors, which were made according to the conditions of the moment . . . are those that we ought to imitate."[19]

On the mainland, governance from principle made use of several time-honored mechanisms. Ironically, Venetians fell back upon procedures endorsed by civil law jurisprudence while excluding the substance of the *ius commune*. In particular, leading authorities sanctioned argument from *intentio*, restoring the superiority of the purpose or spirit of the law over the letter of the law.[20] But where jurists invoked *intentio* as a last resort against blatant miscarriage of justice, Venetians elevated intention to a primary justification for central intervention. On occasion, Venetian *intentio* actually supported local law, canceling bad decisions by local governors, or supplemented the law by filling gaps or closing loopholes: blocking the subterfuges by which Jews acquired land, for example, or those by which countrymen obtained citizenship yet evaded urban obligations.[21] In general, however, appeal to the spirit of the law served to declare a higher Venetian will and override the strict terms of local positive law.

Venetian promotion of arbitration as an alternative to lawsuits similarly raised equity over statute. Mainland law had long accepted private composition, indeed required it in certain categories such as disputes within families. But the councils of the Republic so heavily stressed extrajudicial compromise, and so elegantly refined its procedures in laws of 1433–44, that arbitration was thereafter held to have been accomplished *more veneto*. Again, Venetians were well served by

jurists whose doctrines they otherwise rejected. Their guiding principle came from Bartolus: "In arbitration the judge is not obliged to
follow the letter of the written law but can follow equity and not the
written law." Arbitration cases could be decided either by the law or the
facts of the dispute. Jurists insisted that the law should be followed if it
was certain; but Venetians, having privileged decisions made "according to the conditions of the moment," clearly preferred *de facto* judgment. As the lieutenant of Friuli noted in 1518, it was better to have
"accords and private peaces than trials and rigorous application of the
law."[22]

Appeals presented an apparent obstacle to the imposition of equity. Venetian sovereignty and ultimate responsibility for justice required
that there exist some mechanism to send legal cases for definitive judgment in the capital. Standard doctrine, however, held that the judge of
an appeal was bound to observe the law of the court of first instance.
That doctrine obtained Venetian ratification in 1415, even though
Venetian judges were thereafter obliged to make appellate decisions
according to local statute rather than *equitas*.[23] Characteristically, Venetian councillors did not challenge this state of affairs but instead
favored an alternate routing. Simple petitions to the doge for clemency
equally preserved subjects' right of redress; and petitions could be
decided according to the facts of the case and the judge's perception of
true justice. The judge had no obligation to determine a *supplica* by
recourse to local statute. Indeed, since petitioners generally complained that they had been brought to an unhappy state by the rigors of
statute, the judge had a strong impetus to override positive law in the
interests of mercy. Because petitions permitted the application of equity, they were actively encouraged, and they considerably outnumber
formal appeals in Venetian archives.

In everyday administration, argument from ethical empiricism
led Venetian councils to grant governors the power to act "according to
their conscience," "as best fit[ted] justice and right," and "as equity
demand[ed]" in given judicial cases. That *arbitrium* enabled governors
to supersede local law and judiciaries in the interests of a higher law.
Central magistracies sometimes empowered governors to act with flexibility and not *rigide*, that is, to avail themselves of all judicial options,
statutory and extrastatutory; sometimes to decide a case summarily;
sometimes to remove a case from local tribunals for judgment in Venice; sometimes, indeed, simply to supervise the execution of justice
within local channels. In cases of goods usurped from the Venetian fisc,
for example, the Council of Ten held the power "to give to those
rectors or officials to whom the matter is denounced the faculty and
liberty of proceeding to justice according to their consciences."[24]
Grants of *libertas* or *facultas* were seldom categorical—in fact were

almost always applied to specific cases. Nonetheless the Venetian capacity to decree extraordinary measures was unlimited and could not be gainsaid by local allegiance to fixed norms and procedures.

Venetian "recourse to nonformalistic criteria" was the logical application of an ethico-juridical basis for governance. Whether or not Venetians were sincere and high-minded, that recourse was also politically expedient. Invocation of *conscientia* and *arbitrium* was a peculiarly Venetian strategy for superseding local statutes when these were not in the Venetian interest.[25] It also gave the Republic an open-ended mandate, since there could be few issues that did not in some manner have ethical implications. So Venetian councils rejected perfectly valid Vicentine laws simply because these were "inhumane": the rule that countrymen could be arrested for the private debts of fellow villagers, for example, or the rule that draft animals and agricultural tools could be seized as debt pledges.[26] Grounding law and administration in divine precepts did not require wholesale cancellation or suspension of local law, but it did justify constant Venetian intervention lest positive law infringe the divine.

That grounding reveals, more than any single criterion, the profound divide between Venetian and mainland judicial cultures. Mainland cities had little regard for the conscience and *arbitrium* of judges. In Brescia and several lesser towns, conscience ranked last in the hierarchy of sources of law, behind statute, custom, and the civil law. Elsewhere it entered not at all. Peoples steeped in the civil law tradition feared arbitrary powers as encouraging the arbitrary exercise of authority and the derogation of statute and *ius commune*. Nor did they allow argument from principle to contravene the written law except in cases of gross injustice. The Vicentine jurist Alessandro Nievo once remarked that his judgment went against the authority of Augustine's *City of God*, but that his commission left him no alternative but to follow the *ius commune*.[27]

On the Venetian side there was a strong suspicion that a law grounded in the *ius commune*, however venerable, could not guarantee equity and justice. Marc'Antonio Sabellico, usually a good indicator of Venetian thinking, confessed his distrust of learned jurisprudence and his fears that "clever interpretation of law" amounted to eloquent, skilled but devious argumentation. Equity had to take precedence over law: Francesco Barbaro once intervened on behalf of an aged and ignorant widow against the judgment of the distinguished Vicentine lawyer Matteo Bissari, simply because it was "pious" to do so. As Gaetano Cozzi has concluded, the contrast between center and periphery was a "contrast not so much of legislative content as of ways of conceiving law and justice: seeing as preeminent, that is, either the technical and doctrinal or the political and empirical."[28]

4

Dominion and Empire

Ostensibly, mainland recourse to the *ius commune* simply perpetuated ancient practice. Mainland jurists did little more than reiterate the doctrines of preceding centuries. Maintenance of traditional usage gained additional impetus from the fact that Venetians were unskilled in the civil law. Inertia and political opportunism alone cannot explain jurisprudential conservatism, however. The *ius commune* was grounded in the law of the Roman and medieval empires, and imperial law was inextricably connected to imperial authority. Given Venice's stated independence from the empire and its insular legal tradition, the mainland's preservation of the civil law and invocation of the imperial tradition made a tacit appeal to non-Venetian authorization.

LAW AND EMPIRE

Quattrocento jurists in the region, even the Venetian Pietro Del Monte, repeated medieval commonplaces without reservation: the kingdom of Italy belonged to the emperor, all jurisdictions resided in and were delegated through the emperor alone, all law was ultimately sanctioned by the emperor.[1] The Vicentine Bartolomeo Pagello gave public utterance to that common opinion in an oration before Emperor Frederick III in 1489. The emperor, he declared, was indeed "head of all the lands of the globe, chief of all human affairs." In the West, other rulers might hold lands and office by legitimate title, but the emperor was superior to all princes in rank and glory. Gathered under his *imperium* were the rights, laws, judgments, and jurisdictions of all peoples. Specifically, Frederick III as true emperor was heir to those Roman Caesars who had subjugated the world. Pagello even voiced the hope that once Frederick's son Maximilian had brought the western and northern regions firmly under his power, he might conquer all enemies of Christianity and place all nations under one *imperium*. A later scribe struck out this latter statement in the transcript of the oration, no doubt from concern about its seditious implications. Still, the point had been made.[2] Communal orators made much the same point in every city that Frederick and his predecessors visited on their several passages through the *terraferma*.

Jacob Burckhardt was to dismiss such sentiments and imperial "holiday trips" as anachronisms. Recent historians have judged Quattrocento imperial suzerainty a "dead letter," at most useful for legitimizing aristocratic titles.[3] They are probably right, at least in terms of Frederick's incapacity for effective intervention. At the time, however, peoples of the Veneto took the imperial presence very seriously. Frederick, as Sigismond before him, enjoyed an adulation all out of proportion to his actual power. Certainly Venetian governors and prelates were never honored by anything like the grandiose civic ceremonies organized "to venerate the sacred majesty of the Emperor" during passages in 1436, 1440, 1452, 1468–69, and 1489. On the last of these occasions, the commune of Verona, in preparing "for the arrival of the Sacred Imperial Majesty and for displaying the honor due his majesty, with as much and as careful diligence as is possible, and with that elaboration and opulence and dignity that such an Imperial Majesty merits," ordered flowers, festoons, and rich drapes hung from the windows along the processional route, selected a leading citizen to give the oration, and required the full attendance of the citizenry. The Vicentine welcome a few days later was even more elaborate. The city's streets were covered with cloth and decorated with fountains and festoons "in the antique style." Frederick toured the city under the communal canopy of gold cloth, to the sound of pipes and trumpets, accompanied by clergy, guilds, communal officers, and special floats. "It was a beautiful sight to see, and pleased him greatly."[4]

Such outpourings of enthusiasm were not isolated incidents but, rather, intensifications of deep-seated allegiance to the empire. That allegiance, in turn, was not based on nostalgia. Ongoing imperial authority validated the laws, judges, and notaries that were essential to Vicentine public life and which, by that validation, were independent of Venetian rulership and beyond Venetian supervision. Recognition of imperial authority did not signify anti-Venetian sentiment: Vicentines were quite capable of compartmentalizing their loyalties to empire and Republic. The great Belpietro Manelmi, for example, was simultaneously civilian director of the Venetian army and imperial count palatine. Nonetheless mass displays to honor the emperor were intensely political acts, renewing an overall imperial lordship to which the Venetian Republic was, by its own self-definition, extraneous. Invocation of imperial suzerainty, in general terms, proclaimed that no other legitimation of law could be equally valid, that the ideal of universal empire still captured the hearts of mainland citizens—and that Venetian sovereignty was far from complete.

Imperial grants of noble title were deemed important enough to draw the scrupulous attention of chroniclers. In Vicenza, although records are very incomplete, one patrician was made a count palatine in 1426, two in 1434, one in 1436, one in 1437, two in 1451, seven in 1452, one in 1454, one in 1465, one in 1467. four in 1469, and ten in the banner year of 1489.[5] Undoubtedly there were many other ceremonies of ennoblement, for there were many in the rest of the Venetian mainland.[6]

These titles both conferred and reflected supreme social and political standing. They were fundamental to the transformation of mainland patriciates into true nobilities, for they gave formal distinction from lower orders to individuals and families already distinguished by wealth, political prominence, and ancient lineage. The process of aristocratization will be discussed more fully below (chapters 7 and 8); here it should be noted that imperial title also carried prerogatives that had practical as well as symbolic significance. Knights and their families were exempt from communal restrictions on ornate clothing and lavish funerals. The nobility did not suffer the penalties imposed on citizens domiciled in the countryside. Ennoblement in 1469 gave members of the Thiene family the power to create notaries and *judices ordinari*, legitimate bastards, emancipate sons, manumit slaves, wear the insignia of the imperial eagle, and yearly create two additional knights and two doctors. Matteo Pogliana and his heirs received the same powers in 1489, and in addition, the right to create other counts palatine and appoint guardians. Counts palatine could release convicts from the civil disabilities of formal public shame (*infamia*).[7] These were not hollow jurisdictions. Records indicate that they were constantly exercised, particularly to legitimate bastards and create notaries.

Municipal judges held office precisely because of their training in the Roman law. The legitimacy of the notariate, hence the legitimacy of the legal transactions and judicial sentences that notaries recorded, likewise derived from imperial authorization. Pietro da Unzola, whose *Aurora Novissima* was edited and published in Vicenza in 1485, summed up the common opinion: the privilege of creating notaries belonged to the emperor and his assigns. The single Venetian attempt to assert that power in Vicenza was hastily revoked after communal protest.[8]

In the city of Vicenza, to be sure, the imperial presence was somewhat residual, since notaries were created by their college; but in the past that college had been careful to note confirmation of its statutes by imperial vicars, and the college in Verona, at least, still traced its authority to a grant from Frederick II. Vicentine notaries could not totally forget their origins, since the primary textbook for notarial students was the Justinianic *Institutes*. The standard title for a notary in Vicenza, and in mainland cities generally, remained "notary public by imperial authority" (*publicus ex imperiali auctoritate notarius*), and that title was an integral part of the signature that validated a notarial instrument.

Further indication of imperial loyalties is provided by the *Rua*, a heavily decorated tower that Vicentine notaries carried in civic and religious processions. Little is known of its Quattrocento form save that it was surmounted by the wheel that provided its name. But in the earliest surviving pictures of the *Rua*, dating perhaps from the later seventeenth century, the imperial double-headed eagle stands just below the apex. The lion of St. Mark stands a poor fourth.[9]

Rural notaries, who did not usually belong to the college, were therefore even more dependent upon imperial legitimization. A survey of 1429, for example, revealed that the majority of Vicentine rural notaries owed their offices to privileges issued by imperial counts from Pisa, Lucca, Milan, Verona, Padua, and Treviso; and the document was careful to note which emperor had ennobled those counts. While the survey was evidently preparatory to an attempt by the urban college to restrict creation of notaries except under college auspices, imperial authority was not easily curbed. Indeed, that authority became more prominently displayed as Vicentine patricians acquired imperial patents and freely exercised the prerogatives of their nobility. In 1461, for example, Giacomo Ragona of Vicenza, created count palatine by the Emperor Sigismond, granted a man of Carmignano the right to practice the notariate. His son Girolamo did the same for a rural grammar teacher.[10]

Beneficiaries of imperial privilege openly proclaimed loyalty to the source of their distinction. The testament of "the magnificent and generous Marco Thiene, most splendid knight and Count of Quinto," for example, ordered that his heirs erect a statue of the Emperor Frederick on the right side of his tomb in the cathedral, with a matching figure of the doge to be placed only on the left. The Braschi family had portrait reliefs of Roman emperors placed on the exterior wall of their new palace to commemorate recent ennoblement. Fellow nobles commissioned the image of the imperial eagle on plaques, bridges, buildings, and inscriptions throughout the city. In the list of Vicentine monuments compiled by the seventeenth-century antiquarian Girolamo Gualdo, imperial insignia are as common as those dedicated to St. Mark. Those awarded imperial titles were permitted to add the eagle to coats of arms; by the time Vicentine heraldry was firmly established, some twenty-six families had done so.[11] Every important festival brought out the *Rua*, which celebrated empire above republic.

Venetians too acknowledged the emperor's special status, reserving for him special titles such as *Serenissimus, Imperialis Celsitudo, Dominus Imperator, Optimus et Supremus Princeps Christianorum,* and *Sacra Cesarea Maiestas.* They celebrated his entries into Venice with a pomp and reverence seldom accorded visiting rulers. But Venetians were well aware that, on the mainland, the cult of empire maintained a pole of authority distinct from, even counterbalancing their own. Their magistracies were naturally concerned lest public displays on the mainland serve as catalysts for overtly anti-Venetian actions. They sent ambassadors to greet and guide the emperor on his way, but equally to keep an eye on the festivities. They forbade particularly charged acts of welcome, ordering, for example, that mainland governors not permit any attempt to present Frederick III with the keys to cities visited in the passage of 1489.[12]

Still, that was nearly the extent of Venetian opposition to the cult of empire. Much as they loudly affirmed their own freedom from empire, Venetians declined to mount a direct assault upon the ancient affections of their subjects. They made no attempt to limit ennoblements, for example, or to curb the display of imperial insignia. Councillors knew that, in general terms, it was impossible to eradicate philoimperial sentiments, as it was impossible to supersede mainland laws and jurisdictions grounded in empire, *ius commune* and Roman law. There was little reason to make the attempt, as long as nobody actually revolted in the name of empire and residual imperial institutions continued to function adequately. The Republic did have to pay a price for coexistence, however: preservation of a mainland juridical culture foreign to its own, one often able to compromise its authority.

VENICE AND THE IMPERIAL TRADITION

The first step towards reaching accommodation with that culture was accommodation with its source. The Republic needed to come to terms with the unquestioned imperial lordship of the mainland. If it did not do so, it faced the unpleasant prospect of governing without clear title, which would leave the formal basis for governance dangerously unclear. In that case the Republic could either avoid the issue of its illegitimacy by conceding thorough autonomy to mainland communes, which was inimicable to Venetian ambitions for effective governance, or it could attempt to rule by simple imposition of its will. This latter alternative suggested tyranny and in any case was impossible in a practical sense, since resident Venetian officials were few in number, unconversant with the local situation, and largely dependent upon local agencies for the execution of decrees. The preferred course was regularization of the Venetian position. Imperial lordship had long been been exercised through nomination of local *signori* as imperial vicars; having deposed the Scaligeri and Carraresi and blocked the return of the Visconti, the Republic needed legitimation in its own right.

Strategies to avoid imperial legitimation proved unconvincing. If Venice was indeed New Rome, had been the beneficiary of a *translatio Imperii*, the Republic had no need for a German prince to ratify its mainland possessions. But influential members of the Venetian patriciate were reluctant to use this argument to make concrete political claims. It contradicted the insistence of the myths that Venice had always been outside the imperial sphere. It suggested Rome's imperial mission, thus played into the hands of enemies who charged that Venice was motivated by "lust for domination." It impugned, as well, the official line that the Republic had only accepted invitations to protect the mainland against tyrants. Moreover, metaphoric assertion of Venice as rightful empire did not make it so in law.

The jurists who established Venice's sovereignty appeared to build a better case. The Republic had always been outside the imperial domain because it was built upon the sea, because it recognized no superior authority, or because of the law of prescription. That freedom from empire, said the distinguished Paolo da Castro, then extended to the Republic's territorial dominion: "Since Venetians do not recognize any superior, they take the place of the emperor for their cities and peoples." Bartolomeo Cipolla echoed his words: "Venetians in their lands take the place of the emperor."[13] Substituting its own sovereign power for that of predecessors, Venice would not need separate recognition of its authority on the mainland.

But the argument rested on bad logic, as Carlo Ruini pointed out sharply from his chair at the University of Padua in the early Cinquecento.[14] Medieval authorities such as Bartolus and Baldus had posited a Venetian *exemptio ab Imperio* at a time when Venice held little or no territory on the mainland. The historical argument for Venetian independence, from the circumstances of Venice's foundation or from Barbarossa's concession of 1177, likewise referred to an age when the Republic was purely maritime. In any case proof of independence covered only the city of Venice and not the mainland that it later absorbed. Sovereignty of the urban center could not automatically extend to subsequent annexations from the imperial domain.

Legitimation was not an idle issue, since imperial claims to the *terraferma* were far from moribund. From the moment of mainland expansion, imperial lordship authorized incessant sedition and invasions on behalf of displaced vicars. Disruption did not cease when in 1414 the duke of Milan, another imperial vicar, renounced his claim to be lord of Verona and Vicenza. By then Sigismond of Hungary, King of the Romans and hence emperor elect, was stirring up trouble as suzerain and champion of the Scaligeri and Carraresi. He invoked imperial authority, as well, in issuing new titles and jurisdictions within the Venetian dominion. After a period of quiet, Sigismond returned to the attack in 1435, sponsoring a raid by Marsilio da Carrara and, in a somewhat bizarre move, investing the duke of Coimbra (brother of the king of Portugal) with the entire mainland.[15]

Marsilio failed miserably, and the duke of Coimbra never had a chance. The threat however, convinced Venetians that the time had come to secure proper title to the dominion. This does not represent a drastic reversal of Venetian policy: in the later Trecento, even as its partisans were perfecting the myth of Venetian *exemptio ab Imperio,* the Republic had vainly sought recognition from Charles IV for its rule in Treviso. Now Sigismond, defeated in Italy and occupied by protracted negotiations to end the Hussite wars at home, proved more compliant. In a treaty signed in 1435, Venice promised submission, an oath of fidelity, and annual tribute of a gold cloth worth a thousand ducats in return for a perpetual imperial vicariate on the mainland. The actual investiture took place two years later.[16]

That treaty had important consequences for Venetian rule. It marks, most notably, the beginning of a distinctive Venetian feudal policy. Hitherto largely silent regarding imperial titles and jurisdictions on the mainland, the Republic began to create fiefs for mercenary captains and to regulate extant fiefs only after 1435–37. It had annexed Friuli in the second decade of the century, for example, but only in 1445 forbade the Patriarch of Aquileia to grant fiefs there.[17] That delay indicates Venetian respect for the common opinion that only the emperor or his assigns could licitly ennoble and enfeoff. It indicates, as well, Venetian acknowledgment that its own title was far from legitimate up to that time. After obtaining the vicariate, however, the Republic actively used its imperial sanction to reward followers and punish rebels. Growing sophistication in feudal management culminated in elaborate formularies and ceremonies for creating counts and conferring supreme civil and criminal jurisdiction.[18]

Verona and Vicenza saw little exercise of Venice's imperial vicariate even after 1435–37. This fact further indicates the Republic's regard for imperial legitimation. In a significant loophole, the treaty had specifically excluded these two cities from the Venetian vicariate pending future agreement with the current vicar, Brunoro della Scala. Accord was never reached, and Venetian title to the cities was not secured until 1523. Throughout the Quattrocento, with the Scaligeri still technically in office, Venetian councillors made only limited changes in existing feudal jurisdictions. Only in 1505 was Girolamo Nogarola, owner of the Vicentine vicariate of Bagnolo, made count of Bagnolo by the doge and considered to hold his position by Venetian privilege. Nor was the Republic inclined to establish new jurisdictions in Verona and Vicenza, though it did so freely in other mainland cities where it held clear legitimacy. The first new title was that of count of Guazzo, granted to a loyal Veronese as late as 1502, and the title was purely honorific. The first new fief with significant fiscal or judicial rights, that of Illasi, was established only in 1509, and in any case the central government sharply restricted its jurisdiction a few years later.[19] Until the extreme pressures of the early Cinquecento forced abandonment of a long-time policy of reticence, Venice scrupulously respected its lack of imperial title in Verona and Vicenza.

VENICE AND THE *IUS COMMUNE*

Venetian nobles sent out as governors and judges were initially ill equipped to handle the technical requirements of their offices. Legal education in Venice was undeveloped. The city had no law school of its own, and a small notarial school only after 1446, which was, in any case, frequented exclusively by commoners. Within the capital, Venetians relied upon priest-notaries and notaries "by imperial authority," a situation that was perceived as scandalous but was not corrected. Most nobles were trained only in commerce and practical statesmanship; only twenty received degrees in civil law from the University of Padua in the first half of the century. When patricians tried to become directly involved in mainland affairs, their ignorance of legal discourse proved embarrassing to the Republic, and so in 1453 central councils forbade Venetian nobles (except governors) to speak before municipal councils, in 1479 to plead before local courts.[20]

   The only remedy for unfamiliarity with the civil law was reliance upon outside experts. The Republic had long hired foreign jurists as consultants in cases that required special expertise. In the Quattrocento, too, outside lawyers gave opinions in domestic disputes and served in diplomatic missions abroad.[21] As mainland governance required a larger supply of trained lawyers than the Venetian patriciate could provide, jurists from the *terraferma* accompanied governors as vicars or "judge-assessors." That practice remedied the obvious deficiencies of Venetian administration. Since these jurists had attended the University of Padua, they brought to local administration a thorough training in the Roman law and *ius commune*. Since they came from the Veneto or Venetian Lombardy, from cities with essentially similar laws and procedures, they brought to mainland administration a sensitivity to local custom. And since individual jurists were hired year after year, they provided continuity, experience, and standardized services. The Paduan lawyer Conte Alvarotti, for example, served as vicar of Vicenza in five years of the decade 1498–1507.[22]

To Venetians, however, this system was an imperfect expedient. Because the governor himself seldom had legal training, cases requiring technical interpretation had to be decided by the non-Venetian vicar or assessor. The loyalty of those assistants was beyond question. Still, having a non-Venetian as virtual head of local judiciary ran counter to the preferred principle that the chief judge of subject cities be a representative of the Republic and also—as a noble and a member of the Venetian Great Council—himself a ruler equal in rank to the doge. Employment of mainland jurists represented a dilution of Venetian authority.[23]

Venetians thus found considerable impetus to train future administrators in the civil law. The Quattrocento, in fact, marks the beginning of the Venetian "invasion" of the Paduan law school. Many patricians had notable careers as students: perhaps half the *rectores juristorum* were Venetian. A surprising number went on to become professors. The Venetian *cursus honorum,* in turn, richly rewarded specialized knowledge. Mainland governors were increasingly chosen from the ranks of noble lawyers, as were special commissioners like Barbaro Morosini, who was sent in 1451 to adjudicate the vexatious border dispute between Verona and Vicenza. In the later Quattrocento, jurists were numerous and prominent in the upper ranks of the central government. They served particularly as ambassadors and *avogadori,* the two offices that particularly demanded legal training and forensic skills.[24]

Mainland administration required that the University of Padua produce a sufficient number of well-trained lawyers, Venetian and non-Venetian. Legislation from 1407 onwards established a Paduan monopoly on legal education and threatened severe penalties and loss of recognition to those who studied elsewhere.[25] The Senate made constant efforts to upgrade the law faculty by attracting illustrious outsiders and by keeping high the salaries of those professors who brought particular honor to the university. Venetian supervision of the university was increasingly firm but did not suffocate academic life: the last quarter of the century, in fact, has been called a golden age in Padua's history. Though the legal faculty remains to be studied in detail, it was certainly highly competent and frequently distinguished, to judge from the opinions and treatises of its leading lights.[26]

By the end of the Quattrocento, Venetian expertise in the *ius commune* was far greater than it had been in 1404. Not coincidentally, Venetian administration was relatively free of the gross technical errors that had plagued it in earlier decades. Central magistracies confidently and accurately invoked even the fine points of the civil law: the rules of *praesentatio,* for example, or the law of *lèse majesté,* or the right of an unemancipated son to claim poverty (*inopia*). Roman law tags such as *actor sequitur forum rei* and *audia alteram partem* fill Venetian discourse. When in 1501 Girolamo da Schio quoted Bartolus before the Council of Ten, his erudition was probably not wasted on his audience. Trained advocates became common in Venetian courts, especially the appellate tribunal of the Quarantia; at least five Vicentine lawyers found regular employment there in the limited period 1492–1505 for which accurate records survive.[27]

Gradual Venetian annexation of the civil law tradition can be demonstrated by a single example. The mainland had long maintained a thirty-year period of prescription, derived from the *praescriptio triginta annorum* of the Justinianic Code (C.7.3.9): unchallenged occupation of land for thirty years constituted full ownership. The problem of prescriptive right became acute in the mid-Quattrocento, when aggressive fiscal magistracies demanded restitution of lands usurped from the public patrimony, even though in some cases these had been held peacefully for several generations. Venetian officials initially vacillated concerning the time after which occupation became legitimate ownership, establishing terms of twenty-five, thirty, or fifty years, or even that indefinite period since Venetian acquisition of a city. By the third quarter of the century, central councils had a general standard of thirty years, though they did not specify the source of that standard. In 1496, however, the Council of Ten declared, firstly, that communal lands were subject to the *praescriptio annorum triginta,* and secondly, that it applied the law of prescription established by the *lex communis.*[28] Venetian legal practice had adopted the sources and techniques of its subjects, not vice versa.

Still, the Venetian conversion was at best partial. The incompatibility of Venetian and mainland legal systems remained, both revealing and causing a profound division between center and periphery. Venetian accommodation to mainland ways could not compromise ingrained habits of jurisprudence, particularly when myths boasted of a distinct Venetian law as guarantor of the justice and equity that made the Republic exemplary. There was no possibility, for example, that the *ius commune* would permeate Venice itself. When mass employment of civil lawyers in the capital's courts threatened distinctive Venetian argumentation, senior councils passed stringent laws to limit their number and salaries.[29]

Again, a pivotal case illustrates general orientation. Proposed legal reforms in the 1520s would, in effect, have integrated (or reintegrated) the *ius commune* into Venetian law. Despite supporters as powerful as Doge Andrea Gritti, the project was an abject failure. Gaetano Cozzi interprets that failure as a refusal by Venetian nobles to betray their collegial heritage. In particular, they feared that granting privileged status to legal specialists would compromise the principle of equality within the patriciate. Angelo Ventura prefers a reading based on divisions within the patriciate: lesser nobles refused to cede power to that oligarchy which, with greater educational and patronage resources, could have controlled technical expertise.[30] Either way, Venetian rulers refused assimilation of their legal culture with that of their subjects.

PART II

Privileged Commune, Commune of the Privileged

5

Commune and Governor

Resident Venetian governors held supreme civil and criminal jurisdiction. They were local repositories of that overall Venetian *arbitrium* which was "the authority to create, supply, interpret, and change the law at will." Behind them loomed the majesty of the Most Serene Republic and, if necessary, its troops quartered in the countryside. In theory they had the power to make the Venetian will felt in all aspects of governance. From the start, however, they were inclined and able to do so only in extraordinary cases and in specific sectors such as finance and criminal justice.

Several purely practical considerations suggested that local structures would predominate in ordinary administration. Certainly Venetian administrators could not easily establish an independent presence. They were, for a start, few in number. The senior of the 2 rectors was a podesta (*praetor* to the classically inclined, hence the adjective *pretorian*), roughly in charge of justice and finance. The captain, with competence over Venetian troops and employees of the Republic, had little occasion to intervene in purely local affairs. These rectors brought to Vicenza a skeletal staff of 3 judge-assessors, 1 chancellor, 1 chamberlain, personal servants, and a few constables, to govern a city and countryside that counted well over 100,000 inhabitants.[1] The Vicentine communal administration, on the other hand, consisted of 8 deputies, 12 consuls, 9 judges, 17 *anziani*, dozens of notaries, a Great Council, executive councils of forty and one hundred, and 35 general officials. The commune sent 15 vicars and 107 assistants to govern the countryside. Subordinate to the urban commune were a dozen larger towns, each with councils and courts, and nearly two hundred rural communes with rosters of *decani, merighi,* and *saltari* to keep order.

Sheer inexperience obliged Venetian officials to work closely with civic agencies. Governors arrived ignorant of local law, procedures, and judicial precedents. The Republic deliberately sought ignorance, lest rectors' overfamiliarity with the local situation lead either to a personal power base or to favoritism. The best rectors, wrote Marc'Antonio Sabellico, were those who were "most innocent" of the cities in which they served. In consequence of that policy, no rector had previously served in Vicenza, and none returned for a second term. There

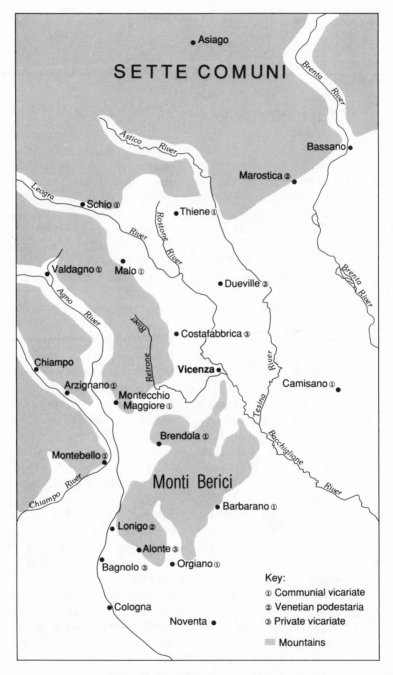

Map 2.
Vicenza in the fifteenth century

was no permanent Venetian administration in Vicenza: the podesta brought assessors, constables, and officials as his personal staff, and they left with him at the end of his term of office. Those assistants too were outsiders. They could not serve in their own cities or places in which they had family, property, or even, after 1446, close friends. They could not serve in consecutive years. After 1471 rectors could not hire anyone who had previously served in the city at any time.[2]

Moreover, local norms defined the actual operation of Venetian administrators. The commissions issued by central councils regulated salaries, fees, personal conduct (no dining with citizens, no leaving town without permission), and staff hiring. They said almost nothing about the specifics of the job. Local statutes alone spelled out an administrator's responsibilities, jurisdictions, and procedures.

Reinforcing those practical considerations were an array of strictures, all endorsed by Venice, which guaranteed the urban commune a considerable capacity for independent action and indicated that the Venetian will would be largely mediated through communal structures. Specific sectors of governance will be examined in later chapters. First, however, it is necessary to examine the general prerogatives of the Vicentine urban commune. That examination must be comparative, rating communal resources relative to Venetian authority, relative to forces in the countryside, and—because that commune was dominated by a single class—relative to the mass of Vicentines excluded from power.

COMMUNAL LAW

Vicentine law held primacy only when not contrary to God, justice, or Venetian honor. Even then, Vicentine law was not necessarily Vicentine in origin. Firstly, *arbitrium* gave central councils the "sovereign and political faculty to declare the law," the "unlimited faculty to formulate the law." Secondly, as Doge Cristoforo Moro reminded his subjects, local statutes and provisions "will have no validity whatever unless we first confirm them." Thirdly, any such confirmation reserved for Venetian councils the capacity to "add to, change, correct, or diminish laws."[3]

Nonetheless the potential for Venetian legislative intervention was little exercised. Most of the time municipal law did not offend God, justice, or the ruler's honor. Nor was the Republic, unlike its Tuscan and Lombard counterparts, inclined towards categorical imposition of law. It ratified local statutes without change, and it made few and insubstantial modifications to local provisions. Venetian decrees, however copious, nearly always addressed individual cases and seldom established generally applicable, permanent norms. Only in the Cinquecento did subject cities gather central decrees into books that paralleled and even outranked local statutes.[4] In the Quattrocento, the law of Vicentine administrators and tribunals was predominantly Vicentine.

Municipal law had three basic components. The first and most frequently cited was statutory law. At the time of submission, statutes of 1339 remained in effect. When these came to be perceived as obsolete, they were replaced by a new set in 1425. The doge's ratification was issued in January of the following year.

Vicentine statutory reform appears anomalous on two counts. Firstly, in Tuscany the central government insisted on immediate compilations of new statutes for subject communes according to nearly uniform models supplied by the capital; and Florence itself ordered a new set of statutes that "aspired to be an organic body of regional legislation."[5] In the Veneto, by contrast, reformed municipal statutes appear well after Venetian expansion and certainly were not dictated by the capital. These demonstrate the widest possible variety in format and content and belie any notion of a Venetian attempt to "render uniform the laws and statutes of subject cities, in conformity with its own political principles."[6] In the capital, there was no attempt to compile a single corpus of Venetian law regarding the *terraferma*. A dozen different magistracies issued decrees for individual cities and only haphazardly extended them to other places in the dominion.

Secondly, in contrast to those of its neighbors, Vicenza's statutes demonstrate little Venetian influence. The central government had directed revisions in Trevisan law since the Trecento. The commune of Padua in 1420 obtained permission from the Venetian government before revising the city's statutes; Venetian rectors appointed and worked alongside the commission of sixteen *reformatores*. Chroniclers gave the podesta Marco Dandolo full credit for promoting reform. Though Verona's statutes of 1450 are said to be "predominantly a Veronese creation," a commission that included a pretorian assessor and met in the presence of the podesta actually compiled them. Venetians participated in the commission that reformed Brescian statutes.[7]

The statutes of Vicenza, on the other hand, were entirely Vicentine. It is true that the prologue gave full credit to the podesta Francesco Barbaro, as it gave him credit for everything from filling the treasury to draining swamps. But comparison of Barbaro to Justinian, Minos, Solon, and Lycurgus was largely flattery. He was untrained in the law and had been in office only a few months. Getting down to specifics, the prologue quoted the declaration of the fifteen *refor-*

matores, who were all native citizens, that their mandate derived strictly from municipal councils: "We were chosen and confirmed with full liberty and authority by the Great Council of Five Hundred of the city [of Vicenza]."[8]

The second component of Vicentine law, provisions passed by civic councils, was, strictly speaking, distinct from statute. Nonetheless all manuscripts and early printed editions of the statutes include copies of provisions, indicating that compilers considered ordinances to have a force nearly equal to that of statute. Editors eventually gathered these additions into a standardized collection and printed them as a fifth book of statutes. Indeed, a dozen Quattrocento council ordinances entered directly into the body of the statutes in later printed editions. Contemporaries did not distinguish between statutory law and the law enacted by municipal councils. As Vicentine ambassadors successfully argued before the Senate in 1415, "by the statutes of the commune of Vicenza, whatever is decided in the Great Council is binding and valid."[9]

The third source of Vicentine law was that custom (*consuetudo*) which had by antiquity and consistent application "obtained the force of law." Juridical opinion considered custom equivalent in strength to statutes, pacts, privileges, or decrees, sometimes more powerful than the *ius commune.* Venetian councils accepted the argument and gave equal protection to all components of Vicentine law. They frequently paired custom with statute and provision, for example, in lists of norms guaranteed inviolable by Venetian *privilegia.* Doge Pasquale Malipiero in 1461 summed up the Venetian position, reminding a recalcitrant podesta that he too was bound to observe local norms: "The provisions and statutes of this most faithful commune, and its customs, shall be maintained."[10]

Vicentines never articulated and recorded their customs, as the Veronese did.[11] This actually increased the power of Vicentine custom. Communal ambassadors found invocation of unwritten custom a favorite tactic in pleading before Venetian magistracies whose grasp of local usage was not strong. Venetian judges could not gainsay a plausible *consuetudo* without either investigating local tradition or appearing to abrogate the most basic of subjects' rights. Usually they accepted ambassadors' claims at face value, even when local custom forced cancellation of Venetian decrees. Through argument from custom, for example, the Vicentine commune blocked increases of taxes and prevented the imposition of new ones, protected extensive local powers to determine exile or criminal pardons, prevented Venetian amendments to municipal legislation, and preserved traditional land tenures despite Venetian efforts at land reform.

Invocation of custom was more than a forensic tactic. It pointed to a vast reservoir of law that lay beyond Venetian understanding and Venetian control. Unlike other sources of law, custom needed no confirmation, admitted no amendment, and by its antiquity and prestige permitted no interference. Moreover, it covered a great deal of territory that other sources did not. The wide gap between written law and the law actually operating in local administration suggests that much governance relied upon custom and therefore relied upon norms immune to Venetian intervention. To take one example, Vicenza had sophisticated rules and procedures for emancipating children, yet municipal statutes gave emancipation a single mention in annulling emancipatory acts that sought to "defend the patrimony against creditors" by the transfer of patrimonial goods to emancipated sons.[12] Certainly this did not abolish emancipation itself. Between the laconic and contingent statute and the well-documented practice of emancipation lay a considerable body of unwritten norms, well known to local jurists and notaries but not to inexperienced Venetians.

Venetians were uneasy at the persistence of customary law, as they were suspicious of the mainland tendency to operate under workable but undeclared systems. So, for example, the Senate in 1451 decreed that all lands held under unwritten, perpetual tenures should be subject to the strict conditions of the twenty-nine-year lease.[13] But Venetian councils seldom categorically impugned the authority of local custom. Rather, as was the case in Venetians' use of technical political terminology, their challenge was oblique. Central councils imposed a variant meaning on *consuetudo* that denatured and devalued local intent.

Vicentines, and Italians generally, followed a long jurisprudential tradition that defined custom as habitual performance so deeply ingrained that it had become "another nature." As performed "for so long that there exists no memory to the contrary," custom did not require any proof and could be contravened only if irrational or patently evil. Custom therefore had two basic attributes, antiquity and good usage.[14] Here Venetians, in a rare rejection of the common opinion, imposed a precisely opposite meaning. They usually qualified *consuetudo* as "newly introduced" or "recently arisen" and further qualified it as "abominable" or "evil" or "corrupt," even "detestable, bad, and perverse" and likely to produce misery or scandal or a host of other ills.[15] This constitutes more than simple linguistic variance. By denying the tradition and licitness of custom, Venetians denied the hallowed status that subjects attached to their customary law. Attaching negative ethical qualities to *consuetudo,* in turn, authorized unlimited intervention in what had been a purely local process.

Venetian rejection of local custom was, in fact, rare and usually proceeded from entirely laudable motives: halting official peculation, or forcing officials to serve personally in their cities, or preventing the alienation of ecclesiastical patrimonies. Occasionally a central council abrogated a patently unjust Vicentine custom, for example the usage that permitted arrest of a countryman for the private debts of his fellow villagers.[16] But in those specific rulings they made a more general, ominous point. The fact that Venetians then argued from *consuetudo*, rather than their usual abstract equity, signals willingness to confront subjects on the latter's own ground and to shift the terms of discourse by imposing definitions unfavorable to traditional law. In doing so they served notice that no guarantees of Vicentine judicial autonomy were entirely safe from interference.

EXECUTIVE MAGISTRACIES

In the Trecento, Veneto rulers had been content to preserve local control of lesser communal offices as long as they could control the greater. This was less true a century later. Venice certainly provided the highest magistrates in the podesta and the captain, and in cities such as Treviso and Brescia those rectors appointed higher officers. In Vicenza, on the other hand, the urban commune elected all other senior officials, notably the eight deputies. In some respects the Vicentine commune's position was actually strengthened after 1404. Where in the Trecento the podesta could fill or change higher civic offices at will, Quattrocento statutes made no provision for the governor's discretionary powers.[17]

Unless he received explicit orders from senior councils to the contrary, the podesta was obliged to collaborate with communal deputies in nearly every act of administration. No act was valid, in fact, without the deputies' participation and approval. The podesta and deputies together extracted from communal urns the names of those filling offices, and they heard requests to be excused from office. They jointly issued commissions for the vicars of the countryside. Together they elected ambassadors destined for Venice and issued letters of credential. The podesta and deputies together convened and presided over municipal councils and screened proposed legislation before presentation to those councils. In judicial affairs they collaborated in quelling disturbances, feuds, discords, and violence in city and countryside, and they combined to reduce fines imposed on paupers who otherwise faced incarceration. The podesta and deputies combined to lease out communal lands, pasturage rights, and the franchise to collect customs revenues.[18]

Vicentine deputies, sometimes working with higher communal

councils, held additional powers not enjoyed by the podesta. Although the podesta and deputies jointly proposed new municipal taxes, the commune retained a veto power since new taxes required two-thirds approval by the deputies and Council of One Hundred. The podesta and deputies together supervised the compilation of tax assessments (*estimi*), but the deputies actually selected the *estimatores*. Whereas the podesta held a general guardianship of communal property, the deputies alone had the power to prosecute usurpations or fraudulent alienations. Only deputies and the Council of One Hundred could licitly alienate municipal property. Deputies by themselves could hear petitions from rural communes, grant tax exemptions, and impose summary fines on those who disobeyed their orders. Together with the Council of Forty, they chose special commissioners to investigate charges of extortion.[19] Records indicate that rectors largely respected those theoretical jurisdictions. The podesta seldom acted independently of municipal officials, and few acts of local government do not bear the imprimatur of the Vicentine commune.

Council proceedings indicate a comfortable collaboration between Venetian and Vicentine officials. The deputies were, as one appreciative podesta noted, "just like brothers." But deputies were not, by that token, automatically deferential to Venetian authority. They took seriously their charge to protect the rights of the Vicentine *respublica*. Hardly a year went by without their sending ambassadors to the capital to protest infringements of communal prerogatives. Usually their targets were non-Venetian officials such as chancellors or chamberlains, or minor Venetian magistrates such as the *auditori nuovi*. If necessary, however, deputies challenged governors directly. In 1490 they angrily confronted the podesta Francesco Basadona and charged him with repeatedly granting illegal pardons that undercut the commune's criminal jurisdiction. A chastened Basadona admitted his ignorance, annulled past infringements, and promised never again to usurp communal functions.[20] The event was, in fact, rather routine. The pages that follow are full of successful Vicentine efforts to reverse the rulings of their Venetian counterparts.

CIVIL JUSTICE

The Vicentine judiciary combined Venetian-directed and purely communal tribunals. The podesta or (more likely) his vicar presided over the most prestigious civil court, the Banco del Sigillo. His *judex rationis*, seated at the Banco della Ragione, specialized in fiscal cases such as property damage, sureties, nonpayment of rent, and property title. On the other hand four communal consuls, the judges of the Eagle (*Aqui-*

la), Ox (*Bue*), Horse (*Cavallo*) and Peacock (*Pavone*), shared all pretorian jurisdictions. The Vicentine judges of the *ingrossatori* (responsible for roads and waterways), clerics, *mariganze* (responsible for rural affairs), and *dazi* (tolls and customs) also duplicated the functions of pretorian assessors. The statutes assumed that pretorian and municipal courts were interchangeable, and surviving records of civil tribunals show little distinction between them. But, again, municipal statutes excluded Venetian officials from important sectors. Communal consuls alone had jurisdiction over wardship, emancipation, and legal representation (procuration).[21]

Even a case heard before the podesta or the assessors might be returned for local judgment. Either party in a civil dispute could request that a jurist give a formal opinion in the case, and the presiding judge had to commit it for *consilium sapientis*. The terms of the opinion then bound the judge's decision: "The podesta of the city of Vicenza, his assessors, and other officials of the commune of Vicenza who are delegated to administer law and justice ought to and are bound . . . to make right sentences in writing, wholly following the opinion of the jurisconsult, if the latter has been sought according to the form of the statutes of the commune of Vicenza." The Republic in 1434 ratified the jurisprudential commonplace that sentences rendered according to a *consilium sapientis* could not be appealed to the tribunals of the capital.[22] The ruling should be placed alongside earlier decisions that, firstly, Venetian law had no bearing on Vicentine cases and secondly, Vicentine law would govern even appeals heard in Venice. The net effect of such strictures was clear: litigants had limited recourse beyond Vicentine municipal tribunals, and no recourse beyond municipal law.

A unique register permits tentative measurement of the relative importance of Vicentine and pretorian magistracies. In a regular public ceremony the communal herald proclaimed that, if a given debtor did not make satisfaction within eight days, or if a given defendant in a civil suit did not appear in court, he would enter into the ban. The herald invariably gave the name of the presiding judge who authorized that proclamation. In the sole surviving *Liber Forbannitorum*, listing 465 citations from the period 1388–1421, Vicentine consuls authorized some 63 percent of citations, pretorian assessors the remaining 37 percent.[23]

CRIMINAL JUSTICE

Distribution of authority over criminal justice is less clear-cut. At least Vicentine urban tribunals held the exclusive right to prosecute crimes: neither rural feudatories nor the Venetian podestas in the outlying towns of Lonigo and Marostica possessed criminal jurisdiction. Nor did the central government claim ordinary jurisdiction except in cases of outright rebellion. This fact alone indicates the privileged position of the Vicentine commune relative to counterparts in the Veneto and relative to subject cities in other Italian states. In Tuscany, Florence reserved to its own courts crimes punishable by death or mutilation and created rural vicariates whose Florentine governors—not judges of nearby cities—held criminal jurisdiction. Numerous Milanese feudatories possessed *merum et mixtum imperium*. Feudatories and a few rural communes in Venetian Lombardy held criminal authority independent of municipal tribunals. So too did Venetian podestas placed in the larger towns of the Trevisan countryside. In Verona, despite communal gains in mid-century, some of the scores of private jurisdictions in the countryside had *pena sanguinis* for at least part of the Quattrocento. The favorable Vicentine situation should be measured over time, as well: many of those Tuscan vicariates and Lombard fiefs were created under the territorial state, thereby vitiating ancient urban jurisdictions. The Vicentine urban monopoly, on the other hand, was firmly established only in the Quattrocento, after centuries in which broad areas of the countryside were privately governed.[24]

While affirming an urban monopoly, Vicentine statutes were not entirely certain whether Venetian or local magistracies held criminal jurisdiction. Several articles assigned the third pretorian assessor, the *judex maleficiorum,* complete authority to investigate criminal complaints, take testimony, hear defenses, make final judgment, and pass sentence. Other rubrics, however, gave the Vicentine consulate (in criminal matters, the four civil consuls plus eight nonjurists) the power to investigate and draw up the formal dossier (*processum*) of charges and evidence. Still another rubric assigned investigation to a mixed body of one consul, a constable of the podesta's staff, the notary of the *judex maleficiorum,* and a communal herald. The implications of these contrasting statutes were not entirely clear even to contemporaries. In 1444, for example, the doge assured the Vicentine commune that the *judex maleficiorum* should not personally accompany the consuls in tours through the countryside, yet seven years later the Senate had the impression that he could indeed do so.[25]

In fact there appears to have been an informal demarcation of competences between Venetian and Vicentine officials. The consulate tacitly ceded powers to investigate in the city, and it established a de facto monopoly over rural crimes by gradually eliminating Venetian judges and officials from the group delegated to ride out to investigate them. In 1443 a consul, a pretorian constable, and the notary of the *judex maleficiorum* made up the team; a decade later, a consul, his notary, and a communal messenger; in 1459 a consul alone; and in 1461 a consul and his notaries.[26] Shortly thereafter a Vicentine orator sought exclusion of the *judex maleficiorum* from a clamorous case of theft in the town of Castelgomberto, since "such criminal acts pertained to the consulate of this city, by right of its privileges." This assertion of communal prerogatives was irregular, since the *privilegia* of 1404 and 1406 said no such thing and the 1425 statutes contained clear statements to the contrary. Nonetheless the doge ratified a system that had become customary. By the end of the century, the *judex maleficiorum* is no longer mentioned in connection with investigation of rural crimes. Moreover, by a custom that survived into the seventeenth century, the *processum* drawn up by Vicentine consuls on their tours of the countryside, that dossier which largely determined subsequent judgment, was inviolable and could not be altered by Venetian judges.[27]

Registers of fifty-one investigations in the period 1489–93 indicate the predominant role played by local consuls. In 10 percent of cases there was no *processum* at all but only judgment on the basis of formal complaints by rural officials. In 31 percent, podesta and *judex maleficiorum* investigated on the basis of public outcry or "clamorous information." In 6 percent, Vicentine and Venetian officials collaborated: the podesta and *judex maleficiorum* investigated, and a consul drew up the *processum*. But in a full 53 percent of cases, Vicentine consuls handled the preliminary stages of prosecution.[28] The proportion of criminal investigations wholly or partially involving the consuls (59 percent) is very close to that of communal participation in the civil cases recorded in the *Liber Forbannitorum*.

The definitive hearing of a criminal case (*expeditio*) classified the crime (as homicide or manslaughter, for example), determined the guilt or innocence of the accused, and passed final sentence. *Expeditio* was made by a body known, confusingly, as the *consolatum:* not in fact the communal consulate alone but a mixed tribunal of the podesta, his assessors, and the full Vicentine consulate. Here Vicentine judges enjoyed a privileged position. Once the *consolatum* had read through the dossier and heard the defenses of the accused, the assembled judges expressed their opinions beginning with the oldest of the judge consuls and proceeding through the judge and nonjurist consuls. Only then did the podesta and his assessors speak. In the majority vote that followed, Vicentines could determine the outcome, since statutes set a quorum of seven consuls and allowed at most four Venetian magistrates. Though the podesta then announced criminal sentences before the general assembly of Vicentines (Arengo), those sentences were valid only if made with the consent of Vicentine consuls.[29]

The Vicentine consulate was, by all accounts, an extraordinary institution. It had survived even Giangaleazzo Visconti's attempt to abolish it, when fierce communal protests led him to rescind the order. Quattrocento counterparts on the mainland had far less authority: Veronese consuls could not draw up the *processum,* could not proceed without supervision of the *judex maleficiorum,* and were excluded from more important criminal cases. The Venetian Republic, in turn, protected Vicenza's "splendid jurisdiction" to the extent of denying central magistracies the power to alter or hear appeals from Arengo sentences. That privilege derived from broad Venetian respect for the consulate's efficiency. As the ex-podesta Alvise Moro reported to the *collegio* in 1500, "justice is administered by twelve consuls, four doctors, and eight laymen. And this they do in a just manner." To Marc'Antonio Sabellico, Vicentine judicial magistracies were the bulwark (*praesidium*) of the citizenry and "governed with the highest justice."[30]

MUNICIPAL COUNCILS

Civic councils were Vicentine in membership and autonomous in operation. That they held powers to enact provisions, elect higher officials, and authorize the reformation of statutes was in itself something of a triumph. Under Trecento *signori* the councils of Treviso ceased to function, those of Padua lost the capacity to make law, and Visconti rulers packed a new *consiglio* for Verona and Vicenza with their officials. The fossil councils of Treviso were actually abolished in 1407, and those of Padua were nearly moribund in the period 1408–30.[31]

The arrival of more tolerant Venetian rule did not assure local control of council membership. In the early Quattrocento the Dominante freely exercised its right to confer Vicentine citizenship, the prerequisite for entry onto municipal councils. The problem arose, however, that new citizens frequently lived outside the city and evaded their share of the urban tax burden. In November 1410 a communal orator complained of this grave injustice to more dutiful original citizens, and the doge obligingly ordered that the Vicentine Great Council henceforth advise on the worthiness of all candidates for citizenship. A ducal declaration of 1440 made local opinion binding, ordering that grants of citizenship should conform to the will of Vicentine councils. The central government in 1460 completed the reconstruction of local prerogatives with a decree that all Venetian grants should henceforth conform to the statutes and ordinances of the Vicentine commune. Those measures established, in effect, the commune's sole capacity to regulate access to municipal power. Venetian concessions of Vicentine citizenship fell sharply in number after 1410, declined further after 1440, and almost ceased after 1460. The Vicentine privilege was greater than that of Padua, where the podesta could independently admit foreigners to citizenship.[32]

Vicentine councils demanded and received a free hand in making law and choosing municipal officials. In 1410 the doge ordered that a ballot with his name was to be inserted in communal urns during elections by lot. If this were drawn, the podesta could appoint the officeholder. By 1424, however, the commune had begun to ignore this "ancient custom," and it apparently disappeared shortly thereafter. When the commune established a Council of One Hundred in 1423, the podesta and deputies chose its members, but this was a one-time event, and right of election passed the next year to the deputies alone. The central government in 1453 forbade Venetian nobles to sit or speak in municipal councils.[33] Two Venetian prerogatives alone remained. The podesta presided over council meetings, and councils had to submit important legislation for ratification, cancellation, or amendment. Vicentines found neither right burdensome. There is no record of the podesta having dominated or imposed his will upon assemblies, and Venetian interference with communal legislation was slight.

Recent historians have concluded that in Verona and Padua, as in Italy generally, civic councils steadily declined in prestige and significance as central governments assumed vital functions. They measure loss of municipal vitality by reduced attendance in councils and by increasing difficulties in finding citizens to assume communal office. This may have been true elsewhere, perhaps, but not in Quattrocento Vicenza. There, participation in Great Council sessions remained steady at about 160 to 180 councillors, and attendance in the Council of One Hundred at 115 to 120. Some of the most lively debates, closest votes, and most important reforms came at the end of the century.[34]

VICENTINE NOTARIES

All governmental discourse took place on Vicentine terms. Administrators and judges might be Vicentine or Venetian, but members of the local College of Notaries drew up official documents. Neither governors nor assessors brought their own notaries into office. The chancellor could not himself compose, copy, or commission instruments. The Vicentine privilege, specifically confirmed in 1408, echoed that of other mainland cities.[35] Indeed, all surviving public records bear the signatures of Vicentine notaries.

Attempts to circumvent or diminish the notarial monopoly proved unsuccessful. Venetian chancellors, in particular, constantly tried to make copies of ducal decrees, judicial documents, and council provisions for public distribution. They may have been ignorant of the limited possibilities of their office or ambitious to pick up some of this lucrative business. Nonetheless a vigilant commune and college always foiled their efforts by appeal to higher Venetian magistracies. On several dozen occasions central councils upheld local rights and overruled those chancellors, ordering that the task of redacting documents in *publica forma* belonged to college members alone. Fiscal magistracies tried to classify communal notaries as adjunct members of the Venetian administration, hence subject to Venetian taxation and supervision, but senior councils ruled in 1452 that notaries were officials of the Vicentine commune and subject solely to local law.[36] In 1469 the doge licensed noncollege Vicentines to practice the notariate. He could base his actions upon the common jurisprudential doctrine that the *princeps* held the power to make notaries, but, in a rare show of disregard for the *communis opinio,* the Vicentine commune successfully protested the attempt.[37] The college thereafter retained the exclusive capacity to create urban and communal notaries.

More to the point, the local monopoly on the notariate ensured that public discourse would be filtered through Vicentine formularies. That requirement, in turn, subjected discourse to the strictures of Vicentine law that underlay formularies. In keeping with the doctrine of jurists that "a notary ought to put in his instruments those things that are in accordance with the mores and customs of the region," Vicentine notaries could not draw up any document that was contrary to municipal statutes.[38] Even when Venetian officials rendered summary judgment or invoked *conscientia,* the language and constructs by which local notaries articulated transactions shaped those decisions. Vicentine notaries, fully as much as jurists, deputies, and legislators, stand as guardians of a privileged local tradition.

6

Commune and Countryside

RECONSTRUCTING COMMUNAL JURISDICTIONS

The territorial state seldom favored the claims of provincial cities to govern their hinterlands. Rulers found a measure of security in subdividing their dominions into isolated units governed directly from the capital. This was especially true when, as was the case in Pisa, the ruler achieved annexation by outright conquest and the subject city remained hostile. Villages, for their part, often welcomed the chance to exchange control by a nearby city for administration from the more distant capital. So Florence "amputated" the *contado* of a Pisa or Pistoia or Arezzo and carved it into vicariates and *podestarie* governed by Florentines. The Visconti recognized extant fiefs while rendering them dependent upon the ruler, and they created several new fiefs. In either case, Visconti support usually enabled feudatories to resist the pretensions of nearby urban communes. Milanese rulers granted separate status, as well, to mountain towns and larger provincial centers. Small towns around Brescia achieved unprecedented (if sometimes short-lived) autonomy first under Milanese, then under Venetian control.[1]

Past Veneto rulers had been equally inclined to disregard urban claims. In the Trecento the Venetian Republic divided the Trevisan countryside into several circumscriptions, each with a Venetian governor and each largely outside the control of the Trevisan commune. Vicenza's rulers were no more sympathetic to urban jurisdiction. Although the municipal commune claimed authority over the entire *districtus,* successive *signori* divided the countryside into a tangle of incomplete and overlapping circumscriptions. The Scaligeri created vicariates on an ad hoc and irregular basis, along with captaincies in larger towns such as Marostica, Schio, Arzignano, and Barbarano. The urban commune governed only some of the vicariates. Scaligeri fiscal officers filled others, and courtiers endowed with judicial powers filled the rest. The Scaligeri named all captains. Some areas, apparently, had neither vicars nor captains.[2]

Visconti domination produced additional statutes in 1390 and 1400 to clarify the election and competences of at least the communally controlled vicariates, but continued Milanese tinkering with jurisdictions tended only to confuse matters further. The original captaincies disappeared, for example, and were replaced by two regional captains (*versus Lonigo* and *versus Marosticam*) endowed with full civil and criminal jurisdiction. The Visconti promptly substituted podestas for those captains in Marostica and Lonigo, downgrading the jurisdiction to merely local competence and lesser civil jurisdiction; but there are still references to captains in 1397.[3]

The case of Schio illustrates the fluidity of the situation and also the exiguity of communal prerogatives. In the early Trecento the Maltraversi family held Schio as a separate county. By 1335, Schio was simultaneously a vicariate controlled by the Nogarola of Verona, whose tenure lasted to 1380. In 1375, Schio also had a captain named by the Scaligeri. The Visconti revived the county in 1387 and granted it to the Veronese Giorgio Cavalli, without abolishing the vicariate. Vicentine councils filled the vicariate in 1393; but by 1396 the same Giorgio Cavalli held the vicariate privately and permanently. The actual situation was probably even more confused.[4]

Extension of Venetian authority after 1404 initially reinforced the region's tradition of fragmented rural administration and irregular urban control. In Verona the Republic gave major towns such as Peschiera, Legnago, Porto, and Soave to feudatories or Venetian governors and tacitly confirmed scores of private jurisdictions. When the Venetian fisc sold off the holdings of the Scaligeri patrimony, new owners received the jurisdictions associated with the lands. Six Venetian podestas administered the major subdivisions of the Padovano. Cologna (claimed by Verona and Vicenza, and trying to belong to Vicenza) and Bassano (claimed by Vicenza and Padua, and trying to belong to neither) received separate status and Venetian podestas.[5] Within the district of Vicenza, Venetian podestas governed the walled towns of Marostica and Lonigo. The Sette Comuni, seven villages on the high plateau around Asiago to the north of the city, soon obtained confirmation of a 1399 privilege that guaranteed their fiscal and economic freedom from the commune of Vicenza in return for a fixed annual fee. The Venetian podesta of Marostica exercised judicial authority in the Sette Comuni.[6]

But dismemberment of the Vicentine *districtus* ended at that point. Within a few years the urban commune had fully vindicated its claim to preeminent authority throughout the countryside. In fact the commune's resurgence began somewhat earlier, with a successful drive to eliminate separate criminal jurisdictions. In 1390 a Vicentine petition asked Giangaleazzo Visconti to revoke a recent privilege that conceded *merum et mixtum imperium* to the Milanese podesta of Lonigo: "This is the destruction of the *podestarie* of Vicenza, the destruction of the jurisdiction of the commune of Vicenza—it is the separation of the limbs from the head!" Vicentines' claim to past control of Lonigo had little historical basis, but Giangaleazzo Visconti accepted the petition. Henceforth the podesta of Lonigo held only civil jurisdiction in cases valued under twenty-five *lire*, and no criminal authority. The urban commune assumed all remaining jurisdiction in Lonigo. Four years later the commune expanded its claims and again received Giangaleazzo's backing: the recently appointed territorial captains, who had been given criminal jurisdiction to pacify an unruly countryside, lost this authority after a Vicentine protest.[7]

The issue was not urban power but urban survival. Purely regional centers such as Vicenza, lacking significant international commerce, would languish and fade without control over the agricultural hinterland.[8] Well aware of that fact, Vicentine municipal councillors in the spring of 1404 acted quickly to extend jurisdiction over the countryside as a whole. They accomplished their goal with surprising ease. In the 1404 *privilegia*, Venice promised that all vicariates currently held by the Vicentine commune should remain under the commune, and that the Republic would not alienate criminal jurisdictions. The *capitula* of 1406 further promised that jurisdictions taken away by the Scaligeri and Visconti would be restored to the urban commune.[9] Again, claims to past mastery of the countryside rested on a gross exaggeration of the historical record, but Venetian negotiators accepted those claims.

The commune quickly eliminated or neutralized rival jurisdictions. The *privilegia* specified Vicentine authority in Arzignano and Schio, neither of which had appeared in the most recent list of communal vicariates. Arzignano, though it had enjoyed separate status as a captaincy and signorial vicariate, apparently passed under Vicentine rule without incident. The town of Montecchio Maggiore, which also had not appeared in the list of communal vicariates of 1400, quietly came under Vicentine control. In 1404 the Thiene family yielded civil and criminal jurisdictions around Camisano to the commune, and the Nogarola ceded some unknown criminal jurisdictions. The Cavalli ceded their county of Schio in 1404; they forfeited any residual claims to Schio in May 1406, when Ludovico Cavalli was implicated in an anti-Venetian plot and his father, Giorgio, was exiled to Candia. When the commune of Schio submitted to Venice a few days later, it asked to be subject to Vicentine civil and criminal jurisdiction, and to receive a Vicentine vicar.[10]

Placement of Venetian podestas in Lonigo and Marostica, which had been independent of the city throughout much of the Trecento, actually favored Vicentine authority. Those rectors' commissions specified that they should govern according to Vicentine municipal statutes, and that greater civil and all criminal jurisdiction should rest with urban tribunals. There remained only the four private vicariates of Bagnolo, Alonte, Dueville, and Costafabbrica (now Costabissara). These consisted of single villages and minor prerogatives, and in any case communal magistracies soon assumed greater civil and all criminal jurisdiction in them. The vicariate of Alonte came to be held only by annual Venetian concession and was abolished altogether in 1445.[11]

The Vicentine experience mirrors, but also anticipates, that of counterparts throughout Italy. Chittolini has noted for Tuscany that, after Florence's initial amputation of rural districts, cities gradually recovered some control over their surroundings. The Visconti's cancellation of the privileges of rural towns and imposition of discipline on Lombard fiefs also redounded to the benefit of urban communes. In particular the great Maggior Magistrato decree of 1441 affirmed the superiority of urban over feudal and rural jurisdictions in major cases and appeals. In the Venetian dominion, the Brescian commune recovered jurisdiction over the countryside in 1439, though rural resistance somewhat canceled its effective authority. In Verona the communal offensive against private jurisdictions reaped tangible results, but only after the fourth decade of the century. As late as 1466 private jurisdictions outnumbered those of the urban commune by a ratio of nearly 3 : 1.[12] In Vicenza, on the other hand, recovery of urban control was substantially complete by around 1410.

How Vicentines established relatively thorough and precocious mastery is something of a mystery. It is not known what induced the Cavalli, Thiene, and Nogarola to give up their rights in 1404 or what induced the Republic to place formerly separate vicariates under Vicentine control. The urban commune had little tradition of rural administration, having previously exercised only sporadic control over a few vicariates. It was certainly no stronger in the early Quattrocento than was Verona or most other Italian cities. The Venetian Republic, as seen in its handling of the Veronese situation in 1405 and the Brescian situation after 1426, was far from hostile to private jurisdictions. In any case relative Vicentine success goes far to explain the city's greater territorial authority for the remainder of the century.

POINTS OF CONTENTION

The commune's supremacy in the countryside faced constant challenge from rural authorities. Venetian podestas in Lonigo and Marostica, in particular, chafed at their lack of criminal jurisdiction. The urban *privilegia* implied that disability, and ducal letters of 1408 and rectors' commissions spelled it out, but it rankled just the same. Their counterparts in Treviso, for example, did hold criminal authority. Insofar as they were obliged to assist Vicentine consuls in investigating crimes and sending malefactors for urban trial, podestas in Lonigo and Marostica actually took orders from local magistrates. They could not even erect pillories for the public humiliation of minor offenders. Several rural podestas, offended at subordinate status, attempted to prosecute crimes on their own initiative. As was so often the case, however, the Vicentine commune enjoyed the support of central Venetian magistracies. On at least a dozen occasions, the doge accepted Vicentine petitions and sternly admonished these podestas not to interfere in *criminalia*.[13]

The Vicentine commune severely limited the civil jurisdiction of those podestas as well. The rules were clear, if unfavorable to the governors of Lonigo and Marostica: they could hear any case valued up to 100 *lire*, but Vicentine tribunals judged greater cases and appeals. More importantly, in 1408 the doge responded to a Vicentine request with a decree that either party to a dispute in Marostica or Lonigo could have the case transferred to Vicentine courts. The independent authority of rural podestas further declined with the doge's order, first handed down in 1414 and several times repeated, that they give full assistance to Vicentine officials in various rural tasks: collecting taxes and debts, executing the sentences of urban courts, inspecting roads and waterways, making surveys of foodstuffs, enforcing textile laws, blocking contraband, and the like. They much resented the obligation to serve, in effect, as agents of the Vicentine commune, and they frequently tried to impede communal officials. Invariably, sharp commands from the capital ordered them to respect urban prerogatives. The doge was adamant that the Republic's own representatives not denigrate basic privileges: "No village or walled town in the district of Vicenza shall be separated from its jurisdiction."[14]

Country towns united in opposition to urban economic privileges, particularly those of the Wool Guild. Most noxious were laws that fine cloth be made only in the city or walled towns (Marostica and Lonigo), that all cloth be finished in the city, that imported wool and cloth pay urban tolls, and that rural producers bring cloth to the city for inspection, weighing, and bonding. At one time or another rural ambassadors, led by representatives of Schio and Marostica, challenged all those privileges before Venetian councils. In 1477, Schio even mounted a counterattack, interpreting the urban monopoly on fine cloth production to mean that cheaper cloth could not be made in Vicenza. Three years later, Schio combined with Arzignano, Cornedo, and Valdagno to seek cancellation of the monopoly of the urban mar-

ket. All those efforts came to naught, as Vicentine ambassadors successfully fought derogation of the city's privileges.[15]

In the process, Schio took the challenge a step farther. To be able
to produce fine cloth, the town had to have walls, which Schio wanted
and was willing to pay for. But walls also had political consequences: in
joining the ranks of Marostica and Lonigo, Schio would likewise receive a Venetian podesta rather than a communal vicar. When central
councils turned down petitions for walls in 1463 and 1468, Schio
openly sought secession from Vicentine jurisdiction by requesting a
Venetian podesta with criminal and civil jurisdiction. Typically of Quattrocento governance, Schio's ambitions were irrepressible. Despite the
doge's order that the town maintain perpetual silence, and despite the
Council of Ten's ferocious warnings against raising the issue further,
Schio renewed its claims in 1469, 1470, 1472, 1476, and 1492–93. But
it was also typical of Vicentine fortunes that the central government
never accepted those claims. Schio remained without walls and received Vicentine communal vicars throughout the century.[16]

The people of Lonigo were particularly incensed by an inequitable
system of direct taxation. As was the case in most territorial states, the
central government demanded a flat contribution from subject cities
and allowed local governments to distribute the burden. In Vicenza the
urban commune compiled separate assessments for city and countryside according to distinct criteria. Statute set the *estimo* of the city at
2,500 *lire* divided among inhabitants, that of the countryside at 250
"hearths" divided among rural communes. Statute also required that
the countryside pay twice as much as the city. The problem lay in the
fact that land was taxed with the owner's place of domicile. When title
to land passed from countryside to city through purchase or the
owner's acquisition of urban citizenship, rural communes received no
compensation for the erosion of their tax base. Indeed, the system
could not compensate for emigration or land alienation. Loss of one
town's tax base could only be remedied by increasing the quota of other
towns, which was unpopular in the countryside, or by abolishing the
two-part *estimo* and fixed urban/rural quotas, which the urban commune would not allow. The system remained intact, and rural landowners shouldered a progressively heavier burden. Michael Knapton
has estimated for the similar Paduan situation that by the end of the
century, on the basis of contributive capacity, the countryside paid
twice as much as the city in direct taxes.[17]

Lonigo appeared to have a safeguard against that erosion: the
1404 articles of its submission to Venice specified that lands currently
in the *estimo* of Lonigo should remain there despite change of ownership. The doge confirmed Lonigo's privilege in 1415. This time, how-

ever, the Vicentine commune vigorously protested that the ruling insulted its powers to confer citizenship and to tax its own citizens. The Venetian Senate offered a compromise: new citizens should pay land taxes with the place where the land was located but should pay taxes on movable goods in the place where the owner had domicile. Emboldened by confirmation of its primary claim, Lonigo in 1418 aspired to full exemption from taxes imposed by Vicenza. The Senate sided with the city and ruled that Lonigo should indeed pay municipal taxes because they did "not intend that the limbs should be separated from the head." It was the beginning of the end of Lonigo's favored status. In 1441 the doge declared that all goods of Vicentine citizens, including land in Lonigo, should be put in the urban *estimo*.[18]

His decision did not end the controversy. In April 1459, Lonigo directly challenged the countryside's two-thirds share of taxes, citing extensive land purchase by urban residents. Having lost that round, Lonigo's orators returned to Venice in July to seek reversal of the ruling of 1441, and they lost again. A generation later the *avogadori di comun* did cancel that ruling in favor of Lonigo's original privilege of 1404, but Vicenza, as always, had more powerful patrons. Two imperial nobles, a lawyer and a knight-jurist, went straight to the Council of Ten, which preserved the urban privilege. The climax of Lonigo's agitation came in 1503. An unprecedented ten orators appeared before the doge and Council of Ten, armed with reams of documents and the alarming statistic that 90 percent of the town's wealth was now owned and taxed with the city of Vicenza, "so that the burden of those lost lands rests upon the shoulders of Lonigans." The doge, trying to please both sides, and clearly not understanding the assessment system, weakly ordered that land transfers be taken into account at the next redaction of the *estimo*, but that the current *estimo* system remain intact. In effect this rejected Lonigo's request, since the urban commune continued to draw up the *estimo* according to traditional criteria that could not take transfers into account.[19]

Marostica protested the exemption from rural obligations of the *passipage*, Vicentine citizens who by ancient custom lived in the countryside but paid taxes with the city. Marostica hoped to gain sympathy for its cause from the fact that some urban citizens too resented the *passipage:* because they often evaded taxes altogether and because they often engaged in agricultural labor, which, by consensus, was unworthy of a true citizen. In 1461, accordingly, Marostica requested that *passipage* should pay taxes with the countryside. When the doge denied that petition and shortly thereafter repeated the ruling that citizens pay taxes with the city rather than place of residence, Marostica launched a flurry of test cases to prove that individual *passipage* were not true citizens by virtue of ignominious rustic labor. That challenge also failed. Vicentine orators demonstrated that these men had long paid taxes with the city and so had behaved like true citizens; honest poverty excused their agricultural pursuits.[20]

Marostica's request of 1461 was, in fact, part of a broad litany of complaints. That *cahier de doléances* demonstrates the persistence and indomitability of the countryside: each article had been rejected in the past, and each was to be raised in the future with similar lack of success. The outcome of the petition, however, demonstrates consistent Venetian support for urban privileges:

1. That the people of Marostica be freed from the burdens imposed by the commune of Vicenza: denied.
2. That citizens of Vicenza who bought rural possessions in Marostica pay land taxes in Marostica, as was true for Padua and Treviso and for Venetian nobles with mainland property:[21] denied.
3. That *passipage* pay taxes with Marostica: denied.
4. That Marostica not pay the expenses of communal officials sent out to investigate crimes: denied [similarly articles 6–8, 10].
9. That the commune of Vicenza not make undue demands in the *estimo:* denied.
11. That Marostica's cloth not be subject to the expense of Vicentine inspection and bonding: denied.
12. That the people of Marostica not be cited for debt before Vicentine courts, but only before their own podesta: denied.
16. That Marosticans be allowed to finish cloth: denied.
18. That when the *estimo* of a town declined because some of its property passed into urban hands, the amount of that decline not be assigned to other towns: denied.

The fifth article of Marostica's complaint moved the argument from real to symbolic grievances. There Marostica asked for a mild reform in the laws governing the Corpus Christi celebration. Though each rural town had its own procession, it still had to contribute wax for candles used in the Vicentine procession and to pay two *solidi* to a communal official who came to collect the wax. Adding insult to injury, the Vicentine commune sold the leftover wax at a great profit. Statutes regulating the procession had originally specified that each rural commune send a representative with a candle whose size varied with the importance of the town. By 1425 the urban commune had increased that obligation by an additional 142 *lire* 12 *solidi* due from the countryside as a whole. The total burden was not great, but forced contribution to Vicentine ceremonies still had a "precise ideological value, expressive of the subordination of the countryside to the city," and drew the resentment of rural communes. Nonetheless the doge replied that

Vicentine statutes should be preserved "for the veneration of the festivity of the Most Holy Eucharist."[22]

Marostica might well have invoked several dozen additional inequities in governance of the countryside, but these were so firmly established that they were evidently not considered worth protesting. For example, urban litigants could summon countrymen before urban tribunals, but rural courts could not summon citizens. *Districtuales* bore the entire cost of billeting Venetian troops and feeding their horses. They alone provided and paid for levies of infantry and laborers for the army, then paid the salary of a Vicentine communal official who led conscripts to the field. The city had the power to demand food from the countryside, at a price set by the commune. By the reformed statutes of 1425, the commune retained its capacity to forbid grain exports to neighboring cities. The doge in 1430 confirmed a communal provision that inhabitants of the countryside send five sheep to the urban market for every hundred raised. Three years later municipal councils passed a requirement that each rural cultivator plant an annual quota of almonds, pears, figs, cherries, apples, and mulberries. When, towards the end of the Quattrocento, Vicenza developed a considerable silk industry, the commune sought to establish a regional monopoly with a ban on the export of silkworms and mulberry trees. The doge supported communal protectionism and even refused a 1488 request of Milan's Duke Ludovico Sforza for some mulberries.[23]

Though rural protest could not be stilled, it was never successful. Communal resources simply overpowered the countryside's claims of injustice. Vicentines could draw upon a conceptual arsenal that consistently privileged the city. The Justinianic Code and canon law, as received from worthies such as Bartolus and Baldus, declared that "towns and villages shall follow the law of the city," and that "citizens rank higher than rustics." Citizens too could invoke the powerful corporate image, to the effect that the head (Vicenza) held directive power over limbs (rural communes), and that the limbs were obliged to provide support to the head.[24]

Above all, Vicentines could draw upon Venetian support. Central councils frequently moved from specific cases to general statements of respect for communal powers. Responding to a protest of Schio and other towns against the *estimo*, for example, the *avogadori di comun* in 1468 declared to the Vicentine podesta, "You shall cause . . . to be carried out and fulfilled whatever is proposed and passed by the said council [of Vicenza] for the good and utility both of this city and of the entire district." The doge in 1485 forbade podestas of Lonigo and Marostica to infringe the Vicentine consulate's monopoly on rural crimes because he was "more disposed to increase the privileges and concessions of this commune [of Vicenza] than to derogate them in any way." Even such a trivial challenge to Vicentine authority as Marostica's complaint of the high costs of road repair drew the judgment that "the provisions and statutes and customs of this most faithful commune shall be preserved." When Marostica complained of the injustices of the *estimo*, the doge raised his refusal to the level of principle: "The customs and statutes of this our most faithful commune of Vicenza shall have full force and shall be observed inviolably."[25] The countryside's laments of unfair treatment could not begin to match the force of the ongoing coalition of central government and local commune.

7

Affirmation of the Patriciate

Study of Venetian governance cannot be confined to relations between the capital and subject communes. If communes held broad powers to resist the claims of Venetian administrators and to govern the countryside, then the distribution of power within the urban commune assumes particular significance. The degree to which realignments of local power benefited specific groups and the extent to which the Republic responded to or orchestrated those relocations, provide critical indicators of overall Venetian policy and Venetian management of local political resources.

Examination of local political movements has a broader historiographic context as well. Recent historians generally accept the notion that a restriction of the urban power base accompanied the rise of the territorial state. Affirmation of a loosely construed elite, the patriciate, sharply eroded the powers of guilds and popular institutions. Within overall consensus, however, the debate on the patriciate has produced a variety of conflicting opinions. The issue of periodization is far from certain. In the second place, historians encounter considerable difficulties in identifying and defining elites. Prosopographic analysis seeks to locate political elites by tracing continuous family membership in civic councils, but it cannot explain what bound a patriciate together, what separated it from relatively powerless groups, how power was secured, what mechanisms preserved its hegemony, what ideologies justified its exclusivity. Furthermore, structural revision did not formalize distinct ruling bodies. Civic institutions did not change appreciably, and political access remained, on paper, open. Guilds retained political representation.[1] Simple membership in municipal councils cannot therefore automatically demarcate the ruling group from the powerless. Historians of Tuscany have long acknowledged the problem.[2] Even in Venice, where the famous *serrata* is generally thought to have effected closure of the political class, recent research has revealed considerable fluidity within upper ranks.[3] Because the fixing of municipal leadership was not absolute or overt, *patriciate* remains a construct based on the intuition of historians rather than the definitions of contemporaries.

The situation in the Veneto presents an additional difficulty. Studies of political closure have concentrated on sovereign cities such as Florence, Lucca, or Venice. They can focus, therefore, upon the simple binary relationship between an emerging elite and the increasingly powerless, and upon the interplay of factions within that elite. In the Veneto, on the other hand, establishment of the territorial state introduced the variable of Venetian intentions in the conflict between local elites and urban underclasses.

Angelo Ventura in 1964 took the lead in linking the new composite polity to local changes. The Republic, he wrote, completed Trecento *signori*'s work of excluding popular elements from power by sponsoring closure of local ruling classes. Venetian councillors' own aristocratic mentality found patriciates more acceptable than agencies of the *popolo*, hence favored local elites as exclusive agents in local administration. John Law, on the other hand, has argued that purely indigenous forces effected the constriction of political classes. Venetian policy was inconsistent, indeed sometimes hostile to overrestriction of local elites.[4] In the larger sense, however, both interpretations support an emerging consensus: study of the Renaissance state as a whole demands study of relocations of authority within its constituent parts.

EXCLUSION OF *POPOLO*

When in 1404 the Vicentine "commune and people" sought outside protection and eventually submitted to Venice, the signature of its documents reflected the bipartite quality of municipal government.[5] Structures of the *popolo* partly complemented, partly duplicated those of the urban commune. In Vicenza the popular party found institutional voice in the Council of Elders (Anziani), elected by guilds and neighborhoods. Trecento statutes, still in effect, charged this council with pacifying the *civitas* and ensuring good governance by the podesta. The Council of the Anziani also acted as a check upon the commune, guarding lest officials and legislation contravene municipal law.

The Vicentine commune did not directly challenge the Anziani after 1404 but quickly made their council a marginal player in public life. Communal statutes of 1425, it is true, gave the Anziani a prominent place in the hierarchy of municipal offices, just after the Great Council and ahead of consuls and miscellaneous officials. Anziani were entitled to sit ex officio on the Great Council and Council of One Hundred, with full voting rights, and they did in fact participate. But the statutes did not provide the Anziani with any mechanism to enforce supervisory jurisdiction and appointed a member of the College of

Jurists to preside over them. That judge also assumed the Anziani's task of registering membership in the communal Great Council. Communal councils in 1486 removed the Anziani's primary function, monitoring communal officers to safeguard local law, and transferred that jurisdiction to "conservators of the laws" elected by communal councils. Thus stripped of independent authority, the Council of the Anziani probably did not meet as a separate body during the Quattrocento. By 1520 the Anziani had been informally excluded from city councils.[6]

It was typical of Quattrocento Italy, certainly of the Veneto, that guilds lost an effective political voice after the later Trecento.[7] Even traditional economic rights came under attack. In Vicenza, an incident of 1410 set the prevailing tendency: communal deputies, with the approval of the doge, ordered the Wool Guild to give up the house that it kept at Santi Apostoli in Venice for the exclusive use of its members, and to make use only of the house on the Riva degli Schiavoni that the commune maintained for all Vicentine merchants. If the Wool Guild set textile regulations in 1421, the commune issued all subsequent laws. A communal official, the *miles artis lane*, supervised the guild after 1431. In 1455–56, breaking with tradition, the Council of One Hundred ordered that the guild could not choose a rector from within its ranks and appointed a member of the College of Jurists as rector. The wool industry, in fact, declined in the later Quattrocento; significantly, the commune did not allow corporate status for its economic replacement, the booming silk industry. Surviving matriculation records demonstrate strict communal supervision of guilds, with regular reviews of statutes and membership lists.[8]

Neighborhoods suffered even greater eclipse. They continued as useful administrative units: the commune listed tax assessments by quarter and *contrade* and distributed some high offices, notably the deputies, evenly by quarter. By the Quattrocento, however, the neighborhoods themselves had no part in elections except for selection of night watchmen and police officers. Neighborhoods and parishes lacked even a ritual identity in games or processions. In Florence, by contrast, neighborhoods as formal entities recruited militia forces, collected some taxes, and organized processions. Florentine neighborhoods were also centers of political maneuvering, with definite repercussions on the communal level. In Venice neighborhoods elected parish priests, recruited sailors, and (before 1379) sponsored festivals.[9]

Vicenza's lack of political subunits cannot be explained simply by the city's small size and relative lack of social complexity. Vicenza counted some 19,000 inhabitants in the later Quattrocento, nearly half the population of Florence. In cities of comparable size such as Verona and

Padua, neighborhoods were prominent organizers of festivals. That lack, on the contrary, testifies to the Vicentine commune's relative success in establishing itself as sole center of public life.

COUNCIL MEMBERSHIP

Vicentine documents strongly suggest a compact ruling group. The same family names appear over and over in lists of municipal councillors and major colleges. Nearly identical lists of notables furnished by the chronicler Battista Pagliarino in the late Quattrocento and the traveler Giovanbattista Dragonzino in the early Cinquecento corroborate that impression. But if identification of the ruling class is simple, definition of that class is not. In Vicenza, as in Italy at large, the patriciate never received formal demarcation from the rest of the citizenry. Communal office remained, on paper, open to all citizens. Even contemporary observers suffered uncertainty in separating elites from the rest of society. Pagliarino and Dragonzino, like their Paduan counterparts Giovanni da Nono, Giovanni Ongarelli, and the pseudo–Giovanni Basili, were reduced to simple listing of local worthies without providing criteria for selection. They opted for mass inclusion rather than leave out any whose claim to prominence might be acceptable. Thus Pagliarino found 271 notable families in Vicenza, some of "low and humble condition."[10]

Closure of the ruling class in Vicenza, measured by a monopoly on political participation by a constant group of families, dates from 1311, when municipal statutes restricted positions on the Great Council to those currently holding seats, or their heirs or assigns. That law was, however, only a potential vehicle for the eventual affirmation of a distinct governing class. Dynastic upheaval, demographic disasters, free alienation and inheritance of seats, the Great Council's insistence on the right to name new councillors, and its initially broad membership in 1311 ensured heterogeneity and rapid turnover throughout the Trecento. In the three surviving lists of the Great Council, many members were obviously of artisan or humble status. Many families lost their seats between one list and the next. Foreign domination brought an influx of bureaucrats, soldiers and merchant-usurers into the upper ranks of Vicentine society. Such future luminaries as the Poiana, Sesso, Nogarola, Macchiavelli, Angiolelli, Fracanzani, Mainente, Ghellini, Chiericati, and Cavalli secured council seats under the Scaligeri, while the Thiene, originally Vicentine, rose to power with Scaligeri patronage. The seventeen-year rule of the Visconti introduced the Monza, Cavalcabò, Muzani, Roma, Anguissola, and Soardi, among others. Several immigrant families from Padua, Emilia, and Tuscany entered municipal councils. Any notion of political closure before the Quattrocento, in Vicenza as in Verona, Padua, and Treviso, is premature.[11]

Closure did take place in the Quattrocento. Without resorting to caste legislation on the Venetian model, the Vicentine patriciate closed ranks and distanced itself from the rest of society. To render the Anziani marginal was an obvious first step. The second was the gradual raising of eligibility requirements for urban citizenship, the prerequisite for participation in municipal government. The commune had somewhat casually conferred citizenship in earlier centuries, sometimes simply on the basis of ten years' residency; its only concern was that the new citizen be enrolled in the urban *estimo*.[12] In the Quattrocento, communal councils more consciously manipulated the law of citizenship, first as an instrument of urban protectionism and later as an instrument of patrician exclusivity.

The commune openly declared that it granted citizenship in order to fill the city with artisans at the expense of the countryside. That policy paralleled the effort to secure an urban monopoly of key functions in the wool industry. When conventional inducements to immigration failed to provide an adequate supply of skilled workers, the commune in 1431 cut the residence requirement for wool workers to five years, with a quota of fifteen grants of citizenship per year. But easy access soon produced the unpleasant consequence that rural artisans secured citizenship yet continued to live in the *territorio,* paying the lesser city taxes or none at all. So in 1437, Vicentine councils required that countrymen granted urban citizenship in the previous twenty-five years live in the city from mid-November through mid-May, for the first forty years of their citizenship. Even this left too large a loophole, and four years later municipal councils forbade new citizens to exercise their trades in the countryside at any time of year.[13]

More than economic and fiscal self-interest stimulated Quattrocento reform of residence requirements. Increasingly, the urban commune endowed citizenship with behavioral rather than material or residential connotations. A successful petitioner for citizenship usually specified that he was "unable to stay in the village because he [did] not know how to perform rural work," that he lived "in a civil manner," that "because of his age he [was] no longer suited to agriculture, and his grandsons [were] more suited to civil than rustic mores."[14] The laws of 1437 and 1441 began to formalize the distinction between the occupation appropriate to the citizen and that appropriate to the rustic.

Venetian nobles shared that distinction and made it law in a monumental Senate decree of 1448. Countrymen were made citizens, the argument ran, so that they might desist from rural trades and perform the work of citizens. But the opposite had happened: new citizens not only did not desist from their trades but continued to perform "mechanical work, just like rustics" and still paid urban taxes which were smaller. Fiscal evasion and ignominious labor insulted dutiful citizens and citizenship itself. So, the decree ordered, new citizens who practiced a rural trade were to be deprived of citizenship. The Senate only implied a definition of a suitable urban trade, but the general attitude was clear. By 1485 an applicant from the village of Zanè found it a mark of favor that he was "dedicated to letters" and ignorant of rural labor, that he would rather die of hunger than carry on such demeaning work. Finally, in 1500 the Republic extended a Paduan law to Vicenza: any citizen working the land "with his own hands" ipso facto reverted to rustic status.[15]

Scorn for *opera ruralia* eventually translated into a disinclination to grant urban citizenship to any countryman. Vicentine concessions dropped sharply from the high point of 1406–9. In part this can be explained by demographic recovery after the terrible losses of the Trecento and early Quattrocento. The commune felt less need to swell the urban work force and sharply cut back inducements to immigration. Later citizenship concessions generally stipulated, for example, that the new citizen be estimated and pay taxes with his former town until the compilation of the next *estimo*. Since this happened only every two decades or so, the clause canceled immediate fiscal advantage. Positive discouragement of new citizenship led the urban commune to attempt to strip new citizens of the exemption, enjoyed by original citizens since 1260, from tolls on goods shipped to Venice. The master Bartolus had insisted that original citizenship and acquired citizenship should confer the same benefits and obligations, but Vicentine councillors were increasingly disinclined to take his advice.[16]

With demographic pressures eased, the commune after mid-century could shift priorities from the economic or fiscal contribution of the would-be citizen to his personal suitability. Patrician councillors now set the distinction between honorable occupations and any form of manual labor, and they discouraged the immigration of artisans no less than cultivators. Early petitioners for citizenship had stressed the utility that a weaver or shoemaker or scribe brought to the city; those after 1450 declared that they were "dedicated to letters" or the law. Furthermore, councils subjected citizenship petitions to increasingly stringent scrutiny. In 1425 statutes set a relatively simple procedure: formal opinion by eight special commissioners followed by a majority vote in the Great Council. By 1485, on the other hand, the applicant from Zanè became a citizen only after approval by both Venetian rectors, communal deputies, two sittings of the Council of Forty (where a two-thirds majority was required), the Council of One Hundred, the Council of Six Hundred (Great Council plus One Hundred), a commission of eight distinguished citizens, and again the Council of Six Hundred.[17]

Foreigners and countrymen never entirely lost the capacity to become citizens of Vicenza. Nor did urban citizens lose the capacity to gain seats on municipal councils. But as the commune made increasingly few grants of citizenship, councils ceased to admit outsiders to membership. Only three cases of entry to councils are known from the Quattrocento, two from the first decade and one from 1426, and in the last case the family had held a council seat in the past.[18] The great influx of the Trecento ended abruptly, and the potentially restrictive provisions of 1311 finally took effect. Unlike the Florentine situation, where quite open attempts were made to disqualify new citizens from public office, however, legislation played a minor role in exclusion. The single Vicentine example of disabling law was a 1437 provision stipulating that any new citizen was ineligible for higher office—territorial vicar, consul, deputy—for thirty years after acquisition of citizenship. This effectively required that a full generation pass before a new family could gain any real power.[19] But no law blocked the new citizen's immediate entry to lower municipal councils or future entry to higher magistracies.

The closure of Vicentine councils was achieved informally. Despite the patriciate's heterogenous composition in 1404, despite endemic vendettas between notable families, and despite the fact that council seats could be alienated by sale or bequest, the Vicentine patriciate displayed a remarkable cohesion in resisting outsiders. When seats became vacant upon extinction of a councillor's patriline, they passed to lateral relatives or to families already represented on the Great Council.[20] Even then only the Great Council was closed: by law the Council of One Hundred and office of deputy were open to all citizens. In fact electors never looked beyond Great Council families and thus effectively disenfranchised the mass of the citizenry. In the rest of the mainland, similarly, patricians established de facto obstacles to reaching municipal power, though never absolute barriers.[21]

Even without formal closure, citizens possessed of council seats increasingly distanced themselves from the mass of citizens without them. Councillors assumed titles drawn from the equestrian and senatorial orders of the later Roman Empire: *Spectabilis* for deputies, *Egregius* for members of executive councils, *Dominus* for members of the Great Council. At the same time citizens not on councils gradually ceased to qualify themselves as *civis*. If urban citizenship conferred the right to political participation, then those permanently (if only de facto) excluded from councils had, in effect, lost citizenship.

PATRICIATE AND CORPORATIONS

Local colleges of jurists and notaries played a key role in the consolidation of the patriciate. Vicenza presents a very different picture from cities such as Venice, Treviso, and Lucca, where political classes feared the technical knowledge of legal specialists and consequently isolated lawyers from the top levels of power.[22] Like their Florentine counterparts,[23] Vicentine lawyers and notaries were simply the better-educated elements of the patriciate and on that basis tended to assume leadership in municipal affairs. Particularly the jurists predominated in embassies and other missions requiring technical skills, and they served as *deputati* in disproportionate numbers.

The colleges of jurists and notaries were privileged corporations, adjuncts to the privileged municipal commune. Since college members usually held council seats, their interests nearly always coincided with those of the commune. The very title *college* distinguished them from guilds (*frataleae*). Lawyers and notaries occupied more prominent places in civic processions. Jurists enjoyed exemption from most municipal taxes, as did their medical colleagues. Their college provided all municipal judges, a dozen or so annually, and the eleven commissioners sent out to investigate (*sindicare*) the performance of territorial vicars. A college member presided over the remnants of the *popolo* as judge of the Anziani; others served as rectors of larger corporations such as the Wool Guild. The College of Notaries supplied the hundred or so communal notaries who drew up public documents and provided notaries for guilds and religious-charitable corporations. The commune in turn protected that college against Venetian attempts to create notaries for the city, and against attempts of the Venetian chancellor to usurp the lucrative business of preparing official documents. Those privileges were typical of legal corporations in the Veneto at large.

Evolution of the colleges paralleled that of the commune: they became in the Quattrocento, as they were not in the Trecento, exclusively patrician. They used the same mechanisms for restricting access to newcomers: the gradual raising of citizenship and occupational requirements. In 1341 an applicant for entry into the College of Notaries had to have been resident in the city for three years; by 1443 he had to be a citizen as well, and resident for twenty-five. The judges, characteristically, were more stringent. Where in 1383 the college required that an applicant have been a taxpaying citizen for ten years, after 1480 his father also had to have been an "original citizen," and after 1486, both father and grandfather. After 1499 his family had to have held citizenship for eighty years. Stipulation of original citizenship was designed to keep out those who had been made citizens—yet another civic disability imposed on *cives creati*. The colleges also made occupational restrictions increasingly severe, lest ignoble trades stain the nobility of the professions. After 1486 no candidate then practising a rural or manual trade could enter the College of Jurists, after 1499 no one could enter who had performed *opera manualia* within the previous fifty years. Such strictures, too, find parallels in the Veneto and in Lombardy.[24]

Favored treatment of sons of college members was not new and was characteristic of all guilds. In the Quattrocento, however, legal corporations more thoroughly exploited hereditary privilege and more openly directed that privilege at the exclusion of outsiders. For most of the century, for example, the College of Notaries maintained a public school for training in the notariate; by 1485 sons of college members paid no fee to attend lectures. Membership in that college became a sort of private property, freely heritable and alienable as any type of patrimony. Notaries were arranged in two tiers, the mass of ordinary members and those inscribed in the lists (*module*) from which communal officers were selected. If a notary in the *module* was selected for office but was unwilling or unable to serve, he could sublet the position to another college member. By 1412 at least sons of those inscribed in the *module* could enter the college for a nominal payment. Soon thereafter notaries in the *module* held the power to bequeath, transfer or sell their places. Through inheritance or transfer, entry into college and *module* often came at a very young age despite numerous provisions in college statutes. In the Arnaldi family, for example, the brothers Andrea, Battista, and Tommaso entered the College of Notaries in 1425 aged seventeen, eleven, and ten years respectively. A second generation of Silvestro di Andrea and Alvise di Tommaso entered the college as infants and were inscribed in the *module* aged five and three respectively.[25]

Legal colleges in Vicenza, like their counterparts throughout Italy, never formally closed access to outsiders. Particularly the notariate was open to those who somehow secured the requisite training and fulfilled citizenship requirements. A few families of the middling patriciate, generally long active in the notariate, sent sons to Padua to become jurists; the Scroffa, Colzè, and Monza are good examples. Still, de facto obstacles to entry into the legal professions effectively kept out complete outsiders. In theory, for example, a commoner could obtain a law degree at Padua and pass the examination of a local college, but declin-

ing provision for poor students ensured that only the scions of established families could complete the university course. Matriculation records of both colleges demonstrate a nearly unbroken succession of a
few dozen families, precisely those families that constituted the patriciate. The single nonpatrician jurist of whom record survives, Andrea da
Bolzano, was not enrolled in the college and apparently practised his
profession exclusively in Venice.[26]

PATRICIATE AND OLIGARCHY

The Vicentine case confirms a corollary of the aristocratization model:
that formation of a privileged ruling body also generated an elite within that patriciate. An emerging aristocracy already carried the seeds of
oligarchy. Since the Vicentine inner circle was not formally distinct
from the patriciate as a whole, however, the historian encounters problems with identification and definition. Even contemporaries could not
easily distinguish the mighty from the general run of patricians. Battista Pagliarino, for example, listed Vicentine notables in order of importance from the "illustrious and powerful" Loschi down to the
Cogonigri "of low condition," but he found no dividing points along
the way.

The problem of identification is, in fact, particularly acute for
Vicenza. Elsewhere in the *terraferma,* replacement of large councils by
far smaller elite councils clearly signals a movement towards exclusivity. The Brescian Great Council, for example, shrank from five
hundred in 1313 to seventy-two in 1421.[27] In Vicenza, however, the
Great Council of Five Hundred survived with legislative powers intact.
Moreover, identification of oligarchy by prosopographic analysis of
higher offices is suggestive but incomplete. Prominent families frequently skipped a generation in top office, and unusually talented
individuals often rose from the ranks for a brief spell in power. Some
families, the Nogarola for example, exerted great influence but seldom
held office.

The creation of deputies *ad utilia* in 1311 took a step towards
oligarchy, but a preliminary step only. The patriciate as a whole stoutly
resisted any attempt by deputies to act independently of municipal
councils. In 1423, at the end of a long period of friction, civic councillors complained that deputies consistently exceeded their authority
by acting from private ambition rather than for the good of the *respublica,* refusing to consult larger councils and imposing taxes without
the necessary consent of the Great Council. Paraphrasing the venerable legal maxim that "what touches all should be approved by all," the

Vicentine commune secured Venetian approval for the creation of a
new Council of One Hundred, located between the deputies and the
Great Council on the legislative *cursus*. The new council evidently
worked well enough and was more efficient than the cumbersome
Great Council but less restrictive than the deputies, to the point where
documents describe much significant legislation as enacted by the One
Hundred and merely confirmed by the Great Council.[28]

Within a decade, proponents of exclusion were ready to try again.
Their vehicle was the Council of Forty, chosen by deputies "from
among the best and highest-ranking citizens." Statutes assigned the
Forty such critical functions as screening proposed legislation, supervising religious and charitable bequests, and electing fiscal officers.
When in 1432 some unknown agency sponsored legislation to abolish
both the Forty and the One Hundred and replace them with a single
Council of Forty, the proposal suggests a coup attempt by the
deputies.[29]

The problem with an oligarchic interpretation of this event is that
the contrary assertion, that the deputies and the Forty were not
oligarchs hostile to the broadly based One Hundred, is equally convincing. All municipal councils passed the provision of 1432, and it is
difficult to imagine the One Hundred or Great Council consenting to
their own exclusion from executive power. The proposal may only
have been an attempt to streamline the profusion of smaller councils.
Certainly it is difficult to see the Council of Forty as oligarchic after
1491 when, to accommodate an increasing number of worthy citizens,
the commune as a whole authorized the Forty to coopt an additional
sixty citizens as a *zonta*. Moreover, the deputies and the One Hundred
were complementary, not antagonistic: deputies selected the One Hundred, and the two combined to elect deputies for the next year. The two
combined in such critical functions as imposing new taxes and approving new entries to the Great Council. Perhaps the demarcation between
oligarchy and patriciate should be located between the deputies and
the One Hundred on the one hand, and the Great Council on the
other—but that would make a mockery of the concept of oligarchy,
since the two groups were nearly equal in size.[30]

It is prudent not to locate that dividing point at all. Preferable is an
image of concentric rings of power, with no clear moment of passage
from one ring to another. The membership of middle circles must
remain ambiguous, since there survives only a single membership list
of the Council of One Hundred and no list of the Council of Forty.
Nonetheless simple prosopography does reveal a profound difference
in composition between innermost and outermost circles and suggests
that a constant body of a few families virtually monopolized executive

offices. The overwhelming majority of deputies came from families that had held power since the thirteenth century: Loschi, Trissino, da Porto, Bissari, Capra, Valmarana, da Schio, and Caldogno. Tax registers indicate that these families were wealthier and possessed of more branches than lesser patricians. Family archives demonstrate that deputies' families had larger landed interests, and that they were more likely to hold patents of imperial nobility.

Of those families that entered councils after 1300, only the Thiene and Trento reached the top by 1500. Most recent arrivals to the Great Council could hope for little more than advancement to the Council of One Hundred, just outside the centers of real authority. Nonetheless, disparities within the patriciates of Veneto cities did not produce the sorts of tension that have been widely observed for Venice: between older and "new" families over election to the dogeship, between oligarchs and ordinary patricians over legal reform, between the "old" and the "young" over reform of the Council of Ten, between the parties to the Interdict Controversy. During the particularly disruptive episode of the wars of the League of Cambrai, for example, fissure within mainland patriciates was not between greater and lesser families but along the quite different fault lines of philo- and anti-Venetian factions.

The potential for intrapatriciate confrontation was certainly present. In Vicenza, for example, the Council of One Hundred, whose membership was largely drawn from families outside the inner circle of power, elected the elite deputies and Council of Forty and theoretically could have displaced the traditional rulership. Yet the One Hundred consistently chose members of traditionally powerful families for higher office. In general terms, lesser patricians acquiesced in disparities in rank while patiently working to raise the ranking of their own families.

That deference and acceptance of a long apprenticeship may explain why older families were prepared to admit families of long-proven respectability and loyalty into a position of parity. Sheer biological necessity also required some openness, since in the long term some great families were bound to die out or fail to produce sons. We may speculate, too, about the effects of threats to overall aristocratic privilege in the Cinquecento and Seicento. On the one hand well-organized rural leagues protested the hegemony of urban communes; on the other hand newly enriched merchants clamored for admission to municipal councils. Faced with external challenges, higher patricians may have been disinclined to risk dissension within the class as a whole by insistence upon rigid separation from the lower patriciate.[31]

It remains to assess the Venetian role in affirmation of aristocracy and oligarchy. Vicentine evidence, supplemented by evidence from other cities of the *terraferma,* suggests an interpretation somewhere between the positions established by Ventura and Law. The initiative for closure was local in every case. The fact that closure took every conceivable institutional form and spread out over the entire Quattrocento makes it difficult to speak of an identifiable Venetian policy. Yet local communes required Venetian consent to establish executive magistracies, restrict eligibility for citizenship, render guilds marginal, and impose political disabilities upon new citizens. Nor was the Republic's contribution restricted to passive ratification of local legislation. Central councils constantly supported restrictive communes by rejecting the protests of countryside and guilds. In that sense the Republic was an active collaborator, if not the instigator, in the formation of the patriciate. At the same time the Republic resisted attempts to formalize local oligarchies. Central magistracies frequently intervened to open up overly exclusive councils, or to prevent excessive constriction of authority: in Vicenza in 1423 and 1432, in Padua in 1446, in Verona in 1426, 1449, and 1455.[32]

8

Consolidation of the Patriciate

Patrician status, because undefined, required justification and legitimation. De facto eminence provided an inadequate guarantee of social demarcation. Aristocratic *mentalité* could not have much value when the boundaries of the aristocracy were so uncertain. For that reason, Veneto patriciates established several indelible marks of distinction: noble title to ratify prominence, behavioral styles to flaunt prominence, and legal norms to reinforce prominence.

PATRICIATE INTO NOBILITY

Logically, the final stage to aristocratization would be passage of the patriciate into a true nobility, as a definite act of closure and a legal separation from lower ranks. Whether that passage actually took place, however, is open to question. Marino Berengo, examining Lucca and Verona, has concluded that nobilization was at best incomplete. Truly noble families, older and with feudal-military origins, remained a cut above the rest of the patriciate. Families of mercantile or professional origin, though possessed of hereditary positions on municipal councils, were not fully assimilated into the upper ranks. *Patriciate* could never be synonymous with *nobility*.[1]

Though his model is persuasive in terms of the undoubted persistence of older, largely feudal families at the head of communal governments, the case study of Vicenza raises two objections. Firstly, the more literal is that Vicentine patricians universally declared themselves noble. By 1500, *Nobilis Vir* was the standard title for all members of municipal councils, regardless of family origin. Battista Pagliarino labeled all 271 of his worthy families *nobili*, even those "of low condition." Secondly, though at any given moment a small body of traditionally powerful families exercised a monopoly on higher office, that elite was not constant over time. The inner circle of 1600 was not that of 1500, certainly not that of 1400, although a few key families always appear. Many lesser patrician families gained parity with the original elite.

The problem of the relationship of patriciate to nobility is that nobility itself had no single definition. As Berengo points out, contemporaries acknowledged a distinctly noble consciousness and agreed that nobility was somehow connected to political exclusivity, but they retained traditionally open political constitutions. Aside from Venice, few cities had an absolutely recognizable nobility. A variety of authorities conferred titles of nobility in an irregular and imprecise manner.

Contemporary theory only adds to the confusion. The debate on true nobility was one of the most brilliant of the fourteenth and fifteenth centuries, but like many debates—republics versus monarchies, the active versus the contemplative life—it tended more to multiply alternate strategies than to produce consensus. Participants agreed with the Aristotelian principle that nobility was incompatible with manual or rustic labor, but they never clarified the relationship of nobility to honest professions. Humanists accepted the nobility of *virtù*, whether divinely inspired (Dante) or individually accomplished (Buonaccorso da Montemagno, Poggio Bracciolini, and successors), but jurists wanted more verifiable criteria and gave the ethical argument a mixed reception. Participants hotly contested but never definitively excluded possible qualifications of descent, wealth, and title. Not everyone accepted the disqualifications of mercantile profession and humble origin.[2]

In the end, participants in the debate justified so many sources of nobility that nearly any claim could find support in standard legal and classical authorities. The Venetian Lauro Quirini, for example, intended to rehabilitate nobility of descent against Poggio's insistence on *virtù* alone but ended by conceding much of his opponent's position and along the way ratified nobility by imperial title. His contemporary, the Veronese Bartolomeo Cipolla, simply gave up the attempt to fix a single standard of nobility and listed twenty-six possible qualifications. Many were mutually contradictory, few were rejected outright, and none was given preference. The Vicentine College of Jurists, towards the end of the century, defined nobility "by reason of behavior, riches, ranks and offices," family antiquity, public reputation for nobility, and freedom from the taint of manual trade. That multiplicity of standards suggests that even the most exclusive bodies could not agree on what set them apart.[3]

Practical typologies, however, considerably simplified the situation. In the first place, argument from *virtù* was simply irrelevant to everyday classification. Following Bartolus, writers of the Veneto deemed all considerations of theological or natural nobility useless for determining precedence in political affairs (*in foro nostro*). The important issue was to determine what separated noble from plebeian. That distinction, declared the Vicentine jurist and editor Daniele Dall'Aqua, consisted solely of a formal act of ennoblement: "Nobility is a rank conferred by a sovereign, by which a person is accepted above honest plebeians . . . No one has rank by his own standing. It is necessary that rank be conferred upon him by another."[4] If a plebeian were to live in all *virtù* for a thousand years, indeed rise to great prominence before his prince, without formal title he would remain plebeian. Dall'Aqua's comments paralleled those of leading theorists in the region, from Verona's Bartolomeo Cipolla to the University of Padua's Giovanni Bertrachini and Jacopo Alvarotti, to Venice's Pietro Del Monte.[5]

Those who examined nobility were well aware of a central paradox: whereas patrician status derived from prominence in municipal councils, noble title generally derived from authorities external to municipal government. This was particularly true of the greatest source of nobility, imperial title. It mattered not at all that the emperor was a purely residual force in Italian politics: by a judgment of Bartolus, repeated into the later Quattrocento, rulers could ennoble even outside their own jurisdictions.[6] Imperial prestige remained strong enough that would-be nobles swarmed around emperors on their several passages through the Veneto, seeking formal recognition. Observers knew that imperial title automatically propelled its holder to the apex of local society, and they carefully recorded the ensuing ceremonies of ennoblement.

Title granted by imperial counts or knights (*equites*) constituted a second-hand sort of imperial nobility. Their capacity to ennoble was specified in the patents of their own nobilization, hence in theory it was uncontestable. Commentators, however, were loath to put all forms of nobility on equal standing. Furthermore, since that capacity was widely exercised, there arose the potential for proliferation of titles and therefore the danger of dilution of status. Bartolus had only reluctantly endorsed this power as derived from custom, which had the force of law. Some successors were less generous: the Veronese Cristoforo Lafranchino wrote a polemic "against abuse of the title and rank of count."[7] Though Vicentines and mainland counterparts generally accepted derivative imperial nobility, they gave it lesser standing as once removed from the ultimate source of ratification.

A rather different legitimation proceeded from the traditional right of communes to create knights. Bartolus had endorsed that custom, concluding that a city could attach to its offices a rank (*dignitas*) that conferred nobility on the holder.[8] Although the standing and mercenary armies of the territorial state had long since replaced communal militias, subject cities continued to apply the title of *miles* to higher officials. In Vicenza, for example, the commune's chief fiscal officer and the eight nonjurist consuls bore the title of *miles*.

Still, nobility was a relative and not an absolute construct. Writers were doubtful that imperial and communal knights occupied the same rank, and they increasingly discovered flaws in communal knighthood. The majority allowed the nobility of municipal office but heavily conditioned its application and value.[9] The fact that communal office was open to all citizens meant that those of inferior condition, or those who exercised contemptible manual trades, could acquire knighthood. It was widely recalled that the despised Ciompi had in a single day created sixty-seven knights, among them a carder, a wine seller, a baker and two grain sellers. Even when *milites* were drawn from more respectable ranks, knighthood still carried military implications: a true knight was one who gladly risked death to defend the *patria*. Dall'Aqua and several commentators noted caustically that the communal knights of their day were merchants utterly ignorant of martial skills and therefore unworthy of their rank. In addition, legal theory cast doubt on the heritability of the communal nobility, since rank attached to the office rather than the officeholder. Bartolus and many successors held that the nobility of a communal *miles* extended only to his great-grandson and no further.[10]

From yet another perspective, writers of the Veneto accepted the judgment of the *glossa ordinaria* that "knowledge ennobles a man." The practical test for wisdom was a university doctorate; by the Quattrocento, Giovanni Bertrachini had revised the standard tag to read "he who is a doctor is noble." Doctors of laws were obvious candidates, to the point where commentators held that anyone teaching law for twenty years automatically became a count. So members of the Vicentine College of Jurists claimed, by the end of the Quattrocento at least, to be ipso facto noble. So too did notaries, though with less confidence. This was the stated reason that colleges forbade practice of manual or rural trades, lest ignoble acts stain the collective nobility of the profession.[11] Not even those who disparaged the law in favor of knighthood or medicine could impugn the jurists' claim to nobility.[12]

That left a large proportion of patrician councillors—those not possessed of imperial rank, or doctorate, or knighthood—in need of noble title. They, too, could draw upon venerable jurisprudential tradition. Bartolus and Bartolomeo Cipolla, most notably, acknowledged the nobility of the senatorial and patrician order. Specifically, prescriptions of the common law declared that municipal councillors could be considered noble. In practice, however, jurists heavily qualified this claim. Bartolus noted that conciliar nobility was a function of local custom, admitted in some cities (Venice) but not in others (Perugia). Conciliar nobility too was *infima*. Moreover the nobility derived from higher office was imperfectly heritable: if progeny were not themselves elected to elite councils, nobility died out with the great-grandson.[13]

Practical flaws further vitiated conciliar nobility. Legal theorists argued from the example of ancient Rome, where patricians and senators had been clearly distinguished from plebeians. Where (as in Vicenza and the rest of the Veneto) councils were technically open, simple possession of a council seat could not automatically define a privileged class. Moreover, trade usually disqualified an individual's nobility; the only admitted exception was Venice, where the sterility of the site left no alternative.[14] On the mainland, even higher councillors usually engaged part-time in commerce, albeit on a large scale. Finally, even if those elected to executive magistracies were definitely noble, the conciliar standard of nobility could only apply to members of general assemblies at the cost of seriously diluting the aristocracy. In 1510 the Great Council of Vicenza, for example, counted some 629 members or around 13 percent of the city's adult male population.[15]

Faced with such disabilities, simple municipal councillors sought supplemental validation for noble status. In Vicenza and several other cities, they found it in the fact that local bishops, by imperial grants dating back to the eleventh century, were also counts, dukes, and/or marquesses. Episcopal vassals were, by definition, noble. The tradition of episcopal nobility was unbroken in the Quattrocento and indeed may have gained importance in the general scramble for legitimation. Hence Vicentine patricians eagerly sought episcopal investiture, even if the fief involved (as was usually the case) consisted merely of the right to collect tithes in small rural parishes. The ceremonies of investiture were as grandiose as if the prize were a county or knighthood: supplicants went down on bended knee, swore fealty and *homagium* and *vassallagium,* and bishops sealed the relationship with grants of golden rings.[16]

The episcopal nobility overcame potential obstacles without difficulty. Cooperative bishops ensured that vacant fiefs did not pass to nonpatricians. Feudatories ignored Bartolomeo Cipolla's comment that newly conferred fiefs did not necessarily signify nobility and preferred Baldus's claim that what mattered was the antiquity of the fief rather than the antiquity of the investiture.[17] In practice, the nobility of episcopal title was uncontestable. Episcopal investiture had, in addition, the useful feature of reinforcing a hereditary noble status, since feudal holdings were generally regarded as fully heritable.

Reliance upon legal theory does not move the historian too far from the everyday business of nobilization. It is true that, in the early stages, Vicentines did not strictly enforce legal prescriptions. To have insisted upon the ignobility of commerce, for example, would have disqualified that majority of patricians which had recently arrived in positions of power and continued to live at least partially from non-landed investments. Force of custom relaxed disabilities of inheritance. Once an unusually gifted or well-connected individual attained high office, his descendants were not denobilized because they remained simple councillors. The nobility of a lawyer could not in theory pass to his uneducated progeny; this disqualification was tacitly ignored. Bartolus's doubts of nobility by descent (*a stirpe seu progenie*) were offset by Baldus's endorsement of such "natural nobility." Both views circulated in the Quattrocento, but that of Baldus prevailed in practice.[18]

Nonetheless, though the Quattrocento represents something of a grace period, the disqualifications raised by jurists remained normative. Legal theory set standards that aspiring nobles were expected to meet, at least within two or three generations. By the mid-Cinquecento, most Vicentine patrician families had done so. Few nobles were then active in trade or any of the professions except law and medicine. By that time, too, members of lesser councils had acquired the greater security of episcopal investiture or occasional election to higher office. Compliant and cash-starved emperors lavishly granted noble titles, easing the position of many families whose claim to aristocracy had been shaky. The stigmas of communal knighthood and derivative imperial title ceased to matter; and in any case these had always been inconveniences rather than outright disqualifications.

Legal theory accurately signals, as well, hierarchies within the nobility. As legitimating authorities were unequal in stature, so patents of nobility were unequal. The theoretical disabilities attached to each title likewise varied in degree and suggested precedence: from imperial counts and knights to municipal *milites*, to doctors, and, finally, to the ordinary run of municipal councillors. Those gradations of title correspond precisely with hierarchies of municipal power. Imperial titleholders clustered in the higher offices of consul, deputy, and ambassador; communal knights and doctors were often found there as well. Lesser titles prevailed in larger, less powerful councils. In both theory and practice feudal-military origin preserved superiority over the nobility of the robe and particularly over the nobility of the simple councillor, as Marino Berengo has accurately pointed out. Precedence of title correlates with other measurements of status as well. Families of imperial nobility tended to be older, have more branches, receive higher tax assessments. Holders of lesser titles were more often drawn from newer arrivals, smaller landowners, families still active in commerce and the notariate.

The model of hierarchy within nobility does, however, require modification. The possibility of long-term upward mobility was greater than a static model of hierarchy might suggest. Berengo is right that the oldest and best families perpetually occupied the highest rank, but prosopography of Vicentine executive councils amply demonstrates that relative newcomers frequently joined these families. Indeed, contemporaries insisted on the capacity to rise into the nobility and within the nobility. As Bartolus noted, a rustic who achieved all qualifications for nobility could never remove the stain of his own rusticity, but his sons and grandsons would be counted among the *nobiliores*, "as happen[ed] every day." One Paduan chronicler of ca. 1430 even furnished a list of wealthy merchants who, if not themselves of the first rank, could still hope for that position for their sons.[19]

Mechanisms of advancement were not complicated, though the hard work, good fortune, and talent required to master them proved beyond the capacity of most Vicentine families. Titles, because acquired, could be upgraded. The stain of recent arrival could be obscured by the patina of longevity; that of commerce could be removed by retirement into rent collection, land improvement, public office, and genteel usury. In time the sons of notaries could become lawyers, and in time the sons of ordinary councillors could aspire to higher office. Construction of palaces and villas and dedication to cultured *otium* considerably blurred distinctions between an older feudal nobility and *arrivistes*. Fanciful genealogies endowed newer families with the desired martial ancestry. Straitened older families did not hesitate to restore their fortunes by opportune marriages with those of lower rank but greater resources.

There have been few case studies of individual noble *case*, but even a single sample illustrates the values, strategies, and means of legitimation available to upwardly mobile families. Though the Arnaldi of Vicenza were major landowners, notaries after 1425, and municipal councillors after 1426, they continued to style themselves only "citizens" even after election to the Council of One Hundred. They called themselves noble, and then only occasionally, after 1452, when they acquired the episcopal fief for the tithes of two tiny hamlets, Nuvoledo and Porcileto. The Arnaldi consistently claimed noble status only after around 1465, with a second generation's withdrawal from the active notariate. In the early Cinquecento the family secured election to top civic offices and hired Palladio to build a country seat. A century after that the Arnaldi secured first papal nobility and then a position on the Venetian Great Council, then married into the ancient feudal families of the Piovene and Orgian. The final touch came with the creation of a pedigree tracing the family's origins to one Arnaldus, captain under the Emperor Otto in the tenth century. The rise of the Verità of Verona seems to have been somewhat more rapid, in part because of the family's success in penetrating the city's cultural leadership.[20]

Transformation of patriciate into nobility was effected quietly. The actual process of nobilization attracted surprisingly little notice. In a given run of documents, a magistrate hitherto known only by his office is suddenly qualified *Spectabilis*, an individual hitherto described only as citizen of Vicenza is suddenly known as *Nobilis Vir*. How nobles acquired titles and what they intended by them seems clear, but their own records reveal little. Certainly nobilization was not accomplished by legislation or constitutional reform. On paper the commune of Vicenza in 1500 was nearly that of 1311, at least as regards eligibility for office. Vicentines, along with colleagues in much of Italy, were reluctant to put aristocratic closure into law, to formalize the widening gap between noble and plebeian. That was only to happen in the Cinquecento, though it was an accomplished fact a century before.

THE FRUITS OF STATUS

The patrician monopoly on public authority constituted a collective patrimony. Like any patrimony, patrician standing required active management. The vigilant defense of group privilege, in this case against intrusive Venetians and disenfranchised Vicentines, forms one of the central themes of Quattrocento governance. But that patrimony also provided political capital for selective investment. The deployment of that capital, in turn, provides a good indicator of the values of the governing class. Mention must be made of the more pleasant opportunities that the political patrimony gave to the patriciate for unchecked display of aristocratic standing and for further aggrandizement of wealth and power.

The splendid Gothic palaces that line Vicenza's streets testify to the opulence and assertiveness of the city's political class. Iconographically they are even more significant: palaces of the Quattrocento are as closed as the patriciate that built them. Traditional Vicentine vernacular architecture had consisted of rather anonymous connected buildings that overhung the sidewalk to provide a continuous portico for general passage. Shops usually occupied the ground floors. Each building encompassed, in effect, both public and private space. Patrician palaces, on the other hand, were often free-standing and set back from walkways. On the street side heraldry, mottoes, and decorative imagery celebrated the owners' rank, especially their possession of imperial nobility. Sheer facades provided no shelter from the elements and banished ignominious commerce, while forbidding portals and barred ground-floor windows isolated occupants from the world at large. Palaces looked inward, to spacious private courtyards. The palaces were, in short, architectural declarations of aristocratization, monuments to a patriciate increasingly magnificent and aloof.[21]

Distinctive patrician behavior is only sporadically documented. Legislation provides a few clues, for example, the grant by municipal statutes to the nobility of exemption from sumptuary laws. Judicial records, on the other hand, provide ample witness of one salient feature of upper-class habits: control of the communal judiciary allowed patricians to indulge a traditional proclivity for personal violence. That proclivity is not unique to the Quattrocento. Notices begin well before 1414, when Cristoforo Nievo and Cristofano Vivaro murdered Antonio Angiolelli, and continue unabated well beyond 1502, when Leonardo Trissino tried repeatedly to murder Giacomo Trento. Nonetheless the Quattrocento produced significant escalation of the frequency and brazenness of patrician violence. Bands of armed retainers grew in size. Because the Vicentine judicial system favored exile over incarceration and enforced exile poorly, noble *banniti* could gather in the countryside and prey on peasants and patrician enemies with impunity.[22]

A model of hotheaded youth has long been associated with this region: Romeo Montagu came from a Vicentine family, and the Vicentine Luigi da Porto first told his story. In the Quattrocento, however, elder and prominent patricians personally carried on family feuds. The same Giacomo Trento, at the height of a distinguished career as communal ambassador and deputy, was ordered by the Council of Ten not to pursue a vendetta with Sebastiano Pagello.[23] Senior patrician malefactors easily evaded punishment by the municipal agencies that they dominated. Only sporadic and ineffectual Venetian intervention served to curb noble lawlessness.

The very rich and powerful Jacopo Muzano, for example, appears in a rash of notices in mid-century. Banned from the city for unknown crimes, he returned to Vicenza in 1454 under the terms of a special Venetian decree. The next year he launched a criminal lawsuit against a pauper from the countryside and intimidated the citizenry into refusing surety and testimony on behalf of his opponent. When he shortly thereafter beat up another man in the communal palace of the city, Muzano packed the courts with relatives and allies and again escaped unscathed. His influence was for sale: in 1456 he promised to have two men released from exile in return for a certain property but took possession and did nothing further. That disdain for law and abuse of authority attracted the attention of the Venetian *avogadori di comun*, but his local reputation did not suffer. He continued to serve the commune as deputy and ambassador throughout these episodes. Deferential historians remembered only his wealth, wisdom, high spirits, and family connections.[24]

Economic benefits of controlling the commune were legion. Scores of councillors enjoyed municipal employment for at least a part of the year, as notaries in the *module*, and perhaps half of the jurists obtained communal offices. *Deputati* enjoyed immunity from most taxes during their two-month terms of office. Fiscal advantages were even more lucrative. Tax law, for example, neatly furthered patrician interests. As was noted above, the commune's successful defense of separate urban and rural *estimi* increasingly penalized inhabitants of the countryside. As regards the fixed quota of direct taxes due from the city, the commune based assessments not only upon property but also upon the value of occupational skills (*industria*). This practice justified inclusion in the tax rolls of those propertyless workers who were exempted elsewhere in Italy. Patrician landowners could more easily conceal rural assets from assessors than could urban artisans whose property was concentrated in the city. Landowners did not pay gabelles on foodstuffs imported from their country estates, but landless Vicentines paid taxes on food bought in urban markets.

With regard to tax assessments, municipal law specified selection of *estimatores* from the "greater, middling, and lesser" citizens. But the "lesser" group, which anyway provided only one-fifth of the assessors, did not give significant weight to lower orders since the threshold for inclusion was so high that the category included very wealthy citizens. The wealthiest 5–10 percent of the population provided the other four-fifths of estimators. Those commissioners then relied upon their own impressions of an individual's contributive capacity rather than upon formal declarations of assets and liabilities. Patrician in membership and independent in operation, commissions of estimators apparently manipulated assessments to reduce the collective tax burden of the patriciate relative to the mass of Vicentines. In one sampling of 2,123 *estimi* from 1453–1505, the burden shouldered by the wealthiest citizens dropped sharply, from 71 percent of the total to 60 percent. The proportion of citizens assigned the highest assessments fell from 21 percent to 13 percent. Since the patriciate did not decline demographically as a percentage of the population, and its share of total Vicentine wealth certainly did not decline, the inescapable conclusion is that commissions of wealthy *estimatores* simply assigned themselves and fellow patricians a lesser burden than real wealth would have warranted. In Vicenza, moreover, everyone in the *estimo* paid taxes.

The Veronese commune, despite efforts by the patriciate to the contrary, preserved a threshold for actual payment that exempted the poorer citizens in the *estimo*.[25]

The patriciate's control of communal legislation and administration assisted the formation of large-scale landholdings. Indeed, the commune functioned as something of an agent for urban landlords. To some extent this situation predates the Quattrocento. It had long been the case, for example, that creditors could summon rural tenants before urban courts, whereas countrymen could not summon citizens before rural tribunals. The communal Camera dei Pegni accepted pledges for arrears of rents and dues and sold unredeemed pledges to compensate the creditor. This office too predates the Quattrocento, though the commune significantly strengthened its powers in 1452–72. By the ancient principle of collective responsibility, if a debtor did not voluntarily produce the pledge, the head of his village had to produce it himself or risk a fine to be paid by the entire village. In any case communal messengers and constables could seize anything short of draft animals and agricultural implements to satisfy debts.[26]

Quattrocento legislation reinforced the position of landowners. A provision of 1407 set a one hundred *lire* fine for tenants who denied possessions or rents to owners. Municipal statutes of 1425 perfected mechanisms for collecting arrears and compensating owners for damage to fields or crops. Statutes codified, as well, the commune's right to set the time of the grape harvest, restricted tenants' rights to break leases, and increased the obligations of rural officials. After 1456 cultivators, when thrown off the land, could not harass new tenants. In 1458 council provisions abolished a favorite trick of cultivators, that of encumbering their lands with mortgages and dowry claims, which took priority over debts to owners. A decade later municipal councils forbade tenants to gather or transport the harvest except in the owner's presence. After 1477 the territorial vicars, chosen from the Vicentine Council of One Hundred, could render summary justice against rural debtors.[27]

Vicentine custom and legislation find ample parallel in the region. In Verona, for example, landlords demanded rents in kind, thus increasing their incomes in a period of rising food prices. In Padua a provision of 1414 permitted forcible collection of debt pledges when citizens had difficulty collecting rents. Urban owners throughout Italy were generally successful in having their farm workers estimated with the city, to the further distress of fellow *districtuales*. In the Veneto that practice was abolished only in 1504 by Venetian order.[28]

Most patricians were not exclusively rentiers. They invested heavily in the wool trade, in urban workshops and real estate, and particularly in usury, as they had at least since the Trecento. Here too communal law gave full backing to owners. The urban monopoly on finishing and retailing wool cloth obviously benefited those patricians who predominated in the financing of partnerships, management of finishing shops, and ownership of market stalls. The commune tacitly tolerated usurious loans of foodstuffs, seed, and money. Notaries cooperated in circumventing canonical prohibitions of usury by use of a double transaction: a patrician fictitiously bought land, then leased the land back to the cultivator. The cultivator could repurchase the land within a specified period of time. In that transaction the purchase price constituted the loan, the annual rent was the interest, and the right of repurchase was the chance to pay off the loan. In fact few cultivators were able to raise the cash for repurchase, and the lender retained ownership of the land.[29]

One final note on patrician power and finance must remain on the level of suggestion. Growing sentiment against usury produced increasingly stringent curbs on its Jewish practitioners. Contracts between the commune and individual lenders had ratified the Jewish monopoly on pawnbroking well into the third decade of the Quattrocento. After that time, however, pressure on Jews built steadily for several decades, fueled by the antiusury sermons of Bernardino da Siena, Bernardino da Feltre, and others. Locally, violently anti-Semitic sermons and treatises from notables such as the suffragan bishop Pietro de' Bruti and the jurist Alessandro Nievo intensified the campaign. In 1443 the commune forbade Jews to practice the trades of goldsmithing and drapery, which restricted their capacity to sell unclaimed pledges. In 1453 the commune persuaded the doge to withdraw his earlier permission for a Jew to live and lend in Schio. From 1475 onwards Vicentines received reports of Christian boys murdered by Jews in Trent, Marostica, Portobuffolè (Treviso), and Friuli; in each case the cadaver became the focus of popular cults. After 1479 all Vicentine contracts with Jewish moneylenders were canceled, and only Jews with Venetian license could lend in city or countryside.[30]

In April 1486, with the doge's approval, the Vicentine commune expelled all Jews from city and countryside. In August the commune established a public pawnshop, the Monte di Pietà, to assume the Jews' traditional activity of petty moneylending. Given the events of the previous half-century, genuine devotion and outrage are sufficient to account for the expulsion. All the same, expulsion did leave patrician moneylenders without competition at a moment of extraordinary demand for scarce liquidity.[31]

The campaign against usury left patricians unscathed. By putting their loans into the form of perfectly innocent (though fictitious) sales and leases, patricians escaped the notoriety attached to open lending. In any case the patriciate faced no real domestic opposition by the 1480s. Nor did the Monte di Pietà seriously compete with their moneylending activities, since the Monte could lend only up to three *lire* for a maximum of six months. Indeed, the Monte became a positive boon to patricians. In 1494 the commune decreed that contributors to the fund should be paid 5 percent annually, the interest to be raised either by the sale of unclaimed pledges or by a general tax on city and countryside.[32] To patricians with spare capital for investment in the Monte, Christian service and profit went hand in hand.

PART III

Center and Periphery

9

Pacification and Security

Thus far Venetian governance of Vicenza has appeared remarkably restrained. Senior magistracies protected local *privilegia* and municipal law even against locally resident Venetian officials. The Republic largely sanctioned the commune's control of guilds and countryside, its exclusion of outsiders, and its effective disenfranchisment of the citizenry. Venetian disinclination to categorical imposition of law, or to imposition of a thorough resident administration, was a concession that the Republic's *arbitrium* and superior jurisdiction would be largely mediated through local institutions.

If enquiry were left at that point, it would ratify the old model of a federal state characterized by minimal central intervention and extensive local autonomy. It would also willfully ignore much available evidence and would contradict most recent interpretation. Ventura, it is true, does not accept Venetian centralization: one of his primary concerns is documentation of Venetian failure to overcome particularism and form a unified state. Nonetheless his description of Venetian "evisceration" and "emptying" of mainland prerogatives leaves no doubt that the *libertas* of subjects was effectively extinguished. Cozzi points to substantial respect for local institutions, given the cultural divide between ruler and subject, but he proceeds to document the Republic's assertion of sovereignty through "capillary" exercise of authority or circumvention of local structures. More recently Michael Knapton has not felt obliged even to posit an initial period of local autonomy. His demonstration of increasingly efficient fiscal and military demands builds upon an already well-established Venetian superiority.

Recent studies suggest, as a common denominator, certain sectors in which Venetian interests were directly at stake. In particular, Venetian control over security and justice, finance, religion, and appeals was likely to have been firm and growing. It is the intention of this section to examine those sectors as regards governance in Vicenza. Several considerations come into play in each: Venetian intentions in intervening, the intensity of intervention, and the scale of encroachment upon preceding Vicentine prerogatives. These are traditional enquiries. This section addresses the other side of the equation as well: Vicentine resources for resisting or deflecting intervention, dysfunctions in Ve-

netian administration that vitiated intervention, limited Venetian ambitions, and a Venetian disinclination to tamper with workable local
institutions.

It is logical to begin with considerations of security and criminal
justice. Simple preservation of the state is the highest imperative of any
ruler and requires suppression of open sedition and mass disorder. In
the Venetian state, the Republic's strong sense of responsibility for
justice intensified that imperative by requiring intervention in any case
that insulted equity, Venetian honor, or divine commands. On the
other hand, the disparity between the judicial cultures of capital and
subjects posed obstacles to the imposition of Venetian will. For those
reasons the repression of disorder provides an unusually sensitive indicator of the policies and politics of mainland governance.

TARGETS OF INTERVENTION

Late one night in the winter of 1498, the Venetian night watch came
upon four servants of Count Ludovico Thiene and demanded their
arms. The servants refused and broke into the family war cry of
"Thiene! Thiene! Flesh! Flesh!" In the ensuing scuffle the watch raised
the Venetian cry of "Marco! Marco!" Servants of Ser Matteo Toso
joined their Thiene brethren, and bystanders on balconies lent support
with more yelling of "Thiene! Thiene! Flesh! Flesh!" But the guard
eventually got the upper hand, apprehended the miscreants, and presented them for trial. The Venetian captain rendered justice.[1]

The incident, trivial though it may have been, provides a lesson in
Venetian judicial intervention. Why the case was removed from conventional criminal procedures and handed over to the captain is a
primary question. The answer is not as obvious as might be thought.

It was only common sense that Venetians alone prosecute threats
to state security. Even municipal law gave jurisdiction over *lèse majesté* to
the podesta. The commissions of the rectors clarified that jurisdiction
somewhat: if anyone plotted or otherwise acted "against our state," the
captain and podesta together were to investigate, draw up the *processum,* and proceed against delinquents as they deemed "most fitting
to God and justice." By logical extension, attacks on Venetian officials
also fell under this rubric. When in 1488 four men wounded a watch-
man in the middle of Vicenza's main piazza, in broad daylight and in
the presence of the captain, central councils gave rectors permission to
prosecute the crime personally. Similarly, the *avogadori di comun* took
the case of vandalism of a tax collector's balcony because the victim was

a "public person." The podesta summarily judged cases of assaults on troops. He also heard lesser civil cases "according to Venetian norms" when local citizens sued pretorian officials. The captain heard similar cases valued over five hundred *lire*. Rectors likewise handled civil suits against troops.[2]

In fact, however, even implicitly anti-Venetian episodes were rare, and Venetian intervention here marks no great subtraction of jurisdiction from municipal tribunals. In the tumultuous period just after initial Venetian expansion, for example, the only two cases of outright rebellion involved noble families of Veronese origin and should be considered within the context of sporadic Veronese uprisings. Later accusations of sedition have an unlikely or even comic ring: the two farmers from the northern hills said to have conspired against the Venetian state, the patrician caught displaying the flag of a Visconti duke who had been dead for fifty years, the rustics who hurled obscenities at an official of the Salt Office. Despite the fact that several Vicentines were suddenly summoned to Venice—the secrecy of the Council of Ten may hide more concrete opposition—there is little hard evidence for serious efforts to throw off Venetian rule. Vicentines did not participate in the endemic revolts of Verona and Padua. Indeed, a Vicentine captured Marsilio da Carrara in 1435 and a party of fellow citizens happily escorted him to prison in Padua.[3]

Still, the line between rebellion and simple violence was often faint. Central councillors took the prudent course and regarded mass disorder in much the same light as overt threats to state security. Violence by or against patricians, notably, might or might not have more serious implications. The central government invariably assumed the worst. Insofar as the Republic supported the patriciate as a closed and privileged body, any attack on a patrician could be construed as an attack on that class which served as Venetian agent in local administration and, by extension, as an attack on justly constituted public authority. When in 1475 two unknowns robbed and severely wounded a servant of the Vicentine noble Gabriele Anguissola, the Senate considered the crime an offense against the Venetian dominion and authorized the podesta to set a very high price on the heads of the malefactors and ban them from all Venetian lands.[4]

Local patricians equally represented the only conceivable internal threat to Venetian rule, as partisans of dispossessed *signori* or outside enemies such as the Visconti. Even when the state itself was not at risk, armed retinues and brazen patrician-on-patrician murders endangered public order and the rule of law. Venetian councils, preferring caution to complacency, therefore saw political implications within ordinary acts of violence. When in 1414 the nobles Cristoforo Nievo

and Cristofano Vivaro murdered the patrician jurist Antonio Angiolelli—on his way to Mass, no less—the *avogadori* decided that the
crime "touch[ed] our State," removed jurisdiction from the podesta
and Vicentine consulate, and committed the case to the Venetian
Quarantia. When Leonello Nievo wounded Cristoforo da Barbarano
in 1473, the Council of Ten sentenced him to exile; when he returned
to commit further depredations in the countryside, the Ten classified
him as a rebel and ordered confiscation of his goods. By the end of the
century, the Council of Ten was closely monitoring aristocratic vendettas even when these had not yet resulted in bloodshed, ordering, for
example, that Sebastiano Pagello and Giacomo Trento not pursue an
incipient feud on pain of perpetual exile and loss of goods.[5]

A further danger of feuding patricians was that they all too easily
linked up with the major disaffected element in Vicentine society, the
bands of exiles that gathered along borders and took entire districts
out of government control for months on end. The numbers of such
banniti were large: in 1426 the Venetian Great Council noted that some
1,200 men had been banned from Vicenza for debt or violence, or
upwards of 1 percent of the total urban and rural population. Within a
quarter-century the situation had deteriorated sharply. The Senate in
1453 declared that 800 men had been banned from Vicenza for homicide alone; since conviction for homicide was one of the least frequent
causes of exile, far exceeded by flight to escape prosecution for debt or
assault, the total number of *banniti* was probably at least three to four
times that figure.[6] Exiles' unruliness alone warranted strong measures
of repression, but the real danger was that breakaway patricians might
give them cohesion and leadership. In the early Cinquecento, for example, the area around Noventa in the southern Vicentine was thrown
into turmoil when the Paduan noble Antonio Dotti had a falling out
with his illegitimate offspring. Both sides gathered retinues of exiles,
and the private armies waged open warfare for several years despite
the best efforts of the Senate and Council of Ten at pacification. After
Antonio was cornered and killed in 1504, the *banniti* remained in Noventa and continued to defy public authority.[7] Among Vicentine nobles, this sort of threat came into sharp relief when in 1502 Leonardo
Trissino, already exiled for the murder of a fellow patrician, stormed
into the village of Costozza with an armed band in an attempt to
murder his father-in-law, Giacomo Trento. Venetian councils granted
the podesta extraordinary powers to investigate, exile accomplices, and
set an extremely high price on Trissino's head.[8] If the implications of
factionalism were not then obvious, they became so in 1509 when the
same Leonardo Trissino entered Vicenza at the head of Maximilian
Hapsburg's army.

Noble vendetta was not the only target of Venetian intervention. When a band of rustics broke the jail in Barbarano to free two of their friends, the doge and Senate classified the crime as *lèse majesté* and authorized extraordinary measures for its punishment. Smuggling too constituted *lèse majesté*. A string of Venetian decrees forbade gatherings of rustics (*adunationes*) for the purpose of committing evil acts, or the bearing of arms before peacekeeping officials, or even the wearing of arms by rustics generally. Several broad categories of offense, notably the carrying of arms at night, were removed from local judiciaries and prosecuted by Venetian governors. Rectors likewise held jurisdiction over disorders that threatened to get out of hand, such as the factional slaughters in Marostica.[9]

Until Trissino's final defection, however, only the most nervous Venetian could have perceived Vicentine crimes as threats to the Republic's dominion. Political security provided only a partial impetus to direct action. A further and perhaps more powerful motive to central intervention lay elsewhere, in the distinctly Venetian ethico-religious approach to administration. Central councils rarely invoked *lèse majesté* but nearly always associated infractions with a cluster of values such as justice, honor, and piety. They moved rapidly from the act to its general significance. The beating of Anguissola's servant had to be punished, for example, "for the sake of justice and the honor of our Dominion." The "tremendous riots and disorders" in Marostica required suppression because they brought shame (*ignominia*) to the Republic. Permitting transgressors to escape punishment through legal technicalities, the doge thundered to the podesta of Brescia in 1491, constituted an offense to justice and a "denigration" of the Venetian state. Councillors constantly acknowledged that their primary responsibility (*debitum*) was to ensure equity and pacification throughout the dominion.[10]

Honor was more than preservation of the Republic's reputation for good justice: it was, at heart, grounded in fulfillment of the divine imperative. Rectors' commissions sounded the theme at the onset of Venetian rule. The captain was to proceed against rebels as seemed to him "most in accordance with God and justice." The podesta was charged with administering justice according to local statutes "insofar as these [were] in accordance with God and justice and our honor." In fact these criteria were virtually interchangeable: Venetian honor rested on establishment of justice as defined in divine commands. Obedience to the police, said the Council of Ten in 1468, was reverence to God and the state alike. Two decades later the Senate declared that evildoers had to be captured "to honor God and preserve the dignity of our state."[11] The local judiciary might be trusted, even granted broad powers in local affairs, but ultimately the Republic answered to God for the behavior of its subjects. Even minor infractions, with no conceivable implications of sedition, endangered the greater security of the state.

Argument from justice and divine imperatives constituted an open-ended rationale for intervention. Though politically convenient, that argument also presented considerable difficulties for everyday governance. Since small injustices had to be punished as severely as great ones, there could be no consistent criteria for chosing which infractions were to receive the attention of the central government. As a result the Republic, with sorely limited governing resources, often became bogged down in minor affairs. It was logical but distracting, for example, that executive councils take up the case of the profanation of an image of the Virgin in an obscure chapel in the northern hills. On four separate occasions in 1450–51, in the midst of war with Francesco Sforza over Milan, the doge became embroiled in a dispute between Vicentine barbers and bath-keepers over the right to shave customers.[12] Recourse to the ethico-spiritual bases of government gave Venice theoretically unlimited power but equally dissipated that power into unproductive pursuits.

LEGISLATIVE INTERVENTION

Justice, Venetian councillors never tired of pointing out, was the foundation of their state. Certainly judicial administration dominates the records of Venetian relations with mainland cities, far overshadowing fiscal, economic, rural, or military concerns. In accordance with conscientious assumption of responsibility for pacification of the mainland, central councils claimed the power to make law for subject communes and to change the law of those communes, lest divine favor be forfeited by the legislative injustices of subordinates. Nonetheless Venetian legislation proved less effective than the Republic's theoretical superiority might suggest.

The law regarding exiles is a particularly instructive case in point, because the problem was so acute and because central policy was so inconsistent. It had long been mainland custom that anyone presenting a returned exile (dead or alive) could, by way of reward, have himself or one of his friends released from the ban. To Venetians this system invited vigilantism and further violence. Accordingly, the doge in 1414 canceled the custom and substituted a simple reward of one hundred *lire* for capture of an exile. Local governments thus lost a convenient means of setting criminals against one another, thereby supplementing meager communal resources for the capture of violent malefactors, and found the ruling an intolerable hardship. In 1426 the communes of Verona and Vicenza successfully petitioned to have their *ordo antiquus* reinstated. Three years later, however, the Senate overturned the custom anew; but in 1438 the Senate reversed itself again with the order that "all our mainland rectors [should] henceforth investigate, proceed, and make condemnations in violent crimes and other criminal cases strictly according to the statutes and ordinances of the city in which they serve." The issue was not even then settled. Despite reinstatement of mainland custom in 1450, 1451, and 1489, the Senate canceled it in 1493 but reinstated it again in 1502. The confusion produced by Venetian legislation was also true of a closely related mainland custom, that an exile who returned to his city of origin could be killed or wounded with impunity. Confirmed in 1450, the custom was sharply restricted in 1489 but reinstated in 1490.[13]

Purely Venetian laws regarding exile proved either too lenient or too harsh. The only remedy was an embarrassing revocation of the offending decree. The first such cancellation came as early as 1413, when free issuance of Venetian pardons flooded Vicenza with ex-*banniti*. Acceding to a communal request, the doge ordered that, in cases of men banned for any crime whose penalty was death, no pardons should be granted except according to the statutes of Vicenza. Two years later the Senate and Quarantia decreed that central councils could not grant pardons to those banned for crimes involving violent factionalism. On the other hand a Senate order of 1489 expelled immediately all exiles who had returned to their cities after having been improperly released from the ban. The Senate canceled the measure within a month after mainland protests that such men had lived quietly for many years in their cities of origin, raising families that would be destitute if the expulsion order were carried out. A more conciliatory policy thereafter was no more successful. Overreadiness of Venetian councils to concede pardons had the effect of permitting *banniti* to secure safe-conducts and return to terrorize their homelands. The Senate remedied the situation in 1502 by canceling all safe-conducts issued without the approval of the Maggior Consiglio.[14]

Such erratic and counterproductive measures suggest that categorical imposition of law was not Venice's strong suit. The councils of the capital readily acknowledged that they were ignorant of local conditions and uncertain of the proper means of suppressing *banniti*. They acknowledged, too, that judicial magistrates were inclined to grant pardons to exiles without knowledge of the original crime, the personal worthiness of the exile, or the pardon's effect on local security. Moreover, the empirical mentality of Venetian councillors did not support global legislation: hard and fast rules could not satisfy the situational imperatives of honor, justice, and equity. The Venetian preference for decisions made "according to the conditions of the moment" suggested a strategy of intervention on a case-by-case basis.

CONTINGENT INTERVENTION

Only rarely did central councils themselves prosecute mainland crimes. For the most part, Venetian magistrates preferred to work through locally resident governors. Often their mandates were rather generic, requiring the podesta not to act too rigidly in a case of rural vendetta, or ordering that he pacify noble feuds, catch rustic murderers, and prevent smuggling. In the case of an ugly barn-burning in Barbarano, central councils commanded him to "impose that justice which [was] appropriate to such a horrendous crime." When the podesta lacked the necessary authority to prosecute an offense, his superiors granted supplemental powers: *arbitrium* to issue pardons, *libertas* or *facultas* to set a high price on the head of a malefactor and to exile him from the entire Venetian dominion.[15]

Technically, orders from the capital freed the podesta from the constraints of local law and judiciaries. *Arbitrium*, as Pansolli has noted, was an invitation to dispense with the *ius commune*. Grants of *libertas* or *facultas* often included a requirement that the podesta proceed according to his conscience, for example when local citizens usurped goods from the Venetian fisc, or when unknowns murdered a Venetian mercenary in the cathedral in 1468. Occasionally Venetian orders actually required governors to bypass local structures. In the 1488 case of assault on the watchmen, the doge authorized rectors to proceed "without the consulate." When the Vicentine vicar of Camisano was assaulted in 1445, the doge required the podesta to form an ad hoc committee to investigate and thereby ignored the consulate's traditional jurisdiction.[16]

In most instances, however, Venetian charges left the podesta the discretion to choose procedures for prosecution. They allowed him to operate outside the communal judiciary but by no means demanded that he do so. Indeed, there were compelling reasons why he might not do so. His own staff was small. By the design of the central government, all members of his staff were initially ignorant of the local situation. He himself rarely had training in the *ius commune* or familiarity with municipal law. The podesta always had to work with at least part of the communal machinery: the notaries who recorded his acts, the messengers who executed his civil judgments, the constables who captured criminals. He had little impetus to dispense with the rest of a large, well-trained and generally cooperative communal machinery. Central magistracies, for their part, actually encouraged governors to work with local judiciaries. Bypassing the law of the commune, noted the Council of Ten in 1444, would only jeopardize the local good will necessary to assure justice: "It should be clearly understood that no small disruption and scandal will result if the pacts, privileges, and concessions granted to our subjects are infringed, because then their hearts will be made angry and many evils may result."[17]

Even if the podesta wished to extricate himself from the local judiciary, local privileges generally prevented him from doing so. The consulate claimed a primary role in criminal cases, particularly in the investigation of rural crimes, and superior Venetian councils consistently supported that claim. Early in 1462, for example, the doge ordered both Vicentine rectors to proceed against one Nicolo da Trissino, who had stolen some notarial instruments. The Vicentine commune immediately dispatched a distinguished ambassador to Venice, who "revealed that such criminal acts belong to the consulate of this city, by virtue of the city's privileges." The doge agreed that the consulate held rural jurisdiction and further declared Vicentine privileges to be inviolate. He revoked his order and committed the case to the consuls.[18]

When the crime was especially offensive, central councils occasionally gave local rectors the authority to investigate and draw up the formal dossier (*formare processum*). Here too the Vicentine judiciary eventually gained a predominant voice. Aside from the fact that notaries were Vicentines bound to draw up documents according to Vicentine formulas, the podesta had to draw up the constituent elements of the *processum*—denunciations, accusations, inquisitions, depositions, testimonies, interrogations, and defenses—according to procedures outlined in municipal law. Even then, with Venetian officials directing investigation (*cognitio*) of a crime, the actual sentence was passed by the tribunal of the *consolatum,* in which Vicentine consuls had numerical superiority. This was true even in politically sensitive cases of patrician vendetta. In 1503, for example, the podesta initially handled Gregorio Nievo's assault on Gian Pietro da Barbarano, but the doge ordered final disposition by the *consolatum.* The next year, the *avogadori di comun* took competence over Francesco Volpe's assault on Marco Gallo; the Council of Ten promptly revoked their mandate and sent the case to judgment by the *consolatum.*[19]

Decisions of the *consolatum* were sacrosanct. They could not be appealed to Venice. In addition, the podesta could not publish any sentence that had not been approved by the consulate. In 1456 the podesta Lorenzo Minot, evidently dissatisfied with one judgment, refused to publish the *consolatum's* sentence and tried to send the case before his own tribunal. The *avogadori* sternly ordered him to obey that decision. A decade later the commune successfully challenged the Council of Ten, which had given the hearing of a criminal retrial to the podesta alone. The Vicentine ambassador declared that, "according to the form of the pact conceded to the commune of Vicenza at the moment of acquisition, reexamination and new judgment belong[ed] to the podesta with his consulate and not to the podesta alone, just as [was] the case with all criminal proceedings." The doge agreed and returned the case to the entire *consolatum*. In 1468, Vicentine orators angrily charged that the podesta Federico Corner had, variously, ordered that no action be taken against malefactors, ordered that condemnations not be read in the *consolatum*, ordered that condemnations made by the *consolatum* not be published, and ordered that convicted men not be molested. The doge forbade all such actions and further ordered the central magistracies of the *avogadori* and *auditori* not to interfere with local criminal sentences. The podesta Francesco Basadona tried in 1490 to circumvent local prerogatives by issuing pardons from *consolatum* sentences but backed down when confronted by communal deputies.[20]

Vicentines were not alone in limiting the exercise of the podesta's *arbitrium*. The situation was much the same in Verona. Indeed, Vicentine archivists recorded several dozen Veronese cases by way of corroboration and analogy. In each, Venetian magistracies initially committed a criminal case to one of the rectors, often with a supplemental grant of *libertas* or *facultas* "to administer justice according to [their] conscience." When the podesta attempted to proceed independently, the Veronese commune sent ambassadors to protest omission of the consulate, and the doge upheld local statutes and privileges with the declaration that the podesta should proceed "with the consulate of this city, which we know by experience will be just and honest." Just as frequently, the Veronese podesta used his mandate to pursue justice through entirely conventional channels. The eventual sentence was handed down "with the will and consent of the judges of the commune of Verona, namely the judge consuls and the knight consuls, or a majority of them."[21]

The most common Venetian intervention in criminal justice, if indeed it can be termed intervention, was simply to send a case back to the local judiciary for normal disposition. This was particularly true in civil disputes but was widespread in criminal cases as well. When the podesta failed or refused to execute the judgments of local courts, the *avogadori di comun* ordered him to do so. When local courts botched a case, central councils ordered the podesta to ensure the observance of local statutes: allow accused men to present defenses, or commit a case to the consulate, or permit a defendant to hire an advocate, or commit a case for *consilium sapientis,* or prevent relatives of interested parties from sitting on the consulate. When a case was so blatantly mishandled as to be irrevocably flawed, the Venetian response was usually to order it returned to its "pristine state," that is, prosecuted from scratch according to the usual procedures. In each such instance, the Venetian mandate was issued specifically "in order that [Vicentine] law be observed." A characteristic case arose in 1455, when a Vicentine condemned in absentia complained to the *avogadori di comun* that he had never been cited before any court, and that the testimony against him had been perjured. The *avogadori* ordered the podesta once again to "administer law and justice" but qualified that mandate by declaring that they themselves were acting "attentive to the law and statutes of Vicenza." They also charged the podesta, "If the matter warrants, you shall reintroduce it before the consulate."[22]

   In this sense, Venetian magistrates intervened as supervisors, guarantors, and consciences of the local system, not as rivals or supplanters. They were certainly unanimous in protecting the rights of the urban judiciary against attempts of Venetian podestas in Marostica and Lonigo to assume criminal jurisdiction, against efforts of the Vicentine podesta to bypass the consulate, and against attempts of convicted men to appeal sentences formulated by the *consolatum.* The special grants of *arbitrium* or *facultas* seem more designed to spur slow-moving governors than to undermine local agencies. The Vicentine judiciary could well be trusted as the primary agency for ensuring justice: the vast majority of infractions were not, after all, directly offensive to God or Venetian honor, and the proportion of politically charged offenses was quite small. The guiding principle of Venetian intervention in local justice was set in the spring of 1456, when the Venetian *judex maleficiorum* failed to hear the defenses of a poor tanner: "The form and order of the statutes shall be observed in all matters."[23]

   To return to the Thiene servants' skirmish with the night watch in 1498: was the case given to the captain because Venetian officials were involved? Because arms laws were infringed? Because patrician consuls could not impartially administer justice? Because the introduction of partisan war cries introduced an element of political insurrection into a common street brawl? Because special efforts were needed to stamp out armed noble retinues? Any or all of these considerations could have served as pretext. Perhaps the answer does not really matter. Venetian *arbitrium* and *imperium* was open-ended, and Venetian honor and sense of justice covered any contingency.

But, in fact, the captain chose to work within traditional communal structures. He formally pronounced sentence before the Arengo, the general assembly of Vicentines "where similar condemnations [were] usually made." He chose, that is, the customary site for publication of the consulate's sentences and chose for his sentence precisely the language and judicial constructs that the consulate used. His recourse to the Arengo held powerful connotations, notably the rule that sentences pronounced in the Arengo could not be appealed to Venice and could not be touched by the *auditori nuovi* or *avogadori di comun*. And the captain acted, he said, "following and wishing to follow the laws and statutes of Vicenza."

10

Fisc and Army

When in the early 1420s Doge Tommaso Mocenigo delivered the famous "deathbed speeches" opposing further territorial expansion, his primary argument was economic. The mainland, he said, was a garden, literally so in providing foodstuffs for Venice and figuratively so in providing artisans, trade goods, markets, and investment capital for the Venetian economy. Subject cities from Verona to Mestre provided 464,000 ducats in taxes to support the Venetian army. Because Venice had lived in peace with its neighbors, the city abounded in gold and silver, industries, shipping, commerce, palaces, rich citizens, and many workers. Offensive war against Milan would jeopardize that wealth. God might withdraw his favor, the Visconti would certainly cut off the flourishing trade with Lombardy, and—if the war were lost—the Republic might lose the mainland dominion itself.[1]

As a military forecaster Mocenigo proved largely inaccurate: a quarter-century of war with Milan was expensive, but the Republic annexed Brescia and Bergamo without damage to its long-term economic interests. He was entirely correct, though, with regard to the riches of the hinterland. Particularly prescient was the judgment that the harvest of the mainland was vital to Venice's economy, that Venice could no longer draw exclusively upon its own capital and the proceeds of maritime trade. If economic gain was not, as historians once thought, a primary motive for *terraferma* expansion,[2] Venetians were skilled and determined in drawing upon the material, human, and financial resources of their subjects.

GOODS AND SUPPLIES

From the beginning of the Quattrocento, Venetian decrees sought to regulate the mainland economy. Many were frankly protectionist, forbidding mainland production of items such as luxury textiles that would compete with Venetian specialties. Others ensured Venice as obligatory entrepot for goods passing in and out of the dominion, to prevent "the destruction of our government's tolls and income, the ruin of our commerce and the voyages of our galleys and ships, and the

distress of our citizens and all the trades and crafts of our city." The list
of items required to pass through Venice grew in the course of the
century until, by a comprehensive law of the early Cinquecento, it
included wool, cotton, spices, sugar, silk cloth, gold and silver work,
alum, wax, figs, fustians, copper, leather, salt fish, and several other
products.[3]

A second set of decrees, the annonary laws, sought to secure an
adequate food supply for the capital. Initially this took the form of
allowing free transport of grain to Venice without payment of tolls or
customs duties and without regard to the export restrictions of local
cities. The principle subsequently extended to poultry, eggs, sheep,
game, and other meats. In years of scarcity the central government
ordered mandatory sales of grain to Venice and restricted commerce in
grain between subject cities, to secure maximum supplies and mini-
mum prices for the capital. After mid-century a string of orders,
largely from the Council of Ten, forbade hoarding or even long-term
storage of wine and grain, to prevent speculation or profiteering. Considerations of state security gave additional impetus to commercial and
annonary legislation. Mainland trade could not be allowed to encour-
age the economies of frequently hostile powers such as Milan and
Austria. Food export, too, aided the enemy. For that reason the Senate
forbade export of sheep to Mantua, and the chiefs of the Council of
Ten issued dozens of decrees against sending wheat to surrounding
states. At first, central councils imposed these restrictions only in war-
time, but after 1500 they did so quite regularly in response to the
ominous buildup of Hapsburg forces.[4]

Military needs required Venetian monopoly of strategic materials,
especially for the Arsenal. Dozens of decrees and letters forbade the
the cutting of timber, ordered the protection of forests and planting of
new trees, and blocked exports of timber to Austria. The central government periodically restricted the export of horses. It exercised strict
control over Vicentine extraction of minerals, not only the nitrates
used in gunpowder but also critical products such as silver, lead, and
vitriol. Venetian magistracies alone could issue mining concessions and
licenses to tax mineral extraction. Vicentine miners received special
protection: their lawsuits were removed from local courts and heard in
Venice.

Arguing from these decrees, historians have concluded that Venetian claims constituted an unprecedented claim on mainland material
resources and provoked open resentment and even active opposition
from subjects. Vicentine evidence tempers this conclusion. Since little
is known of previous economic administration, it is speculative to con-
clude that Venetian demands were greater than those of past *signori*.

Vicentines, though quick to challenge judicial and administrative interference, appear to have accepted Venetian economic orders as entirely
appropriate to a ruler. The only known example of resistance, dating
from 1455, involved Venetian rectors who refused to ship grain to
Venice. Protest by subjects dates only from the Cinquecento and beyond.[5]

Moreover, burdensome or unwelcome decrees were not necessarily executed. By a Senate law of 1488, for example, local citizens
were to accompany an official of the Arsenal on a tour of the countryside, call forth every rustic to testify on the location of oaks, draw up
an inventory of forest owners, and list the amount of oak under cultivation. Each village then had to raise one *campo* of oak for every ten *campi*
of land, plant twenty-five seedlings per year, and carefully maintain
fences and ditches. The law required local podestas to make yearly
inspections of villages and certify full compliance. Implementation of
this order would have drastically disrupted cultivation, and it presup-
posed a governing apparatus beyond the capacity of any fifteenth-
century state. Apparently it was completely ignored. In a similar vein,
the central government several times ordered destruction of the road
over the northern Passo Pertica, much favored by Vicentine and Austrian smugglers. Nothing was done for most of the century. A key
bridge was finally razed in the late 1480s, but local inhabitants quickly
reassembled it. Thereafter the Council of Ten issued a stream of requests to halt grain smuggling to Austria, measures that by their very
repetition seem to have been ineffectual—perhaps because Vicentine
patricians were among the leading exporters.[6]

The model of Venetian exploitation also ignores the economic
benefits that subjects gained by entry into the Venetian state. Above all,
Vicentine producers and merchants now had free access to the Venetian market. The *capitula* of 1404 and 1406 specifically confirmed a
treaty of 1260 that permitted transport of Vicentine goods to the capital without payment of Venetian tolls and customs dues. Subsequent
legislation exempted goods shipped to Venice via Padua or Treviso
from the tolls of those cities. A decree of 1406 granted automatic
Venetian citizenship *de intus* to Vicentine citizens, which gave them the
right to trade freely within the capital. Particularly since the Venetian
wool industry was not yet highly developed, those measures opened an
important market to Vicentine producers. At home, Vicentine con-
sumers benefited from free importation of goods from Venice, also
guaranteed by the treaty of 1260, and from Venetian orders that allowed importation of Veronese woolens at the expense of the protec-
tionist-minded Vicentine Wool Guild. Annonary legislation, in turn,
was a two-edged sword. If Venice could demand Vicentine wheat in

times of scarcity in the capital, Vicentines could draw upon Venetian supplies when food was scarce locally.[7]

THE MONEY SUPPLY

By September 1405, barely two months after Verona's formal submission, the Venetian mint was coining money for Verona and Vicenza. A few months later a decree of the Senate flatly established Venice as sole source of coinage used in the two cities: "we desire that there be expended no other money than the money made in our mint." Thereafter, mainland cities could obtain new issues of coins only by petitioning the Senate or, after 1472, the Council of Ten.[8]

Establishment of a monopoly on coinage was politically necessary: control of currency is an imperative for any state that aspires to sovereignty, and monetary stability was particularly vital for a trade economy such as Venice's. That monopoly was also tremendously lucrative. Local communes had to pay in gold for silver coins, and in gold or silver for copper coins, at a time when the relative value of gold was rising rapidly. Venetian councils fixed those relative values and demanded payment of taxes in gold and silver rather than the debased copper "black money." The Republic both profited from advantageous exchange rates and drained mainland cities of gold in a period of scarce bullion.[9]

Central councils did not altogether remove jurisdiction over counterfeiting and alteration of money from local judicial structures, but the central government alone issued the laws by which such crimes were prosecuted. Municipal statutes were silent on the subject. A Venetian decree, for example, set the penalty for altering and coining money as loss of right hand, loss of eyes, and banishment from the Venetian dominion. Even when the Vicentine judiciary prosecuted monetary crimes, the Council of Ten in particular monitored prosecutions and specified the steps to be taken at each stage. The podesta, not local magistrates such as consuls, drew up the *processum*. Towards the end of the century, Venetian intervention became even more direct. A priest accused of counterfeiting in 1490 was sent to Venetian jails, despite the Vicentine bishop's claim to jurisdiction over clerics. When in 1496 the tailor Alvise de Luco was found altering copper *oboli* to look like silver, the Council of Ten tried and condemned him. Thereafter the Ten heard all known Vicentine cases of counterfeiting, alteration, and alchemy (seen as a cover for adulteration).[10]

Two considerations must slightly qualify a conclusion that, in Reinhold Mueller's term, Venice exercised a true "monetary sovereignty."

Firstly, prohibition of foreign currencies proved unenforceable. To some extent the Republic fell victim to its own policies, as the high price of obtaining coins and the local scarcity of good metal prevented mainland communes from buying adequate quantities of currency. Endemic shortage of liquidity forced subjects to accept foreign monies. The Republic also fell victim to the principles of Gresham's law: inferior coinage from abroad tended to drive out superior Venetian money. Overvaluation of Venetian coinage, indeed, virtually guaranteed continued influxes of currency. But the persistence of foreign monies was not due to value imbalances alone. Hostile powers actively promoted the diffusion of their coins throughout the Venetian dominion in order to profit from the exchange of adulterated or underweight currency for good Venetian money. The duke of Milan in 1429 flooded the dominion with coins equal in face value but inferior in weight; in 1472 his successor planned to send eighty thousand ducats' worth of false Venetian monies to the *terraferma* and encouraged the rulers of Bologna, Ferrara, and Mantua to follow a similar course. The constant complaints of the Senate, and (increasingly) the Council of Ten, that Milanese coins in particular remained in circulation indicate that the problem was never eradicated.[11]

Secondly, money coined by the Venetian mint at least partially respected local particularism. It is true that all the Veronese coins described by Salvaro bear purely Venetian insignia: portraits of the doge, the winged lion, the name of St. Mark or the current doge. On the other hand, documents of 1440, 1444, and 1458 refer to *monete vincentine*. About the same time the Senate spoke of "different stamps for different places," namely Brescia, Bergamo, Verona, and Vicenza. The Republic partially met the threat of 1472 by issuing coins specifically for Verona and Vicenza. Internal records of the mint mention the distinct stamps of coins destined for Treviso, Bergamo, and the Romagna. Numerous references to the "customary stamp" of various cities indicate coinage unique to each city. Sebenico in Dalmatia received coins with the image of St. Mark on one side and that of St. Michael, the city's patron saint, on the other. In 1491, Padua received coins with St. Mark on the obverse and a cross, taken from the city's coat of arms, on the reverse. From the 1490s onwards, in fact, Venetian councillors generally accepted the petitions of subjects to issue coins with images of local patron saints, in order to compartmentalize monetary circulation and drive out false and foreign monies.[12] Monetary sovereignty did not, then, imply monetary unification.

TAXATION

In 1404 and 1406, Vicentines requested that Venice not impose taxes. The commune's strategy seems to have been to ask for maximum advantage in hopes of securing reduced but still favorable terms of submission. Surprisingly, on both occasions Venetian negotiators gave unconditional approval, as they did to a similar Veronese request in 1405.[13]

Perhaps Venetians then felt that other resources guaranteed by the *capitula* would cover costs of administration and defense. Both Vicentine *capitula* assigned to Venice the proceeds of tolls, transit fees, and customs dues, collectively known as *dazi*. These provided the lion's share of communal income, some 65–75 percent if figures from Verona and Padua are any guide. The Republic also assumed the traditional right of *signori* to monopolize salt distribution and force subjects to purchase fixed amounts of salt. This prerogative was slightly less lucrative, yielding the equivalent of 10 percent of Verona's communal income and 20 percent of Padua's. Customary too was the ruler's right to garrison troops in the countryside. In 1413 the doge did promise that the entire Venetian army would not be sent to Vicenza, but he brusquely rejected a communal request that the Republic send only infantry and not cavalry.[14] Vicentine rustics provided billeting, fodder, wood, and pasturage to Venetian troops, as they had to Veronese and Paduan predecessors, subject only to more precise regulation. Traditional levies of infantry, auxiliaries, arms, and horses further reinforced the Venetian army. Vicentines continued to provide food and military supplies to castles and garrisons in the countryside.

Within a decade of mainland expansion, costs of defense far exceeded traditional revenues, particularly since the Republic had carried the war forward into Friuli and provoked invasion by Austrian and Hungarian troops. Given a policy that the *terraferma* finance military and administrative expenses, the central government abandoned its earlier renunciation of new taxes. In 1411, to meet the Hungarian invasion, the Paduan commune offered to pay for maintenance of one hundred lances, and the Paduan clergy offered to pay for one hundred infantry. Shortly thereafter the Republic demanded a similar contribution from Vicenza and other mainland cities and collected the offering as a flat fee per lance and foot soldier. After the war, Venice retained this *dadia delle lanze*, as it came to be known, as an annual tax to support the standing army. Legislation in 1442 fixed Vicenza's share at 15,600 ducats annually, with one-eighth to be paid by the clergy. A second type of direct taxation consisted of forced loans or outright cash levies imposed upon subject cities. Vicentine documents record *mutua* and *subsidia* in 1414, 1416, 1418, 1435, 1437–39, 1472–74, 1487, and 1499, each amounting to some 5,000–10,000 ducats.[15] There is no record of eventual repayment.

The tax quotas established in Venetian decrees, supplemented with fragmentary fiscal data, suggest that old and new taxation constituted a massive drain on mainland resources. The Vicentine commune's quota of the *dadia delle lanze* was about 85,000 *lire* annually, whereas ordinary communal income was about 160,000 *lire* annually. New Venetian demands, in other words, added a 53 percent surcharge to the general tax burden.[16] Subjects had to pay, transport, and provision the large levies of infantry and auxiliaries, contingents that reached as many as two thousand men in 1477 and three thousand men in 1499.[17] Vicentines supplied food and equipment to the garrisons of a half-dozen fortresses. Rural populations bore the cost of the captain's yearly cavalcade around the countryside for inspection of fortifications; he was in the habit of traveling with a retinue of seventy to eighty followers, despite constant orders to the contrary.

The *alloggio*, or obligation to billet cavalry, rested entirely on the countryside. This burden too can be calculated with some precision. The unit of measurement was the lance, consisting of three horses, a rider, and an attendant. By norms of 1442 the men received housing, food, and forty-two carts of wood yearly, and each trio of horses received twelve carts of hay, twelve carts of straw, and one *campo* of pasturage in May and June. Information from the last decades of the Quattrocento indicates that between two hundred and four hundred lances were quartered in the Vicentine annually. Regulations of 1485 commuted the entire obligation to a flat payment of 12 ducats per lance. The countryside then paid around 3,600 ducats yearly, or the equivalent of a 40 percent surcharge to its share of the *dadia delle lanze*.[18]

LOCAL RECALCITRANCE

Whether Venetian taxation constituted exploitation of the mainland is a matter of judgment. Since fiscal policy under previous rulers cannot be gauged, there is no basis for comparison. The impact of Venetian demands in real terms, too, is a matter of speculation. Moreover, a closer look at the way taxes were actually collected suggests that, particularly from the point of view of urban citizens, the situation may not have been as bad as it first appears. The central government lowered some obligations and never collected its full quota of taxes. Of those taxes that remained, the urban commune could at least shift the primary burden onto the powerless sectors of Vicentine society.

The Republic left the task of distributing and collecting the *dazi* to municipalities. Central councils initially tried to establish some sort of fiscal bureaucracy but abandoned the attempt in 1413. "There is no doubt that if *dazi* are collected by special officials in the name of our Dominion, those officials will not have that care and diligence which is characteristic of collectors with a direct interest in *dazi.*" Thereafter Vicentines retained their traditional procedures. Each year local governors auctioned off the right to collect *dazi,* in conformity with local statutes. Already this constituted a victory for the Vicentine commune: in Padua, for example, officials from the Venetian fisc (the Camera Fiscale) auctioned *dazi* collection without mediation by local authorities. After 1447, Venetian nobles could not serve as collectors of the salt tax, and after 1449 they could not collect any *dazi* whatever.[19]

In Vicenza the central government reinforced local control of *dazi* collection. In 1408 a communal judge, the *judex datiorum,* assumed jurisdiction over recalcitrant exactors and cases of nonpayment, clandestine sales, smuggling, and the like. Initially the podesta appointed him, but by the 1420s right of election had passed to the Vicentine College of Jurists. After 1446 communal employees rather than the chancellor or the captain's constable supervised collectors. A decade later central decrees forbade the Venetian *provedditori sopra le camere,* newly created but powerful fiscal magistrates, to levy fines upon Vicentine collectors who failed to hand over the requisite sums. After 1476 the *auditori nuovi* could not intervene in *dazi* cases. Venetian officials could not force collectors to submit their books for review, or to accept Venetian nominees as assistants.[20]

Local control brought relief to the entire Vicentine populace. Communal policy kept *dazi* rates low: by the terms of the articles of submission, the commune retained the schedule of fees set in 1339, before a period of slow but sustained inflation. Even in periods of military crisis and extraordinary need for money, Venetian councils proved reluctant to raise *dazi* rates. The few attempts to do so foundered when mainland communes successfully protested infringements of their *privilegia.* When a ducal letter tried to raise the *dazi* on wine and meat in 1507, the Council of Ten summed up longstanding policy: "We intend that the statutes and ordinances that derive from the privileges given to this city at the time of submission remain firm and inviolate."[21]

Despite collection at low rates, the income from *dazi* fell far short of Venetian expectations. Subjects knew a variety of techniques for evasion. The Senate discovered in 1446 that Vicentines regularly obligated their lands with dowries and mortgages so that these could not be confiscated for debt, then ran up large *dazi* debts against which fiscal officers had no recourse. Vicentine exactors, for their part, took a somewhat casual approach to collecting *dazi.* They could do so almost with impunity: as the Senate noted sourly in 1467, collectors were not subject to Venetian penalties and so did not bother to make prompt or full payment. Nor was the communal judiciary zealous in prosecuting exactors. As a result, collectors' debts to the Camera Fiscale were regular and large: two patrician collectors owed 3,000 and 2,900 *lire* respectively, a partnership owed 1,800 and 1,700 *lire*, a consortium of ten collectors owed a total of 30,437 *lire*.[22] Collectors themselves profited handsomely from lax supervision, but indifferent collection also reduced the rigors of *dazi* payment for the populace as a whole.

Subjects successfully blunted other Venetian demands as well. A ducal letter of 1414 exempted Vicentines under the age of six from the mandatory purchase of salt, and another letter of 1447 reduced penalties on collectors in arrears from 25 percent to 10 percent. After 1442 the commune assigned two local notaries to compile the inventories of cows, sheep, and pigs upon which purchase quotas were based. Notaries performed that task in an erratic manner, and rural communes proved equally uncooperative, making it hard for the Salt Office to collect requisite payments. When in the early Cinquecento the Republic attempted to impose a land tax of five *soldi* per *campo*, a storm of protest from Verona, Vicenza, and Padua forced cancellation of the project.[23]

Most Venetian decrees on the *alloggio* were directed at protecting Vicentine rustics from any demands by troops in excess of the norms of 1442. In fact, Venetian policy tended to reduce the nonmonetary contributions due from the countryside. The Republic in 1444 cut by 67 percent the amount of hay owed to Venetian cavalry, from twelve to four cartloads yearly. The number of horses garrisoned in the countryside fell sharply from 1,299 in 1479 to 1,225 in 1484, to 760 in 1485, to 595 in 1491. Since by all accounts the rural population increased in the latter part of the century, the per capita burden on countrymen lightened considerably. In a similar vein, orders to furnish troops and auxiliaries certainly appear burdensome, but the commune often successfully petitioned the central government to cut back periods of service: because of an impending harvest, or bad weather, or simply because the commune deemed the request excessive.[24]

The record of the primary direct impost, the *dadia delle lanze*, was much the same. Here the Vicentine obligation declined in both absolute and real terms. The initial requirement that Vicenza support one hundred lances and one hundred infantry was capitalized at a monthly charge of 12 ducats per lance and 14 ducats per foot soldier, or 31,200 ducats annually. The commune immediately pleaded poverty and secured a reduction of the cavalry obligation to seventy-five lances or a total of 27,600 ducats yearly, a 12 percent decrease. When Venice set the final quota at 15,600 ducats in 1442, Vicenza owed half its initial contribution. That success was not Vicenza's alone: the quota due from Verona dropped from 18,000 ducats annually in 1417 to 6,000 ducats after 1449.[25]

Moreover, the fall in taxes took place during a pronounced rise in population. That of the city of Verona nearly tripled in the period 1409–1502, and there is no reason to think that the Vicentine experience was appreciably different. All indicators point to an accompanying economic recovery that, while not as spectacular, was still impressive. Given demographic and economic growth, the per capita burden of a declining *dadia delle lanze* would have fallen sharply.[26]

The Vicentine commune retained jurisdiction over the distribution and collection of the remaining obligation. This fact alone reveals the Venetian state as significantly less centralized than the Florentine, where the well-known Catasto of 1427 onwards imposed a uniform system of assessment upon the territorial dominion. In Lombardy, while local officials divided central demands among the populace, ducal officials joined with citizens in adjusting certain quotas. In the Veneto, on the other hand, orders from the central government consistently safeguarded local prerogatives against interference by Venetian officials. In 1426 the doge forbade his chamberlain in Vicenza to take any part in collection of direct taxes. The Senate in 1442 defeated four consecutive proposals that mainland *estimi* be reformed by Venetian nobles. Two decades later the Avogaria di Comun refused to hear appeals about the *estimo* that the Vicentine commune imposed upon the countryside. The doge in 1497 forbade the *auditori nuovi* to become involved in communal *estimi*, and a decade later he admitted that he himself could not interfere in Vicentine assessments.[27]

All Vicentines profited from the ways in which the commune then collected taxes. For example, Venetian grants of tax exemptions, to rural communes on account of poverty and to patricians on account of loyal service, inevitably increased the general burden. So the Vicentine commune in 1414 requested that all citizens and countrymen pay the *onera, factiones,* and *collecta* imposed by the commune. The doge, feeling that the request impugned the capital's right to issue immunities, replied curtly that Venice would provide for exemptions as it saw fit. Within four years, however, the Republic came around to the mainland point of view. Agreeing with a Veronese argument that it was "just and pious" that "what affects all should be funded by all," the doge ordered that Venetian-imposed taxes should be paid by exempt and nonexempt alike. His successors repeated the principle through the century.[28] Local communes could not cancel immunities but did largely neutralize their effect.

In the handing over of the proceeds of direct taxation to the Venetian fisc, massive shortfalls were the norm. As a local chronicler noted in 1490, overall Venetian revenues were rising, but those from Vicenza had fallen by 2,500 ducats yearly. In the period 1506–8, income from the *dadia delle lanze* handed over to the Camera Fiscale averaged some 22 percent less than the quota, and the deficit was growing each year.[29] The Vicentine record on forced loans was no better: the commune failed to pay some 27 percent of a 10,000 ducat *mutuum* in 1438. In a similar vein, the central government required communes to withhold a portion of rectors' salaries and turn the money over to the Venetian fisc. Vicentine arrears reached 20,000 *lire* by 1495 and 27,000 *lire* a year later.[30]

The significance of shortfalls is not entirely clear. It may have been the case that Venetian demands progressively exhausted local resources, that by 1500 subjects were impoverished and unable to pay. This was perhaps true for the countryside, which bore the entire burden of the *alloggio* and suffered an increasingly unfair burden of the *estimo.* Archives hold many examples of rural communes obliged to mortgage or sell common lands and pasture rights because of large debts for salt or direct taxes. The Republic had always forbidden the dissipation of communal patrimonies, but in 1473 it allowed alienation as a last resort because Vicentine rustics had no other way to pay for the latest *subsidium.*[31]

It is unlikely, however, that the urban commune was similarly straitened. Municipal powers to tax the countryside were, if anything, reinforced by 1500. The commune could draw, as well, upon a growing population and rising economy. Furthermore, Venetian demands were no greater in 1500 than they had been a half-century before. More probably, communal arrears in payment of direct taxes to the Venetian fisc resulted from the commune's failure or reluctance to collect the sums required. Communal prerogatives were a license to fiscal evasion and a source of relief to the urban population.

There was not a great deal that the central government could do about tacit resistance. It is true, as Michael Knapton has demonstrated, that the Republic considerably tightened fiscal administration in the course of the Quattrocento. New specialized magistrates such as the *governatori alle entrade, ufficiali alle cazude,* and *provedditori sopra le camere* provided continuity and technical expertise lacking in earlier decades. The Council of Ten generally supervised these magistrates, giving cohesion and thoroughness to a previously disjointed administration. New devices such as the *limitation,* a strict schedule of priorities governing disbursements by each Camera Fiscale, likewise brought order particularly to military finance.[32]

Nonetheless reform measures served more to render the central administration more efficient than to extend Venetian control over local agencies. The chiefs of the Council of Ten, for example, wrote almost daily letters to local rectors ordering payment of salaries to mercenaries, shipment of grain to the army, and collection of tax arrears. These letters testify to the Ten's improved awareness of local conditions. But because orders had to be repeated many times before, with gross delay, they were finally executed, the letters equally testify to the continued incapacity of local governors to fulfilll the demands of the central government. If communes did not pay monies into the Camera Fiscale, it could hardly forward them to designated recipients. If communes did not send supplies to garrisons and the army in the field, governors had few means to force them to do so.

Perhaps, as the Ten so often charged, governors and Camera officials were negligent or corrupt. More likely local officials were both overburdened and powerless. They could not themselves collect taxes. Neither they nor officials from the central government could impose penalties on *dazi* collectors or, after 1455, on collectors of the *dadia delle lanze*. They therefore depended upon the Vicentine commune for full payment of dues. Persistent arrears indicate that local cooperation was not always forthcoming. For its part, the Council of Ten could only exhort local rectors to better performance and issue dire threats of prosecution for nonperformance. It could exert pressure on the Vicentine commune but had little direct jurisdiction over collection of taxes.

THE COMMUNAL PATRIMONY

The Vicentine commune differed from its Paduan counterpart in having a large income of its own. Knapton has concluded that the overwhelming proportion of Paduan revenues was deposited in the Camera Fiscale or sent directly to Venetian repositories.[33] This was certainly not the case in Vicenza: Venetian rule did not deprive the commune of independent sources of funding. In turn, a significant disposable income allowed the Vicentine commune to reduce the purely local taxes that financed municipal services.

In Verona and Padua the Republic quickly liquidated the patrimonies of the Scaligeri and Carraresi. In Vicenza, on the other hand, the *privilegia* guaranteed that the "goods, jurisdictions, and possessions" of the Vicentine commune, either held by the local fisc (*fattoria*) or alienated by previous rulers, should be restored to the commune. The central government fully respected this promise. In October 1406 ducal letters ordered that the *fattoria*, subsequently reconstituted as the Camera Fiscale, turn over to the commune all income-producing properties. Eight weeks later, Venetian fiscal officers formally transferred to their Vicentine counterparts some fifty-four leases bringing in over 1,500 *lire* annually. These leases included houses, pasture rights, mills, market stalls, the right to collect 400 *lire* annually from the Sette Comuni in exchange for a tax exemption, and a large property in Marostica.[34]

This was by no means the full extent of the Vicentine patrimony. A contemporary inventory of goods that the commune had held all along lists market stalls, houses, gardens, sawmills, and warehouses worth nearly 500 *lire* yearly. Incidental documents refer to several miscellaneous incomes: 40 *lire* owed by the town of Torre Belvicino, 30 ducats (ca. 185 *lire*) owed by Folgaria, 10 ducats owed by Arsiero. Probably there were many others. The commune added further revenues in the course of the century. In 1414, Alvise Dal Verme donated to the commune the large Campo Marzo just outside city walls, which was leased out for markets and pasture for some 200 ducats or ca. 1,240 *lire* yearly. When Ludovico Dal Verme rebelled in 1438, the central government assigned to the Vicentine commune the 100 *lire* that his family had collected annually from the Sette Comuni.[35]

A regular and substantial income came from various fiscal privileges. As was the case in Verona, one-quarter of the salt *dazi* remained with the local commune, amounting to some 5,500 *lire* yearly if the Veronese case is any guide.[36] Most important of all, the Vicentine commune and not the Venetian fisc received the proceeds of justice. The final request of the commune in 1406 was that condemnations and fines imposed by local tribunals be assigned to the commune for necessary expenses. Venetian negotiators agreed, specifying that judicial income was to be expended on the city's walls and fortifications.

Whereas Paduan and Veronese data suggest that this income was not extensive, amounting to no more than around six thousand *lire* annually,[37] the Vicentine case indicates the opposite. Civil tribunals imposed thousands of fines each year. More importantly, the Vicentine commune would have received the income from the "criminal" condemnations published in the Arengo. These included the large fines and confiscations imposed on convicted criminals and those who fled to avoid prosecution, the hundreds of lesser fines for trade fraud, and thousands of three-*lire* fines imposed on rural officials who failed to bring debt pledges to the Camera dei Pegni. Even if the commune only partially collected the tens of thousands of *lire* in condemnations imposed each year, net Vicentine income must have been considerable.

Nor did the commune consistently spend that income on fortifications. As early as 1410 the doge complained that the proceeds of justice had been diverted to the upkeep of bridges and roads, and central magistrates repeated the charge throughout the century. Urban defenses remained incomplete or poorly maintained. The commune petitioned in 1409 to finish the southern section of walls, in the Borgo Berico, but failed to follow through. Despite communal efforts in 1435 and 1476 to complete the northern circuit, the Senate noted in 1479 that "Borgo Pusterla has no wall, but only towers." Rectors reported in 1479, "At present the walls and fortresses are in terrible condition, almost in ruin and desolation." Marino Sanudo's crude sketch of the city's main fortress, made in 1483, shows the inner precinct completely built up with private houses. The Council of Ten noted sourly in 1503, "The bridges cannot be raised, the gates are in sad shape, and the towers lack tops."[38]

Despite Venetian efforts to ensure that judicial income be spent on military projects, Vicentines retained control of condemnations. Even when, as in 1445–46, the *auditori nuovi* made the entirely reasonable request that the commune not divert fines away from the upkeep of fortifications, the doge overruled them and ordered respect for the commune's "ancient usage." Central magistrates offered proposals that condemnations finance public works elsewhere, or that convicts be allowed to work off their fines by service to the state, but the projects foundered when the Vicentine commune protested such infringements of its privileges. Councils of the capital forbad the podesta in 1458 and 1483 to issue pardons from or otherwise impede Arengo condemnations. A Senate attempt in 1463 to divert local fines into purchase of supplies for the Arsenal failed after a communal protest. When in the early Cinquecento the Council of Ten called upon Vicenza to devote its judicial condemnations to repair of the strategic northern fortress of Enego, a clearly frustrated captain responded that communal coffers were empty. The necessary funds had to be supplied from other sources.[39]

Even in the crucial military sector, therefore, Venice was not master of the situation. As was symptomatic of fiscal administration generally, Vicentine *privilegia* received consistent Venetian protection even when that was clearly detrimental to Venetian interests. Evidently central magistracies felt that abrogation of those privileges to secure sound fiscal management, perhaps by imposing a centrally directed bureaucracy independent of local communes, would jeopardize local good will and strain Venetian resources. Increasingly frustrated councillors railed at insufficient Vicentine payments but lacked sufficient irritation to impose effective alternatives to local collection.

From the local point of view, protection of fiscal prerogatives had excellent practical consequences. Diversion of judicial condemnations into nonmilitary spending such as bridges, roads, and municipal salaries had the effect of reducing overall fiscal needs of the Vicentine commune, thus reducing municipal taxation. Failure to collect and hand over requisite *dazi* and *dadia delle lanze*, likewise, reduced the fiscal burden on the population at large. In that sense, Vicentine fiscal administration constituted a carefully calculated form of resistance, never so confrontational as to draw significant reforms from Venice. The *privilegia* had become a weapon to protect the commune against unwelcome demands by its ruler.

11

Piety and Morals

THE VICENTINE CHURCH

After 1404 all Vicentine bishops and major abbots were Venetian nobles. The commune in 1406 made a half-hearted attempt to assert some local control, asking that the Republic confer ecclesiastical dignities and benefices solely on clerics of Vicentine origin, but the request was more hopeful than realistic. The Venetian response, a vague promise to exhort future prelates to do the will of the Vicentine commune and citizenry, amounted to a refusal. The central government did several times promise that Vicentine bishops and prelates would be locally resident, but it made no effort to enforce the ruling.[1]

Venetian policy was hardly unusual. Rulers had long inserted their relatives and allies into subject cities, and the Republic claimed nothing that other Quattrocento Italian states did not enjoy. The Republic deemed it politically necessary that key prelacies be held by those loyal to the Republic. Prelacies were, moreover, a fine source of patronage: at the death of Bishop Battista Zeno in 1501, executors found a trove of 22,714 ducats in his palace in Vicenza, a further 60,000 in Padua, and 26,000 more in Ancona. A contemporary chronicler put his total wealth at 130,000 ducats. So, as early as 1405 and especially after a law of 1413, the Senate quite openly made nominations to mainland episcopates and abbeys, and Rome nearly always approved those nominations without fuss. Increasingly, as well, Venetians obtained minor benefices throughout the dominion.[2]

Venetian assumption of ecclesiastical prerogatives did not, however, proceed only from traditional motives of pacification and patronage. The ethico-spiritual basis of governance demanded an unprecedented thoroughness in ecclesiastical supervision. Intervention extended to trivial matters in which the Republic gained no material or political advantage. When senior magistrates suspended their deliberations to discuss the profanation of a holy image in a tiny mountain hamlet, for example, it appears that Venetian assumption of responsibility for the spiritual well-being of subjects derived from more than political expediency.[3]

Characteristic of Venetian governance, indeed, is the degree to which ecclesiastical policy was motivated by a self-interest defined much more broadly than was the case among predecessors or Quattrocento counterparts. The axiom that dominion depended upon divine favor had very real implications. Since any act of impiety jeopardized God's good will towards the Republic, the councils of the capital had to treat affronts to God as seriously as questions of diplomacy and war. The theft of seven chalices from the Vicentine church of San Biagio, the sodomy of a young boy in remote Cornedo, or a routine homicide in a Marostica church provoked the same urgency as outright rebellion or patrician factionalism. Central councils responded to those offenses with similar grants of extraordinary authority to local governors.[4]

A major objective of Venetian ecclesiastical management was placement of suitable clergy in all levels of benefices. Several laws after 1414 sought to restrict passage of benefices into *commende*. Legislation of 1459 made explicit the conjunction of piety and politics, requiring Senate approval for appointments to benefices to ensure honest priests, to give contentment to subjects, and "so that the ecclesiastical benefices of our jurisdiction be conferred on persons faithful and pleasing to us." As was true of other major jurisdictions such as finance, *privilegia*, and the military, senior magistracies actively contended for primary competence over ecclesiastical appointments. By 1485 at least, the Council of Ten had eclipsed the Senate and claimed that holders of benefices needed its license.[5] The Ten, once in power, continued the Senate's policy that all benefices, no matter how insignificant, required careful scrutiny by senior councillors. The order of 1485 arose from a dispute over provision of a priest for a small chapel high in the Valdagno.

Venetian councils equally assumed responsibility for protecting ecclesiastical patrimonies. Vicentine statutes were silent on the subject. A Senate decree of 1412 became the primary law governing transfer of ecclesiastical property: clergy could not use movable goods as pledges, cultivators could not hold church lands under long-term leases, and alienations and exchanges required Senate permission.[6] Though attempts to limit long-term leases ran contrary to Vicentine agrarian custom, hence had little impact, the Senate did succeed in enforcing the principle that the sale or exchange of church lands needed its approval. It exercised that jurisdiction with extraordinary zeal. In the midst of delicate negotiations or potentially disastrous warfare, when the very preservation of the dominion seemed at stake, the Senate constantly paused to consider requests of mainland convents to sell or exchange a few acres of land.

Venetian direction of church affairs substantially reduced the traditional powers of the ecclesiastical hierarchy. In the first place, the central government denied Roman authority in key sectors, or at least subjected papal intervention to Venetian approval. For example, the Republic forbade appeals to Rome by clergy or laity because, as the doge declared in 1445, "our intention has always been that our subjects not be dragged before the Curia." The Senate's demand of 1459 to license holders of benefices directly targeted unworthy clerics who obtained benefices by papal order. A Senate provision of 1472, complaining that foreigners occupying mainland benefices deprived local clergy of the means to eat, study, and "improve themselves" (*farsi valente*), declared that the pope could not grant a benefice to "any foreigner who is not our subject."[7] Venetian and mainland citizens could not petition the Curia or apostolic legates for letters setting aside testamentary bequests. In 1483 the heads of the Council of Ten decreed that rectors could not accept or execute papal or curial letters unless specifically told to do so by a competent Venetian council. The Ten designed that measure to prevent Roman hearing of divorce or annulment cases. Clergy could not post notices of excommunication and interdict without Venetian permission.[8]

In the second place, central councils severely restricted the authority of diocesan bishops. Though bishops were Venetian nobles, they were not regarded as adjuncts of the Venetian administration, nor were they privileged relative to local rectors or even communal judges. Secular rather than ecclesiastical courts held jurisdiction over any case involving temporal interests. So, for example, the *avogadori di comun* and Council of Ten removed from episcopal courts all disputes between rival claimants to benefices and disputes over legacies and pious donations. Episcopal courts could not summon Jews accused of usury, who received summary justice by the podesta.[9] Above all the Republic insisted that clerical lawsuits against laymen be judged in secular rather than episcopal courts. Secular tribunals, notably, heard suits over nonpayment of tithes. Central councils protected Vicentine rustics against the claims of such powerful figures as the abbot of Santa Giustina and the bishop of Padua.[10]

Logically, ecclesiastical tribunals should have adjudicated disputes involving episcopal fiefs. Venetians, however, preferred the Roman law maxim that "the plaintiff shall appear before the tribunal of the defendant" (*actor sequitur forum rei*). On that basis, the doge decreed in 1435, secular courts should resolve disputes between laymen over income from ecclesiastical fiefs. Within two years that maxim produced a Venetian ruling that secular judges should decide any feudal case involving a lay defendant, even if the bishop himself brought suit. Two decades later the doge further reduced episcopal competence with the ruling that bishops retained jurisdiction over title to episcopal fiefs but that disputes over the income from fiefs belonged to lay courts. In 1507 the doge completed a century of encroachment upon episcopal authority with the blanket declaration that "disputes over fiefs [should] be decided by secular judges."[11]

COMMUNE AND CULT

Venetian assumption of primary ecclesiastical responsibility did not reduce the Vicentine commune to a passive spectator in ecclesiastical administration. Assignment of broad categories of cases to secular tribunals did not, for example, automatically indicate assignment to the podesta or his assessors: the communal judge of ecclesiastics retained equal jurisdiction over lawsuits by clerics against laymen. In order that the commune of Vicenza make appropriate provision for maintenance of the divine office, municipal councils in 1409 gave local *provveditori* the power to supervise the financial management of religious institutions. Three citizens and a notary examined accounts of monasteries, hospitals, and charitable foundations and monitored buildings, furnishings, and books. A similar commission of two citizens, elected from the communal Council of One Hundred, directed pious institutions such as the Ospedale de' Proti for impoverished nobles, the Lazzaretto for lepers, and Marcabruno Clarello's endowment for "paupers of Christ."[12]

Even supervision of clerical morals remained partially within the commune's jurisdiction. Pope or doge actually ordered transfers of monasteries and churches from one order to another, but communal *deputati* generally provided the initiative for reforms such as placement of the Servites at Monte Berico, the Girolimini at Monte Summano and San Nicolo in Olmo, and the Observant Franciscans at San Biagio, and the hospital of Borgo Pusterla. The Clarices entered Vicenza when the nuns of San Tommaso transferred lands to the commune, which then handed them over to nuns of the Observant Franciscans. The commune in 1458 moved against the scandalous Conventual Dominicans in the city's principal monastery, Santa Corona, and after five years of embassies and protests secured a transfer of the house to Observants from Verona. The commune likewise sponsored several attempts to reform the lax convent of the Araceli.[13]

The commune also obtained broad powers to direct public religious observance, thereby enhancing its own prestige within Vicentine society at large. Particularly significant was the commune's successful promotion of San Vincenzo as the city's patron saint: as Sergio Bertelli has noted, the patron was a crucial component in establishment of a precise civic identity, reinforcing not only the city as a corporate whole but also the specific power ruling the city. In the Trecento urban devotions had been somewhat unfocused, as Vicentines celebrated several patrons whose relics rested in the city's monasteries: Felice and Fortunato, Leonzio and Carpoforo, and Beato Giovanni Cacciafronte. Giangaleazzo Visconti introduced several others—Santa Maria della Neve, Sant'Ursula, San Gallo, and San Luca—on whose festivals his armies had won victories in the advance on Vicenza. But in the last decades of the Trecento, the Vicentine commune took the initiative in raising San Vincenzo, hitherto a minor figure in local observance, as primary patron. The commune built his church in a prominent site across the main piazza from the communal palace, controlled its endowment, and appointed its clergy. From its steps a Dominican friar, sponsored by the commune, preached every Sunday after dinner.[14]

In the Quattrocento the almost homonymous association of San Vincenzo with the city of Vicenza provided the primary focal point for civic loyalties. Giangaleazzo's saints disappeared from public observance. Though the commune ordered processions to honor several other saints, municipal statutes downgraded their titles to "protectors." The Vicentine commune did not, as did its counterparts in Padua, Treviso, Bassano, and Cologna, adopt St. Mark as a patron.[15] The great processions of Corpus Christi and Santa Spina, carefully organized to remind guilds and countryside of their subjection to communal authority, began at the church of San Vincenzo. There the commune headquartered the Monte di Pietà, in a characteristic conjunction of charity and municipal patriotism.

Other cults likewise celebrated a distinctly Vicentine, primarily communal identity. The commune gave annual gifts and ordered guild processions to the church of Santa Maria Misericordia, built to commemorate heroic Vicentine resistance to a Paduan army. The great shrine of Monte Berico, overlooking Vicenza, based on a vision of the Virgin by the conveniently named "Donna Vincenza" in 1428, was largely a communal project. A communal deputy directed the formal investigation that compiled testimony to miracles on the site, and the commune was instrumental in the placement there of the Brigitines and (later) the Servites. The commune sponsored, as well, the plague church of San Rocco, begun in 1485, and placed there the secular canons of San Giorgio in Alga.[16]

In two regards, Vicentine citizens enjoyed notable authority in the episcopal curia. First, Vicenza had no tradition of priest-notaries, and Venetian bishops did not bring scribes as part of their entourages. Notaries from the Vicentine college drew up instruments of episcopal transactions, notably feudal investitures and leases of church property. Because notaries were primarily trained in municipal law and were forbidden to redact instruments contrary to that law, employment of lay notaries partially imposed local formulas and legal structures upon episcopal administration. Second, as was generally the case in Italy, Roman appointees filled many Vicentine canonries. Most foreign canons were nonresident. But there were many Vicentine canons as well, and several Vicentine archdeacons and archpriests. Since these clerics were resident, they enjoyed by default a major role in the administration of the chapter's considerable patrimony.[17]

Vicentines even made some inroads against subtraction of local revenues by bishops. The city's cathedral, still the center of local observance, badly needed repair by the mid-Quattrocento. In 1465 the commune offered 1,000 ducats for its restoration, which shamed the bishop into offering 1,200, and the combined venture financed the lovely pink and white marble facade that still stands. But the commune had better uses for its funds: the municipal palace also needed restoration. In any case, Vicentines knew a better means to finance cathedral work. Taking advantage of a protracted dispute between the central government and the bishop, Vicentine orators to the doge requested and received the authority to sequester episcopal income for repair of the *duomo:* 500 ducats in 1472, another 500 in 1473, 1,000 ducats in 1475. In fact the commune simply pocketed the money. Restoration had to await another campaign. Even then, in 1505, the first 1,000 ducats came from the estate of the late Bishop Battista Zeno.[18]

PUBLIC MORALS

Venetian rule promoted, in the words of Don Giovanni Mantese, a healthy austerity. There was nothing unusual in the overall Venetian intention: Vicentines too demanded right behavior on spiritual grounds and saw the divine and ethical as a single imperative. But the Republic gave that imperative a more urgent priority than did subject communes. Measures to maintain public morality came largely from the capital. Indeed, this is one of the few areas in which the central government unilaterally imposed legislation upon subjects.

Usury is a case in point. The Vicentine commune does not appear to have regarded usury as a serious danger. Municipal statutes were largely silent on the subject, declaring in a single vague rubric that a usurer's rights were not to be respected.[19] Vicentine councillors took a somewhat lax approach to enforcement of that law: because all patrician fortunes derived at least in part from interest-bearing loans, because patricians so carefully disguised their loans as fictitious sales that they were safe from charges of usury, and (perhaps) because the patricians' standard interest rate of 6 percent was rather low for the time.

Concerted opposition to usury came only from Venice. In 1456 the Senate tried to abolish the collection of interest on loans of wheat and to regulate cash loans disguised as future sales of wheat. In 1458 the Senate forbade rectors to authorize the payment of usurious charges, a measure aimed at the common practice of licensing Jewish moneylenders in the countryside. The great lex Vendramina of 1478, one of the few decrees directed both to the capital and to the mainland and overseas dominion, sweepingly forbade any sort of usurious transaction and authorized the podesta to enforce that ban. Venetian councils thereafter took a direct interest in the extirpation of usury. In one case of 1503, for example, an extraordinary tribunal of podesta and captain handed down the original sentence. Central councils eventually removed the case to Venice, where the Quarantia gave final judgment.[20]

Festivals in Vicenza, as elsewhere, combined religious observance with purely secular celebration. Both Venetian and Vicentine councillors realized that excessive frivolity undermined spiritual intention. As regards the major feast of the Holy Thorn (Santa Spina), for example, both governments sought to channel the more raucous sideshows into decorous, even pious acts. In 1431 the commune replaced the tilting contest (astiludium) with an annual gift of a silver lamp to the monastery of Santa Corona. In 1451, with the cooperation of Venetian councils, the commune abolished the womens' foot race—which had replaced a greased pole contest—in favor of an offering of a silver crown. Nonetheless Vicentines vigorously resisted Venetian efforts to make the day a totally solemn occasion. The Republic tried to abolish the exhibition of flag throwing and divert its expenses to candles for the procession, but it quickly withdrew the order after communal protests. Venetian disapproval led to temporary suspension of the horse race, but in 1460 the communal deputy Valerio Loschi revived and endowed the race "so that the whole day shall be festive."[21]

Vicentines were quite casual about prostitution. The commune had sponsored a central brothel at least since the Trecento. When prostitutes thereafter spread throughout the city, the commune was concerned only that one notorious bathhouse was a fire hazard and that taverns of ill repute served untaxed wine. By the mid-Quattrocento the official lupanarium, located just opposite the city fortress, had grown into a complex of two baths, a large house, and seven smaller houses. Venetians saw the situation as scandalous. In 1454 the podesta forbade innkeepers to admit prostitutes. In 1470 the Venetian bishop bought up the land under the communal brothel and expelled its *meretrices* to the suburbs. The commune's response was nothing short of audacious: orators asked permission to cut a door in city walls to facilitate urbanites' access to the new brothel. The doge refused. By 1480 the commune was attempting to relocate that brothel next to its original site, which happened to adjoin the bishop's garden.[22]

The central government likewise subjected gambling to increasingly strict supervision. In this case local law provided strong precedent. Statutes of 1425 forbade games of hazard, especially dice. Subsequent municipal provisions protected young boys from professional gamblers, abolished the communal tax on dice as blatantly inconsistent with prohibition of the game itself, and extended the ban to card playing. Civic councils empowered consuls to propose necessary legislation before the Council of Forty, and to direct the recovery of monies by losers in games of chance.[23] But all legislation after mid-century came from Venice, beginning with a ducal letter of 1455 directed against players of dice or cards. Two years later the Council of Ten entered the scene with a flat ban on dice play in Venice, the mainland, overseas colonies, and even ships at sea, and it reinforced that ban with ferocious penalties. To ensure that its prohibition was effective, the Ten in 1479 granted the *auditori nuovi* all its authority over gambling and authorized them to make formal inquiry into infractions. By its "charter" of 1468, the Council of Ten had no particular jurisdiction over gambling; evidently its mandate to preserve the security of the state included suppression of gambling. The seriousness of the crime also allowed that council to override the fact that the *auditori nuovi* were expressly forbidden to act as judges of first instance.[24]

The success or failure of Venetian efforts to legislate a better moral tone for Vicenza is not at issue. The sheer fact that the Republic seized the initiative is important and indicates generally sombre governance and insistence on raising personal conduct to a primary concern of public policy. Significant too is that, with the exception of prostitution, the Vicentine commune offered little resistance to Venetian intervention. Usury prohibitions did not harm patricians. Indeed, patricians could use those prohibitions to eliminate competition by Jewish moneylenders. Other decrees of the central government aimed, in the immediate sense, at social pacification: elimination of rowdy festivals and a halt to the brawls and fraud associated with gambling. If the commune resisted the more dour aspects of Venetian rule, on the whole its councillors welcomed the backing of Venetian councils in suppressing disorder. It is entirely possible, as well, that patricians were eager for the respectability appropriate to their new status as aristocrats. In any case, the Vicentine patriciate found that piety and local control went hand in hand.

12

Appeals and Their Limits

Appellate jurisdiction is not a glamorous subject, but it is one that preoccupied Quattrocento governments. Venetians knew that a sound system of appeals and petitions was necessary for the maintenance of justice, "the honor of our Dominion, the observance of law, and the contentment of subjects."[1] Vicentine councillors could not challenge the Venetian capacity to accept appeals, but they could not accept wholesale derogation of the communal judiciary. Efforts to realize those divergent objectives produced considerable friction and adjustment. The documentary records of that struggle occupies a prominent place in surviving archives.

Appellate jurisdiction is, moreover, a highly revealing issue. Because stakes were so high, rulers and subjects gave appeals a top priority and devoted major energies to securing maximum advantage. In the process each side articulated its priorities and demonstrated its resources. The issue gains importance, as well, from the currently accepted notion of the Venetian state's "diaphragm" between capital and periphery, which consisted of a permeable barrier between sovereign central government and privileged local communes. If this was the case, the hearing of appeals marks one of the rare sectors in which the business of governance regularly crossed that membrane. Recent historians have reached a consensus that Venice actively encouraged appeals in order to centralize judicial authority, to offset the local autonomies guaranteed by *privilegia,* and to unify a composite state.[2] Though confirming that overall policy, Vicentine evidence suggests, on the other hand, that administrative dysfunctions and local prerogatives considerably vitiated Venetian intentions.

CONDUITS FOR APPEALS

Certainly Venetian councillors anticipated an influx of mainland judicial cases. To handle this influx the Maggior Consiglio in late 1410 established the magistracy of the *auditori nuovi,* charged with traveling throughout the mainland to hear complaints and appeals. From the start the *auditori nuovi* had a composite and extremely powerful jurisdiction. Like their parent magistracy, henceforth known as the *auditori vecchi,* they heard civil appeals, judging lesser cases on the spot and forwarding ("intromitting") deserving appeals of more important cases to Venice for definitive hearing. On tour in the mainland, they assumed the criminal jurisdiction of the Avogaria di Comun, both hearing appeals from criminal sentences and opening investigations into unpunished crimes. They also held the capacity to investigate ("syndicate") the conduct and judgments of Venetian governors, with the power to hear witnesses and investigate official wrongdoing. Subsequent legislation assigned the *auditori* miscellaneous competences over jurisdictional disputes between courts, disputes over officials' fees, *dazi,* extortion by tax officials, usurpation of common lands, and mishandling of public monies.[3] Marino Sanudo's eyewitness account of a typical hearing, in 1483, demonstrates how far-reaching their authority was:

> In the palace [of Padua], after Pylades the notary with his trumpeter had made proclamations and presented the syndics in tribunal, he proclaimed the command of these *auditori-avogadori-provveditori-syndics* of our Most Illustrious Signoria that, if any person wished to complain of or had knowledge of any extortion, fraud, or violence or to complain about any civil or criminal judicial act made by any podesta, captain, chamberlain, castellan, vicar, judges, chancellors, constables, cavalry, or other officials in the past ten years, he should come forth to make his complaint, and justice shall be done for him. The same happens in every city and fortified place.[4]

The *auditori*'s powers grew in the course of the century. When miscreants began to exploit the loophole that an entire sentence could be set aside for a minor procedural flaw, for example, the *auditori* received the power to judge specific aspects of a sentence rather than send the whole appeal to Venice. Their capacity to hear new testimony expanded, and the value of sentences that they could annul on the spot rose from ten ducats to fifty. After 1421 they not only investigated peculation by Venetian officials but also punished offenders on the spot and ordered restitution. After 1478 they heard appeals in cases of usury, and a year later they acquired the jurisdiction of the Council of Ten in gambling offenses. After 1491 they could, in criminal accusations against Venetian officials, draw up the formal dossier of accusation, evidence, and testimony that guided eventual judgment in Venice. A commission of 1473 summed up a complicated responsibility: "You shall have the liberty to provide, ordain, and regulate all matters that you judge useful to the good state and honor of our Dominion, in all places to which you go."[5]

It took some time for the magistracy to take hold. Business was so slow in the early decades that in 1430 Venetian tribunals allotted some of the *auditori nuovi*'s court time to the more active *auditori vecchi*, who judged purely Venetian appeals. In 1444 the Maggior Consiglio observed, "The appeals that are sent to the *auditori nuovi* are so few and even diminished that these [officials] have an abundance of free time." By 1483, however, appeals had so multiplied that the *auditori nuovi* could not expedite them even with heroic efforts, and the Maggior Consiglio temporarily created the office of the *auditori nuovissimi* to hear lesser cases. The problem of overwork persisted, and central councils either recreated or made permanent the *auditori nuovissimi* in 1492.[6]

The two branches of the *auditori* were not the only magistracies empowered to channel mainland appeals to Venice. The *avogadori di comun*, by a reaffirmation in 1419 of a law of 1352, retained the capacity to hear appeals from criminal sentences that ordered execution, mutilation, life imprisonment, or permanent exile.[7]

BARRIERS TO APPEALS

That elaborate mechanism did not, however, succeed in drawing great numbers of appeals to Venice. There were two reasons for this. Firstly, most appeals remained on the local level. Secondly, the appellate system did not function well enough to satisfy its superiors, which sharply cut back its range and effectiveness.

Both practical and legal obstacles blocked recourse to Venice. Pursuing an appeal was very expensive, counting travel, lodging, and the hiring of lawyers in the capital. Several known appeals cost several hundred *lire*, well beyond the capacity of most Vicentines. Appellants had to post surety for the amount of the original judgment, a requirement that further discouraged litigation.[8] Precisely because paupers could not afford appeal to central tribunals, the *auditori nuovi*'s capacity to make decisions on the spot expanded to cover sentences up to fifty ducats, which encompassed the majority of judgments.

But even then the *auditori nuovi* were a magistracy of last resort. Those inclined to pursue appeals first had to go through the local appellate system. When a Vicentine judge or Venetian assessor handed down the original sentence, the communal judge of appeals heard appeals. If he confirmed the original sentence, that sentence was fixed (*rata*) and could not be further appealed. If he found the appeal reasonable, any second round of appeals went to the podesta or his vicar. When the judge of first instance was the podesta's vicar, appeals went to the podesta, who also had the capacity to declare sentences fixed.[9] The *auditori nuovi,* in those cases, heard only second- or third-level appeals. Only when the podesta himself rendered the initial sentence could a litigant appeal directly to the *auditori nuovi.*

Furthermore, a hearing in Venice was unlikely to change a decision because all appeals were heard according to Vicentine law. As early as 1415 a ducal letter established the principle, derived from Bartolus, that "cases of appeal shall be tried in accordance with those laws and statutes by which the original case should be and was tried." Bartolomeo Cipolla, for one, noted the implications of this ruling: Venetian tribunals had to decide mainland cases according to local statute or the *ius commune* rather than the equity that prevailed in Venetian jurisprudence. Local norms also prevailed if the initial case had been decided by custom rather than statute.[10] Appeals were not, then, a means to diffuse Venetian law on the mainland. Indeed, they imposed mainland law upon the magistracies of the capital. Technically, Vicentines could not appeal from local to Venetian law.

Central councils established respect for local law as a guiding principle of the appellate system. The *auditori nuovi* in particular, declared the Senate in 1430, had to observe the statutes of the place when deciding an appeal. A few decades later the Council of Ten entered the arena with a demand that the *auditori nuovi* respect all pacts, concessions, and *privilegia* of the mainland. The doge in 1480 reinforced the ban on arbitrary decisions by the *auditori nuovi:* "We desire that the statutes and concessions made to this most faithful commune [of Vicenza] be preserved down to the last detail, nor shall they be contravened in any way; indeed they shall remain uncorrupted and inviolate."[11] Indeed, the most ringing endorsements of *terraferma* privileges and law were carried in stern reminders to the *auditori nuovi.*

Above all, central councils obliged the *auditori nuovi* to respect the fact that vast categories of cases could not be appealed to Venice at all. In all mainland cities, for example, either party in a civil dispute could request a formal legal opinion (*consilium sapientis*), which was binding upon the judge. In 1415 the doge extended this procedure from the local to the Venetian judiciary: the *auditori nuovi* too had to commit any appeal for expert opinion and had to render their decision strictly according to the *consilium.* Even so, appellants chafed at having to trek around the state in search of the *auditori nuovi* and pay their 5 percent fee. To alleviate those hardships the Venetian Maggior Consiglio in 1434 passed an ordinance that appeals of sentences made according to a *consilium sapientis* were to be heard not by the *auditori nuovi* but by the podesta. Litigants, at that point, could force the podesta to commit cases for further *consilium,* and, the ordinance continued, "Just as the expert advises, so the podesta shall pronounce."[12] At all junctures, then, appellants could remove a case from hearing by Venetian judges and give it to a local jurist for a binding opinion.

Most important of all, the law of 1434 canceled the *auditori nuovi*'s jurisdiction over sentences rendered according to a *consilium sapientis.* Therefore, litigants could not appeal those sentences to Venice. Venetian councils generally respected that barrier to appeals. Only three instances of appeals of *consilia sapientis* are known to have reached Venice. The Quarantia immediately threw out two of them because such appeals were illegal. It allowed the third only because of massive blundering by the local jurist: the opinion of Antonio Thiene, declared the Quarantia, offended law, justice, two ducal letters, and Vicentine municipal statutes.[13]

"Criminal" sentences could not be appealed through the *auditori nuovi.* These were the sentences published in the general assembly (Arengo) of each mainland city. In Vicenza that category encompassed not only violent crimes but also fiscal infractions such as trade fraud or smuggling and purely civil offenses such as failure to provide debt pledges. Originally, Vicentine statutes forbade the appeal of Arengo sentences to the communal judge of appeals, and Paduan statutes forbade the appeal of Arengo sentences concerned with property usurpation. In 1435 the doge universalized piecemeal prohibitions with a ruling that the *auditori nuovi* could not interfere with Arengo sentences. This left the possibility that the *avogadori di comun* could accept appeals from Arengo sentences, but by 1450 central magistracies had confirmed the complete inappellability of Arengo acts. When local governors began to issue pardons of Arengo sentences, thus allowing appeal through the back door, the doge in 1490 and 1496 revoked past pardons and forbade their issuance in the future. Towards the end of the century, criminals found a loophole and appealed those sentences approved by judges but not yet proclaimed in the Arengo, but the Council of Ten forbade this practice in 1492.[14]

Venetian directives denied appeal in several other major classes of judicial cases. Firstly, by *terraferma* law, seconded by Venetian decree, litigants could submit nearly any civil dispute for binding arbitration. After 1433, Venetian judges had to confirm arbitration sentences, the *auditori nuovi* could not hear complaints against them, and the losing party could not appeal sentences to Venice except with the assent of all six ducal councillors, the three heads of the Quarantia, thirty-five members of the Quarantia, and two-thirds of the Maggior Consiglio. Subsequent legislation closed loopholes in the law. In fact Venetian councils generally declined to hear appeal from arbitration.[15] Secondly, a Senate ruling of 1433 established the principle that, when a dispute received two consecutive concurring sentences in court of first instance and initial appellate court, the losing party could not further appeal the judgment.[16] Thirdly, no Venetian tribunal but only the judge of first instance could hear appeals of interlocutory acts, broadly defined to include all judicial decisions before passage of the definitive sentence: whether to accept testimony, compilation of the *processum*, citation of witnesses and defendants, provision for sureties and defenses.[17] Fourthly, when an accused malefactor fled to avoid judgment, which happened in most cases, local criminal courts sentenced him to banishment until he could be found; the Council of Ten and the Maggior Consiglio both ruled in 1446 that criminals could not appeal sentences *ad inquirendum*.[18] Finally, Venetian decrees forbade the *auditori nuovi* to touch an array of miscellaneous cases: rural vandalism (*danni dati*), sentences against *dazi* collectors, disputes over the *privilegia*, judgments against communal officials, demands for debt pledges, tax assessments, sentences made by pretorian vicars, or cases settled out of court.[19]

In 1450 the Council of Ten gathered the mass of legislation regarding inappellable cases into a single list and made its norms applicable to the mainland as a whole. Blanket decrees of 1454, 1455, 1494, and 1505, all directed against meddling by the *auditori nuovi*, clarified that list, expanded it slightly, and removed loopholes. The highest Venetian magistracies, that is, actively sponsored the progressive constriction of the conduit of appeals. In consequence, the number of appeals that actually reached Venice declined precipitously. After the creation of the Venetian magistracy of the Quarantia Civil Nuova in 1492, for example, most civil appeals would have been heard there, but the surviving register for the period 1499–1505 records only thirty-five Vicentine cases, five yearly.[20]

DYSFUNCTIONS: THE MAINLAND

The *auditori nuovi* heard, but they did not obey. The list of their infractions is long and dreary. Superiors ordered them to commit appeals for *consilium sapientis* in 1415, 1423, 1426, 1435, and 1444, and forbade them to hear appeals of sentences derived from *consilium sapientis* in 1417, 1435, 1450, 1451, 1454, 1474, and 1502. Central councils quashed their interference in such appeals in 1432 and 1468. Senior magistracies enjoined them from hearing appeals of Arengo sentences in 1433, 1435, 1450, 1451, 1453, 1454 (twice), 1455 (twice), 1481, 1492, 1494, and 1507 and canceled attempted intromissions of Arengo sentences in 1450, 1454, 1455, 1460, 1461, 1489, and 1508. In 1433, 1450, 1458, 1482, and 1502, Venetian tribunals ordered them not to interfere with cases that had received two concurring sentences. They were told in 1433, 1450, 1466, 1469, and 1480 not to hear appeals from sentences of arbitration or compromise. Injunctions against hearing other types of appeals—from sentences *ad inquirendum,* interlocutory acts, acts of local officials, sentences of Vicentine or Veronese consuls—date from 1446, 1450, 1454, 1455, 1502, and 1508.

It is not hard to see why the *auditori nuovi* were so prone to error and correction. Their allotted task was nearly impossible to perform correctly. The original mission was ambitious enough: a yearly tour of Treviso, Padua, Vicenza, and Verona, smaller centers such as Feltre, Belluno, Bassano, and Cologna, and the small towns—Marostica and Lonigo in the Vicentine, a half-dozen each in Treviso and Padua—governed by Venetian podesta. As the mainland dominion grew to include Friuli, Istria, Brescia, Bergamo, Crema, Ravenna, Rovigo, and the Polesine, the original itinerary more than doubled. After 1435 they had to visit all prisons as well as hold public hearings.[21] When the value of cases that they expedited on the spot grew to fifty ducats, the volume of business in any one place must have been overwhelming. In each place they had eight days to hear appeals, accept petitions, judge lesser cases, investigate official wrongdoing, and audit fiscal records. In that time they had to master local law and judicial precedents. They were, by design, inexperienced: neither they nor their staffs could serve in consecutive years.

The central government did little to increase their resources to handle the expanded case load. Perhaps senior councils intended the *auditori nuovi* to be a minor magistracy. As Gaetano Cozzi has pointed out, they did not occupy a particularly honorable position within the government. *Auditori nuovi* did not have to be members of the Senate or trained in the law. They tended to be young and at the beginning of their careers. Most were not destined for great careers. There were, as well, practical reasons why the office did not attract the brightest young nobles. The *auditori nuovi* were paid rather less than their colleagues the *auditori vecchi,* who in addition did not suffer the rigors of a long and growing tour of syndication. In the early Quattrocento their salary was cut in half, to a mere sixty ducats annually. A law of 1469 halved their case fees (*carati*), from 5 percent to 2½ percent or less. The Senate acknowledged difficulties in recruitment.[22]

Most of the *auditori nuovi's* infractions probably resulted from ignorance rather than willful meddling. Nonetheless, if the historian can excuse poor performance, their superiors in Venice were not so lenient. The Senate in 1434 mixed sympathy with blame: "Petitions are customarily sent to the *auditori* for their response, but these officials are not (nor can they be) informed as to whether the petitions contain the truth. They respond solely on the basis of what they have heard and thus usually decide petitions to the injury or self-interest of many persons." For the most part central councils expressed only blame. By 1416, the Senate noted, they had not been to the mainland in three years. By 1451 they had not been to Istria in ten years and had never visited Ravenna. In 1494 *auditori* themselves declared that their predecessors had not gone to the *terraferma* for three years, and they asked Senate permission to set forth. Superiors and peoples of the mainland constantly complained that the *auditori* neglected to expedite legitimate complaints, especially those of lesser value that would produce lesser fees. Central councils accused them of corruption, collecting illegal or excessive fees. By mid-century they had developed the "bad custom" of approving all appeals when time was short, thereby causing an overload of Venetian courts. They suspended cases resolved by predecessors or granted safe-conducts to and intromitted sentences against men irrevocably exiled by past rectors. Exasperated superiors ordered them to forward only specific and deserving cases.[23]

Superiors were no more pleased with the performance of the other intermediate appellate magistracy, the Avogaria di Comun. *Avogadori* too proved incapable of remaining within jurisdictional boundaries. In 1464 the Council of Ten declared them the chief perpetrators of "dangerous and pernicious" attacks on the very foundations of the Venetian state by their cancellation of decrees by the Maggior Consiglio, Senate, Council of Ten, and Quarantia. Four years later the Ten similarly ordered them not to interfere in mainland cases beyond their jurisdiction. In 1486 the Ten and doge reprimanded the *avogadori* for suspending ducal letters and interfering with the podesta's judicial authority and ordered them not to hear appeals in *dazi* cases. The *avogadori* too tended towards wholesale approval of appeals without regard to merit or local law.[24]

Infighting between *avogadori* and *auditori* further complicated the hearing of mainland appeals. The two magistracies inevitably overlapped, since both held criminal jurisdiction, and the *auditori* acted "as *avogadori*" (*tamquam advocatores*) in tours of the mainland. In fact they collided, canceling or allowing appeal against each other's decisions. The Senate tried to restore order with a declaration in 1448 that the intromissions of the *auditori nuovi* could not be impeded by other officials, but it actually compounded the problem by reserving the rights of the *avogadori* (*salvo iura advocatorum*). Mutual interference grew worse when the aggressive *avogadori* illegally assumed civil jurisdiction and interposed themselves as intermediaries between the *auditori* and higher Venetian councils. The Maggior Consiglio deplored the "very bad custom" that *avogadori* annulled the intromissions of the *auditori,* and it forbade further actions contrary to Venetian laws and customs. The Council of Ten joined the fray with a harsh decree against the *avogadori*'s interference with decisions of other Venetian councils. But all attempts to impose discipline were in vain: the surviving registers of the *avogadori* abound with attempts to overturn the acts of the *auditori*.[25]

DYSFUNCTIONS: VENICE

The course of appeals was little smoother once a case reached the capital. The *auditori nuovi* acted somewhat as ushers, "leading to council" the cases they had intromitted while on the mainland tour. By law they had to present their cases within three months of the day on which they accepted the appeal. Their actual tour, however, often lasted for six or eight months, and when it had finished, the *auditori* often did not bring appeals before definitive tribunals for several months more. Litigants were kept in Venice awaiting judgment for months on end, which served (so declared the Quarantia) to dishonor Venetian administration and pervert justice. There were many cases, particularly those of lesser value, that the *auditori nuovi* never presented. Senior councils tried to stimulate the *auditori* to greater speed and efficiency by denying them fees from cases not led to council, allowing appellants to introduce delayed cases without benefit of *auditori,* and ordering the *auditori* to introduce appeals in order of their acceptance.[26] Continuing criticism indicates that reforms were not effective.

The cases that did reach appellate tribunals were subject to delay and gross error. The *auditori* had the troublesome habits of examining one side's witnesses while ignoring the other side, failing to cite both parties to Venice, and neglecting to specify which council a cited party was to appear before. Those procedural flaws forced judges to throw out some appeals. Repairing the salvageable still delayed hearing. Frequently the *auditori* simply failed to appear in court. Nor were the *avogadori* more efficient: they were so subject to delay that the *auditori* could take their cases to council when two months passed without action. In Venice too the *avogadori* fought with the *auditori,* throwing out lawful testimony and preventing them from introducing appeals to appropriate tribunals.[27]

Tribunals themselves suffered similar dysfunctions. As the Maggior Consiglio noted in 1443, the Quarantia seldom read appeals and petitions and sometimes did not decide those which it did consider. This failure eroded the Dominante's once-great reputation for justice and jeopardized the divine favor that had brought many cities into the

Venetian state. The Quarantia often failed to produce a quorum. It heard important cases first and allowed lesser cases to languish. Central councils commanded that cases be heard in order of arrival in 1430, 1438, 1439, 1460, 1466, 1472, and 1474, a sign that the Quarantia did not heed the rule. Adding a further problem, appeals against sentences of Venetian rectors often required personal appearances by those rectors, who served long tours of duty on the mainland and could not return to Venice for a year or more. Because the Quarantia also heard purely Venetian appeals and cases from overseas colonies, appellants competed for court time, and personal influence rather than justice tended to determine which cases were actually heard. The Senate, Maggior Consiglio, and Council of Ten took turns apportioning court time and forbidding the importuning of judges so that the Quarantia could do justice "with sincere and uncontaminated mind." A sweeping reform of 1480 forbade absenteeism, raised salaries, imposed a three-day limit for expediting appeals, and addressed problems of time-wasting, subornation, unpreparedness, failure to hear all sides, and raucous behavior in council chambers.[28] Complaints of delays and inequity went undiminished.

Though the Quarantia served as the primary appellate tribunal, the bewildering array of councils authorized to hear mainland cases sweeps away any lingering image of a coherent appellate system. A shadowy body known as the Collegio Solenne delle Appellazioni ("Solemn Appeals College") heard appeals valued under twenty ducats until its abolition in 1493. Until 1425 the doge and six councillors heard appeals of cases valued in the twenty to one hundred ducat range. The Collegio alle Biade ("Grain College"), assumed that jurisdiction, its competence gradually increasing to three hundred ducats. But the Collegio alle Biade was an ad hoc and composite body, its twenty members drawn from twenty different magistracies; it held the more important task of supervising grain supply for the city of Venice and held additional jurisdiction over sentences by fiscal agencies such as the Rason Nuova, Rason Vecchia, and Ufficiali sopra le Camere. Despite reforms of 1472 and 1502, the Collegio alle Biade failed to function effectively as an appellate tribunal. The Maggior Consiglio and Senate accepted extraordinary appeals, and the latter on a more routine basis heard appeals of sentences of the Vicentine captain. The Avogaria di Comun served as definitive court in appeals from the fiscal sentences of the Rason. The office of the Cazude heard cases valued under ten ducats. *Dazi* cases went frequently to the *governatori delle entrade*, but also to the college of the Dodici Savi sopra Dazi, on which the *governatori delle entrade* usually but not always sat. Officials of the Arsenal heard cases of illegally felling oaks, and the *provveditori di sal* heard cases involving salt. Appeals involving soldiers went to the *savi grandi,* or to the *savi di terraferma* if involving harquebusiers, or to the *savi del collegio* if involving laborers working with the army, or to the *prov-veditori sopra le armi.* Sometimes an ad hoc tribunal was assembled from available mid-level officials.[29]

The appellate system was a crazy quilt of magistracies and alter-nate routings, a ramshackle structure whose tangle of accretions and overlapping jurisdictions threatened to overload its fragile founda-tions. The evident inefficiency of that system deeply wounded the pride of Venetians in their administration of justice, "the foundation of [their] state." Senior councils had very high expectations, which malad-ministration constantly betrayed. The *auditori nuovi* received the bulk of criticism, but they were scapegoats for universal disorder. Only a systemwide failure accounts for the fact that, in one block of thirty-five Vicentine cases in the period 1499–1505, the average appeal required twenty-six months between first sentence and appellate sentence, when the law prescribed a six month maximum. Four took over six years, and one lasted thirty-four years.[30]

Delay was bad enough, senior magistrates thought. Wrong deci-sions were a greater offense to God, justice, and Venetian honor. Over-burdened councils issued pardons wholesale, to worthy and unworthy alike: the Maggior Consiglio and Quarantia examined and approved thirty-nine petitions in the afternoon sitting of 15 April 1432, for ex-ample. Automatic pardons allowed malefactors to return to their homes by waiting until the local podesta had left office, then appealing to Venice for clemency. Alternatively, appellants could make the rounds of the capital's tribunals until they obtained a favorable judg-ment. In one case in 1472, for example, the Quarantia overturned a decision of the Vicentine podesta, the Council of Ten committed the case for *consilium sapientis,* the *auditori nuovi* intromitted the original sentence, and the *avogadori* made the final decision—which was simply that the statutes and privileges of Vicenza be observed.[31]

Venetian magistrates were refreshingly candid that decisions were made "without good information." All admitted fault in hearing main-land appeals: podestas "misinformed" on the law of appeals and igno-rant of the merits of petitions; *auditori* ignorant of the inappellability of Arengo sentences and "not well informed" on the truth of petitions; the Maggior Consiglio misunderstanding petitions and wrongly con-ceding pardons; the Senate unaware of local privileges and permitting alienation of Venetian lands; the Quarantia issuing safe-conducts "based on bad information"; *avogadori* ignorant of the facts of a case and the law governing its resolution; the doge himself acting on the basis of "not very good information" and ignorant of Vicentine law on the jurisdiction of the consulate.[32] In each case the magistrate responsible canceled the offending or unwise decision. This happened so often, in fact, that there emerged something of a ritual of apology and reversal, based on the principle of *intentio:* Vicentine orators come before the doge to complain that a given decree has violated local law and privileges; the doge agrees, declares that "our intention is that the statutes and privileges of this city be inviolably preserved" and revokes the order.

The net result of acknowledged central dysfunction was reinforcement of local law and prerogatives. The chastened *auditori nuovi* responded to an indignant Vicentine orator in 1481: "When we wrote our letters, it was certainly not our intention that anything be done contrary to the statutes and ordinances or privileges of this magnificent commune. Therefore we reply that since we desire always to be well regarded in your hearts, we require that nothing should be allowed to derogate those statutes, ordinances, and privileges by virtue of our letters."[33] In particular, Venetian *intentio* upheld the jurisdiction of the consulate, the inappellability of Arengo and *consilium sapientis* sentences, the commune's right to keep judicial condemnations, its power to distribute and collect taxes, and its right to set conditions for citizenship. That intention served, above all, to undermine attempts of lower officials such as the *auditori nuovi* to draw cases from Vicentine to Venetian courts.

REFORM AND REDUCTION

Constant apology damaged the Republic's prized reputation for good justice and impugned the nascent myth of the Republic's efficient and equitable governance. On a practical level, poor handling of appeals wasted the time of higher councils and exasperated their ideal of good governance. Systematic acceptance of local cases clearly did not provide justice and only diverted the tribunals of the capital from more important concerns. It was absurd that the doge become involved in a dispute between Vicentine bath-keepers and barbers. It was unseemly, too, that he then suffer the indignity of canceling earlier judgments after protest by the Vicentine commune.

Senior councils made frequent attempts to ensure that the appellate system work as designed. Appointment of a fiscal coadjutor in 1453 addressed the *auditori*'s problem of an excessive case load, as did creation of the *auditori nuovissimi* in 1483 to handle lesser cases. A major provision in 1491 ordered that half the *auditori*'s time be spent on minor cases, stipulated that all cases be heard in the city of origin, and gave the *auditori* authority to draw up the *processum* in criminal cases. A year later the *lex Pisana* ordered that they decide appeals within three months, tightened up procedures and fee schedules, and recreated the office of the *auditori nuovissimi*. The *lex Marcella* of 1493 dissolved the Collegio Solenne, reaffirmed the *auditori*'s power to deal summarily with cases valued below fifty ducats, and reinforced the three-month rule.[34] Still, repeated attempts at reform did not reduce the backlog or ensure a fair hearing. Annoyance at delay and injustice was even greater by 1500 than at mid-century.

In the midst of those reforms, senior Venetian magistracies adopted a different and more effective strategy: piecemeal dismantling of appellate structures, notably the office of *auditore nuovo*. The orders banning appeal of broad judicial categories drastically reduced the *auditori*'s potential jurisdiction. Within two decades of their creation, the Senate removed the task of preliminary screening of petitions and assigned it to rectors. In 1435 the podesta assumed their capacity to hear appeals of sentences made according to a *consilium sapientis*. He also took their jurisdiction over appeals of the podestas of Marostica and Lonigo. By 1476 the *auditori nuovi* had lost the right to intervene in cases regarding *dazi* of subject cities, fiscal exemptions, immunities, and monies owed to the Venetian fisc. Towards the end of the century, the doge in a specific case and ducal councillors in a general order forbade the *auditori* to interfere with local tax assessments.[35]

Bereft of those powers, the office suffered marked decline. By the Cinquecento the *auditori nuovi* had become a marginal force in mainland administration. If they are indeed emblematic of Venetian policy, their history in the Quattrocento indicates that creation of an intermediate level of governance proved, in the judgment of their superiors, a failed experiment.

13

Reconstructing Local Prerogatives

The record on appeals and petitions is representative of Venetian administration generally. In nearly every sector the quality of governance fell far below the expectations of its directors. Senior councillors were no more kind to their colleagues than to the *auditori nuovi*. Within two years of mainland expansion, the Maggior Consiglio complained: "As everybody knows, our governors, judges, and officials, both in Venice and outside, do not observe council decrees or the terms of their commissions. This causes a great burden to our Republic and vast harm to individuals."[1] Internal criticism was unabated throughout the century, as higher magistracies traded charges of ignorance, meddling, exceeding authority, inequity, corruption, infringement of *privilegia*, and incompetence. Some of these accusations merely reflect departmental infighting, though internecine conflict was itself part of the problem. Others have the ring of truth. Whatever the cause, unanimous Venetian perception of gross mismanagement led to major changes in mainland governance.

Conflict and error were inevitable, given the overlapping jurisdictions of central councils, imprecise chains of command, and the lack of a clear hierarchy. A dozen magistracies could hear appeals and petitions. A score issued orders to the Camera Fiscale. The doge, Council of Ten, Maggior Consiglio, *avogadori di comun,* and Senate all sought exclusive patronage of mainland *privilegia,* and all sought to discipline the *auditori nuovi.* The custom of sending ad hoc emissaries to handle individual cases exacerbated duplication of authority and undermined whatever lines of authority had been established. The common situation in which a given magistracy possessed only partial authority— legislative but not executive powers, for instance—produced delay and confusion until a competent magistracy could be found to complete a decree.

The constant rotation of higher offices presented further obstacles to effective administration. Collegiality had worked well when the Venetian state consisted of the city and a few overseas colonies, but (by the councils' own admission) it proved unable to provide the same good governance after annexation of a vast mainland state. Because overworked councils seldom had time to examine requests in detail, the first party to gain the ear of a Venetian tribunal tended to win the dispute. Because councils seldom knew or respected preceding decisions, the opposing party could just as easily send an embassy to have the decision overturned: thus the doge reversed himself four times within two years in the battle royal between Vicentine barbers and bath-keepers. Despite the presence of permanent secretaries, central magistracies seldom followed up decrees to ensure their execution.

On the local level the yearly changeover of the podesta's staff produced discontinuity and vitiated effective imposition of Venetian will. Most acts of intervention are known simply from the original decrees, and many were probably ignored. In 1439, for example, the village and valley of Chiampo successfully petitioned to secede from the vicariate of Arzignano and form a new vicariate based in San Giovanni Ilarione. There is no record that local officials effected this radical reformation of rural administration. Subsequent documents list Chiampo and San Giovanni Ilarione under the vicariate of Arzignano.[2] Decrees that ordered cultivation of oaks, destruction of smugglers' routes, and improvement of fiscal management suffered the same fate.

Senior magistracies were well aware of such problems and made concerted efforts to streamline mainland administration. In 1462, for example, the Maggior Consiglio forbade officials to hear cases not specifically authorized by their commissions. In 1486 the doge ordered local rectors not to execute Venetian decrees unless these were accompanied by ducal letters affixed with the lead seal, in an attempt to establish the ducal chancery as a clearing house for *terraferma* business. In 1487 the Senate drastically reduced the number of magistracies empowered to make fiscal concessions: charging that too many exemptions had been granted by "simple letters," it voided all *gratie* made without its permission.[3] The Maggior Consiglio introduced some order into the system by its efforts to clarify the relative jurisdictions of higher councils—the great laws of 1468 and 1486 demarcating the Council of Ten and Avogaria di Comun, for example. In 1502 the Senate remedied the overreadiness of councils to concede pardons in criminal cases, thereby permitting *banniti* to secure safe-conducts to return to their homes, by canceling the powers of other councils to issue pardons. Gradual affirmation of the Council of Ten in matters relating to fisc, army, and violent crime undoubtedly increased continuity and efficiency, particularly since the Ten proved remarkably tenacious in day-to-day supervision. Moreover, the fact that the Ten effectively subordinated lesser fiscal magistracies further clarified the chain of authority.

In the judgment of central magistracies, these reforms did not prove satisfactory. Conflicts between Venetian magistracies, and between magistracies of the center and the periphery, were no fewer in 1500 than they had been a half-century earlier. Complaints of revenue shortfalls, unprepared fortifications, smuggling, inept handling of appeals, badly decided petitions, violent exiles, and patrician vendettas were, if anything, more frequent and harsh.

From the point of view of local authorities, however, one thrust of the reform movement had entirely positive consequences. Central magistracies, made aware of dysfunctions in the councils of the capital, frequently placed severe restrictions on their own capacity for intervention in the mainland. Simultaneously they ceded broad powers to the more efficient agencies of local administration.

REINFORCING THE PODESTA

Acknowledged problems with centralized administration led central councils to limit *terraferma* recourse to Venetian tribunals. Most obviously, the Republic considerably expanded the categories of cases that could not be appealed beyond the local level. The Republic took steps, as well, to restrict mainland embassies to Venice. In 1456 the Council of Ten ruled that orators would receive no hearing unless they were equipped with letters of credential issued by rectors. Nor could orators discuss any matter that municipal councils had not authorized. The expressed intent of that legislation was to block petitions of *districtuales* against the Vicentine commune. In effect, it gave civic councils and Venetian governors a veto over embassies. The Senate meanwhile rendered embassies less attractive by limiting pay and frequency of service and forbidding ambassadors to conduct private business before Venetian councils. Later in the century two decrees of the Council of Ten put a further damper on the "bad and perverse custom" of sending orators to Venice "to argue all sorts of trivial things" by limiting the number of ambassadors to four and forbidding the sale of communal properties to finance the trip.[4]

Manifest dysfunctions led central councils, as well, to expand the podesta's power to handle cases formerly expedited by Venetian officials or the *auditori nuovi*. Podestas acquired the capacity to screen petitions (1424), to hear appeals of sentences made from *consilium sapientis* (1435) and to hear appeals from the podestas of Marostica and Lonigo (1456). After 1435 the podesta could settle disputes over lands purchased from the Venetian fisc. Initially, Venetian plaintiffs could summon mainland defendants before Venetian magistrates, even if all litigants were resident on the mainland and the case concerned mainland properties. Citing inconvenience to *terraferma* subjects and the legal maxim *actor sequitur forum rei,* the Senate in 1435 authorized local rectors to render judgment. When the Council of Ten began to pass laws against grain hoarding and speculation, it transferred to the rectors its authority to investigate offenses and to render summary judgments, which could not be appealed to Venice. In the *lex Vendramina* of 1478, which capped a major offensive against usury, the doge specified that all accusations and appeals should be handled by rectors and not by the *auditori nuovi.* After all, the doge told the podesta, in refusing to hear a tangled case involving fiscal exemptions, "Since you are actually there and ought to know this matter well, you should do . . . as seems most fitting to you."[5]

Though petitioners addressed their complaints to the doge or Quarantia, definitive tribunals increasingly and even necessarily sought the advice of the podesta. Venetian councils could not, they readily admitted, know the true facts of a case or the law that should determine its resolution; councillors voted casually or ignorantly, and too often incorrectly. Thus in hundreds of pardons, exemptions, or reductions of criminal sentences, the qualifier "thus the podesta has advised" (*sic consuluit potestas*) justified the eventual verdict. In this sense the podestas no less than the *auditori novi* served as a filter in the flow of business between periphery and center. Apparently central councils nearly always heeded their recommendations.

In several important areas the podesta's *consilium* formed an integral part of the petition. A favorable recommendation accompanied nearly all requests to alienate ecclesiastical lands, for example. Petitions for Vicentine citizenship, communal petitions for ratification of economic legislation, and petitions to be allowed to appeal despite statutes of limitation all required his opinion. In 1442 the Senate decreed that all petitions from civil judgments greater than one hundred *lire* had to receive the advice of rectors and their chancellors before final disposition in Venice. In 1507 the Senate lifted that pecuniary limit and universalized piecemeal decrees with the order that no petition could be judged until Venetian councillors "inspect the nature of each petition, taking particular note of the information sent by the rectors or other magistrates and officials for elucidation of the truth."[6]

Coupled with self-imposed limitation of the central government's independence was gradual expansion of the podesta's authority to decide petitions on his own. In the first such instance, the Vicentine podesta in 1418 asked the Maggior Consiglio for permission to issue *gratie* from fines imposed by his predecessor, since subjects given harsh sentences had been thrown into a vagabondage that reduced the population and cut into judicial income. The Maggior Consiglio granted the request, for his term of office alone, and renewed it for his successor in 1419. In 1420, since it was pleasing to God and useful to the Republic that paupers have local redress, the Maggior Consiglio made that authority permanent. In 1479 the Senate confirmed a suggestion of Vicentine rectors that rectors should judge all petitions from fiscal condemnations, even those published in the Arengo, which could not be formally appealed.[7]

DYSFUNCTION: THE PODESTA

Transfer of power from the central to the local level of governance rested upon a double premise: that central magistracies could not provide good justice and administration, and that officials on the periphery could do a better job by virtue of their sensitivity to local conditions and local law. The first assumption was accurate enough, by the measurement of a highly self-critical Venetian government. The second proved too optimistic. Those councils which delegated authority to lower levels did not create a local machinery able to expedite increased responsibilities efficiently or equitably. The result was a stream of rebukes of subordinate officials and a further shift in power, this time to the commune of Vicenza.

The performance of rectors was no better, in the eyes of their superiors, than that of the *auditori novi*. The excuse that they were overburdened, unprepared, and understaffed received no sympathy. The heads of the Council of Ten, for example, wrote hundreds of letters castigating rectors for failure to hand over requisite taxes. In fact communal prerogatives prevented rectors from control of taxation, but careful assignment of blame was not a Venetian objective. Central councils noted only that rectors acted where they were forbidden and did not act where they were required. As local representatives of the Republic and members of the Republic's ruling caste, the rectors were personally responsible for good administration and solely accountable for failure to secure *ius et iustitia*.

The Republic's deliberate policy of ensuring the rectors' unfamiliarity with Vicentine law and precedents, exacerbated by the lack of a permanently resident staff, undoubtedly explains a good deal of poor administration. Still, rectors may have largely deserved their superiors' charges of incompetence. There is some indication that the terms of mainland administration discouraged the more talented or zealous patricians. Growing competition for posts and growing corruption in elections guaranteed that merit was not the primary criterion in selecting governors. Younger patricians, from whose ranks the Maggior Consiglio selected Vicentine rectors, chafed at apprenticeship in lesser offices. After 1442 central councils reserved the castellanies of Vicenza and Lonigo for poor nobles, whose sole qualification was their poverty. Moreover, conditions of service deteriorated in the course of the century. Higher positions became less remunerative. The salary of the podesta gradually decreased from 1,100 to 800 ducats and that of the captain from 960 to 800 ducats, with no diminution in the staffs that rectors had to maintain out of their own pockets. In 1452 all Venetian officials had to spend an additional six months in office without pay; when the war crisis passed, superiors only reduced the period of gratuitous service to an additional four months, where it remained for the rest of the century. After mid-century all officials in the Venetian administration paid an increasingly heavy tax on their salaries, some 64 percent for rectors and 51 percent for assessors, with additional charges on the additional incomes (*utilitates*) that they could expect to receive. The situation reached the point where the Senate in 1493 complained that, when a noble was elected to mainland office, he first enquired about the position's emoluments before accepting or rejecting—hardly a sign that *terraferma* service attracted dedicated young nobles.[8]

Podesta and captain were frequently absent from the city. They delayed arrival and hastened departure and easily obtained permission to return to Venice for family business. In 1456, after granting seven leaves in four years to Vicentine officials, the Senate moved against this *pessima consuetudo* with a decree that no official could receive license to visit Venice except with permission of all six ducal councillors and three-fourths of the Senate. Permissions declined only slightly. Alternatively, the Council of Ten pulled officials off the job for missions elsewhere: to investigate a murder in Bassano, syndicate the podesta of Verona, lead troops to Friuli, collect taxes, or accompany dignitaries to other cities. In the fiscal emergency that surrounded the loss of Zonchio at the end of the Quattrocento, the Ten ordered that vacancies in local administration remain unfilled, with salaries sent to the war effort.[9]

Sheer inaction was a common charge. Rectors needed months to carry out simple commands, if they executed commands at all. In June 1482, for example, central councils ordered Vicentine rectors to investigate a riot in the village of Mason. By the following February nothing had been done, and superiors transferred the case to communal consuls. Early Cinquecento riots in Marostica show rectors in a particularly unflattering light. Because the Vicentine podesta was busy trading accusations with his Marostican counterpart over who had fomented and who had failed to suppress the violence, the Council of Ten ordered the captain to investigate, calm the populace, draw up the *processum*, and punish the guilty. His reply was a masterpiece of evasion: he would have gone immediately, but the rains were too great; he would certainly have gone when the rains stopped, but by then he had to await the arrival of a successor. In the event, nothing was done.[10]

When rectors did move, their actions frequently required revocation. They freely modified or canceled the decisions of their predecessors and threw administration into confusion until superiors canceled this capacity in 1478. They infringed canon and civil law by violating the right of sanctuary of churches. They failed to hear witnesses, or send a case to the consulate, or cite both sides of a lawsuit, or commit a case for *consilium sapientis*. One podesta prosecuted a man for abduction even though he had signed a marriage contract and was only fetching his fiancée for the wedding. Another misinterpreted a grain export embargo to mean that no grain was to be bought, sold, or transported at all. Several imposed stiff jail sentences for minor crimes "contrary to the order of the law and the quality of the debt."[11] Senior councils overruled podestas who had infringed Vicentine statutes, or impeded communal officials, or refused to respect safe-conducts or *gratie,* or refused to send appeals to Venice. The governors of Lonigo and Marostica required frequent reminders not to involve themselves in criminal cases, which belonged to the Vicentine consulate alone. In 1468 the doge sternly rebuked the podesta Federico Corner for repeated attempts to undermine the *consolatum's* criminal jurisdiction. The judgment of senior Venetian councillors, that a given pretorian sentence was "badly and wrongly made, contrary to law and justice, and contrary to what the podesta can lawfully do," was so common that it became formulaic.

A final area of central criticism was corruption. In 1408 the *avogadori* charged the first podesta of Vicenza, Jacopo Soranzo, with diverting 800 ducats of Venetian money into his own pocket, claiming 507 ducats in expenses that he had not incurred, and making himself creditor for 223 ducats in grain that belonged to the Republic. This state of affairs continued right through the century: the early Cinquecento chamberlain Piero da Canal stole 570 ducats from the fisc. Podestas and vicars charged with auctioning off *dazi* collections illegally accepted these concessions for themselves. Rectors occasionally imposed an illegal fee of 1 ducat for signing judicial sentences. Lesser officials too engaged in peculation. One sent by the Council of Ten to collect the tens of thousands of ducats due on the *tansa* claimed exorbitant expenses of 20 ducats per day and collected a mere 200 ducats. Chamberlains of the Camera Fiscale stole and accepted illegal payments. Chancellors took illegal fees, accepted bribes for issuing safe-conducts, used subterfuges to stay in office beyond the prescribed terms, and used their office to pursue vendettas and further the interests of their relatives. Constables siphoned off tax revenues. Castellans failed to hand over tolls, stole munitions, and collected salaries while not serving in person. Vicars and assessors took excessive fees from court cases.[12]

The most systematic abuse by podestas seems to have been with regard to the allowance for maintaining horses. Despite a flock of regulations, nine articles in pretorian commissions alone, podestas collected allowances for horses that were never purchased, claimed thoroughbred prices for nags, inflated the cost of fodder, and sold broken-down horses to the army at a high price. Matters reached the point where the Senate in 1472 ordered mainland rectors to investigate one another's stables to root out "corruptions and frauds": Vicenza's to probe Verona's, Padua's to probe Vicenza's, and so forth.[13]

FROM PODESTA TO COMMUNE

This dismal litany is not intended to sensationalize the inadequacies of Venetian mainland administration. Inefficiency and corruption were, in any case, widely acknowledged at the time. Pretorian mismanagement has significance, instead, in its effect on Venetian governance. Sensitive to the growing record of abuses, higher councils increasingly restricted the independent authority of podestas. At the same time they transferred broad powers to the local commune.

Severe strictures curbed the prestige and ostentation of governors. Those orders derive from a characteristic Venetian preference for sober demeanor and anonymous government, but they also indicate a certain distrust of the personal ambitions of governors. Rectors could not make speeches upon entering or leaving office, place their coats of arms on public buildings, or wear the "lugubrious clothes" (*vestes lugubres*) that betokened particular solemnity and rank. The podesta could not own a horse worth more than fifty ducats or undertake major renovations of his palace without Senate permission. Though the captain had to go on cavalcades to check fortifications in the countryside, superiors pared his usual retinue of seventy to eighty followers to twenty and forbade the podesta to accompany him.[14] That rectors flouted those regulations,[15] does not diminish their significance as statements of the central government's intent.

To a certain extent checks on the podesta took the form of subjecting rectors more firmly to central controls. For example, senior councils in 1507 hedged the podesta's capacity to issue safe-conducts by requiring the permission of the Maggior Consiglio. While affirming the podesta's right to issue licenses for grain export, the Council of Ten sought to prevent exports to Austria by limiting the amount that he could release.[16] Sending emissaries from the capital or creating specialized magistracies for fiscal administration likewise reduced the jurisdiction of the podesta in those areas where he had proved unable to meet Venetian requirements.

A more common Venetian response to endemic dysfunction was the transfer of jurisdiction to local communes. This notion, it is true, contradicts the consensus of an inexorable erosion of peripheral rights. But the Republic theoretically confirmed Vicentine law and privileges and consistently protected specific Vicentine prerogatives; it is only logical that the trust implicit in those measures should have led to specific grants of jurisdiction once central councils deemed their local agents incapable of good administration. The notion finds confirmation, too, in the experience of other Italian states.[17]

As regards the *dazi*, for example, the Senate openly conceded the inability of Venetian officials to secure full collection and ordered that *dazi* be auctioned off as they had been before an ill-advised experiment in bureaucratization. Subsequent orders ensured that Venetian nobles could not be involved in collection. After the commune reestablished the *judex datiorum* in 1408, neither the Venetian chancellor nor any other Venetian official could impose fines on collectors. Selection of that judge, initially in the hands of the podesta, passed to the Vicentine College of Jurists. When Venetian chamberlains continued to hear the petitions of *dazi* collectors in a corrupt manner, they lost the authority to hear those petitions.

Here the commune only regained traditional powers temporarily assumed by the central government. Even in areas of outright Venetian innovation, authority frequently passed to Vicenza. An obvious example is the *dadia delle lanze*, at first collected by the Venetian chamberlain of the Camera Fiscale, but after 1426 by the commune with no interference from Venetian officials. Senior councils canceled local officials' right to interfere with the *estimi*. They sanctioned, as well, creation of the office of Vicentine chamberlain with competence equal to that of its Venetian counterpart. Communal chamberlains collected all monies due from *dazi* or *dadia delle lanze*. They also had veto power over disbursment of public monies, even those due the Venetian fisc, since they held two of the four keys to the city's coffers.[18]

In judicial affairs there was less scope for transfer of powers, if only because the *privilegia* already ensured a major local role. At least the Republic issued guarantees where none had previously existed: of the inviolability of Arengo sentences and those made *ex consilio sapien-*

tis, of the consulate's criminal jurisdiction, of the inappellability of broad categories of civil cases, of the requirement that Venetian tribunals judge appeals according to Vicentine law. The commune did recover legislative authority in areas in which Venetian intervention proved counterproductive. In 1426, for example, senior councils withdrew laws governing exile in favor of the Vicentine *ordo antiquus.* When further central decrees produced turmoil and violence, the Senate in 1438 voided them and returned jurisdiction to the commune. Even when the Venetian judiciary assumed individual cases, it often returned them to local structures. Symptomatic was investigation of the Mason riots of 1483, initially committed to rectors but returned to the consulate when rectors showed no signs of action.

If the Vicentine commune already held extensive authority over ordinary judicial administration, during the Quattrocento it acquired power over extraordinary mechanisms such as petitions for pardons or special favors. The central government never renounced its capacity to hear and grant petitions and indeed exercised that capacity throughout the century. This was too fundamental an attribute of rulership, and too useful a means of securing justice through direct intervention, ever to alienate entirely. But the central government gradually hedged its powers over *suppliche* with self-imposed limitations and grants to the Vicentine commune of advisory or even veto power. For example, the Dominante frequently granted fiscal exemptions in the first decades after 1404, to relieve paupers and to reward supporters and mercenaries, but in 1414, Vicentine orators were granted their request that all citizens pay direct taxes, exempt and nonexempt alike. In a similar vein, senior magistracies subjected petitions for Vicentine citizenship first to local opinion, then to the will of communal councils, then to the strictures of local law.

Vicentines argued that only the truly deserving should receive fiscal exemptions, lest the immunities of the unworthy heap greater burden upon the worthy. Because central councils could not know the facts behind a petition, rectors customarily and even necessarily gave advice on the merits of fiscal petitions. But the opinion of rectors, argued communal orators, was insufficient to secure just decisions. Only local citizens could know the truth. Thus in 1437 municipal councils passed a law that, whenever petitions for exemption were sent to Venice, they should first be read out before the Vicentine Council of Forty "and examined as to whether they [were] worthy of being granted or not." When the doge ratified the provision, the Vicentine commune gained a mandatory consultative role in petitions. Given the Venetian tendency to follow local advice, this capacity amounted to a virtual veto power.[19]

In 1429 the Maggior Consiglio severely limited the podesta's capacity to issue pardons from monetary condemnations: to cases below one hundred *lire* in value, only after a year had passed from the original sentence, and only when the petitioner had already paid one-fifth of his fine. Henceforth rectors could set terms only of up to five years for payment of fines. In that ruling the Maggior Consiglio added almost as an afterthought the clause "and if [local] council or law is contrary, [the pardon] shall be revoked." Thereafter the rectors' powers to issue *gratie* continued only at the sufferance of local councils. In the case of Vicenza, that sufferance came to an end. In 1490, Vicentine *deputati* confronted the podesta with the stinging accusation that he had issued "certain pardons of condemnatory sentences read out in the Arengo, which [was] contrary to that which His Magnificence [could] legally do." The podesta admitted that he had been poorly informed in granting those pardons. Wishing always to obey the statutes of Vicenza, he revoked past *gratie* and promised never again to contravene local law. His renunciation bound his successors as well; there are no further records of criminal or pecuniary pardons issued by rectors.[20]

Venetian self-limitation curbed other types of *gratie* as well. The doge withdrew his sovereign right to create notaries for Vicenza after a single attempt to do so provoked fierce communal protest. The Senate in 1458 acknowledged that excessive pardons of *dazi* debtors had greatly harmed Venetian income, and that central councils did not observe a previous decree requiring Senate approval for pardons. Its solution lay in the direction of decentralization. Henceforth, declared the Senate, Vicentine councils and Venetian chamberlains, acting together with the city's rectors, should issue all pardons of *dazi* arrears.[21]

Central councils to some extent returned jurisdiction over criminal pardons to local agencies. The Republic could not entirely renounce this fundamental right, but senior councillors soon realized that arbitrary judgments were a very uncertain means to secure justice and made local law a necessary part of their decisions. In 1413 the doge agreed to a Vicentine request that no *gratie* be granted to men banned for serious crimes, except according to municipal statutes on exile and pardon. The broad latitude that remained with Venetian councils was, in local eyes, excessive. The commune complained in 1435 that many homicides were committed with confidence that the perpetrators' friends could easily secure Venetian *gratie* to have them released from the ban. A compliant Maggior Consiglio then established the principle that Venetian hearing of criminal petitions should be preceded by a reading of original trial documents to determine both the facts of the case and the local law by which a decision was to be rendered. When central tribunals continued to ignore this supplementary evidence, and the Maggior Consiglio continued to make bad decisions, Vicentine documentation was made an integral part of the petition *cursus*. The Senate in 1446 ordered that before voting on any pardon, the deciding tribunal first had to read in its entirety that *processum* which had determined the original sentence. Passage then required a two-thirds vote, not the traditional simple majority.[22]

The cumulative effect of these rulings is striking. Not only did the Venetian government agree to abide by Vicentine criminal law, but it also limited the terms of its own debate to the *processum* drawn up by local magistrates. Criminal petitions provide yet another example of Venetian renunciation of the right to rule the mainland independently of the institutions and procedures of mainland governments. Venetians proved willing to be bound by local laws and even insisted that local structures be integrated into—when they did not entirely determine—the decisions of the central authority.

PART IV

The Renaissance Venetian State

14

Unity and Particularism

The Renaissance state has long been a favored field for romantic narrative, a setting for glittering courts, Machiavellian princes, heroic captains, and proud republics. It has always held, as well, more topical significance as first of the modern states. The assumption of modernity has not, of course, led to any great degree of consensus, since there have been nearly as many definitions of modernity as there have been historians of the period. Students have hailed the Venetian state alone as the forerunner or remote inspiration for, variously, the federal republic, the liberal republic, the Fascist state, the antitotalitarian democracy, and the paternal aristocracy.[1] The notion of the Renaissance state as a moment of passage to the modern state remains lively and compelling, despite intense debate and frequent challenge. Indeed, without this presentist impulse, the Renaissance loses its privileged status in the historical curriculum and is reduced to the richly anecdotal: historians have a professional stake in the issue of modernity.

Tests for modernity have come and gone. The best known remains that of Jacob Burckhardt, who located modernity in the self-conscious structuring of the state, in the "state as the outcome of reflection and calculation." Political analysis was, however, the least-developed aspect of his essay on Renaissance culture, behavior, and psychology. The rational and "scientifically organized" qualities of the state remained on the level of assertion, as his account too preferred gaudy episodes of ambition and revenge. The famous "state as a work of art," however commonplace in popular literature, has fallen into disfavor with historians when not refuted altogether. A largely Italian interpretation, seeing formation of regional states as a step towards national consciousness and patriotism, came out of the Risorgimento. The persistence of this reading is demonstrated by the fact that it required definitive refutation by the master Federico Chabod as late as 1956. Since then it has faded from historiographic view. An equally widespread position located in the Renaissance those republics which provided inspiration and models for democratic republics of the nineteenth century and beyond. This image increased in currency and urgency during World War II and the Cold War, when historians explicitly equated Renaissance tyrannies with Nazism and Stalinism and juxtaposed those tyrannies with free republics. In recent years the republican Renaissance, too, has lost favor as historians have attacked its ethnocentrism, ideological deformation, and anachronism.[2]

The single test for modernity that has survived revisionism is a more technical, less value-laden one. Its terms, suggested by Burckhardt, received refinement and thorough application by Chabod, who looked for concrete developments such as bureaucratization, centralization, and internal unification. His own study of the Cinquecento Milanese state provided the stimulus for Angelo Ventura's pioneering *Nobiltà e popolo* and has remained the primary guide for subsequent work on theVenetian territorial dominion.

Ventura and Berengo added further criteria of modernity, albeit negative ones: aristocratization and the "crisis of liberty" that accompanied the destruction of the quasi-democratic commune. Ventura's conclusion was succinct. Venetian leadership was politically unable to reduce local elites, practically unable to impose thorough bureaucracy, and psychologically unable to integrate those elites into a unified ruling class. The state was, from its inception, divided and compartmentalized, its governance tending to erode local freedoms without imposing effective centralization. The fourteenth to sixteenth centuries mark, therefore, definite passage out of the Middle Ages but a failed transition into the modern state.

Argument for modernity is now rare in Italian studies. As recent historians deny the "Renaissance" quality of Italian states in the fifteenth and sixteenth centuries, they eliminate the original impetus to locate aspects of contemporary polities in those states. It is probably also true that searching the past for embryonic forms of present civilization is, to use Julius Kirshner's phrase, a fruitless teleological quest.[3] Nonetheless, the test for modernity is methodologically useful. Chabod's standards, in particular, provide clear criteria for evaluating the overall direction of the state. Recent historiography has, in fact, provided few other guides for establishing a broader perspective. Some general context is necessary if the period is to escape the level of the local and anecdotal.

UNIFICATION: THE MAINLAND

Quattrocento records offer abundant evidence for unification of the Venetian state. Commissions of podesta and captain, regulating their conduct and that of their subordinates, were initially issued for Vicenza, but their substantial repetition for cities that subsequently came under Venetian rule promoted standardized governance. Rectors rotated through the mainland *cursus* of offices, accompanied by assessors who often made careers of *terraferma* service and who had been trained at the dominion's sole center of higher legal education, the University of Padua. The ideal of consistent administration came close to reality.

Courts and law remained localized, but the Republic considerably erased particularism in the actual execution of sentences. Initially, each Venetian rector held jurisdiction only within his *civitas*. Sentences of Vicenza's podesta and assessors, for example, were valid only as far as the borders with Verona, Cologna, Padua, and Bassano. That judicial compartmentalization offered miscreants the opportunity to hide in the dozens of circumscriptions into which the Veneto was divided. Subject communes knew that creation of regional jurisdiction would infringe their prerogatives, but they were willing to pay this price in order to eradicate the troublesome bands of outlaws. Vicenza took the initiative in 1404 with a request that men banned from Vicenza be banned from the entire dominion. The central government then balked at this innovation, but in 1406 it agreed that those banned for "enormous crimes" in Vicenza be exiled from the region as a whole. Extraterritorial jurisdiction proved useful and popular and was soon extended. Reciprocal powers to arrest and impose exile grouped first neighboring cities, then broad swaths of the dominion: Vicenza and Cologna after 1406; Vicenza and Bassano after 1408; Verona, Vicenza, Cologna, and Legnago the same year; Brescia, Salò, Verona, and Vicenza after 1440.[4]

In the early Quattrocento senior councils established the principle that subject cities were not ordered hierarchically: "We intend that equality be maintained between any two communes, and that one not be superior to another." This encouraged Venetian magistracies to impose ordinances throughout the mainland, subjecting all to a common will. It was only fair that a restriction or exaction laid upon one city be applied to others, that a privilege enjoyed by one city be shared by its neighbors. Especially as regards defense, taxation, criminal prosecution, and appeals, it was common sense to standardize *terraferma* practice in order to forestall the jealousy of disadvantaged subjects. It was common sense, too, not to confuse administration by establishing different laws for each city. The capital's councils strictly enforced equality, to the extent of canceling Vicenza's trivial but preferential tariff on barrel staves.[5]

Municipal archives, preserving local notifications of more general edicts, give the false impression that Venetian governance consisted of bilateral relations between the capital and individual communes. A large proportion of Venetian mandates for Vicenza, in fact, applied to the mainland as a whole and should properly be placed within the context of uniform legislation. Blanket decrees were, it is true, rare and confined to major issues such as forced loans, usury, and war. But frequently a Venetian provision addressed a specific problem in one city, and councils subsequently extended that provision to the other cities of the *terraferma*. Most major Venetian legislation reached Vicenza in this manner. A good example is the body of law restricting classes of legal cases that could be appealed to Venice. The law of 1423 on the *consilium sapientis* originally applied to Feltre; that of 1433 on sentences published in the Arengo to Padua; that of 1439 granting the *auditori nuovi* the right to intromit only part of a sentence to Vicenza, Padua, and Udine; that of 1446 on sentences *ad inquirendum* to Verona; that of 1492 on interlocutory decisions to Verona. The global decree of 1450 listing all categories of inappellable sentences originally applied to Padua alone, but a year later the Council of Ten extended it to the mainland as a whole.

Subjects too regarded localized Venetian mandates as normative for the entire mainland. During the Quattrocento the Vicentine commune copied and inserted into municipal archives scores of decrees issued for Padua, Feltre, Verona, and other towns to corroborate Vicentine-directed measures or to fill gaps in Vicentine law. When fire destroyed those archives in 1509, Vicentine councillors reconstructed Venetian regulations by collecting ducal letters addressed to other cities, regarding them as binding upon Vicenza or at least carrying a principle valid for Vicenza. In this sense formation of a common law for the mainland owed as much to the initiative of subjects as to the policies of the Dominante.

Subjects took an active voice in unifying the dominion. Suffering equally the burdens of Venetian intervention and taxation, cities of the *terraferma* suspended ancient animosities and collaborated on various projects, above all on joint embassies to Venice. The pressure exerted by combined forces was considerable and generally forced the capital to preserve local rights and cancel unwarranted intrusions. In 1426, for example, Verona and Vicenza sent orators to protest the depredations of exiles and secured Venetian confirmation of their common *ordo antiquus sive statutum* against ill-informed Venetian legislation. The thoroughly impractical decree of 1489, ordering 10 percent of the dominion planted with oaks, fell before the collective resistance of Verona, Vicenza, Padua, Treviso, and Friuli. When in 1500 the Venetian government ordered a one-third increase in local *dazi* rates, protesting orators arrived "from Padua, Vicenza, Verona, Crema, and then from Brescia, all in agreement," and the fisc again came up empty despite the extraordinary needs of war with the Turks.[6] Unification here was a negative force, coalescing common opposition to the ruler, but it was no less effective for that fact.

Mainland communes and dynasties had often been at odds, but their underlying cultures were similar, their governments and institutions generally compatible. Those cities had, above all, closely related political classes. Consolidation of patrician hegemony was by no means an exclusively Vicentine event: the patriciate there shared values, strategies, and resources with counterparts in Verona, Padua, and beyond. Moreover, strong ties of blood and marriage linked great families of the Veneto. This was especially true for Vicenza, where many of the courtiers, captains, and merchants who accompanied Trecento changes of rulership had put down roots. Vicentine families such as the Nogarola, Bevilaqua, Sesso, Cavalli, and Maffei had branches in Verona; the Abriano, Ovetari, Dotti, Conti, and Ungarelli had cousins in Padua; the Malaspina, Anguissola, Cavalcabò, Monza, Roma, and Dalla Seta had *parenti* in Lombardy. In the Quattrocento patricians carefully sustained those networks by intermarriage throughout the dominion. Even families strictly Vicentine in origin now established kinship with patricians far afield: thus Giovanni da Porto married a Gambara of Brescia in 1458, and Lucia da Schio married Tommaso Benvenuti of Crema sometime before 1493.[7]

Young patricians met, built alliances, and renewed their common culture at the University of Padua. In Padua they received, as well, a common education in the law. Standardized training in the *ius comune* and uniform grounding in principles for interpretation and application of municipal codes fostered uniform governance of mainland communes. Padua as regional training ground was not new, of course; nor was the substantial consonance of legal systems throughout northern Italy. But the university's significance was greatly enhanced when those cities came under a single ruler, especially when that ruler insisted on Padua as the sole source of higher education for the dominion.

UNIFICATION: CENTER AND PERIPHERY

Venetians too studied at Padua, and in ever-increasing numbers. Many absorbed the legal culture of the mainland, and several stayed to teach. Most moved on to careers in *terraferma* administration, where they worked with mainland assessors in presiding over municipal tribunals. Or they went home to prominent positions on councils and courts. Common training of judicial personnel is surely one cause of the perceptible (though still partial) breakdown of the traditional isolation of

Venetian and mainland legal cultures. But Venetians had much to teach as well as learn. Mainland lawyers appreciated the flexibility and ductility of Venetian jurisprudence, and they borrowed freely. For example, Venetian procedure for arbitration and private composition of disputes spread from the capital to subject cities, its origins acknowledged with the title *more veneto*. Vicentines began to imitate, as well, characteristic Venetian empiricism, reasoning from experience rather than the more restrictive written law in novel or unusually difficult situations.[8]

More humanistically inclined Venetians shared with mainland counterparts an education under peripatetic teachers such as Guarino, Barzizza, and Filelfo, often completed at the University of Padua. Patriotic historians of the capital once attempted to identify a distinctly Venetian humanism; recent monographic research has more accurately described the situation as a succession of regional schools, often grouped around Venetian stars but always including a wide circle of mainland partipants. Indeed, ideas circulating on the lagoon participated in a broadly Italian world of classical recovery, the more so when flourishing typographies of the area began to diffuse editions of the classics throughout the peninsula and beyond.

The career of Francesco Barbaro demonstrates the close ties of Venetian cultural circles with scholars outside the Veneto, on the one hand, and mainland humanists, on the other. Author of the *De re uxoria* (written for the younger Lorenzo de' Medici), translations from the Greek, and hundreds of letters to correspondents throughout Europe, Barbaro had studied at Padua just when that university began its Quattrocento takeoff, then moved to Florence, where he worked closely with Leonardo Bruni and Niccolò Niccoli among others. He served as podesta of Vicenza in 1425, bringing with him Flavio Biondo as personal secretary. There he presided over the revision of municipal statutes and arranged for communal employment of the learned George of Trebisond as teacher of Greek. Two of his assessors, the Vicentine humanists Evangelista Manelmi and Nicolò Colzè, recorded his heroism at the siege of Brescia in 1438–39. Vicentine patricians several times made him the subject of flattering orations and public letters, as he reached the highest levels of diplomatic service and became a front runner for the dogeship itself. Brescian and Veronese orators, too, sought him as their cities' patron.[9] His case was certainly unique, but it sums up the vigorous contacts and exchanges throughout the Veneto in the Quattrocento.

Not only scholars and governors met to mingle the cultures of mainland and capital. At any given moment many Vicentines were resident in Venice: merchants based at the *hospitium* that the commune maintained on the Riva degli Schiavoni, lawyers working in Venetian courts, and the scores of artisans who show up in notarial and criminal records. In turn, a number of Venetians established more or less permanent domicile in Vicenza, from the humble farmer Filippo di Nicolo da Venezia in Longare to the noble Venier who maintained a house in Lonigo, the noble Badoer with their *habitatione bella,* and the Lombardi who managed their Vicentine estates from a palace in the city. One scandalous case involved the humanist Filippo Diversi, who set up a school for Venetian nobles in Vicenza but received public insults and beatings from his charges. On occasion central councils banished lesser malefactors to Vicenza. The learned doctor Vitale Lando, for example, served a ten-year sentence in the Pigafetta house in the city center.[10] On a short-term basis the flow of peoples between center and periphery was even greater: governors and officials from the one, ambassadors and supplicants from the other, spouses, merchants, and artisans from both.

Increasing Venetian landownership furthered interpenetration of center and periphery. Venetians purchased some 29 percent of Scaligeri holdings in Verona. Comparable purchases of Carraresi lands and later accretions led to the complaint in 1446 that a third of Padua's taxable wealth had passed into Venetian hands.[11] Large-scale land reclamation and villa construction took place only in the Cinquecento, but already by the mid-Quattrocento several noble Venetians were regular residents on mainland estates.

The Vicentine case may, in this regard, have been something of an anomaly. In Vicenza there were no massive transfers at the time of submission, since the commune acquired the *fattoria*'s holdings. It is true that in 1442 Venetian nobles bought many of the Vicentine properties confiscated from the rebel Alvise Dal Verme, but new owners soon sold the bulk of that land to the Vicentine patricians Bartolomeo Chiericati and Giacomo Valmarana. Most of the land that remained in Venetian hands was concentrated to the southeast of the city, the least productive part of the countryside. Local patricians, notably the da Faenza family, bought the rest of Dal Verme's lands. In any case, this was a one-time event. Subsequent references to Venetian ownership are incidental and sporadic. Only in the early Cinquecento was there a second wave of major transfers, such as the public auction of Francesco Monza's lands in San Pietro Intrigogna to the Venetian noble Pasqualino Moro for 3,060 ducats.[12] This signaled a trend, but one that was slow to mature and was only later a major factor in the Vicentine economy.

Cultural exchanges between Venetians and subjects led to progressive mingling of styles and behavioral norms. The important test here is the impact of those exchanges upon mainland customs: whether cultural hegemony accompanied political domination or whether indigenous habits successfully resisted cultural colonization. The former gains support from the fact that the very language of Vicenza, like that of cities as far from the lagoon as Bergamo, received a "Venetian superimposition" that modified and even replaced the local dialect.[13] Artistic evidence, however, is ambiguous, for architecture and painting point in different directions.

Up to the mid-Quattrocento, Vicentine patricians paid homage to the capital by reproducing the distinctly Venetian Gothic idiom in their palaces. This was true not only of families such as the Thiene, who owed their eminence in large part to Venetian favor (and an annual Venetian pension of one thousand ducats), but also original Vicentine notables such as the da Porto and *arrivistes* such as the Arnaldi and Ragona, who had no known connection with Venice. Flamboyant tracery, trefoil and quatrefoil mullions, ogive arches, and rich application of precious stones look slightly out of place on dry land, an awkward if striking transplantation of foreign styles. A more significant aspect of borrowing is the massing of Vicentine palaces: fortresslike, closed off from the public, inward-looking. It is surely no accident that their plan derived from prototypes in Venice, where the aristocracy had long before reached unprecedented levels of self-consciousness and exclusivity.[14]

Yet the Vicentine taste for the Gothic had ended by the third quarter of the Quattrocento. The Renaissance architecture that then prevailed owed nothing to Venice. The leading architect in the new style was Lorenzo da Bologna (in Vicenza 1476–89), building in an eclectic Tuscan-Emilian idiom. Veronese and Lombard builders brought additional elements from the west. Franco Barbieri interprets that movement away from Venetian styles as a deliberate statement, expressing a rising swell of patrician hostility to Venice. Hard evidence for this view is hard to come by. Antipathy is difficult to prove for Vicenza, especially since Lorenzo's patrons—the Thiene, Arnaldi, and Valmarana—were, if anything, leaders of the pro-Venetian faction. It may simply have been the case that local preferences changed and Venice, late in abandoning its cherished Gothic, could not supply a replacement. Venetian Renaissance styles were themselves eclectic: the master builder Mauro Codussi was a Bergamasque, influenced strongly by Tuscans such as Alberti and Michelozzo. A political explanation for an architectural shift is suggestive, but the question must remain open.

Painting seems to have moved in the other direction. Early and mid-Quattrocento Vicentine artists drew from International Gothic and Veronese models. Later, with the introduction of distinctly Renaissance styles, they borrowed from the Paduan school around Squarcione. Again there was a turning point around 1480, but this time towards Venice. Vicentine painters such as Bartolomeo Montagna, Marcello Fogolino, and Giovanni Buonconsiglio fell under the influence of Giovanni Bellini, and Vicentine painting remained within a Belliniesque style well into the Cinquecento. Major patronage traveled in the same direction: Bellini's great *Baptism of Christ* (ca. 1501) still hangs in its original position in the Dominican church of Santa Corona.

Cultural exchange did not simply consist of acceptance or rejection by subjects of the Dominante's models. The capital demanded as well as supplied. When Venetians moved out among the ruling classes of Renaissance Italy as diplomats, governors, or landlords, their merchant culture proved inadequate to new social standing and political status. Nobles were obliged, and eager, to imitate the manners of mainland counterparts. It was not difficult to master refined learning and eloquent rhetoric, with training by tutors and university professors. Acquiring the refinements of noble leisure was considerably more difficult. The neochivalric was much in vogue, for example, and so celebrations in the capital came to include jousts and tournaments. Venetians were not very experienced in such activities, however, and Paduans or Trevisans frequently sponsored displays. Contestants were drawn from the *terraferma* and neighboring states. The emergent villa culture of the mainland exercised an even more powerful attraction. As local patricians expanded their rural holdings, they upgraded country houses to accommodate lengthening stays in the summer months. Venetians soon followed, whiling away the hours in performance and learned discussion. Harsh criticism of a corrupt and seductive *villeggiatura* by conservatives such as Girolamo Priuli could not stem the tide. Caterina Cornaro's glittering court at Asolo (after 1489) was a portent of things to come.[15]

Direct ties bound the mainland patriciate to some of the greater families of Venice. To take only the Vicentine example, the Orgiano (Aureliano) had branches in Venice and Vicenza. Emilia Brazoduro married Gianfrancesco Sanudo, her countrywoman Fiordelisia Brandolini married Giovanni Versi, Ugolino Sesso was betrothed to the Venetian noblewoman Mabilia Grimani, and Giovanni da Porto married Lucrezia Zeno. This is only a sampling.[16] Intermarriage brought advantages to both sides: prestige to status-hungry Vicentines and rich dowries to straitened Venetian houses. Not so incidentally, marriage extended kinship networks between center and periphery, binding ruler and subject with personal as well as governmental ties.

Indeed, there could be no mutual isolation of Venetian and mainland ruling classes once the Republic made careers in mainland administration available to local patricians. Rapid conquest in Lombardy, the Veneto, Friuli, and Dalmatia soon outstripped Venice's capacity to supply trained officials, particularly as overseas commitments also grew. The obvious solution was to utilize the pools of underemployed, well-educated, and locally knowledgeable subjects. Vicentines, for example, nearly monopolized the position of collateral general of the Venetian army, akin to chief of finance, administration, and munitions. Belpietro Manelmi's tenure of four decades provided a model of vigilance and efficiency. Captains and Venetian councillors alike respected his expertise, and the Senate noted his death in 1455 with great sorrow. His predecessor Antonio Facino and successors Valerio and Ludovico Chiericati, Gian Filippo Orgiano, and Evangelista Manelmi were all Vicentine patricians, as were the vice collaterals Gian Niccolo Manzini, Belpietro and Chierighino Chiericati, Piero Camucci, Andrea Orgiano, and Gian Marco da Arzignano. Basilio della Scola served with great distinction as a military engineer and captain of artillery, receiving a special commendation from the Senate in 1496 for service in the "Gallic wars." Roberto Thiene held a sizable *condotta* in the Visconti wars and later in the campaigns of the Morea, along with kinsmen Uguccio and Giorgio.[17] The *Libri commemoriali* record hundreds of lesser Vicentine careers in the Venetian military.

Vicentine patricians were even more common in the Venetian civil and ecclesiastical administration. The altogether unexceptional Francesco Angiolelli, for example, served as pretorian vicar and assessor in Padua, Belluno, and Crema. His fellow citizens Evangelista Manelmi and Nicolo Colzè served in Brescia. Other patricians appear as castellans, chancellors, pretorian vicars, *governatori alle entrade pubbliche*, governors in the Romagna, envoys to Dalmatia, advisors to Venetian ambassadors, and secretary to the king of Cyprus.[18] Giovanni Chiericati, bishop of Cattaro, and his kinsman Leonello, bishop of Traù and later Concordia, both rose as high in the ecclesiastical hierarchy as was possible for non-Venetians.

PERSISTENT DIVIDE: CENTER AND PERIPHERY

Rewarding and prestigious as those middle-level positions might have been, they were the upper limit for Vicentines in Venetian service. In the same vein, demographic interpenetration and exchanges of ideas and values signal movement towards unification but stop short of it. Governmental policy only partially broke down the compartmentalization of the dominion.

Only members of the Venetian nobility could hold positions of real authority such as podesta, captain, or *provveditore*. That nobility was nearly closed to subjects. The central government occasionally granted patrician status to foreign princes in order to cement alliances or reward service but almost never did so for worthies of the mainland. A proposal of 1411 to open up Venetian rulership by accepting nobles from Zara into the upper administration was a quick failure, and the issue was not again raised. The Senate made the Vicentine Gian Piero Proti a Venetian patrician and appointed him podesta of Verona and captain of Padua; but his case is both unique and very early—he died in 1412.[19] The nobility of the mainland could not aspire to entry into the nobility of Venice, at least not until the seventeenth century, when desperate state finances forced the Republic to accept well-heeled aristocrats such as Vicenza's Angarano, Valmarana, and Arnaldi into the Maggior Consiglio.

In theory, subjects should have enjoyed at least the lesser advantages of inclusion in the Venetian dominion. By a concession of 1406 the Republic regarded Vicentine citizens as Venetian citizens *de intus*. Central provisions soon accorded that status to citizens of Verona, Padua, Treviso, Feltre, and Belluno, shortly thereafter to citizens of Zara, and, eventually, to those of Brescia and Crema.[20] By establishment of a unitary citizenship, the Republic declared its intentions to integrate subjects into a unified state. In more practical terms that citizenship conferred trading rights in Venice, eligibility for public office in the capital, and access to Venice's well-organized charities.

The real impact of that legislation is open to question. A single document suggests that the central government respected at least some of its terms. Around 1450 a Venetian merchants' court and a court reserved for foreigners fought for jurisdiction in a case involving a Veronese citizen. Ducal councillors decided in favor of the merchants' court, since all Veronese (and, specifically, Vicentines, Paduans, and Trevisans) "[were] Venetians *de intus* and should be treated as Venetian citizens, as [was] stipulated in the privileges conferred by [our] Ducal Dominion." But this was an isolated confirmation of the privilege, and in any case it involved only economic privileges. Any aspiration to political access or social integration proved illusory. Venetian intent was clear: in 1450 central councils labeled mainland peoples as "foreign subjects" (*subditi forenses*), with accent on their foreignness. When peoples of the mainland moved to Venice, they suffered explicit disabilities. In 1457, for example, while discussing the magistracy of the Sopraconsoli, which assisted impoverished citizens, the Senate drew a sharp distinction between "resident Venetian citizens," who were eligible for relief, and the Paduans, Vicentines, and Veronese legally domiciled in Venice, who were not.[21] Nor did subjects acquire positions within the bureaucracy of Venice itself.

The universal citizenship promised in 1406 had become a dead letter. The only hope for Vicentines of integration into Venetian society lay in acquisition of an individual grant of Venetian citizenship, but probably no more than a dozen Vicentines secured that privilege in the course of the Quattrocento. That effective refusal to accept subjects signals a salient feature of the Venetian state. In Tuscany, likewise, citizens of recently annexed cities acquired citizenship of the capital and gained eligibility for public office, major guilds, and other civic benefits. But unlike their Venetian counterparts, Tuscan subjects were able to take full advantage of their new-found status.[22]

Disabilities were reciprocal. Venetian nobles could not take part in the municipal councils of the mainland, plead legal cases before communal tribunals, or collect *dazi*. Central councils based those strictures on pragmatic considerations: that Venetian nobles embarassed the Republic by their ignorance and arrogance in legal pleading; that they were too casual in collecting taxes. But more fundamental principles were at work. Venetian policy generally excluded its citizens from Vicentine public life as it excluded Vicentines from access to that of the capital. Two examples illustrate the diaphragm between rulers and subjects, a diaphragm occasionally permeable but in the main resistant to transfer from either side.

The law of the *terraferma* was a territorial law. If a Veronese committed a crime in Padua, he was tried in Paduan courts according to Paduan law. But Venetians and those in their employ held extraterritorial and privileged status. Disputes between Venetian citizens and locals could not be decided by *consilium sapientis* but received summary decision by the podesta or his vicar. The captain heard disputes involving Venetian troops. Rectors judged cases involving the podesta's kin "according to Venetian ordinances." The Venetian *curia forinsecorum* heard lawsuits involving land rights if the plaintiff was a Venetian citizen. In this sense, Venetian citizenship conferred a personal law, rendering Venetians nearly immune from the law or courts of the mainland. Central decrees, then, reinforced the different judicial status of Venetians and mainland subjects and abrogated the principle of territoriality that had long been characteristic of Venetian law.[23]

As a corollary, judgments in any mainland city were valid only within the confines of the *civitas*. In certain categories of violent crime, the sentence of a podesta might be binding in neighboring cities or even the *terraferma* as a whole—but not in Venice. Exile from Venice, on the other hand, automatically denoted exile from the mainland dominion, and local governors had to execute those sentences. In civil cases too, rectors had to enforce sentences, contracts, purchases, and leases made in Venice;[24] but local judges could not compel Venetian magistrates to execute mainland judgments. Jurisdiction of the center extended to the periphery, but the converse was not true.

In addition, when central councils established unitary Venetian citizenship in the heady days after initial mainland conquests, those who set policy may then have entertained the notion of full assimilation of subjects. When the central government thereafter reasserted Venetian exclusivity, however, each subject commune retained a distinct citizenship. The logic of the Republic's endorsement of particularism then led rulers to an extraordinary act of self-limitation, as they gradually ceded the right to regulate membership in subject communes. After 1410, it has been noted, petitions for Vicentine citizenship had to receive the opinion of municipal councils before final hearing in Venice. After 1440 the recommendation of the commune was binding on the Signoria. After 1460 no one could be created a citizen of Vicenza "except according to the statutes and ordinances of Vicenza." At least Venetian policy was consistent. In closing off membership in the capital, the Republic allowed subject cities to close off their own memberships. Citizenship was not only exclusive but mutually exclusive.

The test for unification may fairly stand for other tests of modernization. Formation of bureaucracy, in the sense of disinterested functionaries governing in the name of an impersonal state, made negligible progress. Certainly the Quattrocento saw the creation of specialized magistracies, notably for fiscal management. The Council of Ten increasingly subordinated these magistracies, effectively imposing hierarchy upon a previously fragmented administration. But new magistracies operated on an ad hoc basis, cleaning up the worst dysfunctions of mainland governance, and tended more to absorb functions of extant Venetian magistracies than to supplant local agencies. Nor did those magistracies, in the judgment of their superiors, function much more efficiently than their predecessors. Ordinary administration remained with the skeletal staff of a few rectors, assessors, chamberlains, chancellors, and constables, unchanged in numbers or powers since 1404. The contrast here is with Florence, which blanketed the rural sections of its dominion in particular with "magistracies and offices dependent directly upon the center."[25]

An alternative model locates bureaucratization in the changing position of local notables, reduced from independent actors to subordinate agents within a hierarchically ordered, centrally controlled state. Here, too, the first century of Venetian dominion produced little change. While generally cooperative in commonsense matters such as the suppression of violence, Vicentine patricians retained a fierce independence that extended to frequent, bitter confrontations of Venetian governors and challenges to central intervention. Local patricians never perceived themselves otherwise than as directors of the Vicentine commune. Certainly they never claimed to act for the Venetian state.

Centralization points in the same direction. Venetian supervision was probably more intense by the early Cinquecento than it had been in the preceding century. Witness to this is the barrage of almost daily letters from the Council of Ten, directed especially at tightening up military and fiscal management. But on two grounds it is doubtful that increased vigilance actually produced more effective central authority. Firstly, the Ten's complaints were no less shrill in 1500 than they had been at the inception of those letters three decades before. Fortifications were still in ruinous condition, smuggling across the northern passes was unabated, and arrears in tax revenues were, if anything, greater. Local resources for ensuring compliance were no more effective than they had been a half-century before, and the recalcitrance of communes was hardly diminished.

Secondly, the Ten's undoubtedly greater powers in 1500 do not necessarily indicate serious erosion of local prerogatives. Many, if not all, came from transfer of jurisdictions within the central government, as the Ten progressively crowded out traditional magistracies such as the Maggior Consiglio, Senate, and Avogaria di Comun. Overall Venetian powers in 1500 were not much greater than they had been in 1404. In some sectors—appeals, petitions, local citizenship—they were actually reduced. In others—taxation, criminal justice—local communes had built up a formidable array of *privilegia* to defend against future encroachments. Again the contrast is with Florence. There, as Chittolini has suggested, the Quattrocento produced a radical shift in policy. In early decades, Florence left subject cities as "tributaries," never effecting true annexation; the dominion was a "mosaic of lands loosely aggregated rather than a unitary state structure." This gave way to more incisive central intervention. Imposing law, placing its own officials, and radically reorganizing territorial jurisdictions, Florence built up a comparatively compact, well-articulated regional state.[26]

PERSISTENT DIVIDE: THE MAINLAND

In a similar vein, Venetian policy severely compromised unity among mainland cities. If anything, the Republic sponsored fragmentation by raising formerly subordinate towns such as Cologna, Asolo, and Bassano to independent *podestarie* and placing podestas in larger provincial towns such as Marostica and Lonigo. By the terms of Venetian-backed *privilegia,* each city retained its own commune and municipal law, collected tolls and tariffs, created its own citizens, made its own ordinances, used its own weights and measures, and circulated coins with a municipal stamp. Each dealt directly with the central government. There were no regional confederations or intermediate magistracies such as the captaincies, vicariates, leagues, or federations found in the Florentine state.

Imposition of Venetian decrees for the entire mainland may have standardized administration but, since municipal communes and governors actually executed decrees, uniform law did nothing to bind cities together. Too, Venetian mandates largely addressed special cases and in no way derogated the municipal statutes that directed ordinary governance. These statutes continued to exhibit the widest possible variance from one city to the next, with Venetian confirmations sanctioning jurisprudential particularism. Again the contrast with Tuscany, where the Florentine government both issued and standardized the laws of subjects, is noteworthy.

Specific Venetian decrees frequently reinforced divisions within the mainland. Ostensibly to preserve the sanctity of Paduan agricultural contracts and maintain a sufficient labor force in the Paduan countryside, for example, the doge in 1441 curbed migration between Vicenza and Padua by canceling the authority of Vicenza to offer tax exemptions to immigrants. Communes retained the right to block exports to neighboring cities, though all were "brothers born of common parents." Padua had to ask Vicentine permission even to purchase alabaster for the shrine of San Antonio. Venetian annonary decrees that required free transport of grain to the capital but forbade shipments between cities likewise preserved barriers.[27] Only in 1794 did the central government abolish tolls between cities of the mainland. The principle of equality between subjects, "that one not be superior to another," was as much a force for separation as for unification.

Nor could occasional cooperation on anti-Venetian embassies eradicate ancient enmities. Civic patriotism remained strong, fueled by ongoing hostility to neighbors and former rulers. Vicentines were disinclined to forget old grudges. Doggerel of April 1405, for example, described Vicenza as founded between two dragons, the wild beasts of Padua and the madmen of Verona. A Vicentine patrician crept into the cathedral of Padua in November 1405 and destroyed the ceremonial cart that was symbol of Paduan independence, thus fulfilling Merlin's ancient prophecy and presaging Padua's fall to Venetian troops. When in mid-century Paduans needed Vicentine alabaster, they asked permission in letters so excessively polite that we can be sure that antipathy was far from smoothed over. At the end of the century, Pagliarino's

Croniche pointedly included copies of Vicenza's 1404 letters that expressed terror at the prospect of the city again falling under the "perfidious Paduan enemy." His historical narrative took every opportunity to underscore the cruelty of Paduan lordship and the elation of Vicentines at their liberation.[28] Vicentines subjected Verona to less invective but regarded their neighbor with no greater concilation: the communes never settled a bitter feud over borders and flood controls, despite a century of Venetian attempts at mediation. A single century of common submission to Venice could not erase centuries of friction.

CONFLICT AND ACCOMMODATION

The notion of an ineradicable divide between ruler and subject, variously defined by Ventura and Cozzi, has become something of a commonplace. Most historians, comparing the Venetian experience with the progressive unification that moved most European states towards modernity, have viewed that "profound fracture" in terms of Venetian failure: failure to create a unitary ruling class, to eradicate special (aristocratic) privileges, to attract the loyalty of subjects, to undertake the reforms necessary to keep pace with advances elsewhere. The short-term consequence was a state seething with the hostility of broad sectors of the population, particularly local patriciates resentful of the "humiliating subjection" that denied them any real share in the state. The long-term effect was the stagnation and gradual decay of the state itself, leading to humiliating collapse before Napoleon's armies in 1797. Whereas the Milanese or Florentine states evolved parallel with European counterparts, the Venetian state was stuck in a structural impasse from the moment of its construction.[29]

But that model, teleological and judgmental as it is, puts a terrible and probably impossible burden upon the Venetian state and ruling class. The test for modernity is useful, revealing much of what is distinctive about the state, but the expectation of modernity preordains the state to failure by demanding of its managers a mentality that was not their own. As Gaetano Cozzi has pointed out, it is unfair to blame Venetian nobles of 1500 for failing to create a unitary state when neither they nor anyone else at the time held such an ideal.[30] At the other end of the chronological arc, the Republic was hardly the only state to fall before Napoleon. It is an act of special pleading to single out its rulers for opprobrium.

The Venetian territorial state lasted for nearly four centuries, an excellent record for the time. As the Republic did not maintain its authority by raw force or intimidation, and internal resistance never seriously threatened that authority, stability is as persuasive an interpretation as stagnation. Four hundred years of comparative tranquillity suggests broad accommodation, a pragmatic adaptation by subjects and rulers alike to the situation at hand.

A conclusion of stability does not willfully ignore concerted opposition to Venetian governance. In Padua, notably, patricians kept alive the anti-Venetian struggle even after the possibility of restoring the Carraresi dynasty was extinguished with the execution of Marsilio da Carrara in 1435. Relations with Venice deteriorated to the point of a further plot in 1489 and a communal threat in 1498 to renounce the articles of submission. When in 1483 the Republic tried to melt down a Veronese altarpiece for coinage, outraged citizens threatened to give their town to the enemy.[31]

Nor does the model of accommodation overstate Vicentine compliance. It is true that Vicenza had not been truly autonomous since the early thirteenth century and seems to have lost any impulse towards independence. Early in the century partisans of the Scaligeri and Carraresi fomented revolt in Verona and Padua, with reflex actions in the Vicentine, but Vicentines did not instigate an indigenous anti-Venetian movement. When a Hungarian army marched to the gates of Vicenza in 1413, ostensibly to restore the della Scala to their ancient lordship, it found no welcome. Later incidents of sedition—a minor patrician's plot (in Cremona) to hand Vicenza over to a Milanese army—do not add up to hard evidence for an attempt to throw off Venetian rule.[32]

Nonetheless the Vicentine commune was hardly supine before Venetian authority. The hundreds of communal protests against Venetian infringements of *privilegia* testify to endemic day-to-day conflict. Vigilant lest any slight irregularity provide precedent for future usurpations of prerogatives, the commune confronted any and all Venetian magistracies.

Those specific, often highly technical protests provide a key to the internal dynamics of the state. Resistance to Venetian interference reveals far more than romantic, anachronistic gestures of rebellion. In an extreme reading acts of resistance can be viewed as microrebellions, and perhaps they were so in the sense that all conflict is resistance to authority—but that was not how rulers perceived them at the time. Orators were outspoken, but they never aroused accusations of disloyalty. Confrontation and protest did not add up to *lèse majesté*.

Conflict, rather, was the means towards a general distribution of authority between center and periphery. Only disputation could clarify the initially uncertain boundaries between Venetian and communal jurisdictions. The pacts of 1404 and 1406 were rather generic, confirming both Venetian *arbitrium* and Vicentine *privilegia*. The guiding principle of Venetian governance, that administration should proceed according to local structures as long as these were consonant with divine commands, justice, and Venetian honor, likewise left the relationship only vaguely defined. There always remained broad areas, especially in fiscal and criminal management, where competences overlapped and generated friction. Here conflict allowed adjustment, constantly raising and resolving outstanding issues. In a century without definitive constitutions or comprehensive statements of policy, small confrontations served to define a larger coexistence.

Protest, confrontation, complaint, and embassies are signs of conflict, but they also contained conflict within carefully structured, formalized procedures for resolution and so headed off more overt resistance. The fact that resolution was generally pacific indicates, as well, broad consensus of center and periphery. Accommodation was generous, though never placid, because it was based upon mutually limited ambitions and a realistic acceptance of the possibilities and resources available to each side. Vicentines could not hope for independence, nor did Venetians aspire to absolute mastery. The old model of political formations, that states inexorably tend towards centralization, no longer has much currency. But neither does a central tenet of liberal, especially Risorgimento historiography, that subjected peoples invariably drive towards freedom.

The Republic aimed at the overall security of the state, at maintenance of its own economy and regional preeminence, but not at such thorough control as to divert the resources necessary for Italian and overseas commitments. The central government was content if the hinterland remained relatively pacific and contributed to the capital's larger designs. Judicially, it could allow local agencies a free hand, retaining only the potential for unlimited intervention against threats to state security. It excoriated local violence but felt no need to replace local magistracies. The Republic needed to establish mechanisms for appeal and petitions but could safely pare down those mechanisms when local judiciaries proved sufficiently equitable and magistracies of the capital proved unable to provide superior justice. Fiscally, the massive sums that flowed to the capital adequately served general Venetian interests. If revenues never matched expectations, indeed always fell below established quotas, the unpleasant alternative was expenditure of considerable exertion on substitution of a central bureaucracy for local agencies. Annonary legislation, though widely flouted, secured adequate food supplies for the capital; and thorough enforcement was beyond the capacity of any fifteenth-century state. Having satisfied primary aims, the Republic could empower local communes to handle secondary concerns.

Vicentine patricians were content to secure confirmation of their control of the commune and confirmation of the commune's control of countryside and urban underclasses. Provided with a secure base of power, prestige, and wealth, they had little impetus for greater autonomy. Indeed there is no indication that they seriously entertained such ambitions. The advantages to docility were great; protection of privileges against fractious rural communes and lesser Venetian officials, employment in the Venetian army and *terraferma* administration, the chance to participate in the greater Venetian economy. For their part senior councillors could well entrust local management to the generally loyal, well-educated, and entrenched Vicentine elite. In any case the alternative, that elite's replacement by a professionalized administration, was too costly to contemplate. The Republic had to retain and occasionally deploy the right of intervention to protect the unprivileged from the flagrant abuses of the privileged: hence defense of peasants, widows, and paupers. But in the normal course of events, that protection did not require infringement of the overall *privilegia* of communes and patriciates.

Conflict took place, as well, within an overall climate of loyalty and appreciation that considerably eased friction between center and periphery. Immediately after submission, for example, the commune of Vicenza requested and received the privileged title of *Fidelissima*, which signified special devotion. On several occasions, Vicentines received ducal letters of congratulation for particular acts of support in resisting invasions; each time, municipal notaries copied the letter scores of times, added those letters to previous documents attesting to Vicentine loyalty, and distributed dossiers of allegiance throughout city archives. Archives abound, as well, with such tokens as effusive orations to podestas that extol their services to the city, or poems congratulating a podesta on the birth of an heir.[33] Speakers and writers actively promoted definition of the new dominion on terms favorable to Venice: Vicenza as freely offered to Venice, as firstborn of the Republic's growing brood; Vicentines as dutiful children, as limbs of the body politic obedient to a wise and protecting head, as servants to a benevolent master. The cult of loyalty was enough advanced by the late fifteenth century that Pagliarino organized the second book of his *Croniche* around it: "On the Faithfulness of Vicentines."

Display was not only literary and rhetorical. For example, communes frequently, if illegally, held ceremonies at the end of a podesta's term office, at which local humanists made speeches of thanks for wise and just administration. In one Vicentine witness to this custom, the podesta Domenico Moro paused on his return to write a note of thanks for the "many generous and ample gifts" and to express his pleasure that his "administration of the city was pleasing and well received by that magnificent commune." Other, more concrete records of loyalty filled Vicenza. Along with its counterparts throughout the mainland, the urban commune placed a sculpted lion of St. Mark on a pillar in the main square and celebrated anniversaries of Venetian victories. In a more intimate event, the Vicentine College of Notaries adopted the winged lion as its insignia.[34]

The hostility of other cities' patricians to Venice cannot be discounted. Early humanists such as Ognibene Scola and Guarino indulged in guardedly anti-Venetian orations and letters, and some of their successors were notably cool. There is come evidence, however, that professed Vicentine affection for Venetian rule was not an isolated phenomenon. Trevisans, or at least the most influential among them, welcomed return to the Venetian fold in 1388 and again in 1509, after brief experiences with other rulers. One of the most vivid accounts of the 1435 plot to restore the Carraresi came from a fiercely pro-Venetian Paduan, evidently delighted at the attempt's failure. Varanini has noted the relatively tranquil entry of Verona into the Venetian dominion and the Veronese patriate's lack of resentment of Venetian fiscal administration. Veronese too grew fond of individual Venetian officials.[35] Any model of unremitting antagonism of periphery to center ignores a large part of the evidence. For Vicenza, that evidence all but predominates.

Venetian expressions of appreciation cost the Republic little, but they were not necessarily false for that fact. The doge noted in 1435, for example, that Vicentines' loyalty and prompt obedience was long known, but that their faithfulness and fervor had been so exceptional during the recent conspiracy that they deserved special commendation, praise, and perpetual favor.[36] In fact, Vicentines had captured Marsilio da Carrara and provided a mass escort for the trip to the Paduan jail, all quite spontaneously. Venetian relief at the extinction of the Carraresi, and with them any serious threat to dominion in Padua, was entirely genuine. In a century that saw Venetian forces engaged against Hungarians and later Turks to the northeast, Germans to the north, Milanese to the west, Ferraresi to the south, and Turks overseas, a pacified hinterland was a valued asset.

The sincerity of subjects need not be at issue. Particular acts of loyalty brought immediate rewards. The central government suspended the salt tax in 1413 when Vicentines resisted the Hungarian invasion. Faithful service in the Milanese wars earned cancellation of a forced loan in 1435, drastic reduction of the *dadia delle lanze* quota in 1441, and fiscal subsidies of five thousand ducats in 1444.[37] In the long term, praising the podesta was a good investment in the future, for

rectors passed to higher office in Venice and influenced central decisions. Vicentines particularly heaped praise on Francesco Barbaro, one
suspects, not only for his undoubted brilliance but also for his widely
perceived chances for the dogeship.

But the rhetoric of loyalty had a more profound intent as well.
Effusive displays of affection flattered rulers but also reassured them.
Self-serving or not, persistent and unanimous praise evidently convinced Venetians of the good will of subjects. It also persuaded Venetians of Vicenza's worthiness to retain extraordinary privileges. Specific conflict, then, took place within a climate of professed allegiance.
Rulers could not mistake protest for disloyalty when Vicentines were so
vociferously faithful, hence could more readily accept their petitions.

Still, the fervency and frequency with which Vicentines declared
allegiance suggests considerable sincerity, particularly from patricians,
who were chief beneficiaries of the Republic's protection. Venetian rule
was probably more mild and equitable, and left greater space for local
initiative, than that of the Scaligeri or Visconti. Certainly it was preferable to rule by the Carraresi or Hapsburgs. It offered recompense for
subordination in the form of *privilegia,* administrative offices, and
hegemony over countryside and urban proletariate. Trade was probably better off from expanded access to Venetian markets; patricians
could evade taxes or offload them onto other sectors of the population.

Too, loyalty to Venice did not jeopardize deeply rooted nativist
sentiments. Vicentines found it entirely possible, as one early Cinquecento chronicle demonstrates, to couple fiercely pro-Venetian sentiments with a belief in the continued magnificence of the Vicentine
republic.[38] Subjects continued traditional municipal processions, local
cults, and literary invocations of a glorious civic past, while simultaneously they took evident pride in participation in the great Venetian
enterprise. These were distinct levels of allegiance, seldom in conflict.
Articulate Vicentines never hinted that the coming of Venetian rule
derogated their ancient *libertas.* If they felt so, they were too prudent to
jeopardize Venetian good will by open declaration.

Epilogue

On 11 May 1509 the forces of the League of Cambrai routed Venetian troops at the battle of Agnadello. Three weeks later the army of Maximilian Hapsburg entered Vicenza, led by the Vicentine noble Leonardo Trissino. The commune promptly negotiated the city's submission and paid some of the expenses of the conquering army. All of the most important families quickly went over to Maximilian, and the patriciate as a whole turned out for his formal entry a few weeks later.

The imperial restoration was short-lived. Most patricians were really trimmers, shifting with prevailing winds. As soon as Maximilian left, they began to complain of the high costs and poor behavior of his army of occupation. Once the initial euphoria died down, even the most diehard loyalists saw that Maximilian's dream of restoring direct imperial rule could not be realized. Their suspicions became certainties when Maximilian, lacking the troops and money to occupy the mainland, pulled his forces back towards Austria. In the countryside, meanwhile, Schio had predictably defected to Maximilian, but most peasants stayed loyal to Venice and harassed the retreating Austrian army. No Vicentine expressed regret when Venetian troops reoccupied the city on 12 November. The Vicentine nobles who had entered Maximilian's service, once assured of Venetian clemency, gradually straggled back to the city.[1]

The Venetian return was an obvious opening for radical reform of the dominion. Had senior councillors wished to remedy recent defection and a century of intermittent irritation, they certainly held the power to reduce communal prerogatives, install permanent bureaucratic structures, or at least discipline local nobilities. Yet rulers and subjects chose not to overturn arrangements worked out in the Quattrocento. On 17 November 1509, Venetian officials joined with local *deputati* to present a simple proposal, which the Vicentine Great Council quickly passed. For some 105 years, the commune declared, Vicenza had been governed in a just and pious manner. Now by divine favor it had returned under Venetian protection. The commune would send ten orators to Venice, to request that Venice again take the most faithful Vicenza into its heart and that the doge in his clemency restore the Vicentine commune in its ancient prerogatives, immunities, exemptions, concessions, customs, laws, statutes, and jurisdictions.[2] The embassy departed on schedule, and the doge agreed in full to its petition.

The Republic reconstructed the mainland state, that is, precisely according to original principles. It confirmed both Venetian *arbitrium* and Vicentine *privilegia,* to coexist in uneasy but, on the whole, tolerable consensus for the next three centuries. Rulers imposed no sanctions upon the patriciate as a class and scarcely stripped the commune of its authority in city or countryside. Given precedent governance, and current resources, neither ruler nor subject could realistically hope for any other solution.

Abbreviations

ARCHIVES

Florence
  A.S.F.: Archivio di Stato di Firenze
Padua
  A.S.Pad.: Archivio di Stato di Padova
  Bib. Civ.: Biblioteca del Museo Civico di Padova
  Bib. Univ.: Biblioteca Universitaria
Venice
  A.S.Ven.: Archivio di Stato di Venezia
    Captain Commission: Senato Secreta, Commissioni, Formulari 6, ff. 8v–12v
    Podesta Commission: ibid., ff. 1r–8r
  Marciana: Biblioteca Nazionale Marciana
    Auditori Capitulare: Latin V, 67 (2518) (=Capitulare Auditorum Novorum Venetiarum)
    Auditori Prattica: Italian VII, 1759 (8419) (=La prattica dell'offitio degli Auditori Novi delle sententie)
Verona
  A.S.Ver.: Archivio di Stato di Verona
  Bib. Com.: Biblioteca Comunale di Verona
Vicenza
  A.S.Vic.: Archivio di Stato di Vicenza
    Coll. Not.: Collegio dei Notai
    Corp. Sopp.: Corporazioni Soppresse
    Notai: Fondo Notarile (=Fondo notai defunti)
    Testamenti: Fondo testamenti bombacini
  Arch. Curia: Archivio della Curia Vescovile
  Bertoliana: Biblioteca Civica Bertoliana
    Arch. Fracanzani: Archivio Privato Fracanzani
    Arch. Thiene: Archivio Privato Thiene
    Arch. Torre: Archivio Torre (=Archivio Comunale)
    Gonzati: Camera Gonzati (citations by modern numbers)

PRINTED SOURCES

1404 Capitula: from *Ius municipale vicentinum* (Vicenza, 1707), pp. 305–16

1406 Capitula: from *Ius municipale vicentinum* (Venice, 1567), ff. 180r–85r

Ius municipale vicentinum: Ius municipale vicentinum cum additione partium Illustrissimi Dominij (Venice, 1567)

Privilegia Veronae: Privilegia Magnificae Civitatis Veronae (Venice, 1588)

Statuta Patavina: Statuta Patavina (Venice, 1528)

Statuta Veronae: Statuta Magnificae Civitatis Veronae (Venice, 1561)

CITATIONS

References make use of the following conventions:
 b.: busta (unbound collection of documents)
 f., ff.: folio(s)
 r: recto
 reg.: *registro*
 rub.: rubric
 s.a.: *sub annum*
 s.d.: *sub datum*
 s.v.: *sub verbum*
 v: verso
 #(#): number(s)

The calendar year of most mainland cities began at Christmas, that of Padua (occasionally) on the Feast of the Circumcision, that of Venice on 1 March. All dates have been put in modern form, except when reference is made to a dated document in an unfoliated collection.

Notes

INTRODUCTION

1. Niccolò Machiavelli, *The Prince*, trans. George Bull (Harmondsworth: Penguin, 1961), ch. 3; and see also chs. 12, 20; idem, *The Discourses*, ed. Bernard Crick (Harmondsworth: Penguin, 1970) 1:6; 2:1–5, 19, 21, 30; 3:31; Francesco Guicciardini, *Considerations on the Discourses of Machiavelli*, in *Selected Writings*, trans. Cecil Grayson (London: Oxford University Press, 1965), p. 116. On Machiavelli's view of Venice see Franco Gaeta, "L'idea di Venezia," in *Storia della cultura veneta*, III, 3 ed. Girolamo Arnaldi and Manlio Pastore Stocchi (Vicenza: Neri Pozza, 1982), esp. pp. 605–10; Innocenzo Cervelli, *Machiavelli e la crisi dello stato veneziano* (Naples: Guida, 1974), chs. 2, 3, 7, 8.

2. Raffaino de' Caresini, quoted in Angelo Ventura, "Il dominio di Venezia nel Quattrocento," in *Florence and Venice: Comparisons and Relations* (Florence: La Nuova Italia, 1979), 1:169; similarly Lorenzo de' Monacis, quoted in Angelo Ventura, "Scrittori politici e scritture di governo," in *Storia della cultura veneta*, III, 3, pp. 524–25. In general see Cervelli, *Machiavelli*, ch. 6; Edward Muir, *Civic Ritual in Renaissance Venice* (Princeton: Princeton University Press, 1981), esp. pp. 119–56.

3. John Easton Law, "Un confronto fra due stati 'rinascimentali': Venezia e il dominio sforzesco," in *Gli Sforza a Milano e in Lombardia e i loro rapporti con gli stati italiani ed europei (1450–1535)* (Milan: Cisalpino-Goliardica, 1982), pp. 401–4; James S. Grubb, "When Myths Lose Power: Four Decades of Venetian Historiography," *Journal of Modern History* 58 (1986):72–74.

4. Bernardo Giustiniani, *De origine urbis Venetiarum rebusque gestis a Venetis Libri quindecim*, in *Thesaurus antiquitatum et historiarum Italie*, ed. J. G. Graevius (Louvain, 1722), col. 172; Gaspare Contarini, *De magistratibus et republica venetorum*, in ibid., col. 45; Franco Gaeta, "Storiografia, coscienza nazionale e politica culturale nella Venezia del Rinascimento," in *Storia della cultura veneta*, III, 1, ed. Girolamo Arnaldi and Manlio Pastore Stocchi (Vicenza: Neri Pozza, 1980), p. 18. In general see Cervelli, *Machiavelli*, chs. 6, 8, esp. pp. 293, 394.

5. Samuele Romanin, *Storia documentata di Venezia* (Venice, 1855), 4:45–46, 50–51; Carlo Cattaneo, *La città considerata come principio ideale delle istorie italiane* (Florence: Vallecchi, 1931), pp. 129–30; Lester J. Libby, "Venetian History and Political Thought after 1509," *Studies in the Renaissance* 20 (1973):29–30.

6. Elena Fasano Guarini, "Gli stati dell'Italia centro-settentrionale tra Quattro e Cinquecento: continuità e trasformazioni," *Società e Storia* 21 (1983): 618–19; Jacob Burckhardt, *The Civilization of the Renaissance in Italy*, trans. Hajo Holborn (New York: Modern Library, 1954), pp. 4, 7, 9, 50–51, 61, 72. In general see Giorgio Chittolini, "Alcune considerazioni sulla storia politico-istituzionale del tardo Medioevo: alle origini degli 'stati regionali,'" *Annali dell'Istituto italo-germanico in Trento* 2 (1976):401–7; idem, *La formazione dello stato regionale e le istituzioni del contado* (Turin: Einaudi, 1979), pp. 3–4; idem, "Introduzione" to *La crisi degli ordinamenti comunali e le origini dello stato del Rinascimento*, ed. Giorgio Chittolini (Bologna: Il Mulino, 1979),

p. 8; idem, "Signorie rurali e feudi alla fine del medioevo," in *Storia d'Italia*, ed. Giuseppe Galasso (Turin: UTET, 1981), 4:597.

7. Federico Chabod, "Studi di storia del Rinascimento," in his *Scritti sul Rinascimento* (Turin: Einaudi, 1967), pp. 147–219; Benedetto Croce, *Storia della storiografia italiana nel secolo decimonono* (Bari: Laterza, 1921), pp. 237–53; Walter Maturi, "La crisi della storiografia politica italiana," *Rivista Storica Italiana* 47 (1930):1–19; Nicola Ottokar, "Osservazioni sulle condizioni presenti della storiografia in Italia," in his *Studi comunali e fiorentini* (Florence: La Nuova Italia, 1948), pp. 91–104.

8. Fasano Guarini, "Stati," pp. 618–21, 632–39; Chittolini, "Alcune considerazioni," pp. 410–11; idem, "Introduzione," pp. 19–23.

9. Chabod, *Scritti*, pp. 591–623; Marino Berengo, "Il Cinquecento," in *La storiografia italiana negli ultimi vent'anni* (Milan: Mazorati, 1970), 1:485–89. On Chabod and his contemporaries see *Federico Chabod e la 'nuova storiografia' italiana dal primo al secondo dopoguerra (1919–1950)*, ed. Brunello Vigezzi (Milan: Jaca, 1983), esp. the studies of Sergio Bertelli (pp. 103–28) and Giuseppe Galasso (pp. 163–210).

10. Camillo Manfroni, "Gli studi storici in Venezia dal Romanin ad oggi," *Nuovo Archivio Veneto*, n.s., 16 (1908):362–65; Accademia Olimpica di Vicenza, *Atti*, n.s., 2 (1909–10): appendix (on the history of the Formenton Prize).

11. Grubb, "Myths," pp. 60–72.

12. Marino Berengo, *La società veneta alla fine del Settecento: ricerche storiche* (Florence: Sansoni, 1956), esp. pp. 11–42; idem, "Il problema politico-sociale di Venezia e della sua terraferma," in *La civiltà veneziana del Settecento* (Florence: Sansoni, 1960), pp. 69–95.

13. Angelo Ventura, *Nobiltà e popolo nella società veneta del '400 e '500* (Bari: Laterza, 1964), esp. pp. 5, 33, 39.

14. Gaetano Cozzi, "Ambiente veneziano, ambiente veneto," in *L'uomo e il suo ambiente*, ed. Stefano Rosso-Mazzinghi (Florence: Sansoni, 1973), pp. 93–146; idem, "Considerazioni sull'amministrazione della giustizia nella Repubblica di Venezia (secc. XV–XVI)," in *Florence and Venice*, pp. 101–33; idem, "La politica del diritto," in *Stato società e giustizia nella repubblica veneta (secc. XV–XVIII)*, ed. Gaetano Cozzi (Rome: Jouvence, 1981), 1:17–152; idem, "Politica, società, istituzioni," in Gaetano Cozzi and Michael Knapton, *Storia della Repubblica di Venezia* (Turin: UTET, 1986), pp. 3–252; and see Fasano Guarini, "Stati," pp. 623–24.

15. Giorgio Chittolini, "Governo ducale e poteri locali," in *Gli Sforza*, pp. 27–40; idem, "Le terre separate nel ducato di Milano in età sforzesca," in *Milano nell'età di Ludovico Il Moro. Atti del convegno* (Milan, 1983), pp. 115–28; and works cited in n. 6 above.

16. Philip J. Jones, "Communes and Despots: The City-State in Later Medieval Italy," *Transactions of the Royal Historical Society* 5, no. 15 (1965):95. Sergio Bertelli makes the same point implicitly, carrying his discussion of the "medieval city-state" into the fifteenth century and beyond (*Il potere oligarchico nello stato-città medievale* [Florence: La Nuova Italia, 1978]).

17. William J. Bouwsma, "The Renaissance and the Drama of Western History," *American Historical Review* 84 (1979):1–3; Denys Hay, "Historians and the Renaissance during the Last Twenty-Five Years," in André Chastel et al., *The Renaissance: Essays in Interpretation* (London: Methuen, 1982), esp. pp. 8–9, 14–15.

18. E.g., *Gulielmi Paieli Equitis Oratio* in Marciana, Latin XIII, 90 (4143), ff. 52v–57r; Marino Sanudo, *I diarii*, ed. Rinaldo Fulin et al. (Venice: Visentini, 1879–1903), 7, col. 247.

19. Flavio Biondo, *Italia Illustrata*, in his *Biondi Flavii Forliviensis De Roma Triumphante* (Basel, 1559), p. 379 (though he reversed his opinion in *De origine et gestis Venetorum*,

in Graevius, *Thesaurus*, cols. 24–25); Bertoliana, Arch. Torre 207, fasc. 11, s.d. 19 January 1470; Giacomo Marzari, *La Historia di Vicenza* (Vicenza, 1604), p. 64. The record was set straight by Vettor Sandi, *Principi di storia civile della Repubblica di Venezia* (Venice, 1755), 3:362.

20. Quotas of direct taxes and forced loans from the period 1442–99 show Brescia paying around 23 percent, Padua 22 percent, Verona 16 percent, Vicenza 13 percent, Bergamo 10 percent, Treviso 8 percent, Crema 4 percent, and several minor cities 4 percent (Bertoliana, Arch. Torre 234, fasc. 3, ff. 107v–8r; Bertoliana, Arch. Torre 482, fasc. 9, f. 18r). "Noble cities" is the phrase of Donato Gianotti, *Dialogus de Republica Venetorum*, in Graevius, *Thesaurus*, col. 117.

21. Populations of cities and their districts ca. 1548: Brescia (with Riviera) 343,073; Verona (with Cologna) 167,344; Treviso (with Bassano and Conegliano) 162,603; Vicenza 155,708; Padua 152,163; Bergamo 122,511; Crema 29,132 (Amelio Tagliaferri, "Ordinamento amministrativo della terraferma," in *Venezia e la terraferma attraverso le relazioni dei rettori. Atti del convegno*, ed. Amelio Tagliaferri [Milan: Giuffrè, 1981], pp. 42–43).

22. Machiavelli, *Prince*, ch. 5; and see idem, *Discourses*, 1, chs. 16–18.

23. Chabod, "Studi di storia," pp. 147–48.

CHAPTER 1. CREATING THE TERRITORIAL STATE

Epigraph: speech attributed to Thiene, before the doge, in Marciana, Italian VI, 312 (5990), f. 9r.

1. Galeazzo and Bartolomeo Gatari, *Cronica Carrarese confrontata con la redazione di Andrea Gatari (aa. 1318–1407)*, ed. Antonio Medin and Guido Tolomei, in Rerum Italicarum Scriptores, 2d ed., tome XVII, pt. I, vol. 1 (Città di Castello, 1931), pp. 507–25; documents in Battista Pagliarino, *Croniche di Vicenza* (Vicenza, 1663), pp. 123–32. For secondary accounts see Giambattista Verci, *Storia della Marca trevigiana e veronese* (Venice, 1790), 18, and document 2026; Giovanni Mantese, *Memorie storiche della chiesa vicentina* III, 1 (Vicenza: Istituto San Gaetano, 1958), pp. 129–40; Gigliola Soldi Rondinini, "La dominazione viscontea a Verona (1387–1404)," in *Verona e il suo territorio* (Verona: Istituto per gli Studi Storici Veronesi, 1981), 4:226–27; Italo Raulich, "Per un error di cronisti (l'acquisto di Vicenza pei veneziani)," *Nuovo Archivio Veneto* 5 (1893):383–91.

2. Gatari and Gatari, *Cronica*, p. 513; other conditions listed in Gaetano Cozzi, "Politica, società, istituzioni," in Gaetano Cozzi and Michael Knapton, *Storia della Repubblica di Venezia* (Turin: UTET, 1986), pp. 12–13. Raulich ("Error," p. 387) thinks that Caterina offered only Feltre, Cividale, and Bassano, while Venice held out for Verona and Vicenza. If he is right, Venice already had designs on the mainland. In any case, negotiations foundered.

3. Gatari and Gatari (*Cronica*, pp. 520–22) say the 25th. Vicentine statutes (*Ius municipale vicentinum*, f. 148r) and later chronicles date Venetian deliverance to the 28th, but they probably refer to the end of the siege and the establishment of formal Venetian rule.

4. E. Piva, *Venezia, Scaligeri e Carraresi: storia di una persecuzione politica nel XV secolo* (Rovigo, 1899); Roberto Cessi, "Congiure e congiurati scaligeri e carraresi (1406–1412)," *Atti e Memorie dell'Accademia di Verona*, ser. 4, no. 10 (1910):31–52; John Easton Law, "Venice, Verona and the Della Scala after 1405," ibid., ser. 6, no. 29 (1977–78):157–82.

5. Francesco Barbaro, a leader of the party that opposed further war with Milan,

conceded that he was in the minority (*Centotrenta lettere inedite di Francesco Barbaro,* ed. Remigio Sabbadini [Salerno, 1884], p. 130). He counseled peace with the Milanese only because, as allies, they could be subjected to Venetian domination (*Francisci Barbari et aliorum ad ipsum Epistolae,* ed. Angelo Maria Quirini [Brescia, 1743], App., p. 6). See in general Nicolai Rubinstein, "Italian Reactions to Terraferma Expansion in the Fifteenth Century," in *Renaissance Venice,* ed. J. R. Hale (London: Faber, 1973), pp. 207–8 and n. 82.

6.   Florentine debates and letters in A.S.F., Repubblica, Consulte e Pratiche, reg. 37; A.S.F., Signori, Legazione e Commissarie, Elezioni e Istruzioni, reg. 2; A.S.F., Signori, Missive e Cancelleria, reg. 26; letter to Venice in Verci, *Storia,* doc. 2047. In general see Rubinstein, "Italian Reactions," pp. 197–99.

7.   Lorenzo de' Monacis, quoted in Franco Gaeta, "Storiografia, coscienza nazionale e politica culturale nella Venezia del Rinascimento," in *Storia della cultura veneta,* III, 1, ed. Girolamo Arnaldi and Manlio Pastore Stocchi (Vicenza: Neri Pozza, 1980), pp. 22–23.

8.   Sante Bortolami, "Per la storia della storiografia comunale: il 'Chronicon de potestatibus Paduae,'" *Archivio Veneto,* ser. 5, no. 140 (1975):94–113.

9.   Mantese, *Memorie storiche,* III, 1, pp. 54–56, 59–70; Pagliarino, *Croniche,* pp. 102–3; Gatari and Gatari, *Cronica,* p. 509n; M. E. Mallett and J. R. Hale, *The Military Organization of a Renaissance State: Venice c. 1400 to 1617* (Cambridge: Cambridge University Press, 1984), pp. 7–19; *I libri commemoriali della Repubblica di Venezia,* ed. Riccardo Predelli, Deputazione Veneta di Storia Patria, *Monumenti Storici,* ser. I, Documenti, vol. 3 (Venice, 1878), III, p. 502; Benjamin G. Kohl, "Government and Society in Renaissance Padua," *Journal of Medieval and Renaissance Studies* 2 (1972):207; Verci, *Storia,* docs. 1444, 1462ff. In general see Michael Knapton, "Venezia e Treviso nel Trecento: proposte per una ricerca sul primo dominio veneziano a Treviso," in *Tomaso da Modena e il suo tempo* (Treviso, 1980), pp. 41–78.

10.   *Ius municipale vicentinum,* f. 3v; similarly in Veronese articles of submission and in statutes elsewhere in the *terraferma:* see Giuseppe Biadego, "Documenti della dedizione di Verona a Venezia," *Nuovo Archivio Veneto,* n.s., 10 (1905):420; Gaetano Cozzi, "La politica del diritto," in *Stato società e giustizia nella repubblica veneta (secc. XV–XVIII),* ed. Gaetano Cozzi (Rome: Jouvence, 1981), 1:85, 89, 96.

11.   1404 Capitula, rubs. 1, 3, 15, 34, 36, 39; 1406 Capitula, rubs. 1, 21, 23, 29. Similarly for Bassano, Verci, *Storia,* doc. 2031; and for Curzola, Gherardo Ortalli, "Il ruolo degli statuti tra autonomie e dipendenze: Curzola e il dominio veneziano," *Rivista Storica Italiana* 98, no. 1 (1986):203, 205–06. Visconti rulers, on the other hand, refused to ratify Brescian statutes in 1421; see Antonio Menniti Ippolito, "La dedizione di Brescia a Milano (1421) e Venezia (1427): città suddite e'distretto nello Stato regionale," in *Stato società e giustizia,* 2:31.

12.   Gian Maria Varanini, *Vicenza nel Trecento,* forthcoming in *Storia di Vicenza;* Soldi Rondinini, "Dominazione," pp. 103–10; Cozzi, "Politica, società, istituzioni," p. 206.

13.   A.S.Ven., Podesta Commission, f. 1r; and in general Cozzi, "Politica del diritto," pp. 94–97; Ortalli, "Ruolo degli statuti," p. 210; Cozzi, "Politica, società, istituzioni," pp. 214–15.

14.   The significance of *capitula* for the governance of the territorial state has been underscored for Lombardy (Giorgio Chittolini, "I capitoli di dedizione delle communita lombarde a Francesco Sforza," in *Felix olim Lombardia. Studi di storia padana dedicati dagli allievi a Giuseppe Martini* [Milan: Università degli Studi, 1978]). For Venetian Lombardy and the Veneto see Menniti Ippolito, "Dedizione di Brescia," p. 21 and passim; idem, "'Provedibitur sicut melius videbitur.' Milano e Venezia nel bresciano nel primo '400," *Studi Veneziani,* n.s., 8 (1984):37–43 and passim; Cozzi, "Politica del diritto," pp. 84–86.

15. Quoted in Gian Maria Varanini, *Il distretto veronese nel Quattrocento* (Verona: Fiorini, 1980), p. 129, n. 67.
16. Angelo Ventura, *Nobiltà e popolo nella società veneta del '400 e '500* (Bari: Laterza, 1964), pp. 41–43, 48–49; idem, "Politica del diritto e amministrazione della giustizia nella repubblica veneta," *Rivista Storica Italiana* 94, no. 3 (1982):600; and see Menniti Ippolito, "'Providebitur,'" p. 46; idem, "Dedizione di Brescia," p. 32.
17. Bertoliana, Arch. Torre 61, f. 14r; Bertoliana, Gonzati 572, f. 185r; *Statuta Patavina*, f. 141v. See also John Easton Law, "Verona and the Venetian State in the Fifteenth Century," *Bulletin of the Institute of Historical Research* 52, no. 125 (1979), p. 14; Ortalli, "Ruolo degli statuti," pp. 206–9.
18. Quoted in Aldo Mazzacane, "Lo stato e il dominio nei giuristi veneti durante il 'secolo della terraferma,'" in *Storia della cultura veneta*, III, 3, ed. Girolamo Arnaldi and Manlio Pastore Stocchi (Vicenza: Neri Pozza, 1982), p. 589. Paolo held a similar opinion regarding the Florentine territorial dominion (Julius Kirshner, "Paolo de Castro on *Cives ex privilegio*: A Controversy over the Legal Qualifications for Public Office in Early Fifteenth-Century Florence," in *Renaissance Studies in Honor of Hans Baron*, ed. Anthony Molho and John A. Tedeschi [Florence: Sansoni, 1971], p. 251; and see Mario Sbriccoli, *L'interpretazione dello statuto. Contributo allo studio della funzione dei giuristi nell'età communale* [Milan: Giuffrè, 1969], pp. 37–41).
19. A.S.Ven., Dieci Misti, reg. 12, f. 155r; A.S.Ven., Dieci Misti, reg. 14, f. 30v; Bertoliana, Arch. Torre 188, fasc. 2, ff. 23r–v; Bertoliana, Arch. Torre 62, ff. 417r–v.
20. Bertoliana, Gonzati 572, ff. 185r–86r; Marciana, Auditori Capitulare, ff. 107r, 145r; Bertoliana, Arch. Torre 59, ff. 10r, 44r, 183v, 293v; Marciana, Latin X, 398 (10598), rub. 72; Bertoliana, Arch. Torre 61, f. 248v; Bertoliana, Arch. Torre 1655, #103.
21. Marciana, Auditori Capitulare, f. 148v; Bertoliana, Arch. Torre 61, ff. 264r–v, 292r, 293v–94r; (for Verona) Bertoliana, Arch. Torre 781, ff. 32r–36v; Bertoliana, Arch. Torre 1655, s.d. 15 May 1486; A.S.Ven., Maggior Consiglio 24, f. 83r. On the demarcation of authority between Avogadori and Ten, see Gaetano Cozzi, "Authority and the Law in Renaissance Venice," in *Renaissance Venice*, pp. 303–9.
22. Bertoliana, Arch. Torre 61, ff. 264r–v.
23. Bertoliana, Gonzati 572, ff. 185r–86r; Bertoliana, Arch. Torre 60, ff. 151v–53r; Bertoliana, Gonzati 571, f. 146v.
24. Quentin Skinner, *The Foundations of Modern Political Thought* (Cambridge: Cambridge University Press, 1978), 1:xii–xiii; similarly Brian Tierney, *Religion, Law and the Growth of Constitutional Thought 1150–1650* (Cambridge: Cambridge University Press, 1982), p. x.

CHAPTER 2. DEFINITIONS OF STATE

1. Marc'Antonio Sabellico, *De praetoris officio*, in his *Epistolae familiare necnon orationes et poemata* (Venice, 1502?), ff. 105r–08v.
2. Franco Gaeta, "Storiografia, coscienza nazionale e politica culturale nella Venezia del Rinascimento," in *Storia della cultura veneta*, III, 1, ed. Girolamo Arnaldi and Manlio Pastore Stocchi (Vicenza: Neri Pozza, 1980), pp. 28–30; Eric Cochrane, *Historians and Historiography in the Italian Renaissance* (Chicago: University of Chicago Press, 1981), pp. 63–64, 77–86; and in general Margaret Leah King, "The Patriciate and the Intellectuals: Power and Ideas in Quattrocento Venice," *Societas* 5 (1975):295–311.
3. Quoted in Gaetano Cozzi, "Domenico Morosini e il 'De bene instituta re pubblica,'" *Studi Veneziani* 12 (1970):440. See also Franco Gaeta, "L'idea di Venezia," in *Storia*

della cultura veneta, III, 2, ed. Girolamo Arnaldi and Manlio Pastore Stocchi (Vicenza: Neri Pozza, 1982), p. 589; John Easton Law, "Verona and the Venetian State in the Fifteenth Century," *Bulletin of the Institute of Historical Research* 52, no. 125 (1979):11–12; Aldo Mazzacane, "Lo stato e il dominio nei giuristi veneti durante il 'secolo della terraferma,'" in *Storia della cultura veneta,* III, 3, ed. Girolamo Arnaldi and Manlio Pastore Stocchi (Vicenza: Neri Pozza, 1982), p. 538; Vettor Sandi, *Principi di storia civile della Repubblica di Venezia* (Venice, 1755), 3:353–59.

4. (Francesco Barbaro), *Centotrenta lettere inedite di Francesco Barbaro,* ed. Remigio Sabbadini (Salerno, 1884), pp. 94, 102, 113, 130–32; idem, *Francisci Barbari et aliorum ad ipsum Epistolae,* ed. Angelo Maria Quirini (Brescia, 1743), pp. 8–9, 33, 85, and App., pp. 5–6, 29; idem, *Diatriba praeliminaris . . . ad Francisci Barbari et aliorum ad ipsum Epistolae,* ed. Angelo Maria Quirini (Brescia, 1741), pp. 294–95, 347, 444–45; Evangelista Manelmi, *Commentariolum . . . de obsidione Brixiae* (Brescia, 1728), pp. 57–59, 63; G. Zippel, "Ludovico Foscarini ambasciatore a Genova nella crisi dell'espansione veneziana sulla terraferma (1449–50)," *Bolletino dell'Istituto Storico Italiano per il Medio Evo* 71 (1959–60):229; Hans Baron, *The Crisis of the Early Italian Renaissance* (Princeton: Princeton University Press, 1955), pp. 69, 480–81; Gaeta, "Storiografia," pp. 11–16, 21, 52; idem, "Idea di Venezia," pp. 586–87; Angelo Ventura, "Scrittori politici e scritture di governo," in *Stori della cultura veneta,* III, 3, p. 543.

5. Agostino Pertusi, *La storiografia veneziana fino al secolo XVI* (Florence: Olschki, 1970), p. 286n; Gaeta, "Idea di Venezia," p. 589.

6. Manelmi, *Commentariolum,* p. 41. Vicentines agreed with that assessment: see Bertoliana, Gonzati 166, f. 6v; Bertoliana, Gonzati 220; Marciana, Latin XIII, 90 (4143), ff. 33r–37r, 52v–57r. In general see Barbara Marx, *Venezia—altera Roma? Ipotesi sull'umanesimo veneziano* (Venice: Centro Tedesco di Studi Veneziani, 1978); Gaeta, "Storiografia," pp. 65–75; Franco Gaeta, "Alcune considerazioni sul mito di Venezia," *Bibliotheque d'humanisme et Renaissance* 23 (1961):61–64; David Chambers, *The Imperial Age of Venice* (London: Thames and Hudson, 1970), p. 12; Edward Muir, *Civic Ritual in Renaissance Venice* (Princeton: Princeton University Press, 1981), pp. 103–34; Cochrane, *Historians and Historiography,* p. 84. Lamberto Pansolli (*La gerarchia delle fonti di diritto nella legislazione medievale veneziana* [Milan: Giuffrè, 1970], pp. 224–25) attributes the idea of Venice as New Rome to the mainland jurist Raffaele Fulgosio.

7. Thiene from Marciana, Latin V, 124 (2639), f. 1r. (Pier Zagata), *Cronica della città di Verona descritta da Pier Zagata ampliata e supplita da Gianbatista Brancolini* (Verona, 1745), 2:40; Battista Pagliarino, *Croniche di Vicenza* (Vicenza, 1663), pp. 122–23. For Verona see L. Messagaglia, "La dedizione di Verona a Venezia," *Atti dell'Istituto Veneto* 95 (1935–36):76ff.; Law, "Verona and the Venetian State," p. 12; for Padua see Alfredo Pino Branca, "Il comune di Padova sotto la Dominante nel sec. XV," *Atti dell'Istituto Veneto* 93 (1933–34):330ff.; for Vicenza see the chronicles of "Chronachetta veneziana dal 1402 al 1415," ed. Vincenzo Joppi, *Archivio Veneto* 15 (1879):307; Bertoliana, Gonzati 576, f. 3v.

8. Giambattista Verci, *Storia della Marca trevigiana e veronese* (Venice, 1790), 18, doc. 2055. On Lombard cities see Antonio Menniti Ippolito, "'Providebitur sicut melius videbitur.' Milano e Venezia nel bresciano nel primo '400," *Studi Veneziani,* n.s., 8 (1984):37–38, 43–44.

9. Marciana, Latin VI, 3 (4351), ff. 36r–39v; Marciana, Latin XIII, 90 (4143), f. 34r; similarly in Marciana, Latin X, 118 (3845), #32; (Ognibene da Lonigo), *Omniboni nunc primum edita* (Venice, 1863); Bertoliana, Gonzati 2574–75, s.v. "Altra cronaca in caratteri più antichi"; Bertoliana, Gonzati 162, ff. 32r–34r; Bertoliana, Gonzati 439, f. 18v; Bertoliana, Gonzati 3274, #20.

10. Marciana, Latin V, 124 (2639), f. 1r.
11. Bertoliana, Arch. Torre 207, fasc. 11, s.d. 19 January 1470.
12. In 1404 Vicentines admitted that their action had dubious legitimacy, apologizing to the former Visconti governor that only their desperate plight had led them to break faith (Pagliarino, *Croniche*, p. 131). Only at the end of the century did Pagliarino claim Caterina's license, and from that point the myth passed into the historical record (ibid., p. 140; *Cronicha che comenza dell'anno 1400*, ed. Domenico Bortolan [Vicenza, 1889], p. 1; Sandi, *Principi*, 3:362; Verci, *Storia*, 18:110).
13. Barbaro, *Francisci Barbari . . . Epistolae*, p. 14; idem, *Centotrenta lettere*, pp. 129–30.
14. Menniti Ippolito, "'Provedibitur,'" pp. 41–45; Bruno Paradisi, "Deditio," in *Studi in onore di Arrigo Solmi* (Milan: Giuffrè, 1940), vol. 1; Adolf Berger, *Encyclopedic Dictionary of Roman Law* (Philadelphia: American Philosophical Society, 1953), p. 427. Examples in Bertoliana, Gonzati 572, ff. 194v–95r; Marciana, Auditori Capitulare, f. 144r; A.S.Vic., Corp. Sopp., Collegio dei Notai 51, f. 67v.
15. Marciana, Latin XII, 90 (4143), ff. 33r–37r; A.S.Ven., Captain Commission, rub. 5.
16. Venetian expressions in A.S.Ven., Senato Terra 11, ff. 103r–5r; A.S.Ven., Maggior Consiglio 22, f. 85r; Marciana, Latin V, 124 (2639), f. 1r; Lorenzo de' Monacis, quoted in Pertusi, *Storiografia*, p. 286n; Barbaro, *Centotrenta lettere*, p. 99; mainland expressions in *Ius municipale vicentinum*, f. 2v; Verci, *Storia*, doc. 2055; *Statuta Patavina*, Proemium; *Statuta Veronae*, f. 4.
17. Innocenzo Cervelli, *Machiavelli e la crisi dello stato veneziano* (Naples: Guida, 1974), esp. pp. 11–24; but see the opposing view of Angelo Ventura ("Scrittori politici," ch. 2).
18. Marciana, Latin XIII, 90 (4143), ff. 52v–57r (1471 oration of Guglielmo Pagello); similarly Bertoliana, Arch. Torre 57, ff. 537v–38r; Bertoliana, Arch. Torre 50, #29; Bertoliana, Gonzati Do 36, ff. 48r–49r; Pagliarino, *Croniche*, p. 144; Morosini quoted in Ventura, "Scrittori politici," p. 522.
19. 1404 Capitula, f. 307r; 1406 Capitula, f. 180r. For other cities see Giuseppe Biadego, "Documenti della dedizione di Verona a Venezia," *Nuovo Archivio Veneto*, n.s., 10 (1905):421; Verci, *Storia*, docs. 2048, 2055. On Venice as substituting for bygone *signori* see Carlo Guido Mor, "Problemi organizzativi e politica veneziana nei riguardi dei nuovi acquisti di terraferma," in *Umanesimo europeo e umanesimo veneziano*, ed. Vittore Branca (Florence: Sansoni, 1963), pp. 1–4; Maurice Aymard, "La terre ferme," in *Venise au temps des galères*, ed. Jacques Goimard (Paris: Hachette, 1968), pp. 139–41.
20. As, in the course of the century, the Venetian polity changed its name from commune to dominio; see John Easton Law, "Un confronto fra due stati 'rinascimentali': Venezia e il dominio sforzesco," in *Gli Sforza a Milano e in Lombardia e i loro rapporti con gli stati italiana ed europei (1450–1535)* (Milan: Cisalpino-Goliardica, 1982), p. 404; Giorgio Zordan, *L'ordinamento giuridico veneziano* (Padua: CLEUP, 1980), p. 112.
21. Bertoliana, Arch. Torre 59, ff. 72v–73r.
22. 1404 Capitula, rub. 1; Verci, *Storia*, doc. 2057.
23. Pietro Del Monte, *Repertorium utriusque iuris* (Padua, 1480), s.v. "Dominium"; Bartolomeo Cipolla, *Omnia quae quidem nunc extant opera* (Lyon, 1577), p. 176. They followed precedent: Giles of Rome in the later thirteenth century had similarly confused *dominium* as jurisdiction and property in order to expand the ruler's authority (Brian Tierney, *Religion, Law and the Growth of Constitutional Thought 1150–1650* [Cambridge: Cambridge University Press, 1982], p. 32).
24. E.g., Bertoliana, Arch. Torre 61, ff. 20v–21v; Bertoliana, Arch. Torre 404, fasc. 1, f. 7r; Bertoliana, Arch. Torre 59, ff. 2r–4v, 10r, 121r–v; A.S.Ven., Maggior Consiglio 22, f. 87v. In general see Federico Chabod, "Alcune questioni di terminologia: stato,

nazione, patria nel linguaggio del Cinquecento," in his *L'idea di nazione* (Bari: Later-za, 1961), pp. 146–65; Nicolai Rubinstein, "Notes on the Word *Stato* before Ma-chiavelli," in *Florilegium Historiale: Essays Presented to Wallace K. Ferguson*, ed. J. G. Rowe and W. H. Stockdale (Toronto: University of Toronto Press, 1971), pp. 213–26; Brian Tierney, *Foundations of the Conciliar Theory* (Cambridge: Cambridge University Press, 1955), pp. 51ff.

25. Del Monte, *Repertorium*, s.v. "Imperator."

26. Nicolai Rubinstein, "Italian Reactions to Terraferma Expansion in the Fifteenth Century," in *Renaissance Venice*, ed. J. R. Hale (London: Faber, 1973), p. 201.

27. A.S.Ven., Maggior Consiglio 22, f. 87v; Barbaro, *Francisci Barbari . . . Epistolae*, p. 81; Flavio Biondo, *De origine et gestis Venetorum*, in *Thesaurus antiquitatum et histo-riarum Italiae*, ed. J. G. Graevius (Louvain, 1722), pp. 291–92; idem, *Italia Illustrata*, in his *Biondi Forliviensis De Roma Triumphante* (Basel, 1559), p. 379; Bernardo Giusti-niani, quoted in Patricia H. Labalme, *Bernardo Giustiniani, a Venetian of the Quattro-cento* (Rome: Edizioni di Storia e Letteratura, 1969), p. 115n; Gasparo Contarini, *De magistratibus et republica venetorum*, in Graevius, *Thesaurus*, p. 44; and Guglielmo Pagello, in Marciana, Latin XIII, 90 (4143), ff. 52v–57r.

28. Angelo Ventura, *Nobiltà e popolo nella società veneta del '400 e '500* (Bari: Laterza, 1964), pp. 46–47.

29. "Nam veneta urbs nostra inclita virtute et dignitate latius terris et mare servat imperium" (Lauro Quirini, *De Republica*, in *Lauro Quirini umanista*, ed. Vittore Bran-ca [Florence: Olschki, 1977], p. 125); Vicentine examples in Bertoliana, Arch. Torre 255, fasc. 1, f. 14r; Bertoliana, Arch. Torre 61, f. 317r; Verci, *Storia*, doc. 2057.

30. Barbaro, *Centotrenta lettere*, p. 95 (juxtaposing *populus Brixiensis* with *respublica nostra;* Manelmi, *Commentariolum*, p. LIX (juxtaposing *civitas vestra* with *respublica nostra*).

31. Cipolla, *Omnia opera*, p. 543. For the origins of this idea see J. Gaudemet, "La contribution des Romanistes et des canonistes médiévaux à la théorie moderne de l'état," in *Diritto e potere nella storia europea. Atti in onore di Bruno Paradisi* (Florence: Olschki, 1982), p. 28; Pierre Michaud-Quantin, *Universitas. Expressions du mouvement communautaire dans le Moyen-Age latin* (Paris: J. Vrin, 1970), p. 114.

32. *Ius municipale vicentinum*, ff. 8r–10v, and similarly in Verona (Biadego, "Documen-ti," p. 412). For uses of *respublica* in Vicenza, see Bertoliana, Arch. Torre 61, ff. 74v, 357v–58r; Bertoliana, Arch. Torre 373, fasc. 11, f. 32r; Bertoliana, Gonzati 577, f. 9v; A.S.Ven., Senato Terra 12, f. 131v.

33. Cipolua, *Omnia opera*, p. 544. On the attributes of a *civitas*, see Julius Kirshner, "Civitas sibi faciat civem. Bartolus of Sassoferrato's Doctrine on the Making of a Citizen," *Speculum* 47 (1973):697ff.; Michaud-Quantin, *Universitas*, pp. 111–17; Mario Sbriccoli, *L'interpretazione dello statuto. Contributo allo studio della funzione dei giuristi nell'età comunale* (Milan: Giuffrè, 1969), pp. 27ff.

34. "Licet civitas quando ponitur pro loco finiatur muris, ut hic, tamen quando ponitur pro popolo tunc continentur etiam comittatenses" (Cipolla, *Omnia opera*, p. 484–89, 544); similarly Del Monte, *Repertorium*, s.v. "Civitas"; (Nicolò de Milis), *Repertorium domini Nicolai de Milis* (Venice, 1499), s.v. "Civitas"; (Giovanni Bertrachini), *Reper-torium utriusque iuris Joannis Bertrachinis de Firmo* (Nuremberg, 1483), s.v. "Civitas"; and in general Sergio Bertelli, *Il potere oligarchico nello stato-città medievale* (Florence: La Nuova Italia, 1978), pp. 1–5; Michaud-Quantin, *Universitas*, pp. 111–19.

35. Examples from various cities in Bertoliana, Arch. Torre 172, fasc. 2, ff. 3r–v; Bertoliana, Arch. Torre 404, fasc. 3, ff. 1r–v; Bertoliana, Arch. Torre 59, ff. 43v–44r; Bertoliana, Arch. Torre 61, ff. 169v, 295r–96r; Bertoliana, Arch. Torre 663, fasc. 4, s.d. 21 June 1495. On the multiple meanings attached to *communitas* in the Middle Ages, denoting at most a "more or less institutionalized group" but lacking

any judicial or governmental implication, see Michaud-Quantin, *Universitas*, pp. 147–53.

36. Giacomo Marzari, *La historia di Vicenza* (Vicenza, 1604), pp. 76–78; later examples in Bertoliana, Arch. Torre 59, ff. 72v–73r, 86r–87v, 88r–v, 136r, 177v–8r; Bertoliana, Gonzati 577, f. 25v; A.S. Ven, Maggior Consiglio 22, f. 105r.

37. For Vicenza see Bertoliana, Gonzati 572, ff. 200r–v; Marzari, *Historia*, pp. 76–77; Marciana, Latin XIII, 90 (4143), ff. 33r–37r; Barbaro, *Diatriba*, p. 346–47; for other cities see John Easton Law, "Venice and the 'Closing' of the Veronese Constitution in 1405," *Studi Veneziani*, n.s., 1 (1977):98; *Statuta Veronae*, Proemium; Barbaro, *Diatriba*, p. 346; *Statuta Patavina*, Proemium; Bertoliana, Arch. Torre 61, f. 157v; Verci, *Storia*, doc. 2087.

38. Berger, *Dictionary*, p. 747; examples from Barbaro, *Centotrenta lettere*, p. 94; Manelmi, *Commentariolum*, p. 63; Marciana, Latin XIII, 90 (4143), ff. 52v–57r.

39. Marciana, Latin XIII, 90 (4143), ff. 52v–57r; Barbaro's comments in Manelmi, *Commentariolum*, p. 63; Barbaro, *Diatriba*, pp. 346–48; Barbaro, *Francisci Barbari . . . Epistolae*, App., p. 6. Antonio Loschi in 1423 preferred the image of commendation, likewise taken from Roman social relations (Ludwig Bertalot, *Studien zum italianischen und deutschen Humanismus* [Rome: Edizioni di Storia e Letteratura, 1975], pp. 243–44).

40. For Cologna see Bertoliana, Arch. Torre 778, f. 8v; for Padua see Bertalot, *Studien*, p. 205; for Bassano see Verci, *Storia*, doc. 2031.

41. Pertusi, *Storiografia veneziana*, p. 286n; Contarini, *De magistratibus*, p. 61; Bertoliana, Arch. Torre 61, f. 157r; and *Statuta Veronae*, Proemium. In general see Tierney, *Foundations* passim; idem, *Religion, Law and the Growth of Constitutional Thought*, pp. 19–25 and passim; Michaud-Quantin, *Universitas*, pp. 59–64.

42. Bertoliana, Arch. Torre 407, fasc. 4, ff. 1r–2r; similarly A.S.Ven, Senato Terra 1, ff. 56v–57r. For Padua see Pino Branca, "Comune di Padova," 1:370; for Verona see Law, "Verona and the Venetian State," p. 22.

43. Quoted in Pertusi, *Storiografia*, p. 286n.

CHAPTER 3. DOMINION AND LAW

1. *Ius municipale vicentinum*, f. 80r, and similarly f. 4v; *Statuta Patavina*, rub. 1; Bartolomeo Cipolla, *Omnia quae quidem nunc extant opera* (Lyon, 1577), pp. 466, 467, 510; Pietro Del Monte, *Repertorium utriusque iuris* (Padua, 1480), s.v. "Ius" (Bertoliana, Gonzati 572, ff. 1r–2v (Girolamo da Schio's paraphrase of Del Monte); in general Gaetano Cozzi, "La politica del diritto," in *Stato società e giustizia nella repubblica veneta (secc. XV–XVIII)*, ed. Gaetano Cozzi (Rome: Jouvence, 1981), 1:27–30, 92; idem, "Considerazioni sull'amministrazione della giustizia nella Repubblica di Venezia (secc. XV–XVI)," in *Florence and Venice: Comparisons and Relations* (Florence: La Nuova Italia, 1979), 1:104–5; Mario Sbriccoli, *L'interpretazione dello statuto. Contributo allo studio della funzione dei giuristi nell'età communale* (Milan: Giuffrè, 1969), pp. 131–32, 422–29.

2. Angelo Dal Savio, "Il diritto vicentino nei secoli XIII–XIV," *Atti dell'Accademia Olimpica di Vicenza*, n.s., 1 (1907–8):78, 109; examples in *Ius municipale vicentinum*, f. 101r; Marciana, Latin XIII, 90 (4143), ff. 33r–37r; Bertoliana, Arch. Torre 168, fasc. 16, f. 1r; *Statuto dell'antico e sacro collegio de' nobili giuristi vicentini*, ed. Bartolomeo Bressan (Vicenza, 1877), p. 166.

3. *Ius municipale vicentinum*, ff. 14v–15r; and similarly for Verona, Cipolla, *Omnia opera*, p. 828.

4. Vicentine academic careers from G. Zonta and G. Brotto, *Acta graduum academ-*

icorum gymnasij patavini (1406–1450) (Padua: University of Padua, 1922); Giacomo Marzari, *La historia di Vicenza* (Vicenza, 1604), pp. 130ff.; Battista Pagliarino, *Croniche di Vicenza* (Vicenza, 1663), pp. 172ff.; Barbara Marx, "Handschriften Padauner Universitätsdozenten und studenten aus San Bartolomeo di Vicenza," *Quaderni per la storia dell'Università di Padova* 9–11 (1976–77):129–60; G. Bonfiglio Dosio, "I bresciani Emigli laureati a Padova nel '400," ibid. 8 (1975); Francesco Barbarano, *Historia ecclesiastica della città, territorio e diocese di Vicenza* (Vicenza, 1760), pp. 337–41; Jacobus Facciolati, *Fasti Gymnasi Patavini* (Padua, 1737), bk. 2; Giovanni Mantese, *Memorie storiche della chiesa vicentina*, III, 2 (Vicenza: Neri Pozza, 1964), pp. 821 ff.; G. Gualdo, "La Vicenza Tamisata," Marciana, Italian VI, 141B (5906).

5.   Gero Dolezalek, *Verzeichnis der Handschriften zum Römischen Recht bis 1600* (Frankfurt Max-Planck-Institut, 1972), s.n. Alexander Nievo, Antonius Loschi, Antonius Macchiavelli, Franciscus Macchiavelli, Franciscus Mascarelli, Iohannes da Porto, Michael (Reprandi) da Marostica, Simon da Vicenza. Dolezalek's list of manuscripts is a starting point only. Additional *consilia* of Francesco Macchiavelli, for example, are found in Marciana, Latin V, 2 (2324).

6.   Bressan, *Statuto*, p. 177; similarly in Brescia, Carlo Pasero, "Il dominio veneto fino all'incendio della loggia, 1426–1575," in *Storia di Brescia* (Brescia: Morcelliana, 1961), 2:116ff. A.S.Vic., Corp. Sopp. 2782 preserves records of college examinations.

7.   Inventories from Mantese, *Memorie storiche*, III, 2, pp. 829n–30n, 864, 866n–67n; A.S.Vic., Magistrature Antiche, Banco del Sigillo I, f. 3r; printing from M. Cristoferi, "Editori vicentini del XV e XVI," in *Vicenza illustrata*, ed. Neri Pozza (Vicenza: Neri Pozza, 1976); Mantese, *Memorie storiche*, III, 2, pp. 855–58; G. T. Faccioli, *Catalogo ragionato de' libri stampati in Vicenza e suo territorio nel sec. XV* (Vicenza, 1776), pp. 13, 40, 47, 56, 82, 90; Neri Pozza, "L'editoria veneziana da Giovanni da Spira ad Aldo Manuzio. I centri editoriale di terraferma," in *Storia della cultura veneta*, III, 2, ed. Girolamo Arnaldi and Manlio Pastore Stocchi (Vicenza: Neri Pozza, 1981), esp. p. 235.

8.   Bertoliana, Gonzati 572. Matriculation of 1468 from Bertoliana, Gonzati 579; record of death in Bertolina, Arch. Torre 40, #41. Other glosses in Bertoliana, Gonzati 570 and Incunabulum 166; Marciana, Latin V, 62 (2356).

9.   A.S.Vic., Corp. Sopp. 2782 preserves the college's attendance records for the communal processions of Corpus Christi and Santa Spina, listing those absent and excused as well as those present. For the similar increase in numbers of Trevisan doctors, see Luigi Pesce, *Vita socio-culturale in diocesi di Treviso nel primo Quattrocento*, in Deputazione Veneta di Storia Patria, *Miscellanea di studi e memorie* 21 (Venice, 1983):81.

10. Bertoliana, Arch. Torre 61, ff. 22v–24v; repeated in *Ius municipale vicentinum*, ff. 86v, 148v. The 1410 measure directly attacked the college's exclusivity by permitting recourse to non-Vicentine jurisconsults when a *consilium sapientis* was required and easing criteria for entrance into the college. Later measures to open up the college are found in Marciana, Latin V, 62 (2356), ff. 7v–9r; A.S.Vic., Corp. Sopp. 2782, ff. 17r–18r; Bertoliana, Arch. Torre 61, ff. 57v–59r; A.S.Ven., Senato Terra 3, f. 63v.

11. Especially in Ravenna, Biblioteca Classense, MSS. 450, 484, 485 (multivolume sets); Marciana, Latin V, 2 (2324); Marciana, Latin V, 3 (2652); (Bartolomeo Cipolla), *Consilia criminalia . . . Bartholomei Cepole* (Lyon, 1531), ##7, 16, 18, 31–35, 40, 57, 71.

12. Bertoliana, Arch. Torre 59, unfoliated frontispiece. There is no indication of the author's identity or the date and circumstances of the *consilium*'s composition.

13. Terzi and his Quattrocento predecessors ignored the fact that, elsewhere, Bartolus and Baldus had denied the legitimacy of the Venetian juridical order and the *exemptio ad imperio* (Lamberto Pansolli, *La gerarchia delle fonti di diritto nella legislazione medievale veneziana* [Milan: Giuffrè, 1970] pp. 220–21; Giorgio Zordan, *L'ordinamento giuridico veneziano* [Padua: CLEUP, 1980], p. 215).

14. Jacopo Alvarotti, *Super feudis* (Lyon, 1535), f. 57v; Del Monte, *Repertorium*, s.v. "Veneti"; Pansolli, *Gerarchia*, pp. 219–24, 247; Zordan, *Ordinamento*, p. 215; Franco Gaeta, "Storiografia, coscienza nazionale e politica culturale nella Venezia del Rinascimento," in *Storia della cultura veneta*, III, 1, ed. Girolamo Arnaldi and Manlio Pastore Stocchi (Vicenza: Neri Pozza, 1980), pp. 61–62; Bertoliana, Gonzati 572, ff. 1r–2v (Giovanni da Schio's quotation of Del Monte's *Repertorium*). A later commentator cited a treaty between Charlemagne and the Byzantine emperor stipulating Venice's freedom (Arthur Duck, *De usu et authoritate iuris civilis romanorum in dominiis principum christianorum* [Leyden, 1654], pp. 181–82, 193).

15. Zordan, *Ordinamento*, pp. 219, 227–28; Pansolli, *Gerarchia*, pp. 23–24, 85ff., 107, and ch. 6; Pier Silverio Leicht, "Lo stato veneziano e il diritto comune," in *Miscellanea in onore di Roberto Cessi* (Rome: Edizione di Storia e Letteratura, 1958), 1:203–6; Aldo Mazzacane, "Lo stato e il dominio nei giuristi veneti durante il 'secolo della terraferma,'" in *Storia della cultura veneta*, III, 3, ed. Girolamo Arnaldi and Manlio Pastore Stocchi (Vicenza: Neri Pozza, 1982), pp. 579–81; Giorgio Cracco, "La cultura giuridico-politica nella Venezia della 'Serrata,'" in ibid., II (Vicenza: Neri Pozza, 1976), pp. 238–71.

16. Bertoliana, Arch. Torre 348, fasc. 1, f. 4r; Bertoliana, Arch. Torre 59, ff. 132r, 304v–5r.

17. Marciana, Latin X, 398 (10598), f. 15r.

18. Vergerio quoted in Bruno Dudan, *Sindicato d'oltremare e di terraferma* (Rome: Foro Italiano, 1935), p. 47.

19. A.S.Ven., Maggior Consiglio 22, f. 86v.

20. In the formulation of Riccardo Malombra in the Trecento: "Quicquid fit pro conservatione status reipublice potentius est et preferendum omni statuto reipublice. Ergo illud faciendo non fit non contra statutum, sed secundum mentem statuti" (quoted in Mazzacane, "Lo stato," p. 579). For a good example of the tension between the letter and the *intentio* of the law, see Julius Kirshner, "Ars imitatur naturam. A Consilium of Baldus on Naturalization in Florence," *Viator* 5 (1974):318–19. On *mens* generally, see Sbriccoli, "Interpretazione," pp. 429–36.

21. Bertoliana, Arch. Torre 59, ff. 173r–v; Bertoliana, Arch. Torre 172, fasc. 1, ff. 2r–v.

22. *Ius municipale vicentinum*, ff. 102r–v; Bertoliana, Gonzati 576, ff. 46r–v, 214r–v; Bartolus paraphrased in (Nicolò de Milis), *Repertorium domini Nicolai de Milis* (Venice, 1499), s.v. "Judex"; Del Monte, *Repertorium*, s.v. "Appellatio." On arbitration see Bertoliana, Arch. Torre 59, f. 40r; Bertoliana, Gonzati 577, f. 25v; Mazzacane, "Lo stato," p. 583 ("hacordi et pace che le rigorosita' et processi"); Cozzi, "Politica del diritto," pp. 108–10.

23. Doctrine from (Giovanni Bertrachini), *Repertorium utriusque iuris Joannis Bertrachinis de Firmo* (Nuremberg, 1483), s.v. "Judex"; similarly Del Monte, *Repertorium*, s.v. "Consuetudo"; Bartolomeo Cipolla, quoted in Mazzacane, "Lo stato," p. 597. The Venetian ruling is discussed below, ch. 12.

24. Bertoliana, Arch. Torre 59, ff. 141v–42v.

25. G. Cassandro, "Concetto caratteri e strutture dello stato veneziano," *Rivista di Storia del Diritto Italiano* 36 (1963):43; Cozzi, "Politica del diritto," esp. pp. 46, 82–83.

26. Bertoliana, Arch. Torre 318, fasc. 2, ff. 8r–v; Bertoliana, Arch. Torre 59, ff. 89v–90r.

27. Cozzi, "Considerazioni," p. 106; idem, "Politica del diritto," pp. 91, 95, 99–101; (Alessandro Nievo), *Consilia . . . Alexandri de Nevo civis Vincentie* (Venice, 1566), p. 77.
28. Marc'Antonio Sabellico, *De officio praetoris*, in his *Epistolae familiare necnon orationes et poemata* (Venice, 1502?), f. 107r; Bertoliana, Arch. Torre 61, ff. 76v–77r; Cozzi, "Politica del diritto," p. 20.

CHAPTER 4. DOMINION AND EMPIRE

1. Pietro Del Monte, *Repertorium utriusque iuris* (Padua, 1480), s.v. "Imperator"; Jacopo Alvarotti, *Super feudis* (Lyon, 1535), f. 127r.
2. Bertoliana, Gonzati 166, ff. 51r–55r.
3. Jacob Burckhardt, *The Civilization of the Renaissance in Italy,* trans. Hajo Holborn (New York: Modern Library, 1954), pp. 14–16; Gaetano Cozzi, "Considerazioni sull' amministrazione della giustizia nella Repubblica di Venezia (secc. XV–XVI)," in *Florence and Venice: Comparisons and Relations* (Florence: La Nuova Italia, 1979), 1:105; John Easton Law, "Verona and the Venetian State in the Fifteenth Century," *Bulletin of the Institute of Historical Research* 52, no. 125 (1979):11; Gaetano Cozzi, "La politica del diritto," in *Stato società e giustizia nella repubblica veneta (secc. XV–XVIII),* ed. Gaetano Cozzi (Rome: Jouvence, 1981), 1:80.
4. A.S.Vic., Corp. Sopp. 2782, f. 175r; A.S.Ver., Antico Archivio del Comune, Atti del Consiglio, reg. 64, ff. 227r–v; *Cronica ad memoriam praeteriti temporis praesentis atque futuri,* ed. G. Mocenigo (Vicenza, 1884), s.a. 1489. Those ceremonies are all the more remarkable considering the prevailing low opinion of Frederick personally. In Jacopo Alvarotti's snide judgment, "paucaque de eo a scriptoribus mentio fiat cum pauca memoratu digna reliquerit" (*Super feudis*, f. 88r).
5. Giovanni Mantese, *Memorie storiche della chiesa vicentina,* III, 2 (Vicenza: Neri Pozza, 1964), pp. 775, 779, 804–5; Bertoliana, Gonzati 460, f. 22v; (Manfred Repeta), *Cronaca di Manfredo Repeta,* ed. Domenico Bortolan (Vicenza, 1887), p. 23; Marciana, Italian VI, 30 (5891); A.S.Vic., Notarile, Giovanni Zugian, s.d. 3 January 1461; Sebastiano Rumor, "Il blasone vicentino descritto ed illustrato," in Deputazione Veneta di Storia Patria, *Miscellanea di storia veneta,* ser. 5, no. 2 (Venice, 1899):295–96; *Cronica ad memoriam praeteriti temporis,* s.d. 1452, 1489; S. Castellini, *Storia della città di Vicenza* (Vicenza, 1821), 11–12:216, 251; F. Angiolgabriello di S. Maria, *Biblioteca e storia di quei scrittori cosi della città come del territorio di Vicenza* (Vicenza, 1772), 2:46, 236; Bertoliana, Gonzati 2819, fasc. 2, p. 24; Bertoliana, Gonzati 3379, s.d. 1452, 1454.
6. For Verona see (Pier Zagata), *Cronica della città di Verona descritta da Pier Zagata ampliata e supplita da Gianbatista Brancolini* (Verona, 1745), 2:59, 82, 85; Law, "Verona and the Venetian State," n. 20; idem, " 'Super differentiis agitatis inter districtuales et civitatem.' Venezia, Verona e il contado nel '400," *Archivio Veneto,* ser. 5, no. 151 (1981):27n; chronicles in Marciana, Latin X, 148 (3332), ff. 57v, 63v, 70v; Bib. Com., MS. 1017, f. 80v; MS. 2092, ff. 213r, 217r, 220v–1r; MS. 896, f. 30r; Giulio dal Pozza, *Collegii Veronensis iudicum advocatorum . . . Elogia* (Verona, 1653), pp. 31, 179 and passim. A lavish Paduan record of ennoblement is found in Marciana, Latin XIV, 286 (4302), ff. 209–12.
7. On sumptuary laws, *Ius municipale vicentinum,* ff. 154v–55v; on *passipage,* Bertoliana, Arch. Torre 173, fasc. 6, ff. 11r–13r; on the Thiene, Bertoliana, Gonzati 460, f. 22v; on the Pogliana, Marciana, Italian VI, 30 (5891); on *infamia,* Paolo Sambin, "Gregorio Amaseo e un gruppo di friulani laureati o studenti a Padova nell'ultimo decennio del '400," *Quaderni per la storia dell'Università di Padova* 8 (1975); on creating counts palatine, Mantese, *Memorie storiche* III, 2, pp. 804–5.

8. Petrus da Unzola, *Aurora Novissima* (Vicenza, 1485), ff. 42v–47r; Bertoliana, Arch. Torre 61, f. 255v.

9. Luigi Cristofoletti, "Cenni storici sull'antico collegio dei notari della città di Verona (1220–1806)," *Archivio Veneto* 16–18 (1878–79):325–26; Vincenzo Sansonetti, "Le pubbliche scuole in Vicenza durante il Medio Evo e l'umanesimo," *Aevum* 28 (1952):178; Domenico Bortolan, *Il Collegio dei Notai* (Vicenza, 1917), p. 17; pictures of the Rua bound into Marciana, Italian VI, 312 (5990).

10. A.S.Vic., Collegio del Notai, reg. 114; A.S.Vic., Notarile, Giovanni fu Pasquale Zugian, s.d. 3 January 1461; Mantese, *Memorie storiche*, III, 2, pp. 744n–45n, 775.

11. Thiene from A.S.Vic., Testamenti 41, s.d. 29 December 1475; insignia from Marciana, Italian VI, 141b (5906); heraldry from Rumor, "Blasone," tables 2–20.

12. G. degli Agostini, *Notizie istorico-critiche intorno la vita e le opere degli scrittori viniziani* (Venice, 1754), pp. 124ff.; fulsome orations in (Francesco Barbaro), *Centotrenta lettere inedite di Francesco Barbaro*, ed. Remigio Sabbadini (Salerno, 1884), pp. 85–88; council records in A.S.Ven., Collegio Secreta 7, #47; A.S.Ven., Senato Secreta 19, 23, 34 passim; keys from A.S.Ven., Collegio Secreta, Lettere, unnumbered file for 1480–89, #44. For records and chronicles of imperial passages see T. Toderini, *Ceremoniale e feste in avvenimenti e passagi nelli stati della Repubblica Veneta di duchi archiduchi ed imperatori della augustissima casa d'Austria dall'anno 1361 al 1797* (Venice, 1857), pp. 8–120.

13. Quoted in Lamberto Pansolli, *La gerarchia delle fonti di diritto nella legislazione medievale veneziana* (Milan: Giuffrè, 1970), p. 223; similarly Bartolomeo Cipolla, *Omnia quae quidem nunc extant opera* (Lyon, 1577), p. 161.

14. Pansolli, *Gerarchia*, p. 225.

15. Italo Raulich, "Per un error di cronisti (l'acquisto di Vicenza pei veneziani)," *Nuovo Archivio Veneto* 5 (1893):391–94; *I libri commemoriali della Repubblica di Venezia*, ed. Riccardo Predelli, Deputazione Veneta di Storia Patria, *Monumenti storici*, ser. I, Documenti, vol. 3 (Venice, 1878), III, pp. 191, 196; Giambattista Verci, *Storia della Marca trevigiana e veronese* (Venice, 1790), 19:84 and doc. 2100; Carlo Cipolla, "Note di storia veronese, 10. Diploma in favore dei Sambonifacio," *Nuovo Archivio Veneto* 20 (1900):149–53; Luigi Pesce, *Vita socio-culturale in diocesi di Treviso nel primo Quattrocento*, Deputazione Veneta di Storia Patria, *Miscellanea di studi e memorie* 21 (Venice, 1983):6–7.

16. Documents in Samuele Romanin, *Storia documentata di Venezia* (Venice, 1855), 5:484–93; *Libri commemoriali*, IV, pp. 201–2; Verci, *Storia*, docs. 2180–81. The issue is summarized in Law, "Verona and the Venetian State," pp. 9–11; Gina Fasoli, "Lineamenti di politica e di legislazione feudale veneziana in terraferma," *Rivista di Storia del Diritto Italiano* 25 (1952):67–68.

17. Claudio Povolo, "Aspetti e problemi dell'amministrazione della giustizia penale nella repubblica di Venezia. Secoli XVI–XVII," in *Stato società e giustizia*, 1:178.

18. E.g., "Modus servandus in creatione et in pheodatione solemni comitis instituendi habituri merum et mixtum imperij, et gladij potestatem" (A.S.Ven., Collegio, Ceremoniali, I, ff. 15r–v). See also Giorgio Chittolini, "Signorie rurali e feudi alla fine del medioevo," in *Storia d'Italia*, ed. Giuseppe Galasso (Turin: UTET, 1981), 4:653–55.

19. A.S.Vic., Estimo 1670, ff. 116r–v; Gian Maria Varanini, *Il distretto veronese nel Quattrocento* (Verona: Fiorini, 1980), pp. 155–56; David Chambers, "Marin Sanudo, Camerlengo of Verona (1501–1502)," *Archivio Veneto*, ser. 5, no. 108 (1977):45.

20. On priest-notaries see Giorgio Cracco, "Relinquere laicis que laicorum sunt. Un intervento di Eugenio IV contro i preti-notai di Venezia," *Bolletino dell'Istituto di Storia della Società e dello Stato Veneziano* 3 (1961):179–89; on imperial notaries see A.S.Ven., Collegio, Notariato 13, ff. 196v–200v; A.S.Ven, Maggior Consiglio 24, ff. 59r–v; Marciana, Italian VII, 498 (8147), ff. 29v–30r; on university training see

François Dupuigrenet Desroussilles, "L'università di Padova dal 1405 al concilio di Trento," in *Storia della cultura veneta*, III, 2, ed. Girolamo Arnaldi and Manlio Pastore Stocchí (Vicenza: Neri Pozza, 1982), pp. 616, 619; Patricia H. Labalme, *Bernardo Giustiniani, a Venetian of the Quattrocento* (Rome: Edizioni di Storia e Letteratura, 1969), chs. 3, 5; Vittore Branca, "L'umanesimo veneziano alla fine del Quattrocento. Ermolao Barbaro e il suo circolo," in *Storia della cultura veneta*, III, 1, ed. Girolamo Arnaldi and Manlio Pastore Stocchi (Vicenza: Neri Pozza, 1979), pp. 125–26; prohibitions from Bertoliana, Arch. Torre 59, f. 267r; Bertoliana, Gonzati 576, f. 213v.

21. Giorgio Zordan, *L'ordinamento giuridico veneziano* (Padua: CLEUP, 1980), pp. 128–29; Verci, *Storia*, doc. 2181; *Libri commemoriali*, V, p. 154. The Paduan *legum doctor* Nicolo Pontelmi received the submission of Brescia in 1426 (Carlo Pasero, "Il dominio veneto fino all'incendio della loggia, 1426–1575," in *Storia di Brescia* [Brescia: Morcelliana, 1961], 2:17), and Bartolomeo Cipolla served as Venetian orator to the Diet of Ratisbon (Cipolla, *Omnia opera*, p. 453).

22. Bertoliana, Arch. Torre 781, ff. 42v–43r; A.S.Ven., Avogaria di Comun 3584, fasc. 2, s.d. 7 May 1482; A.S.Ven., Quarantia Civil Nuova 160, ff. 111r, 120r, 140r. The custom of hiring mainland judges was eventually so well established that Cinquecento commentators considered that the office of assessor was reversed for non-Venetians, even though by that time there was a sufficient body of trained Venetians (Cozzi, "Considerazioni," p. 108).

23. Gaetano Cozzi, "Ambiente veneziano, ambiente veneto," in *L'uomo e il suo ambiente*, ed. Stefano Rosso-Mazzinghi (Florence: Sansoni, 1973), p. 104; idem, "Politica del diritto," pp. 103ff.

24. Paduan careers from Jacobus Facciolati, *Fasti Gymnasi Patavini* (Padua, 1737), bks. 2, 3; Gaspare Zonta and Giovanni Brotto, *Acta gràduum academicorum gymnasij patavini (1406–1450)* (Padua: Seminario, 1922); Venetian careers from Bertoliana, Arch. Torre 61, ff. 171v–74r, 264r–v, 322r; A.S.Ven., Avogaria di Comun 3584, fasc. 3, s.d. 12 June 1497; and lists of orators and envoys in A.S.Ven., Senato Secreta.

25. Gaetano Cozzi, "Politica, società, istituzioni," in *Stato società e giustizia*, 2:225–26; Verci, *Storia*, doc. 2072; Bertoliana, Arch. Torre 59, ff. 124r–v; A.S.Ven., Senato Terra 11, f. 99v. In 1410 a Vicentine request for a *studium* of its own was rejected (Bertoliana, Arch. Torre 61, ff. 22v–24v).

26. Dupuigrenet Desroussilles, "Università di Padova," pp. 619–24. On Padua law teaching, see F. K. von Savigny, *Geschichte des Römischen Rechts in Mittelalter* (Heidelberg, 1834), 3:273–301; Hastings Rashdall, *The Universities of Europe in the Middle Ages* (Oxford: Clarendon, 1936), 2:9–21; A. C. Smith, *Medieval Law Teachers and Writers* (Ottawa: University of Ottawa Press, 1975), ##124, 129, 132, 134–35, 138–39, 148, 150, 157.

27. A.S.Ven., Avogaria di Comun 3584, fasc. 6, f. 54v; A.S.Ven., Arch. Torre 59, ff. 141r–v; A.S.Ven., Senato Terra 7, f. 24r; Marciana, Italian VII, 498 (8147), ff. 61r–62r; Bertoliana, Arch. Torre 59, ff. 25r, 299v; Bertoliana, Gonzati 572, f. 195r; A.S.Ven., Quarantia Civil Nuova 160; A.S.Ven., Quarantia Civil Vecchia 98; and in general Pansolli, *Gerarchia*, p. 119.

28. Doctrine from Cipolla, *Omnia opera*, p. 560; cases from Bertoliana, Arch. Torre 59, ff. 92v–93v, 141r–42v, 118v–19r, 361v; Bertoliana, Arch. Torre 61, ff. 239v–40r, 254v–55r; Bertoliana, Arch. Torre 663, fasc. 4, s.d. 20 June 1495; Bertoliana, Arch. Torre 69, f. 273r.

29. Bertoliana, Arch. Torre 59, f. 121v; Marciana, Auditori Capitulare, ff. 57r–58r.

30. Cozzi, "Politica del diritto," sections 4, 5; idem, "Considerazioni," pp. 115–17, 125; Angelo Ventura, "Politica del diritto e amministrazione della giustizia nella repubblica veneta," *Rivista Storica Italiana* 94, no. 3 (1982): esp. pp. 595–96.

CHAPTER 5. COMMUNE AND GOVERNOR

1. The first complete census, in 1557, counted some 143,000 inhabitants (Giovanni Mantese, *Memorie storiche della chiesa vicentina,* III, 2 (Vicenza: Neri Pozza, 1964), pp. 1076–83). That figure may not be much higher than the demographic apex of the Quattrocento: in 1557 there were 19,899 inhabitants of the city, whereas in 1483, according to Mantese (ibid., p. 478), there were 19,000. The Venetian administrations in Padua and Brescia were roughly the same size, for populations perhaps 50 percent larger than Vicenza's (Carlo Pasero, "Il dominio veneto fino all'incendio della loggia, 1426–1575," in *Storia di Brescia* [Brescia: Morcelliana, 1961], 2:111; Benjamin G. Kohl, "Government and Society in Renaissance Padua," *Journal of Medieval and Renaissance Studies* 2 [1972]:215–17).

2. Marc'Antonio Sabellico, *De officio praetoris,* in his *Epistolae familiare necnon orationes et poemata* (Venice, 1502?), f. 106r; A.S.Ven., Podesta Commission, ff. 1v, 2r, 3v; A.S.Ven., Captain Commission, ff. 9v, 11r–v; A.S.Ven., Senato Terra 1, f. 184r; Bertoliana, Gonzati 572, f. 190r.

3. Aldo Mazzacane, "Lo stato e il dominio nei giuristi veneti durante il 'secolo della terraferma,'" in *Storia della cultura veneta,* III, 3, ed. Girolamo Arnaldi and Manlio Pastore Stocchi (Vicenza: Neri Pozza, 1982), p. 598; Gaetano Cozzi, "Considerazioni sull'amministrazione della giustizia nella Repubblica di Venezia (secc. XV–XVI)," in *Florence and Venice: Comparisons and Relations* (Florence: La Nuova Italia, 1979), 1:103, 107ff.; Bertoliana, Arch. Torre 588, fasc. 3, f. 6r; Bertoliana, Arch. Torre 61, ff. 54r–v.

4. For Curzola see Gherardo Ortalli, "Il ruolo degli statuti tra autonomie e dipendenze: Curzola e il dominio veneziano," *Rivista Storica Italiana* 98, no. 1 (1986):209–12, 217–19; for Lombardy see Maria Gigliola di Renzo Villata, "Scienza giuridica e legislazione nell'età sforzesca," in *Gli Sforza a Milano e in Lombardia e i loro rapporti con gli stati italiani ed europei (1450–1535)* (Milan: Cisalpino-Goliardica, 1982), pp. 141–45; John Easton Law, "Un confronto fra due stati 'rinascimentali': Venezia e il dominio sforzesco," in ibid., p. 402.

5. Giorgio Chittolini, *La formazione dello stato regionale e le istituzioni del contado* (Turin: Einaudi, 1979), pp. 294–95, 303–4; idem, "Governo ducale e poteri locali," in *Gli Sforza,* pp. 29–30; registers of statutes in A.S.F., Capitoli, regs. 9, 11, 54–59; A.S.F., Statuti dei comuni soggetti.

6. Angelo Ventura, *Nobiltà e popolo nella società veneta del '400 e '500* (Bari: Laterza, 1964), p. 52. Gaetano Cozzi refutes his claim in "La politica del diritto," in *Stato società e giustizia nella repubblica veneta (secc. XV–XVIII),* ed. Gaetano Cozzi (Rome: Jouvence, 1981), 1:81.

7. For Treviso see Vettor Sandi, *Principi di storia civile della Repubblica di Venezia* (Venice, 1755), 3:214; Ventura, *Nobiltà e popolo,* pp. 131–33; for Padua see *Statuta Patavina,* Proemium; V. Lazzarini, "L'avvocato dei carcerati poveri a Padova nel Quattrocento," in his *Proprietà e feudi offizi, garzari, carcerati in antiche leggi veneziani* (Rome: Edizioni di Storia e Letteratura, 1960), p. 77; Ludwig Bertalot, *Studien zum italianischen und deutschen Humanismus* (Rome: Edizioni di Storia e Letteratura, 1975), p. 204; for Verona see *Statuta Veronae,* f. 5r; John Easton Law, "Verona and the Venetian State in the Fifteenth Century," *Bulletin of the Institute of Historical Research* 52, no. 125 (1979):16; Carlo Cipolla, *Compendio della storia politica di Verona* (Mantua: Sartori, 1976), pp. 178–81; for Brescia see Antonio Menniti Ippolito, "La dedizione di Brescia a Milano (1421) e Venezia (1427): città suddite e distretto nello Stato regionale," in *Stato società e giustizia,* 2:51.

8. *Ius municipale vicentinum,* ff. 1r–2r.

9. Bertoliana, Arch. Torre 57, ff. 537v–38r; similarly *Statuta Veronae,* I, 15.

10. Bertoliana, Arch. Torre 60, ff. 151v–53r. Doctrine from Bartolomeo Cipolla, *Omnia quae quidem nunc extant opera* (Lyon, 1577), pp. 113–16; Pietro Del Monte, *Repertorium utriusque iuris* (Padua, 1480), s.v. "Consuetudo"; (Giovanni Bertrachini), *Repertorium utriusque iuris Joannis Bertrachinis de Firmo* (Nuremberg, 1483), s.v. "Consuetudo"; Daniele Dall'Aqua, *Vocabularius iuris* (Vicenza, 1482), s.v. "Consuetudo." Other Venetian guarantees in Bertoliana, Arch. Torre 482, fasc. 13, s.d. 29 October 1454; Bertoliana, Arch. Torre 217, fasc. 2, ff. 1r–2r; A.S.Ven., Avogaria di Comun 3583, f. 64r.

11. *Statuta Veronae*, II, pp. 187ff.

12. *Ius municipale vicentinum*, ff. 164v–65r. As Thomas Kuehn points out, gaps in statutory law occur because legislators could regard as customary that Roman law which underlay emancipation (*Emancipation in Late Medieval Florence* [New Brunswick, N.J.: Rutgers University Press, 1982], p. 35).

13. Bertoliana, Arch. Torre 59, ff. 141v, 244v–45r.

14. Cipolla, *Omnia opera*, p. 114; Bertrachini, *Repertorium*, Del Monte, *Repertorium*, and Dall'Aqua, *Vocabularius*, s.v. "Consuetudo." In general see Angelo Dal Savio, "Il diritto vicentino nei secoli XIII–XIV," *Atti dell'Accademia Olimpica di Vicenza*, n.s., 1 (1907–8):104–6; and Ugo Nicolini, "Autonomia e diritto proprio nelle città italiane nel Medio Evo," in *Diritto e potere nella storia europea. Atti in onore di Bruno Paradisi* (Florence: Olschki, 1982), pp. 142–48.

15. Bertoliana, Arch. Torre 59, ff. 94r, 118r, 136r; Bertoliana, Arch. Torre 190, fasc. 10, ff. 3v–5r; A.S.Ven., Maggior Consiglio 24, ff. 3r–5r; A.S.Ven., Senato Terra 3, f. 190r; Bertoliana, Arch. Torre 61, ff. 312r–v, 356r–v.

16. Bertoliana, Arch. Torre 318, fasc. 2, ff. 8r–v.

17. *Ius municipale vicentinum*, ff. 8r–10r. For Treviso see Sandi, *Principi*, 3:214; Luigi Pesce, *Vita socio-culturale in diocesi di Treviso nel primo Quattrocento*, Deputazione Veneta di Storia Patria, *Miscellanea di studi e memorie* 21 (Venice, 1983):36; for Brescia see Menniti Ippolito, "Dedizione di Brescia," pp. 47, 49–51. In Verona the local commune successfully resisted Venetian attempts to extend control over appointments and councils (Alda Giuliani Bossetti, "La trasformazione aristocratica dei consigli di Verona durante il dominio veneziano," *Studi Storici Veronese* 3 [1951–52]:45–47).

18. *Ius municipale vicentinum*, ff. 3v, 4r, 9r, 12v–13r.

19. Ibid., ff. 4v, 8v–9v, 10v; 43v–47r; Bertoliana, Arch. Torre 645, #92; Bertoliana, Arch. Torre 167, fasc. 8, ff. 1r–2v; Bertoliana, Arch. Torre 62, ff. 772v–74v; A.S.Ven., Senato Terra 1, f. 27v.

20. Bertoliana, Arch. Torre 61, ff. 233r–34r, 357v–58r. Protests against illegal pretorian interference in criminal proceedings are found in ibid., ff. 293v–94r, 381r–v; Bertoliana, Arch. Torre 684, fasc. 33, f. 4r; Bertoliana, Arch. Torre 186, fasc. 4, f. 2r.

21. Tribunals defined in *Ius municipale vicentinum*, ff. 6r–v, 15v–19v, 20r, 62r–63r; registers in A.S.Vic., Magistrature Antiche 1–4, 2277–81, 3625, 3897. The Banco del Sigillo is not defined in municipal statutes and is a powerful example of the importance of customary (as opposed to written) law.

22. *Ius municipale vicentinum*, f. 98v; juridical doctrine from Bertrachini, *Repertorium*, s.v. "Appellatio"; Cipolla, *Omnia opera*, p. 780. Venetian confirmation will be discussed below, ch. 12.

23. Bertoliana, Arch. Torre 1102, excluding criminal citations.

24. Chittolini, *Formazione*, pp. 36–253, 292–352; Judith C. Brown, *In the Shadow of Florence. Provincial Society in Renaissance Pescia* (New York: Oxford University Press, 1982), pp. 19–20; Giuliano Pinto, "Controllo politico e ordine pubblico nei primi vicariati fiorentini. Gli 'Atti criminali degli ufficiali forensi,'" *Quaderni Storici* 49

(1982): esp. p. 229; Antonio Menniti Ippolito, "'Provedibitur sicut melius videbitur.' Milano e Venezia nel bresciano nel primo '400," *Studi Veneziani*, n.s., 8 (1984):48–57 and passim; Sandi, *Principi*, 3:218–22; Gian Maria Varanini, *Il distretto veronese nel Quattrocento*, (Verona: Fiorini, 1980), ch. 3 and maps 1, 2.
25. *Ius municipale vicentinum*, ff. 6r–7r, 15v–17r, 117r–18v, 120r–22v; Bertoliana, Arch. Torre 61, ff. 124v–25r; A.S.Ven., Senato Terra 2, f. 171v.
26. Bertoliana, Arch. Torre 61, ff. 118v–21r; 312r–v; Bertoliana, Arch. Torre 62, ff. 772v–74v; Bertoliana, Arch. Torre 1655, s.d. 2 October 1461.
27. Ducal ruling in Bertoliana, Arch. Torre 61, ff. 355v–56r; later cases in Bertoliana, Arch. Torre 191, fasc. 1, ff. 16r–v; Bertoliana, Arch. Torre 61, ff. 355v–56r. The commune did not have complete rural jurisdiction: sedition and *lèse majesté* were reserved to Venetian officials, and the podesta retained powers to order torture, commit cases for medical advice, and hear testimony (*Ius municipale vicentinum*, ff. 115v–17r, 120v, 129r). See in general Giacomo Marzari, *La historia di Vicenza* (Vicenza, 1604), pp. 97–99.
28. Bertoliana, Arch. Torre 1141, 1143.
29. On the *consolatum*, see *Ius municipale vicentinum*, ff. 4r–v, 17r, 115v, 118v, 121r–v; Claudio Povolo, "Crimine e giustizia a Vicenza, secoli XVI–XVII," in *Venezia e la terraferma attraverso le relazioni dei rettori. Atti del convegno,* ed. Amelio Tagliaferri (Milan: Giuffrè, 1981), pp. 426–27; examples of judgments in Bertoliana, Arch. Torre 645, #92; Bertoliana, Arch. Torre 186, fasc. 4, f. 2r; Bertoliana, Arch. Torre 189, fasc. 2, f. 18r; Bertoliana, Arch. Torre 1655, #150; Bertoliana, Arch. Torre 61, ff. 118v–21r; Bertoliana, Arch. Torre 190, fasc. 9, f. 43r; Bertoliana, Arch. Torre 684, fasc. 33, f. 4r.
30. Bertoliana, Arch. Torre 630, fasc. 5, s.d. 12 February 1394; Sandi, *Principi*, 3:362–67; quotation from Marino Sanudo, *I diarii*, ed. Rinaldo Fulin et al. (Venice: Visentini, 1879–1903), 3, col. 1052; Sabellico, *De officio praetoris*, f. 81v.
31. Michael Knapton, "Venezia e Treviso nel Trecento: proposte per una ricerca sul primo dominio veneziano a Treviso," in *Tomaso da Modena e il suo tempo* (Treviso, 1980), p. 47; Kohl, "Government and Society," p. 208; Gigliola Soldi Rondinini, "La dominazione viscontea a Verona (1387–1404)," in *Verona e il suo territorio* (Verona: Istituto per gli Studi Storici Veronesi, 1981), 4:154; Ventura, *Nobiltà e popolo*, pp. 133–35; Gaetano Cozzi, "Politica, società, istituzioni," in Gaetano Cozzi and Michael Knapton, *Storia della Repubblica di Venezia* (Turin: UTET, 1986), pp. 206–7.
32. James S. Grubb, "Alla ricerca delle prerogative locali: la cittadinanza a Vicenza, 1404–1509," *Civis* 24 (1984):177–92; for Padua see *Statuta Patavina*, rub. 41.
33. On the doge's ballot see Bertoliana, Arch. Torre 645, #91. On council elections see *Ius municipale vicentinum*, ff. 8r–v. Transfer of elective rights away from the podesta happened elsewhere in the Venetian state, notably Brescia and Bergamo (Ventura, *Nobiltà e popolo*, pp. 109–10, 112–13). On exclusion of Venetians see Bertoliana, Arch. Torre, Catastico IX, f. 84v; Bertoliana, Arch. Torre 59, f. 267r.
34. In general see Sergio Bertelli, *Il potere oligarchico nello stato-città medievale* (Florence: La Nuova Italia, 1978), pp. 102–3; for Padua see Kohl, "Government and Society," pp. 217–18; for Verona (but in succeeding centuries) see Marino Berengo, "Patriziato e nobiltà: il caso veronese," in *Potere e società negli stati regionali italiani del '500 e '600,* ed. Elena Fasano Guarini (Bologna: Il Mulino, 1978), pp. 198, 211–12; for Brescia see Menniti Ippolito, "Dedizione di Brescia," pp. 36–37, 49–50. Gian Maria Varanini, however, doubts widespread absenteeism or loss of powers in the larger council of Verona; see his "Note sui consigli civici Veronesi (secoli XIV–XV). In margine ad uno studio di J. E. Law," *Archivio Veneto*, ser. 5, no. 147 (1979):21–23, n. 39 and appendixes.
35. Bertoliana, Arch. Torre 61, f. 16v; for the *terraferma* see Bianca Betto, *Il collegio dei*

notai, dei giudici, dei medici e dei nobili in Treviso (secc. XIII–XVI), Deputazione Veneta di Storia Patria, *Miscellanea di studi e memorie* 19 (Venice, 1981):70; Kohl, "Government and Society," pp. 209, 217; Luigi Cristofoletti, "Cenni storici sull'antico collegio dei notari della città di Verona (1220–1806)," *Archivio Veneto* 16–18 (1878–79):70; Menniti Ippolito, "Dedizione di Brescia," p. 47.

36.   Successful protests against chancellors in A.S.Vic., Collegio dei Notai, regs. 38, 45 passim; A.S.Ven., Capi dei Dieci, Lettere, s.d. 1504 #247; Bertoliana, Arch. Torre 149, fasc. 10, esp. f. 51r; Bertoliana, Arch. Torre 150, fasc. 3, ff. 9r; Bertoliana, Gonzati 533, ff. 76ff.; A.S.Vic., Magistrature Antiche 3897, s.d. 6 October 1442; Bertoliana, Gonzati 1517, s.d. 13 June 1496; protests against the central government from Bertoliana, Arch. Torre 149, fasc. 10, ff. 38r, 40r.

37.   Del Monte, *Repertorium*, and Bertrachini, *Repertorium*, s.v. "Notarius"; (Nicolò de Milis), *Repertorium domini Nicolai de Milis* (Venice, 1499), s.v. "Notarius"; Bertoliana, Arch. Torre 61, f. 255v; Bertoliana, Gonzati 1517, s.d. 1469.

38.   Cipolla, *Omnia opera*, p. 114 (paraphrasing Baldus); *Ius municipale vicentinum*, f. 47v–52r.

CHAPTER 6. COMMUNE AND COUNTRYSIDE

1.   Elena Fasano Guarini, "Le istituzione," in *Livorno e Pisa: due città e un territorio nella politica dei Medici* (Pisa: Nistri-Lischi, 1980), pp. 31–35; idem, "Città soggette e contadini nel dominio fiorentino tra Quattro e Cinquecento," in *Ricerche di storia moderna*, ed. Mario Mirri (Pisa: Pacini, 1973); Giorgio Chittolini, *La formazione dello stato regionale e le istituzioni del contado* (Turin: Einaudi, 1979), esp. pp. xviii–xxii, 292–352; idem, "Signorie rurali e feudi alla fine del medioevo," in *Storia d'Italia*, ed. Giuseppe Galasso (Turin: UTET, 1981), 4:647–48; idem, "Le terre separate nel ducato di Milano in età sforzesca," in *Milano nell'età di Ludovico Il Moro. Atti del convegno* (Milan, 1983), pp. 115–17; Antonio Menniti Ippolito, "'Providebitur sicut melius videbitur.' Milano e Venezia nel bresciano nel primo '400," *Studi Veneziani*, n.s., 8 (1984):40, 48–71.

2.   Treviso from Vettor Sandi, *Principi di storia civile della Repubblica di Venezia* (Venice, 1755), 3:218–22; Vicenza from Bertoliana, Arch. Torre 777, ff. 3r–8r, 18r–26r; Giovanni Mantese, *Memorie storiche della chiesa vicentina*, III, 1 (Vicenza: Istituto San Gaetano, 1958), pp. 121–22, 424–46; Gian Maria Varanini, *Vicenza nel Trecento*, forthcoming in *Storia di Vicenza*.

3.   Bertoliana, Arch. Torre 777, ff. 54v–56r, 75r–76r, 118r–20v.

4.   Bertoliana, Arch. Torre, Catastico 24, s.v. "Vicari," s.d. 21 November 1311; Giovanni Mantese "La scoperta dell'inventario di Bailardino Nogarola," in *Studi in onore di mons. Turrini* (Verona, 1973), pp. 61–63; Bertoliana, Arch. Torre 48, ##84, 86; Bertoliana, Gonzati 2819, fasc. 1, p. 98; and works cited in preceding notes.

5.   Sandi, *Principi*, 3:399–435; Gian Maria Varanini, *Il distretto veronese nel Quattrocento* (Verona: Fiorini, 1980), ch. 2; Chittolini, "Signori rurali," p. 654; Giambattista Verci, *Storia della Marca trevigiana e veronese* (Venice, 1790), 18, docs. 2031, 2045, 2060, 2064; Bertoliana, Arch. Torre 202, ff. 14r–19r; Bertoliana, Arch. Torre 778, ff. 1r–8v.

6.   Initial privilege in Bertoliana, Arch. Torre 777, ff. 88r–90r, confirmed in Bertoliana, Arch. Torre 648, fasc. 2, s.d. 20 February 1404; subsequent confirmations in Bertoliana, Arch. Torre 412, fasc. 2, ff. 10r–11v; G. B. Zanazzo, "L'arte della lana in Vicenza (secc. XIII–XV)," Deputazione Veneta di Storia Patria, *Miscellanea di storia veneta*, ser. 3, no. 6 (Venice, 1914): docs. 31, 39–42, 48–49; Bertoliana, Arch.

Torre 61, ff. 61r–v, 205r. In 1459 the Venetian *collegio* allowed the commune of Vicenza to appoint a vicar over the Sette Comuni but withdrew the privilege a year later (ibid., ff. 214v–15r; Bertoliana, Arch. Torre 307, fasc. 1, ff. 9r–v).

7. Bertoliana, Arch. Torre 777, ff. 62r, 75r–76r.

8. Marino Berengo, "La città di antico regime," in *Della città preindustriale alla città del capitalismo,* ed. Alberto Caracciolo (Bologna: Il Mulino, 1975), p. 50.

9. 1404 Capitula, rubs. 5, 15; 1406 Capitula, rubs. 6, 25. In Brescia, by contrast, the urban commune failed to gain authority over the countryside at the time of annexation; see Antonio Menniti Ippolito, "La dedizione di Brescia a Milano (1421) e Venezia (1427): città suddite e distretto nello Stato regionale," in *Stato società e giustizia nella repubblica veneta (secc. XV–XVIII),* ed. Gaetano Cozzi (Rome: Jouvence, 1985), 2:25–29, 46–48.

10. S. Castellini, *Storia della città di Vicenza* (Vicenza, 1821), 14:123; Bertoliana, Gonzati 460, s.d. 7 October 1403; Bertoliana, Arch. Torre 61, ff. 11r–13r; A.S.Ven., Avogaria di Comun 3646, f. 5v; and see John Easton Law, "Venice, Verona and the Della Scala after 1405," *Atti e Memorie dell'Accademia di Verona,* ser. 6, no. 29 (1977–78):159–60, 167–68.

11. A.S.Ven., Senato Secreta, Commissioni, Formulari 6, ff. 45r, 65r; James S. Grubb, "Patrimonio, feudo e giurisdizione: la signoria dei Monza a Dueville nel secolo XV," in *Dueville: storia e identificazione di una comunità del passato,* ed. Claudio Povolo (Vicenza: Neri Pozza, 1985), 1:300–301; Bertoliana, Gonzati 2819, fasc. 2, p. 14; Bertoliana, Arch. Torre 61, ff. 135r–v.

12. Chittolini, *Formazione,* pp. xxi–xxiii, 313–18; idem, "Signorie rurali," pp. 665–69; idem, "Terre separate," pp. 117–19, 122–24; Menniti Ippolito, "Dedizione di Brescia," pp. 56–58; Varanini, *Distretto veronese,* ch. 3.

13. A.S.Ven., Senato Secreta, Commissioni, Formulari 6, ff. 45r, 65r; Bertoliana, Arch. Torre 777, f. 101r; Bertoliana, Arch. Torre 61, ff. 18v–19r, 21r–22r, 311r–v, 317r–19r, 394v–95r; Bertoliana, Gonzati 571, f. 146v; Bertoliana, Arch. Torre 253, fasc. 2, 4; Bertoliana, Arch. Torre 255, fasc. 1–5; Bertoliana, Arch. Torre 363, fasc. 2.

14. Bertoliana, Arch. Torre 777, ff. 101r, 102v–3r; Bertoliana, Arch. Torre 363, fasc. 2, ff. 1r–2r; Bertoliana, Arch. Torre 61, ff. 32r–34r, 361r–v, 394v–95r.

15. Zanazzo, "Arte della lana," docs. 16, 38, 43–46, 50–59; Bertoliana, Arch. Torre 61, f. 51v; Bertoliana, Arch. Torre 253, fasc. 5, rub. 16.

16. Bertoliana, Arch. Torre 361, fasc. 1; Bertoliana, Arch. Torre 61, ff. 249v–50r, 253v–54r, 263v–64r, 281r, 360r–v.

17. Michael Knapton, "I rapporti fiscali tra Venezia e la terraferma: il caso padovano," *Archivio Veneto,* ser. 5, no. 117 (1981), p. 44; idem, "Guerra e finanza (1381–1508)," in Gaetano Cozzi and Michael Knapton, *Storia della Repubblica di Venezia dalla guerra di Chioggia alla riconquista della terraferma* (Turin: UTET, 1986), pp. 322–23.

18. Bertoliana, Arch. Torre 645, #88; Bertoliana, Arch. Torre 172, ff. 3r–v; Bertoliana, Arch. Torre 57, ff. 537v–38v; Bertoliana, Arch. Torre 255, f. 9r. In Verona, similarly, the central government first favored, then downgraded rural privileges (John Easton Law, " 'Super differentiis agitatis Venetiis inter districtuales et civitatem.' Venezia, Verona e il contado nel '400," *Archivio Veneto,* ser. 5, no. 151 [1981]:21–22). In Brescia, on on the other hand, the Republic accepted the right of towns to tax citizens (Menniti Ippolito, "Dedizione di Brescia," pp. 44–45).

19. Bertoliana, Arch. Torre 60, ff. 147r–48r; Bertoliana, Arch. Torre 482, fasc. 13, s.d. 11 June 1486, 29 July 1503. The Republic provided some redress in the Cinquecento by reducing the countryside's share of the overall quota for direct taxes (Michael Knapton, "Il Territorio vicentino nello Stato veneto del '500 e primo '600: nuovi equilibri politici e fiscali," *Civis* 24 [1984]:36–38).

20. Bertoliana, Arch. Torre 60, ff. 151v–53v; Bertoliana, Arch. Torre 173, fasc. 11, ff. 1r–5r; Bertoliana, Arch. Torre 172, ff. 1r–22v.

21. There was some justice to this claim. By a Senate order of 1446, Venetians who henceforth purchased land on the *terraferma* would pay taxes with the place in which the lands were located (Bertoliana, Arch. Torre 61, f. 337v).

22. Varanini, *Vicenza nel Trecento*, pp. 152, 253–57; statutes of 1389 in Bertoliana, Arch. Torre 777, ff. 108r–10r; *Ius municipale vicentinum*, ff. 147v–48r. On similar protests in Lombardy, see Chittolini, "Terre separate," pp. 119–21.

23. *Ius municipale vicentinum*, ff. 165r–v; Bertoliana, Arch. Torre 61, ff. 32r, 34r, 64v, 74v–75v, 341r–v, 376r–77r; Giovanni Mantese, *Memorie storiche della chiesa vicentina*, III, 2 (Vicenza: Neri Pozza, 1964), pp. 632–34.

24. Bartolomeo Cipolla, *Omnia quae quidem nunc extant opera* (Lyon, 1577), p. 544; (Giovanni Bertrachini), *Repertorium utriusque iuris Joannis Bertrachinis de Firmo* (Nuremberg, 1483), s.v. "Civis"; Pietro Del Monte, *Repertorium utriusque iuris* (Padua, 1480), s.v. "Civis"; Bertoliana, Arch. Torre 61, ff. 43r–44v; Bertoliana, Arch. Torre 255, fasc. 1, f. 9r; Bertoliana, Arch. Torre 307, fasc. 1, f. 14r. The image was widespread on the mainland: see *Privilegia Veronae*, p. 1; Bianca Betto, *Il collegio dei notai, dei giudici, dei medici e dei nobili in Treviso (secc. XIII–XVI)*, Deputazione Veneta di Storia Patria, *Miscellanea di studi e memorie* 19 (Venice, 1981):199, 204, 209; Giorgio Chittolini, "Governo ducale e poteri locali," in *Gli Sforza a Milano e in Lombardia e i loro rapporti con gli stati italiani ed europei (1450–1535)* (Milan: Cisalpino-Goliardica, 1982), p. 35.

25. Bertoliana, Arch. Torre 61, ff. 249v–50r; Bertoliana, Gonzati 571, f. 146v; Bertoliana, Arch. Torre 60, ff. 151v–53v.

CHAPTER 7. AFFIRMATION OF THE PATRICIATE

1. Marino Berengo, *Nobili e mercanti nella Lucca del Cinquecento* (Turin: Einaudi, 1965), p. 31; Giorgio Politi, *Aristocrazia e potere politico nella Cremona di Filippo II* (Milan: Sugarco, 1976), p. 33; Angelo Ventura, *Nobiltà e popolo nella società veneta del '400 e '500* (Bari: Laterza, 1964), pp. 275–80.

2. Nicolai Rubinstein, "Oligarchy and Democracy in Fifteenth-Century Florence," in *Florence and Venice: Comparisons and Relations* (Florence: La Nuova Italia, 1979), 1:100; Philip Jones, "Economia e società nell'Italia medievale: la leggenda della borghesia," *Storia d'Italia*. *Annali* I: *Dal feudalismo al capitalismo* (Turin: Einaudi, 1978), pp. 304–5, 342, 352–53; Emilio Cristiani, *Nobiltà e popolo nel comune di Pisa. Dalle origini dal podestariato alla signoria dei Donoratico* (Naples: Istitituo Italiano per gli Studi Storici, 1962), pp. 36–37; Michele Luzzatti, "Momenti di un processo di aristocratizzazione," in *Livorno e Pisa: due città e un territorio nella politica dei Medici* (Pisa: Nistri-Lischi, 1980), pp. 120–22; idem, "Famiglie nobili e famiglie mercantili a Pisa e in Toscana nel basso medioevo," *Rivista Storica Italiana* 86 (1974):447–48.

3. Jean-Claude Hocquet, "Oligarchie et Patriciat à Venise," *Studi Veneziani*, n.s., 17–18 (1975–76):401–10; Stanley Chojnacki, "In Search of the Venetian Patriciate: Families and Factions in the Fourteenth Century," in *Renaissance Venice*, ed. J. R. Hale (London: Faber, 1973), pp. 51–58; idem, "Political Adulthood in Fifteenth-Century Venice," *American Historical Review* 91 (1986):798–99, 801.

4. John Easton Law, "Venice and the 'Closing' of the Veronese Constitution in 1405," *Studi Veneziani*, n.s., 1 (1977):76–94; Gian Maria Varanini, "Note sui consigli civici veronesi (secoli XIV–XV). In margine ad uno studio di J. E. Law," *Archivio Veneto*, ser. 5, no. 147 (1979):5–19.

5. Battista Pagliarino, *Croniche di Vicenza* (Vicenza, 1663), pp. 123–32; 1404 Capitula,

pp. 305–6; for other cities see Giuseppe Biadego, "Documenti della dedizione di Verona a Venezia," *Nuovo Archivio Veneto*, n.s. 10 (1905):414–15; Giambattista Verci, *Storia della Marca trevigiana e veronese* (Venice, 1790), 18, docs. 2048, 2055.

6. *Ius municipale vicentinum*, ff. 8r, 11r, 12r, 15v, 22v–23r, 174r–76r; Bertoliana, Arch. Torre 62, ff. 496v–98r, rub. 1.

7. Giorgio Chittolini, "Introduzione," to *La crisi degli ordinamenti comunali e le origini dello stato del Rinascimento*, ed. Giorgio Chittolini (Bologna: Il Mulino, 1979), p. 24 and passim; John M. Najemy, *Corporatism and Consensus in Florentine Electoral Politics, 1280–1400* (Chapel Hill, University of North Carolina Press, 1982), esp. ch. 8; Ventura, *Nobiltà e popolo*, pp. 32, 53, 93, 108, 133; Benjamin G. Kohl, "Government and Society in Renaissance Padua," *Journal of Medieval and Renaissance Studies* 2 (1972):212; Varanini, "Note," p. 12.

8. Chittolini, "Introduzione," n. 106; G. B. Zanazzo, "L'arte della lana in Vicenza (secc. XIII–XVI)," Deputazione Veneta di Storia Patria, *Miscellanea di storia veneta*, ser. 3, no. 6 (Venice, 1914):61, 73, and docs. 11, 13, 27–28, 30, 33–35; Bertoliana, Arch. Torre 61, ff. 209v, 230v, 286v, 289r, 291v.

9. For Florence see Ronald F. E. Weissman, *Ritual Brotherhood in Renaissance Florence* (New York: Academic Press, 1982), pp. 6–10; Richard C. Trexler, *Public Life in Renaissance Florence* (New York: Academic Press, 1980), p. 252; Dale Kent, "The Florentine *Reggimento* in the Fifteenth Century," *Renaissance Quarterly* 28 (1975):576–638, esp. p. 592; Dale and Francis Kent, *Neighbors and Neighborhoods in Renaissance Florence: The District of the Red Lion in the Fifteenth Century* (Locust Valley, N.Y.: J. J. Augustin, 1982). For Venice see Frederic C. Lane, *Venice, a Maritime Republic* (Baltimore: Johns Hopkins University Press, 1973), pp. 12, 49, 98–99; Edward Muir, *Civic Ritual in Renaissance Venice* (Princeton: Princeton University Press, 1981), pp. 140–56.

10. Pagliarino, *Croniche*, ch. 6; Giovanbattista Dragonzino, *Nobiltà di Vicenza*, ed. Franco Barbieri and Flavio Fiorese (Vicenza: Neri Pozza, 1981), p. 25; da Nono from Bib. Univ., MSS, 55, 65; pseudo-Basili from Bib. Univ. MS. 1667; Ongarelli from Bib. Civ., MS. 2610. On the last three see Giovanni Fabris, "La cronaca di Giovanni da Nono" (reprint, Padua, 1940), esp. pp. 1–5.

11. Ventura, *Nobiltà e popolo*, pp. 118–19; council lists in Bertoliana, Gonzati 566, ff. 116r–17v; Bertoliana, Arch. Torre 35, doc. 45; A.S.Vic., San Bartolomeo, reg. 12, doc. 1689; and in general Gian Maria Varanini, *Vicenza nel Trecento*, forthcoming in *Storia di Vicenza*; Pagliarino, *Croniche*, ch. 6. For other cities see Gigliola Soldi Rondinini, "La dominazione viscontea a Verona (1387–1404)," in *Verona e il suo territorio* (Verona: Istituto per gli Studi Storici Veronesi, 1981), 4:161; Luigi Pesce, *Vita socio-culturale in diocesi di Treviso nel primo Quattrocento*, in Deputazione Veneta di Storia Patria, *Miscellanea di studi e memorie* 21 (Venice, 1983):240–69; Kohl, "Government and Society," pp. 209–11.

12. Trecento norms in Bertoliana, Gonzati 566, bk. II, rubs. 37–38, and bk. IV; Bertoliana, Arch. Torre 777, f. 45v. For the similar Brescian case see Giorgetta Bonfiglio Dosio, "La condizione giuridica del *civis* e le concessioni di cittadinanza negli statuti bresciani del XIII e XIV secolo," *Atti dell'Istituto Veneto* 137 (1978–79):528–29.

13. Zanazzo, "Arte della lana," docs. 16, 18; Bertoliana, Arch. Torre 61, ff. 70v–72r; Bertoliana, Arch. Torre 60, ff. 59r–v; Bertoliana, Arch. Torre 181, fasc. 1, ff. 10r–11r; Bertoliana, Arch. Torre 172, fasc. 2, ff. 4r–6v. A similar Veronese law dates from 1415 (John Easton Law, "'Super differentiis agitatis inter districtuales et civitatem.' Venezia, Verona e il contado nel '400," *Archivio Veneto*, ser. 5, no. 151 [1981]:19, 25–26).

14. Bertoliana, Gonzati Do 36, fasc. 2, ff. 2r–22r; A.S.Ven., Grazie 20, f. 11r.

15. A.S.Ven., Senato Terra 2, f. 65v; Bertoliana, Gonzati Do 36, ff. 41r–43v; Bertoliana, Arch. Torre 173, fasc. 1, ff. 7r–8v.

16. The Council of Ten rejected the proposal (Bertoliana, Arch. Torre 61, ff. 348r–v). On disabilities imposed on new citizens, see Julius Kirshner, "Civitas sibi faciat civem. Bartolus of Sassoferrato's Doctrine on the Making of a citizen," *Speculum* 47 (1973):695–702; idem, "'Ars imitatur naturam,' A Consilium of Baldus on Naturalization in Florence," *Viator* 5 (1974):289–90 and passim.

17. The undated provision raising requirements is found in Bertoliana, Gonzati 576, f. 3r. Though requirements for citizenship were about the same in Verona, the *cursus* was far simpler and, apparently, less discriminatory against artisans (Law, "'Super differentiis agitatis,'" p. 17; *Statuta Veronae*, p. 60).

18. Ludovico Vistarini after 1404 (1404 Capitula, rub. 12); Franceschino Trento around 1410 (Pagliarino, *Croniche*, p. 282; Bertoliana, Arch. Torre 61, f. 306v); Andrea Arnaldi in 1426 (Bertoliana, Gonzati 153, f. 18r; but see Bertoliana, Gonzati 566, ff. 116r–18v).

19. The original provision specified thirty years (above, n. 13), but the doge's ratification cut it back to twenty. By 1443 the commune was ignoring the doge by returning to a thirty-year limit (Bertoliana, Arch. Torre 60, ff. 96r–v). This restriction was raised to a full century in 1567 (Ventura, *Nobiltà e popolo*, p. 279). On disabilities in Florence, see Kirshner, "'Ars imitatur naturam,'" pp. 299–303; idem, "Paolo di Castro on *Cives ex Privilegio:* A Controversy over the Legal Qualifications for Public Office in Early Fifteenth-Century Florence," in *Renaissance Studies in Honor of Hans Baron*, ed. Anthony Molho and John A. Tedeschi (Florence: Sansoni, 1971), pp. 238ff.

20. A good example is Count Giovanni Thiene's purchase of a council seat from Girolamo Tomasini in 1496 (Bertoliana, Archivio Thiene, Catastico Co. Adriano, doc. 406).

21. Verona's "closing" in 1405 abolished a great council in favor of a small one but did not restrict access. Subsequent rotation of council seats among a small number of families was the product of informal collusion rather than formal exclusion. Likewise the common system whereby outgoing councillors elected their successors, seen most clearly in Vicenza after 1422 and Padua after 1430, effected only a de facto closing (Ventura, *Nobiltà e popolo*, pp. 59–84, 96–98, 122–25; Law, "Verona and the 'Closing,'" passim). There may have been complete closure in Chioggia, accomplished in stages over the Quattrocento (Carlo Bullo, "Della cittadinanza di Chioggia e della nobiltà de' suoi antichi consigli," *Archivio Veneto* 10 [1875]:326–31).

22. Berengo, *Nobili e mercanti*, pp. 53–64; works of Ventura and Cozzi cited in ch. 4, n. 30. In Treviso, the College of Judges dropped in 1443 to the "grado minore," alongside the artisan guilds, see Bianca Betto, *Il collegio dei notai, dei giudici, dei medici e dei nobili in Treviso (secc. XIII–XVI)*, in Deputazione Veneta di Storia Patria, *Miscellanea di studi e memorie* 19 (Venice, 1981): 167, 178, 424.

23. Lauro Martines, *Lawyers and Statecraft in Renaissance Florence* (Princeton: Princeton University Press, 1968), esp. chs. 4–8; but see also Dale Kent, *The Rise of the Medici: Faction in Florence, 1426–1434)* (Oxford: Oxford University Press, 1978), p. 120.

24. Notaries from Bertoliana, Gonzati 533, ff. 79r, 94r–v; jurists from *Statuto dell'antico e sacro collegio de' nobili giuristi vicentini*, ed. Bartolomeo Bressan (Vicenza, 1877), rub. 39; A.S.Vic., Corp. Sopp. 2782, ff. 113v, 136r, 138r, 252r–53v. For other cities see Maria Gigliola di Renzo Villata, "Scienza giuridica e legislazione nell'età sforzesca," in *Gli Sforza a Milano e in Lombardia e i loro rapporti con gli stati italiana ed europei (1450–1535)* (Milan: Cisalpino-Goliardica, 1982), p. 131; Betto, *Collegio*, pp. 28, 39, 121 (rubs. 35, 38), 205.

25. College from Francesco Fortunato Vigna, *Preliminare di alcune dissertazioni intorno alla parte migliore della storia ecclesiastica e secolare della città di Vicenza* (Vicenza, 1747), pp. 81–83; Arnaldi from A.S.Vic., Collegio dei Notai, reg. 9; reg. 89, f. 266; reg. 91, s.d. 1450; Bertoliana, Gonzati 535, f. 120r. On patrimonialization in general, see Ventura, *Nobiltà e popolo*, pp. 348–65.

26. For Padua see François Dupuigrenet Desroussilles, "L'università di Padova dal 1405 al concilio di Trento," in *Storia della cultura veneta*, III, 2, ed. Girolamo Arnaldi and Manlio Pastore Stocchi (Vicenza: Neri Pozza, 1981), p. 616; for Andrea see A.S.Ven., Quarantia Civil Nuova, reg. 160; A.S.Ven., Quarantia Civil Vecchia, reg. 98. In general see Sergio Bertelli, *Il potere oligarchico nello stato-città medievale* (Florence: La Nuova Italia, 1978), pp. 128–29; Berengo, *Nobili e mercanti*, pp. 62–63; Betto, *Collegio*, pp. 41, 169.

27. Antonio Menniti Ippolito, "La dedizione di Brescia a Milano (1421) e a Venezia (1427): città suddite e distretto nello Stato regionale," in *Stato società e giustizia nella repubblica veneta (secc. XV–XVIII)*, ed. Gaetano Cozzi (Rome: Jouvence, 1985), 2:35; Varanini, "Note" passim; Ventura, *Nobiltà e popolo*, pp. 112–13, 131–32, 140–43.

28. Bertoliana, Arch. Torre 168, fasc. 16, f. 1r. Important legislation in Bertoliana, Arch. Torre 787, ff. 3r–4r (reforms of fiscal offices); Bertoliana, Arch. Torre 61, ff. 210r–11v (reforms of rural jurisdictions); Zanazzo, "Arte della lana," docs. 27, 29 (reforms of the wool trade).

29. Bertoliana, Arch. Torre 217, fasc. 3, ff. 6r–9v; and see also *Ius municipale vicentinum*, ff. 33r–v, 34v, 35v, 38r.

30. Bertoliana, Arch. Torre 318, fasc. 2, ff. 4r–v; *Ius municipale vicentinum*, ff. 8r–9r. The *deputati* pool plus One Hundred (with Anziani) would total 165 councillors; Great Council records show a consistent membership of around 170.

31. On challenges to patrician or urban authority, see Michael Knapton, "Il Territorio vicentino nello Stato veneto del '500 e primo '600: nuovi equilibri politici e fiscali," *Civis* 24 (1984):193–275; Sergio Zamperetti, "Per una storia della istituzioni rurali nella terraferma veneta: il contado vicentino nei secoli XVI e XVII," in *Stato società e giustizia*, 2:59–131; Marino Berengo, "Patriziato e nobiltà: il caso veronese," *Rivista Storica Italiana* 87 (1975):499–500. For an earlier period Cristiani speaks of a fusion of "nobiltà feudale" and "nobiltà cittadino" in a common front against the *popolo* (*Nobiltà e popolo*, pp. 36–37; and see also Jones, "Economia e società," pp. 244, 252–57, 352–53).

32. Law, "Venice and the 'Closing,'" pp. 81, 94–101; Varanini, "Note," pp. 19–23 and table 2; Ventura, *Nobiltà e popolo*, pp. 79–84, 88, 96–97.

CHAPTER 8. CONSOLIDATION OF THE PATRICIATE

1. Marino Berengo, "Patriziato e nobiltà: il caso veronese," *Rivista Storica Italiana* 87 (1975):191–97 and passim; idem, *Nobili e mercanti nella Lucca del Cinquecento* (Turin: Einaudi, 1965), ch. 4, esp. pp. 235–45, 257.

2. Dante Alighieri, *Il convivio*, ed. G. Busnelli and G. Vandelli (Florence: Le Monnier, 1964), bk. 4; Buonaccorso da Montemagno, *De nobilitate* (partial), ed. and trans. Eugenio Garin, in *Prosatori latini del Quattrocento* (Milan: Ricciardi, 1952), pp. 142–65; Poggio Bracciolini, *De nobilitate*, in his *Opera omnia* (Basel, 1538; reprint, Turin: Bottega d'Erasmo, 1964), pp. 64–83; Lauro Quirini, *Tre trattati sulla nobiltà*, in *Lauro Quirini umanista*, ed. K. Krautter, P. O. Kristeller, and H. Roob (Florence: Olschki, 1977). Secondary studies are Francesco Tateo, *Tradizione e realtà nell'Umanesimo italiano* (Bari: Delade, 1967), pp. 355–421; Aldo Vallone, "Il concetto di nobiltà e

cortesia nei secoli XIV e XV," *Atti della R. Accademia Nazionale dei Lincei*, ser. 7, no. 9 (1954):8–20; Danilo Marrara, *Riseduti e nobiltà. Profilo storico-istituzionale di un'oligarchia toscana nei secoli XVI–XVIII* (Pisa: Pacini, 1976), pp. 8–13; P. O. Kristeller, "Introduction" to *Lauro Quirini umanista*, pp. 67–102.

3. Bartolomeo Cipolla, *De imperatore militum diligendo* (Rome, ca. 1475), unfoliated; Bartoliana, Arch. Torre 1763, s.d. 16 April 1499.

4. Daniele Dall'Aqua, *Vocabularius iuris* (Vicenza, 1482), s.v. "Nobilitas" (quoting Bartolus); Bartolus de Saxoferrato, *Commentaria*, IV (Venice, 1581), *Ad duodecimum librum codicis*, Lex prima (*De dignitatibus*), rubs. 52, 56, 59–62, 64; idem, *Repertorium in lecturas Bartoli* (Venice, 1557), s.v. "Nobilis."

5. Cipolla, *De imperatore militum diligendo;* idem, *Omnia quae quidem nunc extant opera* (Lyon, 1577), esp. pp. 117–19; (Giovanni Bertrachini), *Repertorium utriusque iuris Joannis Bertrachinis de Firmo* (Nuremberg, 1483), s.v. "Nobilitas"; Jacopo Alvarotti, *Super feudis* (Lyon, 1535), f. 58r; Pietro Del Monte, *Repertorium utriusque iuris* (Padua, 1480), s.v. "Nobilitas"; *Vocabularius utriusque iuris tam civilis quam canonici* (Milan, 1492), s.v. "Nobilitas."

6. Bartolus, *De dignitatibus*, rubs. 79–80; idem, *Repertorium*, s.v. "Miles"; *Vocabularius utriusque iuris*, s.v. "Nobilitas."

7. Cited in Giambattista Carlo Co. Giuliari, *Della letteratura veronese al cadere del secolo XV* (Bologna, 1876), p. 218. See also Bartolus, *De dignitatibus*, rub. 84.

8. *De dignitatibus*, rubs. 44–45, 78, 81; and see Egidio Rossini, "La professione notarile nella società veronese dal comune alla signoria," *Economia e Storia* 18 (1971):25.

9. Gaetano Salvemini, "La dignità cavalleresca nel comune di Firenze," in his *Opera*, ed. Ernesto Sestan (Milan: Feltrinelli, 1972), esp. p. 113; Emilio Cristiani, *Nobiltà e popolo nel comune di Pisa* (Naples: Istitute Italiano per gli Studi Storici, 1962), pp. 72–78, 89–90; idem, "Sul valore politico del cavalierato nella Firenze dei secoli XIII e XIV," *Studi Medievali*, ser. 3, no. 3 (1962):365–71; Giovanni Tabacco, "Interpretazioni e ricerche sull'aristocrazia di Pisa," ibid., pp. 707–27; Tateo, *Tradizione e realtà*, p. 338. Bartolus, for example, classified civic office the lowest (*infima*) sort of nobility, purely a function of local custom (*De dignitatibus*, rubs. 63, 83, 95; and see also Ludovico Bolognini, continuation of Signorolo degli Omodei, *Utrum preferendus sit doctor an miles*, in *Tractatus universi iuris* [Venice, 1584], 18, f. 25v, rub. 57).

10. Salvemini, "Dignita cavalleresca," pp. 128–30; Vallone, "Concetto di nobiltà," pp. 12–13; Cristoforo Lafranchino, *Utrum praeferendus sit doctor an miles*, in *Tractatus universi iuris*, 18, rubs. 32–34; Bolognini, continuation of Omodei, rubs. 92–95; Dall'Aqua, *Vocabularius*, s.v. "Nobilitas" and "Miles"; Michele Savonarola, *Libellus de magnificis ornamentis regia civitatis Padue*, ed. Arnaldo Segarizzi, in Rerum Italicarum Scriptores, 2d ed., tome XXIV, pt. 15 (Città di Castello, 1902), pp. 31–32, 41–42; Bartolus, *De dignitatibus*, rub. 35.

11. Bertrachini, *Repertorium*, s.v. "Nobilitas"; Cipolla, *Omnia opera*, p. 117; idem, *De imperatore militum diligendo*, rub. 26; Del Monte, *Repertorium*, s.v. "Nobilitas"; Lafranchino, *Utrum praeferendus sit doctor an miles*, rubs. 19, 42, 57; Giovanni da Platea, *Repertorium*, appendix to *Super tribus ultimis libris codicis* (Lyon, 1537), s.v. "Doctor"; Bartolus, *Repertorium*, s.v. "Doctor." Vicentine claims in Bertoliana, Arch. Torre 1763, s.d. 16 April 1499; Bertoliana, Gonzati 533, ff. 164v–66r. Trevisan corporations also claimed nobility; see Bianca Betto, *Il collegio dei notai, dei giudici, dei medici e dei nobili in Treviso (secc. XIII–XVI)*, Deputazione Veneta di Storia Patria, *Miscellanea di studi e memorie* 19 (Venice, 1981):106; Luigi Pesce, *Vita socio-culturale in diocesi di Treviso nel primo Quattrocento*, ibid. 21 (Venice, 1983):103. In general see Tateo, *Tradizione e realtà*, pp. 390–421.

12. On the debate over the precedence of law or medicine, see Coluccio Salutati, *De*

nobilitate legum et medicinae, ed. Eugenio Garin (Florence: Valsecchi, 1947); and texts edited by Garin in *La disputa delle arti nel Quattrocento* (Florence: Valsecchi, 1947); secondary studies in idem, *La filosofia* (Milan: Vallardi, 1947), pp. 207–12; idem., *L'umanesimo italiano* (Bari: Laterza, 1965), pp. 39–46. On the debate over the precedence of law or knighthood, in addition to works by Signorolo, Lafranchini, and Bolognini cited above, see Salvemini, "Dignità cavalleresca," pp. 130–34.

13. Da Platea, *Repertorium,* s.v. "Nobilitas"; Bartolus, *De dignitatibus,* rubs. 35, 46, 82, 102; Cipolla, *De imperatore militum diligendo,* rub. 18.

14. Cipolla, *De imperatore militum diligendo,* rub. 18. There remained a zone of uncertainty between large-scale commerce, which could be acceptable for a noble, and manual trade, which was definitely not. The difference between a passive investor in the wool trade and a wool entrepreneur or between the latter and the owner of a large wool shop was not clear. Observers did not draw the line between noble and ignoble trade.

15. Council lists in Sebastiano Rumor, "Il blasone vicentino descritto e illustrato," in Deputazione Veneta di Storia Patria, *Miscellanea di storia veneta,* ser. 5, no. 2 (Venice, 1899):286–94; population figures of 19,000 inhabitants in 1483 from Giovanni Mantese, *Memorie storiche della chiesa vicentina,* III, 1 (Vicenza: Istituto San Gaetano, 1958), p. 380.

16. In Vicenza in 1451 citizens dressed as duke, count, and marquess paraded before a new bishop during the ceremony of entry "per mostrar che il Vescovo di Vicenza ha questi titoli di Duca, Conte e Marchese" (*Cronica ad memoriam praeteriti temporis praesentis atque futuri,* ed. G. Mocenigo [Vicenza, 1884], s.a. 1451); episcopal investitures in Arch. Curia, Feudi, regs. 14–29; and see Gina Fasoli, "Per la storia di Vicenza dal IX al XII secolo," *Archivio Veneto,* ser. 5, nos. 36–41 (1945–47):228–37. For other cities see Pietro Rasi, "I rapporti fra l'autorità ecclesiastica e l'autorità civile in Feltre (1404–1565)," ibid. 13 (1933):113, 118, 120; G. Biscaro, "Le temporalità del vescovo di Treviso dal sec. IX al XIII," ibid. 18 (1936): esp. pp. 27–28; Joanne M. Ferraro, "Feudal-Patrician Investments in the Bresciano and the Politics of the *Estimo,*" *Studi Veneziani,* n.s., 7 (1983):33; Tabacco, "Interpretazioni e ricerche," p. 710.

17. Cipolla, *De imperatore militum diligendo,* rub. 26; Baldus from Alvarotti, *Super feudis,* f. 57v.

18. Dall'Aqua, *Vocabularius,* s.v. "Nobilitas"; Alvarotti, *Super feudis,* f. 57v; Cipolla, *De imperatore militum diligendo,* rubs. 3, 12, 14, 15, 17, 19, 21–24.

19. Bartolus, *De dignitatibus,* rub. 52; Bib. Univ., MS. 1667, ff. 22r ff.

20. Arnaldi notariate from Bertoliana, Gonzati 535, f. 47r, 50v; council seat from Bertoliana, Gonzati 153, f. 18r; Council of One Hundred from Bertoliana, Arch. Torre 62, ff. 772v–74v; investiture from Arch. Curia, Feudi, reg. 22, ff. 36v–37v, 40r–v; territorial vicariate from Bertoliana, Arch. Torre 309, fasc. 7–8; villa from Howard Burns, "Le opere minori del Palladio," *Bolletino del CISA Andrea Palladio* 21 (1979):15–16; titles from Rumor, "Blasone," pp. 296–97; genealogies from Bertoliana, Gonzati 3334, pp. 125–59; Bertoliana, Gonzati 3337, pp. 123–30; Bertoliana, Gonzati 2984, ff. 346v–48r. Verità from Alison A. Smith, "Il successo sociale e culturale di una famiglia veronese del '500," *Civis* 24 (1984):299–317.

21. As noted for Florentine palaces; see Richard A. Goldthwaite, "The Florentine Palace as Domestic Architecture," *American Historical Review* 77 (1972):977–1012; idem, *The Building of Renaissance Florence. An Economic and Social History* (Baltimore: Johns Hopkins University Press, 1980), pp. 13–16.

22. Immunities from *Ius municipale vicentinum,* ff. 154v–55v; violence from James S. Grubb, "Catalysts for Organized Violence in the Early Venetian Territorial State,"

in *Bande armate, banditi, banditismo e repressione di giustizia negli stati europei di antico regime,* ed. Gherardo Ortalli (Rome: Jouvence, 1986), pp. 389–96.

23. A.S.Ven., Dieci Misti 29, f. 161v; A.S.Ven., Capi dei Dieci, Lettere, 1503, #104. In 1505 someone threw a spear from the window of his house, nearly killing the patrician Ludovico Aimerico (A.S.Ven., Avogaria di Comun 3372, s.d. 13 March 1505.

24. A.S.Ven., Consiglio dei Dieci, Misti 14, ff. 157r, 160r, 194r; A.S.Ven., Avogadori di Comun 3583, fasc. 2, ff. 25v, 38v, 115r⁻v; Battista Pagliarino, *Croniche di Vicenza* (Vicenza, 1663), p. 301; Giacomo Marzari, *La historia di Vicenza* (Vicenza, 1604), p. 145.

25. James S. Grubb, "Patriciate and *Estimo* in the Vicentine Quattrocento," in *Il sistema fiscale veneto: aspetti e problemi (XV–XVIII secolo),* ed. G. Borelli, P. Lanaro, and F. Vecchiato (Verona: Libreria Universitaria, 1982), pp. 153–58 and table 1; *Ius municipale vicentinum,* ff. 10v, 45r. The Veronese system was much the same; see Amelio Tagliaferri, *L'economia veronese secondo gli estimi dal 1409 al 1635* (Milan: Giuffrè, 1966), pp. 34, 64; Gian Maria Varanini, "Note sui consigli civici veronesi (secoli XIV–XV). In margine ad uno studio di J. E. Law," *Archivio Veneto,* ser. 5, no. 147 (1979):25–26; Paola Lanaro Sartori, "Radiografia della soglia di povertà in una città della terraferma veneta: Verona alla metà del XVI secolo," *Studi Veneziani,* n.s., 6 (1982):esp. p. 47.

26. Vicentine regulations in Bertoliana, Arch. Torre 787, ff. 3r–4r; *Ius municipale vicentinum,* ff. 23r–32r, 35v–38r; and citations for arrears in Bertoliana, Arch. Torre 1108–10, 1111–12. In general see Gian Maria Varanini, "Tra fisco e credito: note sulle camere dei pegni nelle città venete del Quattrocento," *Studi Storici Luigi Simeoni* 33 (1983):215–46.

27. Bertoliana, Arch. Torre 777, f. 94r; Marciana, Latin V, 62 (2356), f. 1r; Marciana, Italian VII, 2401 (10509), s.d. 28 September 1458; Bertoliana, Arch. Torre 61, f. 257v; Bertoliana, Arch. Torre 59, f. 146v; and *Ius municipale vicentinum,* bk. I passim.

28. John Easton Law, "'Super differentiis agitatis Venetiis inter districtuales et civitatem.' Venezia, Verona e il contado nel '400," *Archivio Veneto,* ser. 5, no. 151 (1981):14; *Statuta Patavina,* rub. 36; Bertoliana, Arch. Torre 213, fasc. 8, f. 6r. This was a widespread phenomenon (Giorgio Chittolini, *La formazione dello stato regionale e le istituzioni del contado* [Turin: Einaudi, 1979], p. xxviii).

29. On patrician usury in Vicenza, see James S. Grubb, "Patrimonio, feudo e giurisdizione: la signoria dei Monza a Dueville nel secolo XV," in *Dueville: storia e identificazione di una communità del passato,* ed. Claudio Povolo (Vicenza: Neri Pozza, 1985), 1:281. In general see Giuliano Pinto, "Note sull'indebitamento contadino e lo sviluppo della proprietà fondiaria cittadina nella Toscana tardomediavale," *Ricerche Storiche* 10 (1980):3–19; Gigi Corazzol, "Prestatori e contadini nella campagna feltrina intorno alla meta del '500," *Quaderni Storici* 26 (1974):445–500; idem, *Fitti e livelli a grano. Un aspetto del credito rurale nel Veneto del '500* (Milan: Franco Angeli, 1979); idem, "Sulla diffusione dei livelli a frumento tra il patriziato veneziano nella seconda meta del '500," *Studi Veneziani,* n.s., 6 (1982):103–28.

30. General accounts and background are Giovanni Mantese, *Memorie storiche della chiesa vicentina,* III, 2 (Vicenza: Neri Pozza, 1964), pp. 480–83, 651–56; Mariano Nardello, "Il prestito ad usura a Vicenza e la vicenda degli ebrei nei secoli XIV e XV," *Odeo Olimpico* 13–14 (1977–78):80–120; Daniele Carpi, "Alcune notizie sugli ebrei a Vicenza," *Archivio Veneto,* ser. 5, no. 68 (1961):18–21; S. G. Radzik, *Portobuffolè* (Florence, 1984). Contemporary printed works are listed in G. T. Faccioli,

Catalogo ragionato de' libri stampati in Vicenza e suo territorio nel sec. XV (Vicenza, 1776), pp. 26–27, 77–81, 181–82, 214–24; documents in Bertoliana, Arch. Torre 61, ff. 53v, 86r–89v, 118v–21r, 202r–v, 259v–60r, 283r–v, 320v; Bertoliana, Arch. Torre 59, ff. 303r–v.

31. Reinhold C. Mueller, "L'imperialismo monetario veneziano nel Quattrocento," *Società e Storia* 8 (1980):292–97.
32. Bertoliana, Arch. Torre 61, ff. 363r–66v.

CHAPTER 9. PACIFICATION AND SECURITY

1. Bertoliana, Arch. Torre 349, fasc. 6, ff. 15r–16r.
2. *Ius municipale vicentinum,* ff. 129r–v; A.S.Ven., Captain Commission, ff. 8v, 12r; Marciana, Latin X, 498 (10598), para. 48; A.S.Ven., Senato Terra 10, f. 119r; Marino Sanudo, *I diarii,* ed. Rinaldo Fulin et al. (Venice: Visentini, 1879–1903), 3, col. 1401; A.S.Ven., Podesta Commission, f. 1r.
3. A.S.Ven., Avogaria di Comun 3646, ff. 5v, 89v–90r; John Easton Law, "Venice, Verona and the Della Scala after 1450," *Atti e Memorie dell'Accademia di Verona,* ser. 6, no. 29 (1977–78):159–60, 167–68; A.S.Ven., Grazie 21, f. 35v; A.S.Ven., Dieci Misti 14, ff. 162r, 164r; Bertoliana, Arch. Torre 1108, f. 216r; L. Bertalot, "Padua unter venetianischer Herrschaft 1435," *Quellen und Forschungen aus italianischer Archiven und Bibliotheken* 24 (1932–33):188–206.
4. A.S.Ven., Senato Terra 7, f. 67r.
5. On Nievo and Vivaro see A.S.Ven., Avogaria di Comun 666, s.d. 30 May 1414, 27 August 1414; A.S.Ven., Avogaria di Comun 3646, fasc. 2, ff. 59v–60r; on Leonello Nievo see A.S.Ven., Capi dei Dieci, Lettere, 1473, #90; 1474, #369; 1475, #399; 1476, ##7, 41, 49.
6. A.S.Ven., Maggior Consiglio 22, f. 66v; A.S.Ven., Senato Terra 3, f. 85v. On exile, see ch. 8, n. 22.
7. Bertoliana, Arch. Torre 59, ff. 133v–34r, 178r, 213v–15r; A.S.Ven., Capi dei Dieci, Lettere, 1500, #417; 1501, ##108, 132; 1502, ##44, 223, 232; A.S.Ven., Lettere di Rettori 223, #24; A.S.Ven., Dieci Misti 29, ff. 58v, 77r, 161r–v; A.S.Ven., Senato Terra 14, ff. 198r–99r.
8. A.S.Ven., Capi dei Dieci, Lettere, 1502, #409; 1507, #321; A.S.Ven., Capi dei Dieci, reg. 223, ##10, 12; A.S.Ven., Dieci Misti 29, f. 129v; Giovanni Mantese, *Memorie storiche della chiesa vicentina,* III, 2 (Vicenza: Neri Pozza, 1964), pp. 54–59; A.S.Ven., Senato Terra 12, f. 83r; Domenico Bortolan, "Leonardo Trissino celebre avventuriero," *Nuovo Archivio Veneto* 3 (1892):5–46.
9. On Barbarano see A.S.Ven., Senato Terra 7, ff. 24r, 29r; Bertoliana, Arch. Torre 59, f. 25r; on *adunationes* see ibid., ff. 66r, 121r–v, 299v–301r, 305r; on arms, see Bertoliana, Arch. Torre 61, ff. 80v–81r, 118v–21r, 241v–42r; Bertoliana, Arch. Torre 60, ff. 128r–v; Bertoliana, Arch. Torre 777, ff. 95v–96v; on Marostica, see A.S.Ven., Dieci Misti 29, f. 19r; A.S.Ven., Capi dei Dieci, Lettere, 1502, #174; A.S.Ven., Capi dei Dieci, reg. 223,#15.
10. Marciana, Italian VII, 498 (8147), f. 84r; Bertoliana, Arch. Torre 59, ff. 17r, 304v–05r.
11. A.S.Ven., Captain Commission, f. 12r; Bertoliana, Arch. Torre 61, ff. 369r–v; Bertoliana, Arch. Torre 59, ff. 300v–301r.
12. Sanudo, *Diarii,* 5, col. 268; A.S.Ven., Senato Terra 7, f. 95v; Bertoliana, Arch. Torre 61, ff. 158r, 161r.

13. Bertoliana, Arch. Torre 61, ff. 33r–34r, 56r–v, 101r–v, 106v–07r, 164v–65r, 168v–69v, 343r–v; Bertoliana, Arch. Torre 59, ff. 49r, 133v–34r, 178r, 229r; A.S.Ven., Senato Terra 12, ff. 47v–48r.
14. Bertoliana, Arch. Torre 61, ff. 28v–30r, 38r–39r; A.S.Ven., Senato Terra 10, ff. 171r, 176v; A.S.Ven., Senato Terra 14, f. 85v.
15. Typically, the Council of Ten gradually replaced the Senate as source of supplemental grants. The Barbarano case is found in A.S. Ven., Senato Terra 5, f. 192v.
16. Lamberto Pansolli, *La gerarchia delle fonti di diritto nella legislazione medievale veneziana* (Milan: Giuffrè, 1970), p. 113; cases in Bertoliana, Arch. Torre 59, ff. 141v–42v; A.S.Ven., Senato Terra 5, f. 11r; A.S.Ven., Senato Terra 10, f. 119r; Bertoliana, Arch. Torre 61, f. 135r.
17. Bertoliana, Arch. Torre 59, ff. 107v–08r.
18. Bertoliana, Arch. Torre 61, ff. 229r–v.
19. Bertoliana, Arch. Torre 1655, docs. 150, 153.
20. A.S.Ven., Avogaria di Comun 3583, f. 181v; Bertoliana, Arch. Torre 61, ff. 240r–v; Bertoliana, Arch. Torre 684, fasc. 33, f. 4r; Bertoliana, Arch. Torre 61, ff. 357v–58r.
21. Bertoliana, Arch. Torre 781, ff. 22r–36v, 40v, 44r–45v, 49r–v; Bertoliana, Arch. Torre 196, fasc. 3, ff. 1r–9r; Bertoliana, Arch. Torre 62, ff. 636r–37r; Bertoliana, Arch. Torre 192, fasc. 4, ff. 2r–3v.
22. Bertoliana, Arch. Torre 61, ff. 108v, 170r–71v; A.S.Ven., Avogari di Comun 3583, fasc. 2, f. 142r. Examples of such remanding of cases back to local channels are found throughout A.S.Ven., Avogaria di Comun 3583 and 3584.
23. A.S.Ven., Avogaria di Comun 3583, fasc. 2, f. 161r.

CHAPTER 10. FISC AND ARMY

1. Text in Marino Sanudo, *La vita dei Dogi*, in Rerum Italicarum Scriptores (Milan, 1733), 22, cols. 949–58; and *Documenti finanziari della Repubblica di Venezia, Bilanci generali*, ser. 2, vol. 1, pt. 1 (Venice, 1912), pp. 94–97, 577–80. On the text and its corruption, see Hans Baron, "The Anti-Florentine Discourses of the Doge Tommaso Mocenigo (1414–23): Their Date and Partial Forgery," *Speculum* 27 (1952):323–42.
2. Gino Luzzatto, "L'economia veneziana dopo l'acquisto della terraferma," *Bergomum* 38 (1964):59–61; and see Michael Knapton, "Il Consiglio dei Dieci nel governo della terraferma: un' ipotesi interpretativa per il secondo '400," in *Venezia e la terraferma attraverso le relazioni dei rettori. Atti del convegno*, ed. Amelio Tagliaferri (Milan: Giuffrè, 1981), pp. 242–43.
3. Bertoliana, Arch. Torre 59, ff. 32v–33v, 194v–95r; A.S.Ven., Senato Terra 11, ff. 50r–v.
4. Import laws from A.S.Ven., Podesta Commission, f. 4r; A.S.Ven., Senato Terra 3, f. 171r; A.S.Ven., Senato Terra 4, f. 137r; A.S.Ven., Senato Terra 9, f. 161r; A.S.Ven., Senato Terra 10, f. 9v; export restrictions throughout the series A.S.Ven., Capi dei Dieci, Lettere. In general see Angelo Ventura, *Nobiltà e popolo nella società veneta del '400 e '500* (Bari: Laterza, 1964), pp. 380–85; Knapton, "Consiglio dei Dieci," p. 251 and n. 25; idem, "Il fisco nello Stato veneziano di terraferma tra '300 e '500: la politica delle entrate," in *Il sistema fiscale veneto: problemi e aspetti (XV–XVIII secolo)*, ed. G. Borelli, P. Lanaro, and F. Vecchiato (Verona: Libreria Universitaria, 1982), pp. 130–31.

5. A.S.Ven., Senato Terra 3, f. 171r.
6. Oak from A.S.Ven., Senato Terra 10, ff. 115r, 137r; Bertoliana, Arch. Torre 61, ff. 397v–400r; Passo Pertica from ibid., 164r–v, 235r–36r, 257r, 354v, 388v–39v, 391v.
7. On exports see 1404 Capitula, rub. 35; 1406 Capitula, rub. 9; Bertoliana, Arch. Torre 60, ff. 223v, 267r–v; G. B. Zanazzo, "L'arte della lana in Vicenza (secc. XIII–XV)," Deputazione Veneta di Storia Patria, *Miscellanea di storia veneta*, ser. 3, no. 6 (Venice, 1914): docs. 16, 26; Giambattista Verci, *Storia della Marca trevigiana e veronese* (Venice, 1790), 18, doc. 2053; on citizenship see Bertoliana, Arch. Torre 60, f. 14r; on Venetian wool see Domenico Sella, "The Rise and Fall of the Venetian Woollen Industry," in *Crisis and Change in the Venetian Economy in the Sixteenth and Seventeenth Centuries,* ed. Brian Pullan (London: Methuen, 1968), pp. 111–12; on imports see Zanazzo, "Arte della lana," doc. 14; Bertoliana, Arch. Torre 61, ff. 40r–43v, 51v.
8. V. Padovan, "Documenti per la storia della zecca veneta," *Archivio Veneto* 18 (1879):132–33; A.S.Ven., Capi dei Dieci, reg. 223, #5; Giorgetta Bonfiglio Dosio, *Il "Capitolare dalle broche" della zecca di Venezia (1358–1556)* (Padua: Antenore, 1984), pp. 126–28. On the Ten's assumption of jurisdiction, see idem, "Controllo statale e amministrazione della zecca veneziana fra XIII e prima metà del XVI secolo," *Nuova Rivista Storica* 69 (1985):470–71.
9. In 1404 the official rate was set at 3 *lire* 15 *solidi* in silver money per gold ducat; by 1455 it was 5 *lire* 14 *solidi,* and by 1472 it was 6 *lire* 4 *solidi* (1404 *Capitula,* rub. 7; Bertoliana, Gonzati 2547, s.d. 20 November 1455; Bertoliana, Arch. Torre 587, fasc. 5, s.d. 3 October 1472). This represents about a 1 percent annual rise in the relative value of gold. See in general Reinhold C. Mueller, "L'imperialismo monetario veneziano nel Quattrocento," *Società e storia* 8 (1980):277–97.
10. Venetian laws in A.S.Ven., Marostica Commission, para. 30; A.S.Ven., Podesta Commission, ff. 4r–v; A.S.Ven., Captain Commission, f. 12r; A.S.Ven., Senato Terra 2, f. 2r; A.S.Ven., Dieci Misti 19, f. 59r; Marciana, Italian VII, 498 (8147), ff. 1r–6r; Bertoliana, Gonzati 576, ff. 51v–53v, 56v, 64v, 84r, 195r; Bertoliana, Arch. Torre 59, ff. 73v–76v, 226v–27r, 388r–v; cases in A.S.Ven., Capi dei Dieci, Lettere, 1473, ##106, 116, 164–65; 1474, ##365, 373; 1477, #327; 1489, #230; 1490, #103; 1496, #327; 1507, #70; A.S.Ven., Dieci Criminali I, ff. 39r–44r, 45r, 53r, 62v–63r, 85r.
11. On prohibitions see A.S.Ven., Senato Terra 2, f. 2r; A.S.Ven., Capi dei Dieci, Lettere, 1489, #202; 1500, #171; 1508, #404; and in general Vittorio Giuseppe Salvaro, "La moneta veneziana in Verona dal 1421 al 1495," *Atti e Memorie dell'Accademia di Verona,* ser 4, nos. 22–25 (1921–23):99, 103–11; Reinhold C. Mueller, "Guerra monetaria tra Venezia e Milano nel Quattrocento," in *La Zecca di Milano,* ed. G. Gorini (Milan, 1984), pp. 341–55; idem, "La crisi economico-monetaria veneziana di metà Quattrocento nel contesto generale," in *Aspetti della vita economica medievale* (Florence: Olschki, 1985), pp. 541–56; idem, "Imperialismo monetario," pp. 284, 292–93.
12. A.S.Ven., Senato Terra 1, ff. 12r, 147r; Bonfiglio Dosio, *"Capitolare dalle brocche,"* pp. 120–21, 137, 171, 211, 225, 234, 239, 242, 251–53, 260–61, 275; Padovan, "Documenti," *Archivio Veneto* 18 (1879): docs. 53, 63, 64, 65 (2), 66 (3); ibid. 19 (1880):docs. 8, 11; Bertoliana, Arch. Torre 61, ff. 207v–08r; Mueller, "Imperialismo monetario," p. 294.
13. 1404 Capitula, rub. 20; 1406 Capitula, rub. 7; *Privilegia Veronae,* p. 1, rub. 4.
14. 1404 Capitula, rub. 19; 1406 Capitula, rub. 16; Michael Knapton, "I rapporti fiscali tra Venezia e la terraferma: il caso padovano," *Archivio Veneto,* ser. 5, no. 117 (1981),

tables 2A, 2B; Gian Maria Varanini, "Il Bilancio della Camera fiscale di Verona nel 1479–80. Prime osservazioni," in *Il sistema fiscale veneto*, table 1; Bertoliana, Arch. Torre 61, ff. 28v–30r.

15. On the *dadia* see Bertoliana, Arch. Torre 404, fasc. 1, ff. 7r–9v; Bertoliana, Gonzati 2547, ff. 11r–19r; Bertoliana, Arch. Torre 407, fasc. 1; Bertoliana, Arch. Torre 630, fasc. 8; Bertoliana, Arch. Torre 587, fasc. 5, s.d. 30 November 1417; on *subsidia* and *mutua* see Bertoliana, Arch. Torre 407, fasc. 1; Bertoliana, Arch. Torre 61, ff. 32r–33r, 271r; Bertoliana, Arch. Torre 482, fasc. 9, f. 18r; Bertoliana, Arch. Torre 373, fasc. 2, ff. 32r–34r; Bertoliana, Gonzati 572, f. 195v, 197v; Bertoliana, Gonzati 2547, ff. 19v–22v; and in general Knapton, "Rapporti fiscali," pp. 18–19, 25, 50; idem, "Fisco nello Stato veneziano," pp. 33–34, 37–38; idem, "Guerra e finanza (1381–1508)," in Gaetano Cozzi and Michael Knapton, *Storia della Repubblica di Venezia dalla guerra di Chioggia alla riconquista della terraferma* (Turin: UTET, 1986), pp. 301–3; Varanini, "Bilancio," p. 293.

16. A.S.Ven., Collegio Secreta, Lettere, file for 1436–38, ff. 75r, 77v, 79r, 85r mentions the Vicentine commune's *introitus ordinarius* of 13,600 *lire* per month or 26,000 *lire* for two months, or about 160,000 *lire* annually. The commune's share of the *dadia delle lanze* (13,650 ducats) converts to 84,630 *lire* at the eventual exchange rate of 124 *solidi* per ducat. Though communal figures are fragmentary and do not permit precise analysis, comparison with Veronese and Paduan data suggests that they are reasonably accurate. Adding together "ordinary income" and the *dadia* quota, Vicenza would have collected about 245,000 *lire* in gross annual income, or about 39,500 ducats. Verona's gross income was 49,400 ducats (Varanini, "Bilancio," table 1; excluding the *dazio del sale*), that of Padua 65,000 ducats (Knapton, "Rapporti fiscali," table 2A).

17. A.S.Ven., Senato Terra 7, f. 159v; Marino Sanudo, *I diarii*, ed. Rinaldo Fulin et al. (Venice: Visentini, 1879–1903), 3, cols. 7, 9ff.

18. On the *alloggio* see Bertoliana, Arch. Torre 234, fasc. 1, ff. 1r–12r; Bertoliana, Gonzati 2547, ff. 10r–11r; Bertoliana, Arch. Torre 60, ff. 42r–v; Bertoliana, Arch. Torre 61, ff. 117r–18v, 123v–24r, 167r, 272v–73r, 315r–16r, 353r–v; Bertoliana, Arch. Torre 211, fasc. 3; Bertoliana, Arch. Torre 630, fasc. 7, 11; and in general M. E. Mallett and J. R. Hale, *The Military Organization of a Renaissance State: Venice c. 1400 to 1617* (Cambridge: Cambridge University Press, 1984), pp. 131–37. The calculation is based on a mean of 300 lances; the countryside's two-thirds share of the *dadia delle lanze* amounted to 9,100 ducats annually.

19. Bertoliana, Arch. Torre 59, ff. 349r–v; Knapton, "Rapporti fiscali," p. 37; Bertoliana, Arch. Torre 59, ff. 180v–81r, 349r–v; A.S.Ven., Senato Terra 2, f. 29v; A.S.Ven., Podesta Commission, f. 2r.

20. On the *judex datiorum* see Bertoliana, Arch. Torre 61, ff. 70r–v; Bertoliana, Gonzati 569, ff. 55v–56r; A.S.Vic., Magistrature Antiche 3897, fasc. 1, s.d. 27 January 1429, 18 August 1408; on Venetian officials see Bertoliana, Arch. Torre 61, ff. 52r, 146r–v, 218v; A.S.Ven., Avogaria di Comun 3583, fasc. 2, f. 59v; A.S.Ven., Senato Terra 7, ff. 113r, 130r; Bertoliana, Arch. Torre 59, ff. 25v–26r; Ceferino Caro Lopez, "Gli auditori nuovi," in *Stato società e giustizia nella repubblica veneta (secc. XV–XVIII)*, ed. Gaetano Cozzi (Rome: Jouvence, 1981), 1:274.

21. 1404 Capitula, rub. 36; 1406 Capitula, f. 184v; Bertoliana, Arch. Torre 645, doc. 88; Zanazzo, "Arte della lana," doc. 15; A.S.Ven., Senato Terra 3, f. 55v; A.S.Ven., Capi dei Dieci, Lettere, 1507, #200. For Verona see *Privilegia Veronae*, pt. 1 rub. 4; Varanini, "Bilancio," pp. 288–90; for Bassano, see Verci, *Storia*, doc. 2031; and in general Knapton, "Fisco nello Stato veneziano," p. 29; idem, "Guerra e finanza," pp. 330–31.

22. A.S.Ven., Senato Terra 1, f. 189v; A.S.Ven., Senato Terra 5, f. 183v; Bertoliana, Arch. Torre 61, ff. 196v–97r, 220v; arrears from A.S.Ven., Grazie 20, ff. 65r, 71r; A.S.Ven., Grazie 21, ff. 11r, 31r, 39r; A.S.Ven., Grazie 23, ff. 5v, 33v; Bertoliana, Arch. Torre 404, fasc. 1, ff. 12r–v.

23. Bertoliana, Arch. Torre 61, ff. 114r–v, 127v–29v, 148r–v, 151r–52r, 229r–v, 238r–v; *campatico* from Gian Maria Varanini, "Altri documenti su Marin Sanudo e Verona (1501–1502)," *Studi Storici Luigi Simeoni* 30–31 (1980–81):5; Knapton, "Rapporti fiscali," pp. 8–9, 53–54; idem, "Fisco nello Stato veneziano," pp. 26, 29; Sanudo, *Diarii*, 3, cols. 1327, 1406–7, 1438, 1463, 1493, 1531, 1605; Bertoliana, Arch. Torre 412, fasc. 5, ff. 15r–v.

24. Bertoliana, Arch. Torre 61, ff. 107v–08r, 114v, 116v, 207r.

25. Vicentine documents cited above, n. 15; Varanini, "Bilancio," table 2.

26. David Herlihy, "The Population of Verona in the First Century of Venetian Rule," in *Renaissance Venice*, ed. J. R. Hale (London: Faber, 1973), table 3; Amelio Tagliaferri, *L'economia veronese secondo gli estimi dal 1409 al 1635* (Milan, Giuffre, 1966), table 4. Vicentine demographic data confirm this trend (Franco Brunello, "Fraglie e società artigiane a Vicenza dal XIII al XVIII secolo," in *Vicenza illustrata*, ed. Neri Pozza [Vicenza: Neri Pozza, 1976], p. 102).

27. Bertoliana, Arch. Torre 61, ff. 57r–v; A.S.Ven., Senato Terra 1, ff. 52r–53v; Bertoliana, Arch. Torre 61, ff. 249v–50r; Bertoliana, Arch. Torre 59, ff. 12r–13v; Bertoliana, Gonzati 576, ff. 204r–v.

28. Bertoliana, Arch. Torre 61, ff. 32r–33r, 81r–83r; Bertoliana, Gonzati 2547, s.d. 3 June 1442; Bertoliana, Arch. Torre 630, fasc. 8; Bertoliana, Arch. Torre 482, fasc. 13; Bertoliana, Arch. Torre 59, f. 237r–38r; Bertoliana, Arch. Torre 412, fasc. 5; Bertoliana, Arch. Torre 373, fasc. 2, ff. 32r–v; Bertoliana, Arch. Torre 587, fasc. 5, s.d. 19 November 1417. Brescia, by contrast, did not receive the right to cancel exemptions; see Antonio Menniti Ippolito, "La dedizione di Brescia a Milano (1421) e Venezia (1427): città suddite e distretto nello Stato regionali," in *Stato società e giustizia*, 2:30–32, 43–44.

29. Bertoliana, Arch. Torre 61, ff. 220v–21r; Bertoliana, Gonzati 3379, s.d. 1490; Bertoliana, Arch. Torre 404, fasc. 6. On similar difficulties in collection throughout the Veneto and Lombardy, see John Easton Law, "Un confronto fra due stati 'rinascimentali': Venezia e il dominio sforzesco," in *Gli Sforza a Milano e in Lombardia e i loro rapporti con gli stati italiani e europei (1450–1535)* (Milan: Cisalpino-Goliardica, 1982), p. 407; Mallett and Hale, *Military Organization*, p. 131; Knapton, "Rapporti fiscali," pp. 35, 51.

30. A.S.Ven., Capi dei Dieci, Lettere, 1494, #145; 1496, #275; see also 1501, #335; 1502, ##123, 219, 319; 1507, #112. The situation was as bad elsewhere (ibid., 1498, #63; 1501, ##179, 274; 1502, ##345, 388; 1503, ##310, 395.

31. Bertoliana, Arch. Torre 61, f. 270v; Bertoliana, Arch. Torre 59, f. 118r. A good example is Longare's alienation of common pasturage rights to pay debts on the salt tax (Bertoliana, Arch. Torre 373, fasc. 11).

32. Knapton, "Consiglio dei Dieci" passim; idem, "Rapporti fiscali," esp. pp. 21–22, 32–35, 63–65; idem, "Fisco nello Stato veneziano," esp. pp. 27, 39; idem, "Guerra e finanza," pp. 307–10.

33. Knapton, "Rapporti fiscali," pp. 39, 42; similarly in Brescia (Menniti Ippolito, "Dedizione di Brescia," pp. 45–46).

34. Giulio Sancassani, "I beni della 'fattoria scaligera' e la loro liquidazione ad opera della Repubblica Veneta (1406–1417)," *Nova Historia* 12 (1960):100–157; Vittorio Lazzarini, "Beni carraresi e proprietari veneziani," in *Studi in onore di Gino Luzzatto* (Milan: Giuffrè, 1950), 1:274–88; 1404 Capitula, rubs. 10, 17, 19; 1406 Capitula,

rubs. 6, 16; Bertoliana, Arch. Torre 778, ff. 21r–23r; Bertoliana, Arch. Torre 663, fasc. 1, ff. 10r, 13r–14v.

35. Bertoliana, Arch. Torre 318, fasc. 1; Bertoliana, Arch. Torre 61, ff. 9r–11r, 62v–63r, 222r–v, 227r–v; Giovanni Mantese, *Memorie storiche della chiesa vicentina,* III, 2 (Vicenza: Neri Pozza, 1964), pp. 493–94, 522–24; Bertoliana, Arch. Torre 778, ff. 99r–108v; Bertoliana, Arch. Torre 412, fasc. 2, ff. 10r–11v; Bertoliana, Arch. Torre 648, fasc. 2, s.d. 20 February 1404.

36. Varanini, "Bilancio," p. 289 and table 1. Verona's share of the proceeds would have amounted to some 7,400 *lire,* and Vicentine taxes were usually set at about 75 percent of Verona's (Bertoliana, Arch. Torre 482, fasc. 9; A.S.Ven., Senato Terra 1, ff. 54r–v). Padua raised much more, proportionately, from the salt tax (Knapton, "Rapporti fiscali," table 3).

37. Varanini, "Bilancio," table 1; Knapton, "Rapporti fiscali," table 2A.

38. Bertoliana, Arch. Torre 61, ff. 21v–22r, 85v, 273r–v, 278v–79r; A.S.Ven., Senato Terra 8, f. 81v; Bertoliana, Arch. Torre 61, ff. 344v–46v; Marino Sanudo, *Itinerario di Marin Sanuto per la terraferma veneziana nell'anno 1483,* ed. Rawdon Brown (Padua, 1847), p. 108; A.S.Ven., Capi dei Dieci, reg. 223, #17.

39. Bertoliana, Arch. Torre 61, ff. 199r–v, 344r–v; A.S.Ven., Senato Terra 1, f. 173v; Bertoliana, Arch. Torre 191, fasc. 1, ff. 4r–5r; Bertoliana, Arch. Torre 189, fasc. 2, f. 18r; Bertoliana, Arch. Torre 1655, doc. 120; Bertoliana, Arch. Torre 756, fasc. 12, s.d. 14 December 1463; Bertoliana, Arch. Torre 191, fasc. 1, ff. 42r–43r, 44r; A.S.Ven., Capi dei Dieci, reg. 223, ##17–19.

CHAPTER 11. PIETY AND MORALS

1. 1404 Capitula, rub. 13; 1406 Capitula, rub. 14; Bertoliana, Arch. Torre 645, doc. 88, rubs. 16, 19.

2. On Zeno see *Cronicha che comenza dell'anno 1400,* ed. Domenico Bortolan (Vicenza, 1889), s.d. 1501; Angelo Ventura, "Considerazioni sull'agricoltura veneta e sulla accumulazione originaria del capitale nei secoli XVI e XVII," *Studi Storici* 9 (1968):679; Giovanni Mantese, *Memorie storiche della chiesa vicentina,* III, 2 (Vicenza: Neri Pozza, 1964), p. 162. In general see Gaetano Cozzi, "Politica, società, istituzioni," in Gaetano Cozzi and Michael Knapton, *Storia della Repubblica di Venezia dalla guerra di Chioggia alla riconquista della terraferma* (Turin: UTET, 1986), pp. 233–34, 240–43; C. Cenci, "Senato veneto: 'Probae' ai benefizi ecclesiastici," in *Promozioni agli ordini sacri a Bologna e alle dignità ecclesiastiche nel Veneto nei secoli XIV–XV,* ed. C. Piana and C. Cenci (Florence: Collegio San Bonaventura, 1968).

3. Marino Sanudo, *I diarii,* ed. Rinaldo Fulin et al. (Venice: Visentini, 1879–1903), 5, col. 268; similarly A.S.Ven., Senato Terra 7, f. 95v.

4. A.S.Ven., Senato Terra 8, f. 194v; A.S.Ven., Dieci Misti 29, ff. 34v–35r; A.S.Ven., Senato Terra 14, f. 189v.

5. A.S.V., Senato Terra 4, f. 100r; examples of earlier supervision of benefices in A.S.Ven., Senato Terra 1, f. 100r; Bertoliana, Arch. Torre 61, f. 133r; examples of the Ten's intervention in A.S.Ven., Capi dei Dieci, Lettere, 1484, #450; 1485, ##56, 334, 474. See also Cozzi, "Politica, società, istituzioni," pp. 236–37, 241.

6. Bertoliana, Arch. Torre 59, ff. 110r–v.

7. Bertoliana, Arch. Torre 61, f. 145r; Bertoliana, Arch. Torre 59, ff. 122r–v. On the basis of the latter principle the Senate blocked passage of the bishopric of Verona into Roman-appointed *commenda* at the death of the incumbent (A.S.Ven., Senato

Terra 2, f. 193v). On the background of the 1472 ruling see Cozzi, "Politica, società, istituzioni," pp. 239–40.

8. Marciana, Latin X, 398 (10598), f. 15v; Bertoliana, Arch. Torre 61, f. 145r; A.S.Ven., Capi dei Dieci, Lettere, 1483, ##371, 374; A.S.Ven., Avogaria di Comun 3584, fasc. 3, s.d. 5 June 1497; Bertoliana, Arch. Torre 61, f. 133r; Bertoliana, Arch. Torre 59, f. 125v.

9. Vicentine cases in A.S.Ven., Avogaria di Comun 3372, s.d. 12 November 1502; A.S.Ven., Avogaria di Comun 3583, fasc. 2, f. 42v; A.S.Ven., Avogaria di Comun 3584, fasc. 6, f. 48r; A.S.Ven., Capi dei Dieci, Lettere, 1504, ##167, 169, 189; A.S.Ven., Dieci Misti 30, f. 140r; usury laws from Bertoliana, Arch. Torre 61, ff. 86r–89v, rub. 8.

10. Bertoliana, Arch. Torre 59, ff. 296v–97r (case from Treviso); Bertoliana, Arch. Torre 61, ff. 39v, 76r, 79v–80v, 83r–v, 101v–02r, 127r–v, 146v–47r, 149r–v, 247r–v. Vicentine cases involving Paduan prelates arose because much of the northern Vicentine lay within the diocese of Padua; see Pierantonio Gios, "Il vicario generale Niccolò Grassetto e il clero padovano dell'alto vicentino," *Archivio Veneto,* ser. 5, no. 157 (1984):7–8.

11. Bertoliana, Arch. Torre 61, ff. 83r–v, 101v–02r, 186r–v, 197r–98r; Bertoliana, Arch. Torre, Catastico XXIV, s.v. "Feudi," s.d. 18 September 1507.

12. Bertoliana, Arch. Torre 61, ff. 21v–22r, 27v–28v, 67v–70r; Mantese, *Memorie storiche,* III, 2, pp. 675–80; Bertoliana, Gonzati 533, ff. 132r–46v.

13. Mantese, *Memorie storiche,* III, 2, pp. 376, 385–86, 389, 403–04, 414–15, 427–28; idem, *Correnti riformistiche a Vicenza nel primo Quattrocento* (Vicenza, 1958), pp. 881, 915, 931–32; Bertoliana, Arch. Torre 61, f. 366r; *Ius municipale vicentinum,* f. 164v; *Cronica ad memoriam praeteriti temporis atque futuri,* ed. G. Mocenigo (Vicenza, 1884), s.d. 1464; Bertoliana, Arch. Torre 61, ff. 239r–v; A.S.Ven., Senato Terra 3, f. 83v.

14. Sergio Bertelli, *Il potere oligarchico nello stato-città medievale* (Florence: La Nuova Italia, 1978), p. 155; Bertoliana, Arch. Torre 777, f. 68v; Mantese, *Memorie storiche,* III, 1, pp. 128–29, 626–33.

15. *Ius municipale vicentinum,* ff. 147r–48r; and for other cities see *Statuta Patavina,* Proemium; Bianca Betto, *Il collegio dei notai, dei giudici, dei medici e dei nobili in Treviso (secc. XIII–XVI),* Deputazione Veneta di Storia Patria, *Miscellanea di studi e memorie* 19 (Venice, 1981):388; Giambattista Verci, *Storia della Marca trevigiana e veronese* (Venice, 1790), 18, doc. 2031; Bertoliana, Arch. Torre 778, f. 8v.

16. Bertoliana, Arch. Torre 567, fasc. 27, pp. 1–13; Bertoliana, Arch. Torre 777, f. 94r; Sebastiano Rumor, *Storia documentata del Santuario di Monte Berico* (Vicenza: San Giuseppe, 1911), esp. pp. 397–428 and doc. V; idem, *La chiesa votiva di S. Rocco* (Vicenza, 1915); Mantese, *Memorie storiche,* III, 2, pp. 283–84, 372–78, 575–76, 594, 822–25, 995–97.

17. Notices of Vicentine notaries, canons, archpriests and archdeacons in Mantese, *Memorie storiche,* III, 2, pp. 203–25; Vicenza, Arch. Curia, Feudi passim; Verci, *Storia,* docs. 2099, 2104.

18. Mantese, *Correnti riformistiche,* p. 915; idem, *Memorie storiche,* III, 2, pp. 893–99, 925; A.S.Ven., Dieci Misti 30, f. 140r.

19. *Ius municipale vicentinum,* f. 91r.

20. Bertoliana, Arch. Torre 59, ff. 86r–87r, 141r–v, 188r–v, 355v, 338v; Bertoliana, Arch. Torre 61, ff. 212r–v; A.S.Ven., Senato Terra 4, f. 91v; 1503 case from A.S.Ven., Quarantia Civil Nuova, reg. 160, f. 113r.

21. Bertoliana, Arch. Torre 61, ff. 115v–16r, 182r; A.S.Vic., Collegio dei Notai, reg. 45, s.d. 30 June 1445; Mantese, *Memorie storiche,* III, 1, pp. 393–94; ibid., 2, pp. 508–9.

22. Bertoliana, Arch. Torre 61, ff. 191r, 259v–60r, 291r; *Cronica ad memoriam praeteriti temporis*, s.d. 1470; Mantese, *Memorie storiche*, III, 1, p. 399; ibid., 2, p. 511.
23. *Ius municipale vicentinum*, ff. 7r, 136v–37r; A.S.Ven., Senato Terra 3, ff. 44v–45v; Bertoliana, Gonzati 571, f. 137v; Bertoliana, Arch. Torre 61, ff. 142v–45r, 176r–79v, 214r.
24. Bertoliana, Gonzati 576, ff. 152r–v; Bertoliana, Arch. Torre 59, ff. 136v–37r; A.S.Ven., Capi dei Dieci, Lettere, 1474, #203; Marciana, Auditori Capitulare, f. 158r; and see Bertoliana, Arch. Torre 59, ff. 121r–v.

CHAPTER 12. APPEALS AND THEIR LIMITS

1. A.S.Ven., Maggior Consiglio 22, f. 13r.
2. Bruno Dudan, *Sindicato d'oltremare e di terraferma* (Rome: Foro Italiano, 1935), pp. 56–57, 86–92, 112–13; Michael Knapton, "Il Consiglio dei Dieci nel governo della terraferma: un'ipotesi interpretativa per il secondo '400," in *Venezia e la terraferma attraverso le relazioni dei rettori*, ed. Amelio Tagliaferri (Milan: Giuffrè, 1981), p. 255; Ceferino Caro Lopez, "Gli Auditori Nuovi," in *Stato società e giustizia nella repubblica veneta (secc. XV–XVIII)*, ed. Gaetano Cozzi (Rome: Jouvence, 1981), 1:261–64, 290; Gaetano Cozzi, "La politica del diritto," in ibid., pp. 114–21; idem, "Ambiente veneziano, ambiente veneto," in *L'uomo e il suo ambiente*, ed. Stefano Rosso-Mazzinghi (Florence: Sansoni, 1973), p. 108.
3. Authorizing legislation in Marciana, Auditori Capitulare, ff. 1r–33v and passim; Marciana, Auditori Prattica, A, bks. I–VII; Bertoliana, Gonzati 572, ff. 183r–v; A.S.Ven., Maggior Consiglio 24, ff. 35v–36v.
4. Marino Sanudo, *Itinerario di Marin Sanuto per la terraferma veneziana nell'anno 1483*, ed. Rawdon Brown (Padua, 1847), pp. 22–23.
5. Dudan, *Sindicato*, pp. 109–10; jurisdictions from Marciana, Auditori Capitulare, ff. 36r–37r, 46r–47r, 65v–67r, 125v–27r, 130r–31r, 143r–v, 158r, 161v; Marciana, Auditori Prattica, A, bk. I, s.d. 9 February 1477 and bk. III, s.d. 3 December 1445; A.S.Ven., Senato Terra 7, f. 76v; A.S.Ven., Senato Terra 11, ff. 58v–59r; *Privilegia Veronae*, p. 17; John Easton Law, "Verona and the Venetian State in the Fifteenth Century," *Bulletin of the Institute of Historical Research*, 52, no. 125 (1979):18–19; Caro Lopez, "Auditori Nuovi," pp. 272–73, 296–97; Bertoliana, Gonzati 576, ff. 124r–25r.
6. Caro Lopez, "Auditori nuovi," p. 276; A.S.Ven., Maggior Consiglio 24, ff. 35v–36v; A.S.Ven., Senato Terra 11, ff. 103r–05r; Bertoliana, Arch. Torre 59, ff. 2r–4v.
7. Marciana, Auditori Capitulare, ff. 14v, 192v; Caro Lopez, "Auditori Nuovi," p. 265.
8. Bertoliana, Arch. Torre 61, ff. 108v–09r, 167r–v, 185r–86r, 226v, 227v–28v; A.S.Ven., Grazie 23, ff. 8r, 16r.
9. *Ius municipale vicentinum*, ff. 22v, 100r.
10. Initial ruling from Bertoliana, Arch. Torre 59, ff. 41r–v; later confirmations in Bertoliana, Arch. Torre 61, ff. 57v–59v; *Statuta Patavina*, ff. 29v–30v; Cipolla from Aldo Mazzacane, "Lo stato e il dominio nei giuristi veneti durante il 'secolo della terraferma,'" in *Storia della cultura veneta*, III, 1, ed. Girolamo Arnaldi and Manlio Pastore Stocchi (Vicenza: Neri Pozza, 1979), p. 597; Pietro Del Monte, *Repertorium utriusque iuris* (Padua, 1480), s.v. "Consuetudo"; (Giovanni Bertrachini), *Repertorium utriusque iuris Joannis Bertrachinis de Firmo* (Nuremberg, 1483), s.v. "Judex."
11. Bertoliana, Gonzati 576, ff. 125r–v; *Privilegia Veronae*, pp. 15, 18; Marciana, Auditori Capitulare, ff. 102r–04r, 107r–09r; Bertoliana, Arch. Torre 61, ff. 285v–86r, 291v, 295r–96r.

12. Vicentine law in *Ius municipale vicentinum*, ff. 82v, 90v–93r, 97v–98v, 102v; ruling of 1415 in Bertoliana, Arch. Torre 59, ff. 41r–v; charges to the *auditori* in Bertoliana, Arch. Torre 61, ff. 57v–59r; *Statuta Patavina*, ff. 29v–30v; Marciana, Italian VII, 498 (8147), ff. 162v; charges to the podesta in A.S.Ven., Maggior Consiglio 22, f. 102v; *Statuta Patavina*, ff. 30v–31r; Bertoliana, Arch. Torre 61, ff. 67v–70r, 94v–95r; *Statuta Veronae*, II, pp. 107–8. On the *consilium sapientis* in the mainland, see Cozzi, "Politica del diritto," pp. 106ff.; on the obligation of judges to commit cases and respect the *consilium*, see G. Rossi, *Consilium sapientis iudicale* (Milan: Giuffrè, 1958), pp. 143ff.

13. A.S.Ven., Quarantia Civil Nuova 160, ff. 67r, 68v; Bertoliana, Arch. Torre 61, ff. 171r–v.

14. *Ius municipale vicentinum*, f. 22v; Marciana, Auditori Capitulare, ff. 38v–39r; Bertoliana, Arch. Torre 61, ff. 81r–v, 357v–58r, 381r–v; Marciana, Italian VII, 498 (8147), ff. 30v–31r; Bertoliana, Arch. Torre 59, ff. 44v–45r; Bertoliana, Gonzati 572, ff. 202r–v; Bertoliana, Arch. Torre 62, f. 485v.

15. Bertoliana, Arch. Torre 59, ff. 39v–40r; Bertoliana, Arch. Torre 62, ff. 435r–v. For laws encouraging arbitration, see *Ius municipale vicentinum*, ff. 100v–103r; Bertoliana, Gonzati 577, f. 25v; A.S.Ven., Maggior Consiglio 23, f. 113v; Bertoliana, Gonzati 576, ff. 46r–v. Examples of Venetian refusal to accept appeals from Vicentine arbitration sentences are found in A.S.Ven., Avogaria di Comun 3583, ff. 191v, 197v, 218v. Inappellability of arbitration sentences, except in cases of gross inequity, was a commonplace of jurists (Bartolomeo Cipolla, *Omnia quae quidem nunc extant opera* [Lyon, 1577], p. 780; Bertrachini, *Repertorium*, s.v. "Appellatio"; (Nicolò de Milis), *Repertorium domini Nicolai de Milis* [Venice, 1499], s.v. "Arbitri").

16. Marciana, Auditori Capitulare, ff. 38v–39v; Marciana, Italian VII, 498 (8147), ff. 133v, 194r; Bertoliana, Arch. Torre 59, ff. 43v–44r; Cozzi, "Politica del diritto," p. 111.

17. Marciana, Auditori Prattica, B, f. 43r.

18. Bertoliana, Arch. Torre, Catastico IX, s.v. "Consolatus," s.d. 20 March 1446; A.S.Ven., Maggior Consiglio 22, f. 156v. In Milan in the period 1385–1429, about two-thirds of accused criminals fled (E. Verga, "Le sentenze criminali dei podestà milanese, 1385–1429," *Archivio Storico Lombardo* 28 [1901]:39). Vicentine criminal records demonstrate a similar proportion.

19. Marciana, Auditori Prattica, A, bk. II; Marciana, Italian VII, 498 (8147), ff. 162v–63r.

20. Decrees in Bertoliana, Arch. Torre 189, ff. 289r–v; Bertoliana, Arch. Torre 61, ff. 159v–60r, 189v–91r, 202v–03r, 205r–v, 314v; Bertoliana, Gonzati 572, ff. 202r–v; Marciana, Auditori Capitulare, ff. 107r–9r, 191v–92r; appeals tabulated from A.S.Ven., Quarantia Civil Nuova, reg. 160.

21. Vittorio Lazzarini, *Proprietà e feudi, offizi, garzoni, carcerati in antiche leggi veneziane* (Rome: Edizioni di Storia e Letteratura, 1960), p. 91.

22. Gaetano Cozzi, "Considerazioni sull'amministrazione della giustizia nella Repubblica di Venezia (secc. XV–XVI)," in *Florence and Venice: Comparisons and Relations* (Florence: La Nuova Italia, 1980), 2:112–13; idem, "Politica del diritto," pp. 117ff.; Marciana, Auditori Capitulare, ff. 152v–54v; Caro Lopez, "Auditori Nuovi," pp. 284–85.

23. Marciana, Auditori Capitulare, ff. 114v–15r, and ff. 37r, 94r, 173r, 175r, 185v; A.S.Ven., Senato Terra 2, f. 160r; A.S.Ven., Senato Terra 11, ff. 58v–59r; Bertoliana, Arch. Torre 59, ff. 2r–4v, 11v–12v, 191v–92r; A.S.Ven., Senato Terra 4, f. 146v; Bertoliana, Arch. Torre 59, ff. 7v–8v; Caro Lopez, "Auditori Nuovi," p. 286; A.S.Ven., Maggior Consiglio 22, ff. 145r–v.

24. Bertoliana, Arch. Torre 59, ff. 10r, 27v–28r; Bertoliana, Arch. Torre 62, ff. 520v–21r; Bertoliana, Arch. Torre 482, fasc. 13, s.d. 11 June 1486; A.S.Ven., Maggior Consiglio 24, ff. 20r–v.
25. Marciana, Auditori Capitulare, ff. 5r, 75r, 137r, 196v; Caro Lopez, "Auditori Nuovi," p. 278; A.S.Ven., Avogaria di Comun, 3372, 3377, 3401.
26. Marciana, Auditori Capitulare, ff. 120v, 121v; A.S.Ven., Maggior Consiglio 22, ff. 103v, 138v. Of the thirty-five surviving records of Vicentine appeals heard by the Quarantia, seven (20 percent) were introduced directly by plaintiffs (A.S.Ven., Quarantia Civil Nuova 160).
27. A.S.Ven., Maggior Consiglio 22, ff. 103v, 146v–47r, 165r; Marciana, Auditori Capitulare, ff. 43r, 68v–69v; A.S.Ven., Senato Terra 14, f. 151v; Marciana, Auditori Prattica, A, bk. VI; Caro Lopez, "Auditori Nuovi," pp. 296–97.
28. A.S.Ven., Maggior Consiglio 22, ff. 85r, 103v, 121v, 128r–v, 146v–47r; A.S.Ven., Maggior Consiglio 24, ff. 3r–5r; Marciana, Auditori Capitulare, ff. 49v–50r, 125v, 131v, 155v–57r, 162v–63r; Marciana, Auditori Prattica, A, bk. III; A.S.Ven., Senato Terra 2, f. 152r; A.S.Ven., Maggior Consiglio 24, ff. 3r–5r; Caro Lopez, "Auditori Nuovi," pp. 298–303.
29. On the Collegio Solenne, see Bertoliana, Arch. Torre 59, ff. 11v–12v; Caro Lopez, "Auditori Nuovi," p. 272; on the Collegio alle Biade see Marciana, Auditori Capitulare, ff. 72v, 78v–79r, 125v, 158r, 205r; A.S.Ven., Maggior Consiglio 22, ff. 80v, 82r; A.S.Ven., Maggior Consiglio 24, ff. 8r–v; on the captain, see A.S.Ven., Maggior Consiglio 22, f. 80r; Marciana, Auditori Capitulare, f. 68r, A.S.Ven., Senato Terra 10, f. 151r; A.S.Ven., Avogaria di Comun 3646, ff. 89v–90r; on the Avogaria see A.S.Ven., Maggior Consiglio 22, f. 80v; on miscellaneous tribunals see A.S.Ven., Maggior Consiglio 24, ff. 35v–36v; Marciana, Auditori Capitulare, ff. 142v, 174v; Marciana, Auditori Prattica, A, bk. II, and B; Bertoliana, Arch. Torre 59, ff. 27v–28r; A.S.Ven., Senato Terra 7, f. 128r; Bertoliana, Arch. Torre 61, ff. 167r–v.
30. From A.S.Ven., Quarantia Civil Nuova 160.
31. A.S.Ven., Grazie 23, ff. 24r–27v; Bertoliana, Arch. Torre 61, ff. 264r–v.
32. Bertoliana, Arch. Torre 61, ff. 124v–25r, 196r–v, 199v–200r, 221r–22r, 229r–v, 238v–39r; A.S.Ven., Senato Terra 14, f. 81r; Bertoliana, Arch. Torre 59, ff. 277v–78r; A.S.Ven., Avogaria di Comun 3583, ff. 195v, 199v; A.S.Ven., Senato Terra 1, f. 199v; Marciana, Auditori Capitulare, f. 64r; A.S.Ven., Podesta Commission, f. 5v; A.S.Ven., Senato Terra 1, f. 157v.
33. Bertoliana, Arch. Torre 61, f. 291v.
34. A.S.Ven., Maggior Consiglio 22, f. 98v; Marciana, Auditori Capitulare, ff. 125v, 143r, 152v, 161v, 215v; A.S.Ven., Maggior Consiglio 24, ff. 35v–36v; Bertoliana, Arch. Torre 59, ff. 2r–4v, 11v–12v; A.S.Ven., Senato Terra 11, ff. 58v–59r, 103r–05r.
35. Bertoliana, Arch. Torre 59, ff. 12r–13r, 277v–78r; *Ius municipale vicentinum*, ff. 200v–201r; Bertoliana, Arch. Torre 61, ff. 207v–208r; Marciana, Auditori Capitulare, ff. 159v–60r; Bertoliana, Gonzati 576, ff. 54v–55r; A.S.Ven., Senato Terra 7, f. 113r; Bertoliana, Arch. Torre 60, f. 236r.

CHAPTER 13. RECONSTRUCTING LOCAL PREROGATIVES

1. Bertoliana, Arch. Torre 59, ff. 142v–43r.
2. Bertoliana, Arch. Torre 61, ff. 110r–12r; Giovanni Mantese, *Memorie storiche della chiesa vicentina*, III, 2 (Vicenza: Neri Pozza, 1964), pp. 29, 1079–80; James S. Grubb, "L'economia rurale e gli estimi del territorio di Vicenza (1519–1606)," *Annali veneti: società cultura istituzioni* 1 (1984):106.

3. A.S.Ven., Senato Terra 9, f. 170r.
4. Bertoliana, Arch. Torre 225, fasc. 4, f. 1r; Bertoliana, Arch. Torre 60, f. 168r–v; Bertoliana, Arch. Torre 361, fasc. 1, ff. 15r–v; Bertoliana, Arch. Torre 61, ff. 220r–v; A.S.Ven., Senato Terra 4, f. 135r; Marciana, Italian VII, 498 (8147), ff. 22r, 58r, 203r.
5. Bertoliana, Arch. Torre 59, ff. 86r–v, 130r, 187v–88r, 302r–v; Bertoliana, Arch. Torre 61, ff. 85r–86r, 113v.
6. Economic laws from Bertoliana, Arch. Torre 777, f. 92r; G. B. Zanazzo, "L'arte della lana in Vicenza (secc. XIII–XV)," Deputazione Veneta di Storia Patria, *Miscellanea di storia veneta*, ser. 3, no. 6 (Venice, 1914), docs. 9–12, 14, 32, and p. 292; Bertoliana, Arch. Torre 61, f. 286v; statutes of limitations (canceling the jurisdiction of the *auditori nuovi*) from Bertoliana, Arch. Torre 59, ff. 245v–46r, 297v–98r; Marciana, Auditori Capitulare, ff. 114v–15v; 1442 ruling from A.S.Ven., Senato Terra 1, f. 77v; 1507 ruling from Bertoliana, Arch. Torre 59, f. 143r.
7. A.S.Ven., Maggior Consiglio 22, ff. 18r, 23r, 28r; Bertoliana, Arch. Torre 61, f. 158r; fiscal petitions from ibid., ff. 344r–46v; A.S.Ven., Senato Terra 4, f. 106r.
8. Patrician conduct from Gaetano Cozzi, "Domenico Morosini e il 'De bene instituta republica,'" *Studi Veneziani*, n.s., 8 (1970):421; Donald Queller and Francis Swietek, "The Myth of the Venetian Patriciate: Electoral Corruption in Medieval Venice," in *Two Studies on Venetian Government*, ed. Donald Queller (Geneva: Droz, 1977), pp. 99–166; Robert Finlay, *Politics in Renaissance Venice* (New Brunswick, N.J.: Rutgers University Press, 1980), pp. 196ff.; Stanley Chojnacki, "Political Adulthood in Fifteenth–Century Venice," *American Historical Review* 91 (1986):796, 806–07; castellanies from A.S.Ven., Maggior Consiglio 22, f. 135r; salaries from A.S.Ven., Podesta Commission, f. 5r; A.S.Ven., Captain Commission, f. 8v (and marginal amendments to each); additional service from Bertoliana, Arch. Torre 59, ff. 222v–25v; A.S.Ven., Senato Terra 5, f. 56r; Marciana, Latin X, 398 (10598), para. 64; taxes from A.S.Ven., Governatori alle Entrade Pubbliche, reg. 377; Marciana, Latin X, 398 (10598), unfoliated leaves at end; Senate complaint from A.S.Ven., Senato Terra 12, f. 12v.
9. A.S.Ven., Senato Terra 3, f. 190r; complaints of absenteeism, even failure to serve personally, in A.S.Ven., Senato Terra 1, f. 18r; A.S.Ven., Senato Terra 10, f. 11v; Marciana, Italian VII, 498 (8147), f. 73v; Council of Ten from A.S.Ven., Capi dei Dieci, Lettere, 1501, #39; 1508, #109; Bertoliana, Arch. Torre 59, ff. 227v–28v; Marino Sanudo, *I diarii*, ed. Rinaldo Fulin et al. (Venice: Visentini, 1879–1903), 3, cols. 7–9, 53, 314ff.
10. Mason from Bertoliana, Arch. Torre 572, ff. 200v–201r; Marostica from A.S.Ven., Capi dei Dieci, Lettere, 1502, #176; A.S.Ven., Capi dei Dieci, reg. 223, ##15, 17.
11. A.S.Ven., Avogaria di Comun 3583, f. 64r; A.S.Ven., Capi dei Dieci, Lettere, 1488, ##81, 91; Marciana, Auditori Capitulare, ff. 161v–62r; Bertoliana, Arch. Torre 59, ff. 70r, 303v–04r.
12. Soranzo from A.S.Ven., Avogaria di Comun 3646, fasc. 1, ff. 51r, 52v; fasc. 2, f. 36r; A.S.Ven., Avogaria di Comun 666, s.d. 6 June 1411, 14 August 1411, 13 October 1411, 20 September 1412, 4 August 1413; da Canal from Sanudo, *Diarii*, 6, cols. 398, 418; rectors' misdeeds from Bertoliana, Arch. Torre 59, ff. 180v–81r; Marciana, Auditori Capitulare, ff. 118r–19r; officials' corruption from Bertoliana, Arch. Torre 61, ff. 100r, 221r–v, 340r–41r, 279r–80v; Bertoliana, Arch. Torre 59, f. 94r; A.S.Ven., Avogaria di Commun 3377, s.d. 28 March 1503; A.S.Ven., Dieci Criminale I, f. 63v; A.S.Ven., Senato Terra 1, ff. 184r, 190v; A.S.Ven., Senato Terra 13, f. 57v; A.S.Ven., Capi dei Dieci, Lettere, 1487, #33; Marciana, Latin X, 398 (10598), para. 83.
13. Bertoliana, Arch. Torre 59, ff. 227v–28v; A.S.Ven., Podesta Commission, ff. 1v, 2r,

5r–7r, 8r; and in general M. E. Mallett and J. R. Hale, *The Military Organization of a Renaissance State: Venice c. 1400 to 1617* (Cambridge: Cambridge University Press, 1984), pp. 137–40.

14. Marciana, Latin X, 398 (10598), para 19, 53; A.S.Ven., Podesta Commission, ff. 6r–v, 7r; A.S.Ven., Captain Commission, ff. 10v, 12r–v; A.S.Ven., Marostica Commission, para. 48, 59; Marciana, Italian VII, 498 (8147), ff. 51r, 101r; Bertoliana, Arch. Torre 59, ff. 226r, 288r; A.S.Ven., Senato Terra 8, f. 47r; A.S.Ven., Senato Terra 4, f. 80v; Marciana, Latin X, 398 (10598), para. 44; A.S.Ven., Capi dei Dieci, Lettere, 1484, #254; Marciana, Auditori Capitulare, ff. 99v, 176v.

15. On ceremonies of entry and departure, see (Francesco Barbaro), *Francisci Barbari et aliorum ad ipsum Epistolae,* ed. Angelo Maria Quirini, (Brescia, 1743), p. 319; (Francesco Barbaro), *Centotrenta lettere inedite di Francesco Barbaro,* ed. Remigio Sabbadini, (Salerno, 1884), p. 106; Mantese, *Memorie storiche,* III, 2, p. 475n; Sanudo, *Diarii,* 6, col. 345; Angiolgabriello di Santa Maria, *Biblioteca e storia di quei scrittori cosi della città come del territorio di Vicenza* (Vicenza, 1772), 1:76, 83, 242; Bertoliana, Arch. Torre 61, ff. 233r–34r. On sculpted arms and inscriptions, see Marino Sanudo, *Itinerario di Marin Sanuto per la terraferma veneziana nell'anno 1483,* ed. Rawdon Brown (Padua, 1847), pp. 30, 33, 45, 51, 77, 90, 91, 107, 113, 116, 128, 134, 138, 140. Entry ceremonies were common enough that Marc'Antonio Sabellico gave advice to podestas on appropriate behavior (*De officio praetoris,* in his *Epistolae familiare necnon orationes et poemata* [Venice, 1502?], ff. 106r–v).

16. Bertoliana, Arch. Torre 59, ff. 229v–30r; Pompeo Molmenti, "I bandi e i banditi della repubblica veneta," *Nuova Antologia,* ser. 3, fasc. 13–14, 16 (1893):146–47; A.S.Ven., Capi dei Dieci, Lettere, 1483, #398.

17. Giorgio Chittolini, *La formazione dello stato regionale e le istituzioni del contado* (Turin: Einaudi, 1979), pp. xxi–xxiii, 313–18; Elena Fasano Guarini, "Considerazioni su giustizia, stato e società nel ducato di Toscana del Cinquecento," in *Florence and Venice: Comparisons and Relations* (Florence: La Nuova Italia, 1980), 2:161.

18. A.S.Ven., Podesta Commission, ff. 3r, 4r; Marciana, Latin X, 398 (10598), paras. 30, 35–37, 40; and see A.S.Ven., Captain Commission, f. 9v.

19. Bertoliana, Arch. Torre 61, ff. 102r–v.

20. Bertoliana, Arch. Torre 61, ff. 63r–v, 357v–58r.

21. A.S.Ven., Senato Terra 4, f. 95r.

22. Bertoliana, Arch. Torre 61, ff. 28v–30r; A.S.Ven., Maggior Consiglio 22, f. 105r (reinforced in Bertoliana, Arch. Torre 61, ff. 118v–22r); A.S.Ven., Senato Terra 1, f. 199v.

CHAPTER 14. UNITY AND PARTICULARISM

1. James S. Grubb, "When Myths Lose Power: Four Decades of Venetian Historiography," *Journal of Modern History* 58 (1986):46–49. On the various meanings given the Renaissance in the past century, see Federico Chabod, "Storia del Rinascimento," in *Cinquant'anni di vita intellettuale italiana. Scritti in onore di Benedetto Croce,* ed. Carlo Antoni and Raffaele Mattioli (Naples: Edizioni Scientifiche Italiane, 1950), 1:127–207.

2. Federico Chabod, "Esiste uno Stato del Rinascimento?" and "Y a-t-il un Etat de la Renaissance?" in his *Scritti sul Rinascimento* (Turin: Einaudi, 1967), pp. 593–601, 605–10; Hans Baron, "A Struggle for Liberty in the Renaissance: Florence, Venice and Milan in the Early Quattrocento," *American Historical Review* 58 (1953):284–85;

Frederic C. Lane, "At the Roots of Republicanism," reprinted in *Venice and History: The Collected Papers of Frederic C. Lane* (Baltimore, Johns Hopkins Press, 1966), p. 521; and in general Grubb, "Myths," pp. 49–60; Giorgio Chittolini, "Alcune considerazioni sulla storia politico-istituzionale del tardo Medioevo: alle origini degli 'stati regionali,'" *Annali dell'Istituto italo-germanico in Trento* 2 (1976):401–7.

3. Julius Kirshner, "Between Nature and Culture: An Opinion of Baldus of Perugia on Venetian Citizenship as Second Nature," *Journal of Medieval and Renaissance Studies* 9 (1979):108.

4. 1404 Capitula, rub. 32; 1406 Capitula, rub. 27; Pompeo Molmenti, "I bandi e i banditi della repubblica veneta," *Nuova Antologia*, ser. 3, fasc. 13–14, 16 (1893):146–47; *Statuta Patavina*, rub. 65; *I libri commemoriali della Repubblica di Venezia*, ed. Riccardo Predelli, Deputazione Veneta di Storia Patria, *Monumenti storici*, ser. I, Documenti (Venice, 1878), IV, pp. 238–40; Bertoliana, Arch. Torre 61, ff. 15v, 18r–v, 147r.

5. Bertoliana, Arch. Torre 205, fasc. 2, ff. 19r–v (similarly for fiscal exactions: A.S.Ven., Collegio Secreta, Lettere, unnumbered register for 1436–38, f. 75r); A.S.Ven., Senato Terra 3, f. 60v.

6. A.S.Ven., Senato Terra 10, ff. 115r, 137r. Other examples of joint protest in Bertoliana, Arch. Torre 59, ff. 141v–42r; A.S.Ven., Dieci Misti 29, f. 118r; Marino Sanudo, *I diarii*, ed. Rinaldo Fulin et al. (Venice: Visentini, 1879–1903), 3, cols. 1219, 1366; A.S.Ven., Dieci Misti 14, f. 70r.

7. Bertoliana, Arch. Torre 50, doc. 4; *Cronica ad memoriam praeteriti temporis praesentis atque futuri*, ed. G. Mocenigo (Vicenza, 1884), s.d. 1458. Intermarriage might be too intense: Giovanni Thiene's marriage to Nicolosa Conti of Padua was ruled consanguineous (Bertoliana, Arch. Thiene, Catastico #251).

8. E.g., Bertoliana, Arch. Torre 307, fasc. 1, f. 14r.

9. G. Gualdo, "Francesco Barbaro," in *Dizionario biografico degli italiani* (Rome, 1964), 6:101–3; Giovanni Mantese, *Memorie storiche della chiesa vicentina*, III, 2 (Vicenza: Neri Pozza, 1964), pp. 774, 787; Evangelista Manelmi, *Commentariolum . . . de obsidione Brixiae* (Brescia, 1738), pp. 1–65, 66–68; (Francesco Barbaro), *Diatriba praeliminaris . . . ad Francisci Barbari et aliorum ad ipsum Epistolae*, ed. Angelo Maria Quirini (Brescia, 1743), pp. 319–22, 344–46; Ludwig Bertalot, *Studien zum italianischen und deutschen Humanismus* (Rome: Edizioni di Storia e Letteratura, 1975), 2:263.

10. A.S.Ven., Avogaria di Comun 3583, ff. 249v, 375v; A.S.Ven., Avogaria di Comun 3584, fasc. 1, s.d. 14 January 1481; A.S.Ven., Senato Terra 4, f. 77r; Marino Sanudo, *Itinerario di Marin Sanudo per la terraferma veneziana nell'anno 1483*, ed. Rawdon Brown (Padua, 1847), pp. 109–10; idem, *Diarii*, 3, col. 389; Bertoliana, Arch. Thiene, Catastico Co. Adriano, #107.

11. Vittorio Lazzarini, "Beni carraresi e proprietari veneziani," in *Studi in onore di Gino Luzzatto* (Milan: Giuffrè, 1950), 1:375–78; Giulio Sancassini, "I beni della 'fattoria scaligera' e la loro liquidazione ad opera della repubblica veneta (1406–1417)," *Nova Historia* 12 (1960):102–3; Michael Knapton, "I rapporti fiscali tra Venezia e la terraferma: il caso padovano," *Archivio Veneto*, ser. 5, no. 117 (1981):9; Vittorio Lazzarini, "Antiche leggi intorno ai proprietari nella terraferma," in his *Proprietà e feudi, offizi, garzoni, carcerati in antiche leggi veneziane* (Rome: Edizioni di Storia e Letteratura, 1960), esp. p. 9.

12. Dal Verme sales from Bertoliana, Arch. Thiene, Catastico, ##119, 127–28 and Sacchetto Turchio, Processo BBB; Bertoliana, Arch. Thiene, Catastico Co. Adriano, ##107, 188, 219, 235–36, 327, 550; Bertoliana, Arch. Fracanzani, Cata-

stico I, #234; Bertoliana, Arch. Torre 373, fasc. 2; Bertoliana, Arch. Torre 412, fasc. 5; Bertoliana, Arch. Torre 688, fasc. 4; Monza sales from Bertoliana, Arch. Torre 668, fasc. 3, s.d. 16 May 1506.

13. Gaetano Cozzi, "Ambiente veneziano, ambiente veneto," in *L'uomo e il suo ambiente*, ed. Stefano Rosso-Mazzinghi (Florence: Sansoni, 1973), pp. 97, 100.

14. Franco Barbieri, "Case e palazzi gotici," in *Vicenza illustrata*, ed. Neri Pozza (Vicenza: Neri Pozza, 1976), pp. 124–27; idem, *Pittori di Vicenza 1480–1520* (Vicenza: Neri Pozza, 1981), esp. pp. 9–11; idem, "L'architettura gotica civile a Vicenza," *Bolletino del CISA Andrea Palladio* 7 (1965):167–84; idem, *Vicenza gotica: il privato* (Vicenza: Neri Pozza, 1981).

15. Jousts from Giambattista Verci, *Storia della Marca trevigiana e veronese* (Venice, 1790), 18:235–37, and docs. 1994, 2176; villas from Alberto Tenenti, "The Sense of Space and Time in the Venetian World of the Fifteenth and Sixteenth Centuries," in *Renaissance Venice*, ed. J. R. Hale (London: Faber, 1973), p. 21; catalogue of villas in Martin Kubelik, *Die Villa im Veneto. Zur typologischen Entwicklung im Quattrocento* (Munich: Suddeutscher Verlag, 1977).

16. *Libri commemoriali*, 10:181; A.S.Ven., Avogaria di Comun 3372, s.d. 9 August 1502; A.S.Ven., Quarantia Civil Nuova 160, ff. 57v, 93v; A.S.Ven., Cancelleria Inferiore, Doge, Lettere I, fasc. 4, f. 89r; A.S.Ven., Senato Terra 4, f. 61r; Mantese, *Memorie storiche*, III, 2, p. 823; Bertoliana, Arch. Torre 708, fasc. 13, ff. 1r–2r.

17. M. E. Mallett and J. R. Hale, *The Military Organization of a Renaissance State: Venice c. 1400 to 1617* (Cambridge: Cambridge University Press, 1984), pp. 85, 87, 102–11 ("Aureliano" refers to the Orgiano family); Sanudo, *Diarii*, 6, col. 264; Mantese, *Memorie storiche*, III, 2, pp. 51–53, 459, 779–80; Bertoliana, Arch. Torre 61, ff. 265v–66r; A.S.Ven., Senato Terra 3, ff. 144v, 146v; military careers from A.S.Ven., Senato Terra 12, f. 179v; B. Scola, *Di Basilio della Scola soldato bombardiero architetto ed ingeniere militare* (Vicenza, 1888); A.S.Ven., Capi dei Dieci, Lettere, 1495, #258; 1508, #478; A.S.Ven., Dieci Misti 14, f. 128r; A.S.Ven., Senato Terra 4, f. 28r; A.S.Ven., Senato Terra 5 passim; A.S.Ven., Senato Terra 2, f. 181v; *Libri commemoriali*, s.v. "Thiene."

18. A.S.Ven., Grazie 20, ff. 78v, 87v; A.S.Ven., Collegio Secreta, Commissioni, reg. for 1408–13, ff. 2r, 51v; A.S.Ven., Collegio Secreta, Lettere, reg. for 1436–38, ff. 21r, 251r; A.S.Ven., Collegio Secreta, Lettere, reg. for 1480–89, ##29–30; A.S.Ven., Senato Misti 56, f. 64r; A.S.Ven., Capi dei Dieci, Lettere, 1484, #347; 1501, #341; A.S.Ven., Senato Terra 3, f. 18r; A.S.Ven., Senato Terra 10, f. 157v; A.S.Ven., Senato Terra 11, f. 42v; *Cronica ad memoriam praeteriti temporis*, s.d. 1472, 1477; A.S.Ven., Governatori alle Entrade Pubbliche 377, fasc. 2 (Clemente Thiene), fasc. 5 (Zuane Bissaro); Battista Pagliarino, *Croniche di Vicenza* (Vicenza, 1663), p. 282; Sanudo, *Itinerario*, p. 88.

19. Angelo Ventura, *Nobiltà e popolo nella società veneta del '400 e '500* (Bari: Laterza, 1964), pp. 170–72; idem, "Il dominio di Venezia nel Quattrocento," in *Florence and Venice: Comparisons and Relations* (Florence: La Nuova Italia, 1979), 1:186; Pagliarino, *Croniche*, p. 194. Though 113 foreigners were given patrician status in the fourteenth and fifteenth centuries, they were excluded from sensitive council sessions (Giorgio Cracco, "Patriziato e oligarchia a Venezia nel Tre-Quattrocento," in *Florence and Venice*, n. 68).

20. Bertoliana, Arch. Torre 60, f. 14r; Marciana, Italian VII, 498 (8147), f. 162r; *Libri commemoriali*, X, pp. 45–46; Vittorio Lazzarini, "Una bolla d'oro di Michele Steno," *Nuovo Archivio Veneto* 14 (1897):366–70; Bertoliana, Arch. Torre 62, ff. 477v–78r; Verci, *Storia*, 19:10–11; Antonio Menniti Ippolito, "La dedizione di Brescia a Milano (1421) e Venezia (1427): città suddite e distretto nello Stato regionale," in

Stato società e giustizia nella repubblica veneta (secc. XV–XVIII), ed. Gaetano Cozzi (Rome: Jouvence, 1985), 2:40.

21. Marciana, Auditori Capitulare, ff. 89v–90v; A.S.Ven., Senato Terra 2, f. 152r; Bertoliana, Arch. Torre 59, ff. 122r–v, 153v–54r; Bertoliana, Gonzati 576, ff. 227r–v.

22. Stephen Ell, *Citizenship and Immigration in Venice, 1305–1500* (Ph.D. dissertation, University of Chicago, 1976), p. 250, gives the figure of thirty-three total grants of Venetian citizenship to Vicentines in the period 1305–1500. Precise breakdowns for Padua and Verona (pp. 146–47) indicate that Trecento grants were about double those of the Quattrocento. For Tuscany see Julius Kirshner, "Paolo di Castro on *cives ex privilegio:* A Controversy over the Legal Qualifications for Public Office in Early Fifteenth Century Florence," in *Renaissance Studies in Honor of Hans Baron,* ed. Anthony Molho and John E. Tedeschi (Florence: Sansoni, 1971), pp. 229–30, 234 and passim.

23. A.S.Ven., Podesta Commission, f. 1r, and Captain Commission, f. 8v; Marciana, Italian VII, 498 (8147), ff. 42v, 154v; Bertoliana, Arch. Torre 618, fasc. 43, s.d. 24 January 1458; and see A.S.Ven., Cancelleria Inferiore, Doge, Lettere I (letters to mainland rectors ordering execution of Venetian civil sentences against mainland defendants). In general see Gaetano Cozzi, "La politica del diritto," in *Stato società e giustizia,* 1:27–28.

24. Bertoliana, Arch. Torre 59, ff. 303v–04r.

25. Giorgio Chittolini, *La formazione dello stato regionale e le istituzioni del contado* (Turin: Einaudi, 1979), p. 309; Elena Fasano Guarini, "Considerazioni su giustizia, stato e società nel ducato di Toscana nel Cinquecento," in *Florence and Venice,* 2:143–44.

26. Chittolini, *Formazione,* esp. pp. 292–302.

27. Bertoliana, Arch. Torre 60, f. 111v; alabaster from Bertoliana, Arch. Torre 61, ff. 156v–57v; grain provisions from Bertoliana, Arch. Torre 59, ff. 87v, 88r; A.S.Ven., Capi dei Dieci, Lettere, 1483, ##470, 575.

28. Mantese, *Memorie storiche,* III, 2, pp. 477–78; Galeazzo and Bartolomeo Gatari, *Cronica carrarese confrontata con la redazione di Andrea Gatari (aa. 1318–1407),* ed. Antonio Medin and Guido Tolomei, in Rerum Italicarum Scriptores, 2d ed., tome XVII, pt. I, 1 (Citta' di Castello, 1931), pp. 573–74; Gian Maria Varanini, *Vicenza nel Trecento,* forthcoming in *Storia di Vicenza;* Bertoliana, Arch. Torre 61, ff. 156v–57v.

29. Ventura, *Nobiltà e popolo,* p. 46; Marino Berengo, "Il problema politico-sociale di Venezia e della sua terraferma," in *La civiltà veneziana del Settecento* (Florence: Sansoni, 1960), esp. p. 90; Amintore Fanfani, "Il mancato rinnovamento economico," in ibid., pp. 27–67; Cracco, "Patriziato e oligarchia," esp. pp. 88–89; and in general Grubb, "Myths," pp. 60–77.

30. Cozzi, "Domenico Morosini," p. 436.

31. Michael Knapton, "Il Consiglio dei Dieci nel governo della terraferma: un'ipotesi interpretativa per il secondo '400," in *Venezia e la terraferma attraverso le relazioni dei rettori. Atti del convegno,* ed. Amelio Tagliaferri (Milan: Giuffrè, 1981), p. 245; idem, "Rapporti fiscali," p. 56; Benjamin G. Kohl, "Government and Society in Renaissance Padua," *Journal of Medieval and Renaissance Studies* 2 (1972):219; John Easton Law, "Un confronto fra due stati 'rinascimentali': Venezia e il dominio sforzesco," in *Gli Sforza e Milano e in Lombardia e i loro rapporti con gli stati italiani ed europei (1450–1535)* (Milan: Cisalpino-Goliardica, 1982), p. 405; Reinhold C. Mueller, "L'imperialismo monetario veneziano nel Quattrocento," *Società e Storia* 8 (1980):296–97.

32. A.S.Ven., Grazie 21, f. 35v; A.S.Ven., Dieci Misti 14, ff. 162r, 164r; Verci, *Storia,* 19:86–87; Paolo De Peppo, "'Memorie di veneti cittadini': Alvise Dardani, Cancellier Grande," *Studi Veneziani,* n.s., 8 (1984):416; and see above, ch. 9, n. 3.

33. Bertoliana, Arch. Torre 61, ff. 22v–24v; dossiers of thanks in Bertoliana, Gonzati 572, ff. 195v–200v; A.S.Vic., Corp. Sopp., Collegio dei Notai 38, ff. 6v–7r; Bertoliana, Arch. Torre 61, f. 326r; literary praise in Marciana, Latin VI, 3 (4351), ff. 36r–39v; Marciana, Italian XI, 110 (7238), ff. 5r–6r, 6v–7v; Marciana, Latin XIV, 244 (4681), ff. 43v–60v; Bertoliana, Gonzati 6.9.3, #14; Mantese, *Memorie storiche*, III, 2, p. 774; Bertalot, *Studien*, 2:243–44, 257, 263.

34. Moro from Bertoliana, Arch. Torre 61, ff. 233r–34r; insignia from *Cronica ad memoriam praeteriti temporis*, s.d. 1473; Domenico Bortolan, *Il collegio dei notai* (Vicenza, 1917), p. 29; Bertoliana, Arch. Torre 778, f. 8v; Bianca Betto, *Il collegio dei notai, dei giudici, dei medici e dei nobili in Treviso (secc. XIII–XVI)*, Deputazione Veneta di Storia Patria, *Miscellanea di storia veneta* 19 (Venice, 1981):25; *Statuta Patavina*, Proemium; Verci, *Storia*, docs. 2029, 2031; Antonio Zambelli, *Leone di S. Marco a Verona sulla colonna di Piazza Erbe* (Verona, 1886).

35. Humanist opposition from Manlio Pastore Stocchi, "Scuola e cultura umanistica fra due secoli," in *Storia della cultura veneta*, III, 1, ed. Girolamo Arnaldi and Manlio Pastore Stocchi (Vicenza: Neri Pozza, 1980), pp. 117–19; affection from Michael Knapton, "Venezia e Treviso nel Trecento: proposte per una ricerca sul primo dominio veneziano a Treviso," in *Tomaso da Modena e il suo tempo* (Treviso, 1980), p. 62; Gian Maria Varanini, "Il bilancio della Camera fiscale di Verona nel 1479–70," in *Il sistema fiscale veneto: problemi e aspetti (XV–XVIII secolo)*, ed. G. Borelli, P. Lanaro, and F. Vecchiato (Verona: Libreria Universitaria, 1982), p. 293; idem, "Dal comune allo stato regionale," in *La storia* (Turin: UTET, 1985), 2:11, 25; idem, "Altri documenti su Marin Sanudo e Verona (1501–1502)," *Studi Storici Veronesi Luigi Simeoni* 30–31 (1980–81): esp. pp. 6–7; Kohl, "Government and Society," p. 220; Bertalot, *Studien*, 2:189–208; Mario Brunetti, "Treviso fedele a Venezia nei giorni di Cambrai," *Archivio Veneto*, ser. 5, no. 23 (1938):56–82; Jeannine Guerin–Dalle Mese, *Una cronaca vicentina del Cinquecento* (Vicenza: Accademia Olimpica, 1983).

36. Bertoliana, Arch. Torre 61, ff. 84r–v.

37. Verci, *Storia*, 19:90; Bertoliana, Arch. Torre 61, f. 132v; Bertoliana, Arch. Torre 373, fasc. 2, f. 33r.

38. Bertoliana, Gonzati 416.

EPILOGUE

1. Giuseppe Faggin, "Giangiorgio Trissino e l'Impero," in *Convegno di studio su Giangiorgio Trissino*, ed. Neri Pozza (Vicenza: Neri Pozza, 1980), pp. 23–37; Paolo Preto, "Orientamenti politici della nobiltà vicentina negli anni di Giangiorgio Trissino," in ibid., pp. 44–48; idem, "L'atteggiamento della nobiltà vicentina dopo la Lega di Cambrai nelle relazioni dei rettori," in ibid., pp. 433–37.

2. Bertoliana, Arch. Torre 630, fasc. 5, s.d. 17 November 1509.

Index

Unless otherwise indicated, citations of magistracies refer to those of Vicenza.

About the Author:
James S. Grubb teaches history at the University of Maryland,
Baltimore County.

Designed by Sheila Stoneham.
Composed by the Composing Room of Michigan, Inc.,
in Baskerville with display lines in Optima.
Printed by Thomson-Shore, Inc., on 50-lb. Glatfelter Offset
and bound by John H. Dekker and Sons, Inc., in Holliston Roxite.